Praise for *Judaism and Justice*

"An important book written at a moment in which the future character of American Jewish life is being determined. With eloquence and wisdom he demonstrates that the pursuit of justice is not simply one more strategy to engage Jews but the very heart and soul of Judaism. In an age when Jewish life is turning inward Schwarz's insights will inspire readers to remember the dream of why we are here ... to repair our world. And that changes everything."

—Rabbi Irwin Kula, president, CLAL–National Center for Learning and Leadership

"Comprehensive and dynamic ... teachings on Judaism's passion for social justice. A work that touches and teaches, even as it constantly reminds us that ethics is at the heart of Judaism's concerns."

—Rabbi Joseph Telushkin, author, *A Code of Jewish Ethics* and *Jewish Literacy*

"Offers a valuable framework for understanding the internal tension so many Jews deal with—survival vs. social justice. The book makes clear that this is not an either/or proposition but an 'and' imperative. The Jewish community cannot afford to ignore its survival needs nor can the community justify its existence without a deep commitment to social justice. Sid Schwarz's well researched, compelling and insightful book has an important message for our generation."

—Edith Everett, philanthropist and community activist

"A thoughtful, sophisticated, and ultimately deeply spiritual account of the connection between Jews, Judaism and social justice. A work that every Jewish communal leader, rabbi, educator, and individual seeking to understand what Judaism has to say in and to the contemporary world must read. As he did in his masterful first book, *Finding a Spiritual Home*, Rabbi Schwarz opens a window into some of the most creative activity taking place in American Jewish life today and shows how the Jewish community can again be a source of moral inspiration, fellowship, and profound meaning for contemporary Jews. In *Judaism and Justice* Rabbi Schwarz brings to bear his own decades of experience as both a leader in the Jewish community relations field and a Jewish educator *par excellence* to demonstrate why a passion for social justice is critical to ensure the very 'continuity' that the community so ardently seeks."

—Dr. Jonathan Woocher, CEO, Jewish Education Service of North America; author, *Sacred Survival: The Civil Religion of American Jews*

"Sid Schwarz's book is long overdue. By providing a social justice interpretation of the classical texts, an analysis of the organized Jewish community's views on public policy, and an exploration of the emergent Jewish social justice movement, Schwarz covers the depth and breadth of the Jewish social justice story. From his decades of experience as a social change leader in the Jewish community, Schwarz has a profound understanding of the ties that bind Jews to this vital work. A must read for anyone seeking to understand this phenomenon and what Jews might contribute to social change in the years to come."

—Simon Greer, president & CEO, Jewish FundS for Justice

"A comprehensive and sophisticated analysis of the role that social justice plays in defining the commitments of North American Jews. Drawing on the theological ideals of particularity and covenant embedded in the classical Jewish concepts of Exodus and Sinai, Schwarz illuminates the modern Jewish condition and argues how a passion for justice is necessary for a widespread renaissance of Judaism among contemporary American Jews. Judicious and intelligent throughout, it constitutes a valuable contribution to modern Jewish thought and history."

—Dr. David Ellenson, president, Hebrew Union College-Jewish Institute of Religion; author, *After Emancipation: Jewish Religious Responses to Modernity*

"A powerful answer to the question of whether Judaism can make life worth living. The book is rich with classical Jewish sources as well as history and sociology. There is much to learn about Jewish life, especially the story of Jews in the United States. Yet, most compellingly, Sid Schwarz is a storyteller out to inspire us to live a meaningful life by rolling up our sleeves and grasping a world that needs healing."

—Dr. David Elcott, executive director, Israel Policy Forum; author, *A Sacred Journey: The Jewish Quest for a Perfect World*

"Rabbi Sid Schwarz's passion and love for his people and all of humankind comes through powerfully in this volume. It speaks the message that the test of community is how it embraces the most vulnerable. In *Judaism and Justice* Rabbi Schwarz shows the way with mind, soul and heart. Bravo!"

—Rabbi Avi Weiss, Hebrew Institute of Riverdale, founder and *rosh yeshiva*, Yeshivat Chovevei Torah Rabbinical School

"Sidney Schwarz—rabbi, activist, and social justice educator—draws upon all these roles to provide the rationale and context for Jewish social justice engagement in twenty-first century America. *Judaism and Justice* makes the case for a socially conscious and Jewishly informed involvement on the part of all those who care about repairing the world."

—Dr. Steven M. Cohen, research professor of Jewish social policy, Hebrew Union College-Jewish Institute of Religion

"A must read for anyone concerned about Judaism, justice, or both. Schwarz, who has decades of experience in linking Judaism and justice in the lives of young Jews coming from all kinds of Jewish backgrounds, here describes how and why Judaism and justice have and should be linked. This is a reasoned but passionate call to tie our concerns for the Jewish future with our work for a better future for all. With his advice, we just might succeed in doing that."

—Rabbi Elliot N. Dorff, PhD, professor of philosophy, University of Judaism; author, *To Do the Right and the Good* and *The Way Into* Tikkun Olam *(Repairing the World)*

"A powerful way to teach the history and meaning of the American Jewish commitment to *tikkun olam.* By framing the commitment in his innovative concept of the tension between Jewish Sinai and Exodus impulses, Schwarz has given the Jewish community a way to understand its social justice commitment and to measure it. With eloquence and without an iota of artifice or hyperbole *Judaism and Justice* will inspire Jews to make the world a better place in the years and decades to come."

—Rabbi Steven Gutow, executive vice president, Jewish Council for Public Affairs

JUDAISM
and JUSTICE

Also by Rabbi Sidney Schwarz

Finding a Spiritual Home:
How a New Generation of Jews Can Transform the American Synagogue
  (Jewish Lights)

*J*UDAISM
and JUSTICE

The Jewish Passion to Repair the World

Rabbi Sidney Schwarz
Foreword by **Ruth Messinger**

JEWISH LIGHTS Publishing
Woodstock, Vermont

Judaism and Justice:
The Jewish Passion to Repair the World

2006 First Printing
© 2006 by Sidney Schwarz
Foreword © 2006 by Ruth Messinger

For information regarding permission to reprint material from this book, please mail or fax your request in writing to Jewish Lights Publishing, Permissions Department, at the address / fax number listed below, or e-mail your request to permissions@jewishlights.com.

Library of Congress Cataloging-in-Publication Data
Schwarz, Sid.
Judaism and justice : the Jewish passion to repair the world / Sidney Schwarz ; foreword by Ruth Messinger.
p. cm.
Includes bibliographical references and index.
ISBN-13: 978-1-58023-312-5
ISBN-10: 1-58023-312-0
1. Justice (Jewish theology) 2. Justice—Biblical teaching. 3. Social justice—Religious aspects—Judaism. 4. Jewish ethics. I. Title.
BM645.J8S35 2006
296.3'8—dc22

2006021180

10 9 8 7 6 5 4 3 2 1

Jacket design: Tim Holtz

Manufactured in the United States of America
❀ Printed on recycled paper.

Published by Jewish Lights Publishing
A Division of LongHill Partners, Inc.
Sunset Farm Offices, Route 4, P.O. Box 237
Woodstock, VT 05091
Tel: (802) 457-4000 Fax: (802) 457-4004
www.jewishlights.com

To my wife and life partner, Sandy:

My heart has come to trust your intuition (v. 11).
The Torah of kindness that comes from your lips continues to guide
me (v. 26).
My words of praise are not sufficient (v.28).
—INSPIRED BY THE *EISHET CHAYIL*, "WOMAN OF VALOR,"
PROVERBS CHAPTER 31

Contents

Foreword

Ruth Messinger

It is appropriate that in these early years of the twenty-first century Jews take a new look at who we are, where we have traveled, and how best to use our faith to address the challenges of our time. As Sid Schwarz makes clear in this timely, thoughtful, and perceptive book, a detailed examination of the role of social justice in Judaism is central to this inquiry and offers us valuable insights and new directions for our work. It turns out that working in various settings to help repair and improve the world offers entry and reentry points for Jews who find meaning in these activities and who can, through this work, develop a new appreciation for Judaism.

Judaism and Justice examines the pendulum swings between the particular and the universal throughout Jewish history and offers us an analytic framework for understanding the sources of social justice in both ancient and modern Judaism. We are thoughtfully reminded to look at our own roots, to see that at times we have been primarily concerned with the self-protective, survival needs of our people—the tribal perspective—and at times much more imbued with a universal and altruistic outlook, driven to work not only for ourselves but for others—our covenantal consciousness. We are urged to see that these two strands have and will continue to coexist, but that this is a time to invest heavily in our social justice work.

Sid Schwarz is not only a distinguished rabbi, teacher and writer—he is both a pioneer and a veteran in the arena of Jewish social justice work. In his founding of PANIM: The Institute for Jewish Leadership and Values in 1988, he created a vehicle that is training the next generation of Jews to be leaders and activists with a deep love of Judaism and a passionate commitment to social responsibility. Through its various programs PANIM has touched the lives of thousands of young Jews, helping them fully embrace the legacy of prophetic Judaism and inspiring them to become a force for justice and peace in the world.

As this book chronicles so well, there are many other groups that are exploring Jewish tradition and Jewish text as they grapple with issues of urban poverty, environmental activism, how best to serve others, local organizing, and global change. They are attracting a generation of young Jews eager for these experiences. AVODAH: The Jewish Service Corps is now placing new college graduates in urban poverty agencies in three cities, and the Jewish Coalition for Service, which had six member organizations when it was formed five years ago, now has more than fifty program affiliates. The New Israel Fund has worked diligently for more than two decades to support projects in Israel that address such issues as human and civil rights, gender equity, and poverty, and to meet the needs of all citizens of Israel regardless of their religion. Hazon, a much newer organization, has attracted a substantial following not only for its environmentally-focused Israel and U.S. bike rides, but for its community healthy-food projects, and MAZON continues to respond to hunger crises across the United States, in Israel, and elsewhere on behalf of the American Jewish community.

We at American Jewish World Service are also driven by the social justice message of Judaism. In the last decade we have seen our commitment to Jews as global citizens take hold in the North American Jewish community. The idea that there is a faith-based argument for Jews to address poverty, oppression, and hunger in the developing world resonates with a growing universe of individuals and is most evident in the service programs we run for Jews from high school through retirement— Jews who give a week or up to a year of their lives to help people in the poorest parts of the world create a better future for themselves.

The strong response from the Jewish community against the ongoing genocide in Darfur demonstrates this increasing commitment to social action. Working through Jewish federations, community relations councils, individual congregations of all denominations, campus Hillels, national organizations, and all of the newer social justice organizations, AJWS was able to rally tens of thousands of Jews to new levels of activism—signing postcards, holding speak-outs, organizing buses to attend a large rally in Washington, D.C. During this period the Jewish community gave meaning to the phrase "Never again!" as it worked to end the violence in Sudan and rescue the people of Darfur from a continuing attack on their right to exist. Jews showed themselves ready to stand, to speak, and to work for global justice.

Much recent thought, time and money have been invested by Jews in the questions of Jewish continuity: What will keep Jews attached to Judaism? How will we command new attention from "lapsed" members of our faith? What role will Judaism play in the lives and activities of Jews? This book contains many of the answers. We need just such an activist Judaism now because the universe is broken, because there are domestic and international situations that demand our attention. Social justice work is an entry point to a stronger Jewish life for many young people, a way to bring much of the next generation back to Judaism. We have in this book not only a full explication of these ideas, but a guide to who is doing this work and how more of it might be done. It reminds us of the heritage of social justice work in the Jewish tradition and argues brilliantly for the importance of reviving a prophetic Judaism that motivates Jews to help heal the world in the twenty-first century.

Acknowledgments

I recently told an acquaintance that I was working on a new book. He expressed some amount of envy and then asked me what writing a book felt like. I replied that it was like running into a brick wall over and over again and having either the stupidity or the perseverance to try to find an opening until you ran into your next brick wall.

This project had several false starts, and I owe a debt of gratitude to many who believed that I had a book to write if only I could find it. My initial intention was to write a curriculum to be used in conjunction with the work I oversee at PANIM: The Institute for Jewish Leadership and Values. Joshua Perry, an alumnus of PANIM and a friend, worked closely with me on that project. David Behrman of Behrman House publishers encouraged the work and then did me a huge favor when, after reviewing our first draft, he said to me: "Sid, you have a lot to say on this topic. Don't hide it under the restricted and neutral tones of a curriculum." Never was a rejection so liberating.

I was fortunate to be granted a sabbatical from PANIM in the summer and fall of 2004, which allowed me the luxury to read, think, and write the major part of this book. For that I am indebted to the board of PANIM, which has, since my founding of the organization in 1988, provided me with the support and encouragement to dream big and do big—to advance our mission of inspiring and training the next generation of leadership of the American Jewish community with a unique integration of Jewish learning, values, and social responsibility. I would like to single out the respective chairs of the board with whom I have had the privilege to work: Aaron Goldman (*z'l*), Norman Pozez, Mark Levitt, Ellen Waghelstein, Laura Katz Cutler, and Mike Rappeport.

Joshua Perry was a full partner in the development of Part II, chapters

3–8, and I came to trust his excellent choices of texts and critical literary eye. Rabbi Mark Levine and Jonathan Brodie read over early drafts of this book, and I benefited from their feedback. Erica Brown, a brilliant teacher and colleague, was most generous with her time, reading the full manuscript twice and providing excellent feedback and suggestions to me. Dr. Elliot Dorff, who has set the highest standards with his own scholarship, gave me the confidence that the book was of a caliber worthy of wide distribution. Rabbi David Saperstein was generous with his time, providing excellent feedback on issues touched upon in the book about which he had personal knowledge and insight. David Cohen also read the manuscript and shared with me his insider view of the universe of Washington politics. Rabbi Steven Gutow gave me the benefit of his close reading of the manuscript as well. Craig Sumberg was particularly helpful to me in sharpening the language of the book, seeing to it that the words conveyed what I wanted to say. Holli Hartman worked on the technical part of manuscript preparation. Samantha Slater assisted me in the creation of the index of organizations at the back of the book.

I spoke to dozens of people in the research phase of the book. Their names appear in the back of the book in the list of interviews. I trust that I did justice to what they shared with me. I take full responsibility for the thesis and conclusions that I drew from them and from the various sources cited in the book.

Finally, I want to thank Stuart M. Matlins, publisher and editor in chief of Jewish Lights, for the role he played in bringing this book to fruition. Jewish Lights has become a phenomenon of significant note in the renaissance of American Jewish life over the past few years. Though this book was not typical of the kind of volume Jewish Lights puts out, Stuart trusted my assertion that social justice, no less than spirituality, was a critical point of entry for Jews into Jewish life. I trust that the reception of the book bears out my claim. And I would like to thank Lauren Seidman, senior project editor at Jewish Lights, for her exceptionally thoughtful and careful efforts to help bring this book to the reader.

To my wife, Sandy, to whom this book is dedicated, and to my children, Danny, Joel, and Jennifer, who often sacrificed time with me so that I could give birth to this book, I owe unending gratitude. I love each of you very much.

Introduction

This book explores the relationship between Judaism, social justice, and the Jewish identity of American Jews. After thirty-plus years working in the Jewish community, I have become increasingly fascinated by what causes some Jews to make Judaism and the Jewish community central to their lives while others see Judaism as irrelevant. Significantly, one thread that seems to connect affiliated Jews and the organized Jewish community, and Jews whose ties to that community are far more tenuous, is a commitment to make the world a better place—a passion to repair the world. *Judaism and Justice* examines the origins of this commitment and explores how it has shaped the behavior of the Jewish community and of the Jewish people.

There are numerous ways to measure Jewish identity and commitment. The 2000 National Jewish Population Survey rated people with membership in two or more Jewish organizations as "highly affiliated"; those with one membership as "moderately affiliated"; and those with no ties to any Jewish organization as "unaffiliated." Using those definitions, they found that 28 percent of American Jews were highly affiliated, another 28 percent were moderately affiliated, and 44 percent were unaffiliated. If one uses synagogue membership as the yardstick, 60 percent of American Jewry is unaffiliated. Yet ask a different question and you get a very different picture. A 1989 American Jewish Committee survey found that 96 percent of its random sample was "proud to be a Jew." Eighty-six percent of that same sample said "being Jewish is something special." Obviously a lot of people who have some positive feelings about being Jewish do not join Jewish organizations. Their identification with the Jewish people is, at best, a matter of consciousness that does not translate into tangible memberships or financial support. Their affiliation with the Jewish people is, at best, a potential.

In my book *Finding a Spiritual Home: How a New Generation of Jews Can Transform the American Synagogue* (Jewish Lights), I explored how such "potential" Jews, many of them spiritual seekers, might be drawn back to Judaism. I profiled one synagogue from each of the four denominations of American Judaism that had successfully attracted these Jews and developed a composite picture of a new paradigm synagogue that I called the "synagogue-community." The book argued that, to the extent that American synagogues can transform themselves into synagogue-communities, there are tens of thousands of Jews ready to join their ranks. Large numbers of Jews are engaged in serious religious and spiritual searches. The challenge of the American synagogue today is to find ways to make itself hospitable to such seekers.

I believe that what is true in the realm of religion and spirituality is also true in the realm of social justice. The Jewish community has the ability to capture the passions of American Jews who care deeply about social justice. The limited success that it has had in doing so owes to the way the Jewish community has positioned itself in the American public square over the past fifty years. This book will explore the organized Jewish community and its public affairs agenda from the end of World War II through the opening years of the twenty-first century. I use the term *organized Jewish community* to refer to the institutions under the umbrella of the national Jewish federation system that engages in central fundraising from the community and allocates those dollars to fund local and overseas Jewish needs as well as projects in the state of Israel.

This book will also look at the emergence of an alternate universe of smaller Jewish organizations during this period that were singularly focused on issues of social justice. These latter organizations have succeeded in attracting to their ranks many Jews who were disinclined from participation in the large, establishment structures of the organized Jewish community. It is as yet unclear whether the success of these Jewish social justice organizations will lead to a repositioning of the organized Jewish community or, instead, result in drawing away from the organized Jewish community the very Jews who might be able to impact that system's agenda and profile. Clearly, however, we live in a time when the contours of the Jewish community are shifting. The American Jewish community's support for Israel, affiliation with Jewish communal institutions, and commitment to issues of broader social concern are all elements contributing to the emerging realignment of the Jewish community.

Few commitments unite Jews as much as a commitment to create a more just and equitable society. A 1988 *Los Angeles Times* poll asked Jews to name "the quality most important to their Jewish identity." Half of the sample cited "a commitment to social equality." In contrast, only 17 percent cited a commitment to Israel and another 17 percent cited religion. Two years later, a Jewish public opinion poll conducted by the Cohen Center at Brandeis University found that while 20 percent of Jews said that the most important factor in determining their vote for a candidate for public office was his/her position on Israel, 40 percent said that social justice would be the deciding factor. This survey data suggests that the more prominent social justice becomes on the agenda of the organized Jewish community, the more likely it is that many American Jews will be motivated to pursue ties to that ethnic/religious identity. To the extent that social justice is relegated to a peripheral pursuit in Jewish institutions, American Jews can and will find other outlets for their social justice interests.

I do not come to this book as an objective academic, though I use the tools of my academic training to offer the reader a cogent analysis of the subject at hand. I am a participant observer. My political baptism came early. In the midst of the Vietnam War, pressure mounted on Congress to extend the right to vote to eighteen-year-olds. If they are old enough to die for the country, went the argument, they are old enough to vote. The Twenty-sixth Amendment to the Constitution extending the franchise passed in July 1971. As a high school student, I was already writing a monthly column on politics from a youth perspective for a local newspaper on Long Island, New York. I turned eighteen in October 1971 and was promptly appointed the first eighteen-year-old committeeman for the Nassau County Democratic Party. At the University of Maryland, I was deeply involved in campus protests against the war in Southeast Asia. I was one of a handful of student leaders designated to negotiate with the school administration about the infringement of civil liberties caused by university efforts to quell the demonstrations. Majoring in political science, I was fairly certain that I would run for public office.

Life would take me in another direction. I made my first trip to the Soviet Union in the summer of 1970 with United Synagogue Youth

(USY), the Conservative movement's youth group. Speaking and advocating for the freedom of Soviet Jews became a deep life commitment for me. I was also strongly influenced by the surge of Jewish pride that followed Israel's victory in the Six-Day War. My involvement in Jewish campus life, my work as a youth leader and educator in local synagogues, and my summers staffing Jewish camps and trips to Israel led to my decision to become a rabbi.

I was first able to bring together my love of Judaism and my passion for social and political issues when I accepted the post of executive director of the Jewish Community Council of Greater Washington D.C. in 1984. As the umbrella public affairs arm of the Jewish community, I had the opportunity to work not only on issues of Soviet Jewry and Israel, but also in the fields of intergroup and interfaith relations, civil liberties, church-state separation, and economic and social justice. My last day on the job was December 6, 1987, which was the same day as the Summit Rally for Soviet Jewry on the Mall in Washington. I had the privilege of playing a small role in helping to organize the single largest gathering of Jews ever assembled for a political rally—250,000. They gathered in freezing weather from across the United States to send a message to Soviet Premier Mikhail Gorbachev, who was in town to meet with President Ronald Reagan. Jews, and the world, would never sit silent as long as Jews were denied the right to emigrate and/or to live freely as Jews within the Soviet Union. On Monday morning, President Reagan used the front page news about the rally to emphasize to Gorbachev the wide popular support he had for his demands for Soviet reforms.

Within a year, Jews would be free to leave a country that had imprisoned them for close to a century. Subsequently, almost a million Soviet Jews would emigrate to Israel and to the West. Within two years of the rally, the Soviet Union was no more. It would be hard to make a more compelling case for the relationship between religious identity, a commitment to justice, and political activism. There was a direct correlation between an international human rights campaign to free Soviet Jews, the successful mobilization of hundreds of thousands to attend a political demonstration in Washington, D.C., and the eventual ability of Jews to either emigrate from the Soviet Union or freely practice their religion without leaving the country. Once, after telling of my involvement in the Soviet Jewry movement to a group of Jewish teens, a young woman approached me after the talk. "My family emigrated from Russia to

America in 1991," she told me. "Thank you for helping us get out." I didn't think that I deserved the thanks, but I understood what she meant. It underscored for me how political activism could positively affect human suffering and human lives.

In 1988 I founded PANIM: The Institute for Jewish Leadership and Values. Its mission is to contribute to the renewal of American Jewish life through the integration of Jewish learning, values, and social responsibility. This book is part of that effort. Most of our programs focus on Jewish teens. In addition to running the largest Jewish community service program in the country for teens (the Jewish Civics Initiative), PANIM also brings in more than 1,000 students each year for leadership seminars (*Panim el Panim*) that reinforce Jewish identity via social and political activism. Working with Jewish youth week in and week out, I don't need surveys to tell me how central social justice is to the Jewish identity of young Jews. What is missing is the ability for most Jews to link their belief in principles like equality, justice, tolerance, and peace with their Jewish heritage. When it is done effectively, however, the synthesis both deepens the commitment of Jews to social justice and strengthens their pride in their Jewish identity.

Even more telling in this regard is the work I have done with adults. Having worked in Washington, D.C., for more than twenty years, I have had the privilege of meeting and working with hundreds of extraordinary people who commit themselves, day in and day out, to making our society more just and the world a safer and more peaceful place. These individuals work as elected officials, congressional staffers, in the executive branch, and in hundreds of nonprofits devoted to every issue from human rights to children in poverty. Seeing how many of these individuals are Jewish makes me marvel at the statistic that Jews are less than 3 percent of the American population. While only a small fraction of the Jews I meet are formally affiliated with the Jewish community, it doesn't take long for the conversation to get around to Jewish identity (after all, I am a rabbi and the "confession" syndrome extends far past the Catholic Church). When it does, I see how much these people identify their day-to-day work as a manifestation of their Jewish self-perception. Often they have a hard time articulating how their work and their Jewish identity connect. Many have had little formal Jewish education. Yet these rather assimilated Jews seem to know enough about Jewish custom, belief, and practice (if only through movies, books, and television) to be proud of it and to find ways to connect their life and work to Judaism.

About ten years ago several people whom I had met in my public affairs work and who had significant positions in the public interest universe of Washington, D.C., asked me whether I would be willing to do some teaching to a group of their Jewish colleagues who had limited Jewish backgrounds. I was sufficiently intrigued that I took them up on their offer. We gathered a group of about forty Jews who were active in social and political issues. A few were affiliated but most were not. We studied classical Jewish texts, and I tried to connect the teachings of our tradition with the issues that they wrestled with each and every day. I learned at least as much as they did, for over time I saw how hungry Jews are for sources of wisdom that might guide them in their public and private lives. Being highly educated and cosmopolitan, most Jews access and are open to many sources of wisdom. But when the wisdom comes from their heritage, it touches a place deep in their souls. Suddenly, modern, assimilated Jews are speaking ancient words from Jewish sacred texts, and they find themselves standing with their ancestors at Sinai, receiving the Torah for the first time.

This book is about what I call the "Sinai consciousness" of contemporary Jews and how it plays out in the world of social and political issues. It is the book I wanted to be able to give to my class of Jewish policy wonks who needed a quick and dirty on "what from Jewish tradition relates to the things I care about." As such, Part I asks a big question: What is the purpose of Judaism? It is not a conventional question. Volumes have been written about Jewish history, customs, festivals, and laws. This book begins with a question that precedes those specifics: Where is Judaism trying to take its adherents? In probing that question, this book presents a theory of Jewish identity that emanates from the two most formative events in Jewish history, the exodus from Egypt and the revelation of law at Mount Sinai.

Part II offers an interpretation of the classical sources of Judaism—the five books of Moses and seven core rabbinic principles—through the prism of social justice. The chapters explore those elements of the Jewish tradition that establish the foundation for the millennial Jewish commitment to social justice. There is no pretense that the interpretations and values chosen for this book represent the entire Jewish tradition. The interpretations of the five biblical books and the Jewish values highlighted were chosen for their relevance to issues of social and political importance in the world. Part II is thus an extended definition of what I mean when I employ the terms *Sinai impulse, prophetic Judaism,* and *social justice.* These are principles or values that a person might use to guide his or her thoughts and actions as they relate to the myriad complex issues that face our communities, our nation, and our world.

Part III looks at how the American Jewish community positioned itself in the American public arena. This is a piece of the story that can be easily overlooked by many whose social justice stances place them outside of the framework of the organized Jewish community. From the outside looking in, the Jewish community is often experienced as defensive and reactionary. There are elements of truth in this. And yet, as someone who has stood on both sides of the ramparts, I can say that there is a dynamic to the evolution of the Jewish community in America that needs to be taken seriously and understood. By looking at three issues—civil rights, Soviet Jewry, and the support for Israel—the reader will better appreciate how Jewish organizations balance the need to protect and ensure the survival of the Jewish people with the desire to be faithful to the values outlined in Part II.

Finally, Part IV looks at exciting new developments in the American Jewish community that point in the direction of a Jewish renaissance. More and more Jews are finding ways to live their values in Jewish contexts. This section of the book profiles the recent burst of energy in the field of Jewish social justice and explains it in the context of the maturation of the American Jewish community. Whereas a Jew in the 1960s who wanted to be on the cutting edge of social justice often left the Jewish community to do so, by the dawn of the twenty-first century such a person had an exciting array of options to live out the prophetic mandate within the framework of the Jewish community. What remains to be seen is whether the universe of the organized Jewish community, with its considerable institutional, political, and financial clout, can find a way to work with the much younger and much less organizationally mature universe of Jewish social justice groups. In the final chapter, I suggest some reasons why this reconciliation is of critical importance for both parties.

A final word about terminology. A good many authors have addressed themselves to elements of what this book examines using different terminology. These terms include: Jewish liberalism, prophetic Judaism, Jewish political behavior, Jewish community relations, Jewish defense, Jewish social action, and Jewish social justice. There is both overlap and distinctiveness in these terms. My term of preference is Jewish social justice. It is not synonymous with liberalism. My definition of social justice behavior is framed by the Jewish principles and values of mutual responsibility, loving the stranger, compassion, willingness to act in the face of evil, and speaking truth—values explored at some length in Part II. Such values are not the exclusive province of liberals or progressives. The book tries to avoid portraying the issue on a left/right axis, with the left on the side of social justice and therefore the good and everyone who does not agree with that position representing something bad.

Similarly, my use of the term social justice is not synonymous with the universalism side of the old universalist/particularist dichotomy. In my discussion of the organized Jewish community I will look at this dichotomy, but I do not begin with a bias that the particularist choice is antithetical to what social justice demands. Indeed I hope to redefine the terms of a dilemma that has been a source of some controversy and ill will in the Jewish community for half a century—to what extent must the Jewish community focus its energies on the protection and survival of the Jewish people and to what extent should time and resources be devoted to issues of injustice and inequity in the world?

I believe that this dilemma is a theme that runs throughout Jewish history, until this very day. There is no right and wrong side to this dilemma. There is, however, much misunderstanding that leads to communal dysfunction. The thesis developed through this book invokes two seminal moments in Jewish history—Exodus and Sinai—to help explain attitudes and actions along this divide. *Exodus consciousness,* as it plays itself out in Jewish history and Jewish identity, fortifies the survivalist impulse in Jews and in the Jewish community even as it contains elements of concern for the "other." *Sinai consciousness,* as it plays itself out in Jewish history and Jewish identity, fortifies a more altruistic and universalistic impulse in Jews and in the Jewish community even as it contains elements of the Jewish people's uniqueness in the world.

In the end, my belief is that Exodus consciousness and Sinai consciousness are intended to be complementary and interdependent. A Jewish community without one or the other has lost its way. My hope is that this book might shine a light on that more holistic and integrated path.

I THE JEWISH CONDITION

1

The Purpose
of Judaism

Judaism is a big topic. Having taught converts to Judaism, I have tried to understand Judaism through the eyes of the uninitiated. It can be overwhelming. There are our sacred texts. There is history, philosophy, and literature. There are all the customs that revolve around life cycle, holidays, and ritual observance. There are religious practices unique to Jewish communities in countries all around the world. What is it that unites the Jewish people?

At a time when more Jews ask the question "Why be Jewish?" well before they are even interested in pursuing the question "How shall I be Jewish?" it is incumbent on us to frame some good answers. Our "market" has been schooled on instant messaging, media sound bites, and MTV images. While the educator in me wants to respond to the skeptical inquisitor who asks me "Why be Jewish?" by offering a dozen basic books, the pragmatist in me knows that this is a nonstarter. There are too many alternatives making claims on the time and attention of the potential Jew. There is a need for us to state succinctly just what it is that Judaism offers the contemporary Jew if we are to have any chance of staking claim to his/her loyalty.

Core Principles

Judaism is a rich tradition that can take a lifetime to understand, particularly its finer nuances. Jewish sages of the past faced similar challenges but tried to capture the essence of Judaism in easily understood and remembered formulas. In the second century, Simeon the Righteous offered one of the most memorable formulas, the three "pillars" of Judaism—*Torah* (study), *avodah* (service or worship), and *gemilut chasadim* (acts of lovingkindness) (*Ethics of the Ancestors* 1:2). One generation later, the sage Hillel, when confronted with a challenge from a Roman soldier, boiled Judaism down to one principle: "What is hateful to you, do not do to others." "The rest is commentary," he said, "now go and study." Maimonides (twelfth century) framed Judaism in thirteen key principles. Joseph Albo (fifteenth century) formulated three core principles and six dogmas that derived from those principles.

While there are disadvantages in any attempt to reduce Judaism to bite-size formulas, to a generation with a short attention span, the advantages outweigh the disadvantages. When I ask students, "What is the purpose of Judaism?" I am met with mystified faces. Sometimes, the more Judaically knowledgeable the person, the more confused he or she becomes. Indeed, for Jews who have been raised in Judaically rich homes, who have benefited from a solid Jewish education, and who have adopted Jewish lives filled with prayer, ritual practice, learning, and good deeds, the value of a Jewish lifestyle is obvious. Yet even for such a Jew, there is the danger of losing the forest through the trees. "What is the purpose of it all?" is a question that helps focus and center us.

Most American Jews are affluent, well educated, living lives filled with all kinds of opportunities … and Judaically illiterate. If they have had any exposure to Judaism, it might have been in an afternoon Hebrew school or with some obligatory lessons that were required to qualify for a bar or bat mitzvah. As they come into adulthood, the little they remember of their Jewish education is uninspiring. Just as they reach an age when they can begin to appreciate some of the depth, beauty, and wisdom of Judaism, they are ready to chuck the whole thing. They become educationally unavailable because they do not see the relevance of the rudimentary synagogue skills and the handful of Bible stories they learned to the rest of their lives. This is a recipe that often leads to weak and tentative ties to the organized Jewish community and to the dismissal of a heritage of wisdom that might actually add meaning to their lives. Imagine if this constituency of Jews had emerged from their brief exposure to Jewish education with a clear and memorable message of the purpose of Judaism. Perhaps, then, like Hillel's Roman soldier, they might have considered taking up the challenge to "go and study" at some later time when they became mature adults.

Justice and Holiness

Based on my reading of Judaism, there are two compelling answers to the question "What is the purpose of Judaism?" The first purpose is based on Genesis chapter 18, when God expands on the initial charge to Abraham to go forth from his land to the land that God will show him and there make Abraham into a great nation. In verse 18:19 God adds a critical prerequisite that will enable Abraham to fulfill his destiny. He is to obey God's commandments and "extend the boundaries of righteousness and justice in the world," *la'asot tzedakah umishpat.* The second purpose is based on God's revelation to Moses, which is recounted in Exodus 19:6. The Jewish people are told to be "a kingdom of priests and a holy nation," a *mamlechet kohanim* and *goy kadosh.*

This is not a bad start. Why be Jewish?—because it is a heritage that extends the boundaries of righteousness and justice in the world and invests our world with holiness. I think that I might now have the attention of more than an occasional Roman soldier.

The priesthood in biblical Israel was responsible for the sacrificial service in the portable Tabernacle in the desert and, later, in the Temple in Jerusalem. In post-biblical Judaism, particular ritual practices and prayer took the place of the sacrificial service. These would be the practices that would keep Jews separate and distinct from the other people among whom they would live in the diaspora. The Hebrew word for holiness—*kedusha*—comes from a root that means separate and apart. The brilliant paradox of Judaism is that it combines a demand for holy apartness with the expectation that Jews will be totally engaged with the world around them. Both the observance of ritual laws and acting with justice and compassion to others fulfill God's commandments.

The seminal biblical text that connects the ideas of justice and holiness is Isaiah chapter 58, a section that is read, not coincidentally, as the haftarah on Yom Kippur. The holiest festival in the Jewish calendar, Yom Kippur is the very day on which the tradition demands proper alignment between a day of prayer and fasting and the ethical behavior that Jews are supposed to manifest throughout the year.

> Is not the fast that I desire the unlocking of the chains of
>   wickedness,
> the loosening of exploitation,
> the freeing of the oppressed,
> the breaking of the yoke of servitude?
> Is it not the sharing of your bread with those who starve,
> the bringing of the wretched poor into your house,
> or clothing someone you see who is naked
> and not hiding from your fellow human being in their time of
>   need?
> [Behave this way and] Then shall your light burst forth as the
>   dawn,
> your waters of healing will flourish again,
> your righteousness will go before you and God's glory will be
>   behind you.
> Then, when you call out to God, God will respond, "Here I
>   am" (Isa. 58:6–12).

In this memorable passage, Isaiah points to the gap that he observed between the ritual observance of his day and the ethical behavior of those who participated in those rituals. Speaking on behalf of God, Isaiah's objective is not to dismiss the importance of ritual, but rather to press the point that full-hearted faith requires that ritual and ethical behavior complement each other. Either dimension, standing alone, is insufficient and fails to meet God's expectations. It is this twin standard that determines God's judgment of Jews on the day of atonement.

Much has been made of the distinction in Judaism between those laws that are between a person and God and those that are between people and people. The former tend to get categorized as "ritual laws," such as keeping the Sabbath or keeping the laws of *kashrut* (dietary laws). The latter tend to get called "ethical laws," such as giving charity or visiting the sick. Early Reform Judaism emphasized the importance of the latter and the irrelevance of the former. In creating a faith that would allow Jews to easily integrate into general society, the particularities of ritual law seemed to be an unnecessary impediment. Conversely, Judaism's legacy of bringing prophetic principles of justice into the world was a source of pride.

This dichotomy is not always helpful. Even as Reform Judaism has spent the past few decades trying to reclaim parts of the Jewish tradition that the early architects of the movement dismissed, to most liberal Jews, the ethical principles of Judaism have a self-evident value that the more particular parts of Judaism do not. It is against this backdrop that contemporary Jews need to reassess the relationship between justice and holiness.

The Torah calls the Jewish people an *am segulah,* a treasured and exceptional people (Deut. 14:2). It complements the notion of *goy kadosh* (Exod. 19:6), a nation that is holy and apart. With its origins rooted in a pagan Near East, the monotheistic faith that Abraham and his offspring created would eventually give birth not only to Judaism, but to Christianity and Islam as well. If the core principles of Judaism were to survive, the Jewish people needed to shape a culture and a lifestyle apart from the surrounding nations. The biblical admonition against "whoring after other Gods" (Judg. 2:17, 8:33), and later prohibitions against intermarriage between Jews and non-Jews, led to a body of customs that distinguished Jews from others. Such laws were driven by the need to keep Jews as a people apart, a holy nation.

Holy Apartness Reconsidered

In the modern, Western world, many Jews came to believe that this "holy apartness" was an unfortunate holdover from an earlier era when Jews were consigned to ghettos, persecuted, and even killed. They believed that, in a world that welcomed Jews and made "our" Ten Commandments a basis for Western notions of morality and ethics, there was no longer a need for Jews to be a people apart. The liberal/universal bias of so many modern Jews led to either a polite, benign neglect of the idea of holy apartness or an outright rejection of the idea as incompatible with modernity and pluralistic societies.

Mordecai Kaplan, the founder of Reconstructionist Judaism and one of the seminal Jewish thinkers of the twentieth century, totally rejected the concept of the Jewish people's "chosenness," in part because it was unsupported by his understanding of God. But he also felt that the ethnic chauvinism implicit in it contributed to the rivalries and conflicts between peoples throughout world history. If religion were to be a force for social good, Kaplan argued, all religions should eliminate those elements of their belief systems that have led them to assert that their faith was somehow superior to others. As the most ancient of all Western religious traditions, Judaism should be the first to cast off the notion of Jews being "the chosen" of God.[1]

At the dawn of the twenty-first century, this liberal/universalistic ethic is being challenged by many thoughtful people. The contemporary world has been shocked by the sudden surge of radical Islamic fundamentalism, which sees Western, liberal democracy as an evil, surpassed only by the evil of Zionism, Israel, and the Jewish people. All are regarded as infidel forces that need to be eliminated by any means possible. Nor is this the only threat to the values and ideals that Judaism brought into the world. Increasingly it is obvious that secular American culture is not the neutral setting it was thought to be a century ago, a setting that would allow for a multiplicity of faiths and ethnic groups to coexist, leading to a rich cultural mosaic in a tolerant and pluralistic America. This country's affluence and its love affair with consumerism has created a culture that is at odds with Judaism's emphasis on justice and holiness.

For several generations, many American Jews were convinced that American values were more or less the same as Jewish values. The logical extension of that assumption was that it was not worth the time to learn the language of Jewish values since America provided much the same set of values. It was a license for Jewish illiteracy. It went without saying that Jewish holy apartness was not only chauvinistic and exclusivist but also un-American. Why should Jews hold themselves apart from an America that gave them unparalleled freedom and economic opportunity? We should drink deeply and fully from the cup of American society.

It was these assumptions that lay behind Mordecai Kaplan's rejection of the idea of chosenness. Hoping for a world in which all religions might undergo the same kind of reconstruction that he was proposing for Judaism, Kaplan envisioned a world parliament of religions at which the people who brought the idea of chosenness into the world—the Jews—would voluntarily relinquish that claim. In return, all the other religions of the world, which had created their own versions of tribal chauvinism, would also voluntarily relinquish their claims on exclusive truth.

World events of recent years have been hard on Kaplan's brand of liberal universalism. Though we might continue to admire the sentiments that he set forth, most of the Western world has been rudely awakened to a global struggle in which democracy, freedom, and pluralism are identified by adherents of radical Islam as a scourge that must be eradicated from the world. Judaism, of course, does not escape indictment by these same extremist elements.

Now it seems clear that Judaism has some wisdom that is in short supply, both in the world as well as in America. Increasing numbers of Jews, and a not insignificant number of non-Jews, are coming to see that within Jewish texts, there are truths and insights that are badly needed in the world. It is also clear that, throughout history, Jews have had some measure of success in making these values operative in their communities. Ironically, at the dawn of the twenty-first century, it seems that we have not traveled so far down the road from our ancestors who understood that Judaism was "counterculture," offering a way of thinking and living that was embraced by few others in the world. Whereas once the cultural norm from which Judaism dissented was paganism, today it might be religious fanaticism, hedonism, or secularism.

From this perspective, the idea of holy apartness has newfound appeal. There may well be no other way for the values and ideals envisioned by Judaism to be expressed and carried forward in the world, even if those ideals are not yet embraced by the society at large. For much of Jewish history, the biblical expression *am levado yishkon* (Num. 23:9), Israel as "a nation that dwells apart," was descriptive. Today it has become prescriptive. Unless the Jewish people succeed in holding onto some parts of the values and ideals of justice and holiness, over and against societies and cultures that have either rejected or ignored those ideals, there is no way for those principles to endure. It can only be done by reclaiming the importance and value of the Jewish people being holy and apart.

Jewish Mission

The prophet Isaiah describes the Jewish people as a "light of the nations" (*l'or goyim;* Isa. 42:6). The phrase is often rendered as "light unto the nations" even though the Hebrew doesn't yield that precise definition. Yet the more popular translation reveals the way the Jewish people have long understood that phrase from Isaiah—the Jewish people have a mission in the world to be a beacon of morality for others to emulate. In fact, many proponents of the mission-of-Israel concept interpret the very exile of the Jewish people from the land of Israel as the silver lining in what is otherwise a dark cloud in Jewish history. The Reform theologian Kaufman Kohler framed it this way in the early twentieth century:

> To help in the redemption of the world by righteousness is his [the Jew's] messianic mission. Nor is it sufficient to claim the title of priority for these principles of social justice. He must substantiate his mission by its practice in so large a measure so as to become from a mere materialistic pursuer of wealth, which he has so often been declared to be, the very banner bearer of idealism, to command the world's admiration and emulation.[2]

How did the Jewish people come to see themselves as the "banner bearer of idealism" in the world? Religions begin with foundational myths, a master story that gives adherents in successive generations a sense that their allegiance to and practice of a particular faith is connected to generations that came before them and generations that will come after they are gone. What we will now explore is how the master story of the Jewish people imprinted on Jews for all time a deep commitment to be that "banner bearer of idealism" as well as those aspects of the Jewish people's historical experience that sometimes made it difficult to do so.

2

The Exodus-Sinai Continuum of Jewish Life

Religions do not exist in a vacuum. They are rooted in a historical narrative and a contemporary circumstance. Adherents to a religion shape their religious identity at least as much on these twin factors as they do on the tenets that appear in the sacred texts of the same tradition. In the case of the Jewish people, it is the twin experiences of the exodus from Egypt and the covenant with God forged at Mount Sinai that help explain much of the way the Jewish people have engaged with the world in the millennia since those formative events.

From Slavery to Freedom

The Jewish people have been shaped by the historical consciousness that they were born in slavery. The story of the Jewish enslavement in Egypt, recounted in the biblical Book of Exodus, is seared into the memory of Jews via the annual observance of Passover. A Jew need neither be learned nor frequent a synagogue to know the story of their ancestors building the pyramids of Pharaoh as slaves until they escaped under the leadership of Moses, an experience that the children of Israel saw as a redeeming act of God.

Part of the genius of the rabbinic sages was to take the central parts of the Jewish historical narrative and concretize them in annual festivals replete with memorable rituals, symbols, liturgy, and pageantry. The festival of Passover is one of the most beloved and observed festivals in the Jewish annual cycle. The rituals and melodies of the Passover seder are especially designed to capture the attention of children, forming memories that last a lifetime.

There are several ways that the Passover story affects Jews. First, it sets the stage for the motif "from slavery to freedom" (*me'avdut leherut*) that runs throughout Jewish history. Whenever the Jewish people experienced persecution, oppression, or expulsion, they relived the experience of their ancestors in Egypt. Precisely because the Exodus story concludes with the redemption of the Jewish people from Egyptian bondage, Jews throughout history, in the midst of the most dire circumstances, believed that they, too, would ultimately be redeemed from their suffering.

Second, because the motif of slavery to freedom played itself out in Jewish history over and over again, Jews came to see the trajectory of their history as essentially redemptive, or messianic. There would always be a better tomorrow. For religious Jews, this was an article of faith. God's hand was active in history. The redemption of Jews from a specific circumstance was a sign of God's love for his chosen people. When Jewish suffering persisted, that suffering was understood by the rabbis as a divinely directed punishment. Since all of history is under God's dominion, it must be that God is punishing his people for a reason, presumably because they have not been faithful to the covenant at Sinai. And yet, that very theology fortified the belief that, in the end, evil would be vanquished and the world will come to enjoy a state of peace and harmony (Isa. 14:17). This sense of hope, deeply embedded in the soul of the Jew, is reflected in the national anthem of the state of Israel, *Hatikvah,* the hope.

Third, the Jewish people have internalized the verse that appears in Exodus 23:9: "You shall not oppress the stranger for you were strangers in the land of Egypt." This commandment is reinforced again and again in the Jewish tradition, leading Jews to have a particular concern for the "stranger in their midst." Deeply rooted in the collective consciousness of the Jewish people is the sense of being "the outsider."

The Jew as Outsider

The status of Jews as outsiders is based on more than just the biblical origins of the Jewish people. In the year 70 CE, the Romans destroyed the second Temple in Jerusalem and Jews effectively lost their political sovereignty. Banished from the land of Israel, Jews needed a survival strategy. In a remarkable historical transformation, credited in the Talmud to Johanan ben Zakai, the Jews set up an academy outside of Jerusalem, in Yavneh, and began the process of making their national identity portable. The rabbinic sages in the centuries following the fall of Jerusalem—through their interpretations of the laws of the Torah—provided Jews with a carefully defined way of life. This body of Jewish law, called halacha, provided specific guideposts for daily life. In addition, a corpus of legends (*aggadah*) developed that provided the mythic narratives that inform and enrich every civilization. Both of these bodies of literature were used as a prism through which Jews of every generation came to understand their individual and collective existence. It tied them not only to generations of Jews that preceded them, but also to Jews across the globe. This expanded body of Torah provided Jews with the tools to survive a diaspora that lasted almost 2,000 years.

Jews were able to survive the loss of their ancestral land and language because wherever they lived, they clustered in communities that accepted the authority of the rabbinic sages. The sages used halachic decisions and *aggadic* teachings to connect the Jews of their generation with the master narrative of Jewish history. In addition, Jews developed communities that had well-developed social structures, addressing a wide range of individual and communal needs. In many ways, Jews were living out the biblical admonition to be "a nation that dwells apart" (Num. 23:9). Jews throughout the Middle Ages enjoyed an advantage that many non-Jews did not. Within their semi-autonomous communities, with their own political, judicial, and social welfare system, they were able to create both the intellectual and social structures that gave them a sense of purpose and a way to survive.

Jewry in Freedom

As much as these semi-autonomous communities helped Jews negotiate a less than hospitable climate during the Middle Ages, it was a system that would not survive the transition to modernity. Just as feudalism and the system of guilds would give way to the emergence of the modern nation-state, so, too, did the communal governance system of Jewish communities need to adapt to new circumstances.

One of the seminal moments in Jewish history took place in 1807 when Napoleon Bonaparte convened an assembly of rabbis from across Europe and dubbed it, in the grandiose way only an emperor might, "the Sanhedrin." Though the actual Sanhedrin had not actually met since the fifth century CE, there was a method to Napoleon's madness. Desperately wanting to unite Europe under his political authority, he needed to break down the medieval feudal system that had clergy, nobility, artisans, and peasants each with their separate arrangements with local authorities. Laying the foundations for the modern nation-state, Napoleon understood that effective governance over a vast territory would require laws that applied equally across the spectrum of the subject population. He was willing to grant the subject population certain rights in exchange for their political loyalty and the fulfillment of certain financial obligations to his empire. The Jews represented a political entity that functioned semi-autonomously throughout the empire and that stood in the way of Napoleon's ultimate design. Napoleon did not love the Jews; rather the Sanhedrin was Napoleon's clever ploy to break down Jewish separateness and to make the Jews like everyone else.

Nevertheless, his offer was not an ungenerous one. In return for defining Jewish identity as a faith and not as a separate national or ethnic community with loyalties different than other people in the empire, Jews would acquire full citizenship and the rights attending that status. It was the Jews' ticket out of the ghetto, an entry pass into the emerging, modern European nation-state. It was also a break with almost 2,000 years of diaspora Jewish history. If Judaism represented a creative tension between holy apartness and an expectation that Jews would be fully engaged in the world they inhabited, medieval Europe hardly provided the opportunity for the second part of the mandate. The new arrangement offered by Napoleon to the Jews held out the possibility that they might engage with gentile society in a way that had happened only rarely in their history.

The rabbis were given a series of questions that clearly had right and wrong answers from Napoleon's perspective. Napoleon's Sanhedrin gave the emperor the answers he wanted and did so in a way that carefully respected existing halachic guidelines. Among the Sanhedrin's rulings were: prohibiting polygamy; requiring a religious bill of divorce (*get*) to be accompanied by a prior civil divorce; ruling that a mixed marriage would be binding on Jews from a civil/legal perspective, even if not recognized by Jewish law; requiring Jews to regard their country of residence as their fatherland, living by its laws as full citizens and pledging loyalty to its political authority; and calling on Jews to treat their fellow non-Jewish citizens according to universal laws of moral conduct, treating them as they would fellow Jews in all business matters including the exacting of interest on monetary loans. Effectively, these rulings set the groundwork for full Jewish participation in the modern nation-state.

Ever since Napoleon's historic Sanhedrin, Jews have wrestled with the trade-off represented by these rulings. Was Judaism simply a profession of faith or were there national and historical elements that meant that the Jews would always be "a people apart"? If Jews were being offered an opportunity to join the international brotherhood of humanity, free from all of the limitations and disabilities that characterized their diaspora existence for centuries, should the offer be spurned for the sake of perpetuating Jewish historical consciousness and group identity? Could Jews engage with gentile society without losing their distinctiveness? Might this new status be the messianic "end of days" foretold by the Bible or was it a modern version of the Golden Calf, a false idol that appeared to offer redemption but that was, in fact, a betrayal of the biblical mandate that Jews remain a people apart?[1]

It was not until the twentieth century that theories of democratic and cultural pluralism emerged in the United States that changed the terms of Napoleon's offer. These new ideas suggested that a democracy did not require all cultural, religious, and ethnic identities be relinquished. America, it was argued, was a cultural mosaic, not a melting pot. But even before these theories gained prominence in America, laws guaranteeing the separation of church and state and the free exercise of religion allowed the United States to forge a society far more hospitable to Jews than was Europe. This new "social contract" allowed Jews to reach a level of prominence and prosperity in America that was unprecedented in any other country of their historical experience. But it also opened the door to the highest level of assimilation in Jewish history.

The period between the emancipation by Napoleon and the end of World War II was a time of great ferment in the world, and in the Jewish community it brought about many new forms of Jewish identity. Reform Judaism was born in Europe as an attempt to provide the kind of faith that would preserve essential parts of the Jewish religion but without the national and historical dimensions that would stand in the way of full integration of Jews into their European host countries. Conservative Judaism would emerge as a reaction to Reform, trying to balance some of the stringencies of Orthodox Judaism with the demands of living as members of multireligious societies. Within the revolutionary political movements of eastern Europe were many Jews seeking to find secular ways to advance a messianic vision of society. And within those revolutionary movements existed the kernel of the idea for Jews to create a society of their own.

History, however, does not run in straight lines. The opportunity provided by modernity for Jews to integrate themselves into European society was intoxicating, and many Jews seized it. Some went so far as to convert to Christianity. But the Holocaust turned back the historical clock, tapping into the Church's demonization of the Jews that dated to the first centuries of the Common Era. Cutting the cancerous Jews out of the European body politic was an idea that found ready acceptance among many in Christian Europe.

In the years after the Holocaust, the debate over Jewish identity reemerged. If Zionism was an alternative for Jews seeking to escape persecution, could there be another form of Jewish identity for those Jews living in relative freedom? The Zionists were convinced that Jews were at risk of either physical annihilation in countries where anti-Semitism raged (such as the Soviet Union) or assimilation in societies that offered Jews a full embrace (such as much of Western Europe and the United States). Indeed, there is much in the history of the Jewish communities of the world since World War II that bears out the Zionist analysis. At the same time, it is hard to ignore the thriving Jewish communities around the world today that offer a wide array of Jewish identity options. It is here that probing the meaning of the twin impulses of Jewish identity—Exodus and Sinai—will prove illuminating.

Exodus: Political/Ethnic Consciousness

Nations search their past for symbolic starting points because such origins help to define the master narrative of a people. America as a participant in Western civilization can be said to have begun with Columbus's discovery of the New World. America as a nation free of European control can be dated to the victory of the colonies against Britain in the Revolutionary War. America as a democracy can be dated to the framing of the U.S. Constitution.

The Jewish people's narrative also has several possible starting points. While Abraham is the first Jew for bringing the idea of monotheism into the world, it is the Exodus story that represents the beginning of Jewish national consciousness. A group of slaves that might not have had much in the way of ethnic homogeneity shared a common predicament (slavery) and a common oppressor (the Egyptians). What shapes the national consciousness of the people that the Bible calls "the children of Israel" (*b'nai yisrael*) is the pairing of that enslavement experience with the Israelites' escape to freedom. Their consciousness was forged not only by an experience of common suffering, but, more importantly, by a shared experience of redemption. Immediately after the redemption of the Israelites at the Red Sea, Moses impressed upon them the significance of what they just experienced: "Remember this day that you went out from the house of bondage, by virtue of the strong hand of God were you redeemed" (Exod. 13:3).

This is a verse that is used again and again in the Bible, in rabbinic writings, and in the liturgy that Jews recite in worship. Its power to shape the consciousness of the Jewish people cannot be overestimated. It is not only that the experience of the Exodus is passed down through the generations via the festival of Passover, it is that the sacred literature of Judaism uses that experience as the foundation for Jewish peoplehood. It is impossible to know what elements of the Exodus story, passed down via the biblical account, were known to those who were enslaved. The biblical account is a theological interpretation of those events recorded centuries after their occurrence. Even if it were a contemporaneous account, it is unlikely that the average slave would have been aware of the high drama being played out between Pharaoh and his upstart nemesis, Moses. But what could not have escaped the notice of the common slave was that the political regime that oversaw their enslavement was being challenged by some combination of a spokesperson for the enslaved (Moses), environmental calamities (the plagues), and, perhaps, by a God who was more than a match for the deities of Egypt. By the time the slaves followed Moses out of Egypt and escaped the pursuing Egyptians, they were well on the road to nationhood. The Bible records the moment with: "When Israel saw the wondrous power that God employed against the Egyptians, the people were in awe of God, expressed their loyalty to God and to his servant, Moses" (Exod. 14:31).

All the elements of political consciousness were now in place: a common history (Egyptian slavery), a founding myth (being redeemed from the Egyptians by a God more powerful than any other), and a leader (Moses). The Exodus dimension of Jewish existence would continue to be central to the Jewish people throughout their long history. For a time, it would play itself out in the form of political sovereignty, as it did with the ancient kingdoms of Israel and Judea. In the twentieth century, the Exodus dimension would manifest again with the creation of the modern state of Israel.

But the Exodus consciousness described here transcended conventional political arrangements. The Jewish people manifested this consciousness during their wandering in the desert, in their early settlement in the land of Israel arranged by tribal affiliation, and during the two millennia that Jews existed in the diaspora. Exodus consciousness caused Jews to identify with each other regardless of the fact that they might be living thousands of miles apart, under different political regimes, speaking different languages, and developing variations on Judaism that often synthesized elements of traditional Jewish practice with the specific gentile culture in which they lived. This consciousness also meant that Jews took care of one another, not only when they lived in close proximity, but even when they became aware of Jews in distress in other locales. During the time that Jews lacked political sovereignty, they became a community of shared historical memory and shared destiny. They believed that the fate of the Jewish people, regardless of temporal domicile, was linked. This is what explains the success of the Zionist movement, the historically unprecedented resurrection of national identity and political sovereignty after 2,000 years of dispersion. The Exodus consciousness of the Jewish people was the glue that held the Jewish people together. It was the secret to Jewish survival.

For the children of Israel, however, there was a dimension of national identity that transcended political consciousness—an encounter with sacred purpose that would create a direct connection between the slaves who experienced the Exodus from Egypt and the vision that drove the patriarch, Abraham.

Sinai: Spiritual/Religious Consciousness

Scholars, clergy, and lay readers alike can debate the veracity of the Bible's account of the revelation of the Torah at Mount Sinai (Exod. chs. 19–20), but no one doubts its mythic power. Chapter 4 deals at greater length with ways one might understand this piece of Jewish history. Here I need to address the significance of the moment.

If the Exodus gave the collection of slaves that left Egypt a sense of a common past and a shared destiny, the experience at Sinai made it abundantly clear that the people Israel were expected to live out a higher calling. If the Jewish people thought that their redemption from bondage was "a free ride," the covenant entered into at Sinai was a rude awakening. It made many demands on the Jewish people and they would often be judged to fall short of those demands.

> You have seen what I did to the Egyptians, how I bore you on eagle's wings and brought you to me. Now then, if you will obey me faithfully and keep my covenant, you shall be My treasured possession among all the peoples.... You shall be to Me a kingdom of priests and a holy nation (Exod. 19:4–6).

God reminded the children of Israel that they were redeemed from slavery to be God's treasured people on the condition that they obey God's laws and live faithfully in accordance with the covenant.

Throughout the centuries, part of the Jewish people's loyalty to the covenant manifested itself in their observance of ritual laws. Over time, the level of ritual observance would wax and wane. But the ethic of Sinai had greater resonance and staying power than the observance of any particular ritual law. It conveyed to Jews throughout the generations that their task was to replicate, in the temporal world, the kingdom of heaven. While in some religious traditions this phrase would take on otherworldly meanings, Jews combined it with a rich body of core values that guided their behavior in this world. Jews became a people of compassion; the rabbinic term used is *b'nai rachamim*. They were guided both by their history of persecution and their understanding of the revelation at Sinai to lend their hands and their hearts to the most vulnerable members of society, both

Jewish and non-Jewish. The Talmud states: "If anyone has compassion on all created beings, then it is certain evidence that he or she is from the seed of Abraham, our forefather."[2] Compassion for others defines the Jew.

Classical rabbinic commentators focus attention on the way that the children of Israel responded to the giving of the Ten Commandments from God through Moses and the laws that follow in chapters 20–24 of the Book of Exodus. Repeatedly the Israelites proclaim that they will obey all that God has asked of them. It culminates with the famous phrase *naaseh v'nishma,* "we will do and we will obey" (Exod. 24:7), which the commentators take as a sign of ultimate obedience. The commitment to follow the laws, even before they were fully revealed, represents the highest form of religious obedience. It is the standard that God and Moses demand and expect.

There are other significant features regarding the Sinai moment that make it central to the essence of Judaism and to the consciousness of the Jewish people. First, the revelation is given in the desert, in a place lost to history. The sanctity of the revelation will not inhere in the physical place but in the message. Second, the revelation is given not to a subset of priests but to the entire nation. It is the possession of the entire nation of Israel. Third, the covenant is entered into by a free people in an act of volition. The Hebrew word *avodah* carries two meanings. It is the root for the word "slavery," experienced by the Israelites in Egypt. It also carries the meaning of "serving God," a behavior that will be demanded of the Israelites at Sinai. The difference between the two, however, is that "servitude" is coerced whereas "service" is an offering of the hearts of the faithful.

The German-Jewish philosopher Leo Baeck beautifully articulated the concept of a people with a sacred purpose when he wrote:

> A difficult task was assigned this people [Israel] in history. It is
> so easy to listen to the voices of idols, and it is so hard to
> receive the word of the One God into oneself. It is so easy to
> remain a slave, and it so difficult to become a free man. But
> this people can only exist in the full seriousness of its task....
> Man lives within the universe and within history. This people
> [Israel] understood that history and the universe testify to a
> oneness, and reveal a totality and order. One word has dared to
> be the one expression for that which keeps everything together:
> "covenant."[3]

Baeck's characterization typifies Jewish self-perception from the earliest stages of Jewish history. He is describing what I am calling here "Sinai consciousness." Even if we cannot verify God's revelation to the Jewish people at Sinai and his "choosing" of the people Israel, the fact that they lived with a belief that they were the chosen people led them to conduct themselves in such a way that they more than earned the label. In other words, the Jewish people lived at a higher moral level to fulfill the expectation of the covenant.

It must nonetheless be noted that whatever combination of gratitude, fear, and/or religious ecstasy evoked the full-hearted response from the Israelites at Sinai, they would soon stray far from the expectation. The further they got from their enslavement in Egypt and from the revelation at Sinai, the more they complained about the conditions of the wilderness and the more they fell short of covenantal expectations. One of the themes of this early history of the Israelites is unworthiness, and it provides the theological justification for all subsequent travail of the people: the forty years in the desert, the problems that beset the early Israelite monarchies, the chastisements of the prophets, the military defeats at the hands of Israel's neighbors, and, ultimately, the loss of Jewish sovereignty and the exile of the Jewish people from the land of Israel.

The contemporary political philosopher Michael Walzer, in his seminal work *Exodus and Revolution,* points to the gap that almost always exists between the vanguard of a revolution and the masses who are supposed to benefit from the change in political circumstance. While the vanguard is filled with high theory about the ultimate meaning of the revolution and the ultimate destiny of those who have been liberated, the masses are driven by more basic concerns. Will we eat better? Will we enjoy better living conditions? Will we be able to raise our families in relative peace and security? Perhaps it explains why the promise of bringing the children of Israel to "a land flowing with milk and honey" (Exod. 3:8) is mentioned even before the struggle with Pharaoh commences. The willingness to engage in revolution is based on the people's belief that it will lead them to a better life.[4]

On the heels of the Exodus, the children of Israel, filled with gratitude, have good reason to expect that all of their self-interested needs will be met. They promise Moses and God anything and everything ("we will do and we will obey"). But the covenant at Sinai requires a people who are deeply committed to both justice and to holiness. Sinai consciousness can only be fulfilled over the course of many generations, for the proof of fulfillment is revealed only to the extent that the people who accept the challenge "teach the words diligently to their children" (Deut. 6:7). From a theological perspective, the history of the Jewish people is about bridging the gap between the materialist and self-interested longings of the people and the sense of sacred purpose articulated by Moses, as well as by the prophets and rabbis who would follow him.

Exodus-Sinai in Historical Perspective

Central to the understanding of Judaism and the Jewish people is the tension that exists between being the people of the Exodus and being the people of Sinai. The two dimensions are by no means mutually exclusive. In fact, they are meant to be complementary. Yet time and again, history has shown that one impulse conflicts with the other. Specifically, every nation is challenged to find a way to survive. To do so, nations find ways to organize themselves socially, economically, and politically. They acquire a piece of territory that they defend against others who covet it. They develop a particular culture unique to themselves. All of these are the elements of nationhood. And just as with other nations in history, the elements of the Jewish people's unique culture—which includes their Sinai consciousness—come to be subservient to the demands on the nation to ensure its physical survival.

We can see the inherent conflict between the Exodus and Sinai tendencies in the two verses identified in Chapter 1. To be the "holy nation" of Exodus 19:6, the Jewish people will adopt practices that set them apart from the rest of the world. But to fulfill God's charge to Abraham—to extend the boundaries of righteousness and justice—will require that the Jewish people become fully engaged with the world around them, with Jews and non-Jews alike.

And yet we also see how the tendencies are reconciled in the Jewish tradition. Despite the fact that Abraham brings into the world a theology that forces him to leave his father's house and forge an uncharted religious path, the rabbinic commentators admire Abraham for the fact that he does not wall himself off with his own clan. A nineteenth-century commentator, Rabbi Samson Raphael Hirsch, reflects the standard rabbinic perspective on Abraham. Admiring Abraham's behavior in his appeal for the sinners of Sodom and Gomorrah, Hirsch said:

> A righteous person who lives in an atmosphere like Sodom is not permitted to abandon the nation and to close himself off in his own world thinking that he will fulfill his obligation just in order to save himself and his family.[5]

A similar tension between Sinai consciousness and Exodus consciousness can be found in the early history of Zionism. The early Zionists saw two threats to the future of the Jewish people. One was the allure of assimilation in those Western countries that granted the Jews a certain level of political emancipation. What would keep the Jews committed to any group consciousness without the hostility and rejection of the host culture? The second challenge was the deep-seated anti-Semitism of Europe, a culture that the Zionists were sure would never fully tolerate Jews in their midst. The response of the political Zionists, led by the likes of Theodore Herzl, was to solve the problem of the Jews by finding them a homeland.

A small but influential group of thinkers who were contemporaries of Herzl had another answer. These "spiritual Zionists" were as concerned about the future of Judaism and the soul of the Jewish people as they were about saving Jewish lives. They, too, sought to establish a Jewish homeland for the Jewish people but their priority was focused on the establishment of a society that fulfilled the highest ethical and moral principles of Judaism. Some, but not all, of these spiritual Zionists were Orthodox. The most prominent of this group was Ahad Ha'am (Asher Ginzberg), who was steeped in traditional Jewish learning but was a non-Orthodox Jew who considered himself part of the Jewish enlightenment movement (*Haskalah*).

As the Zionist movement evolved, and even after the establishment of the state of Israel, it is easy to see these two strands of thought, political and spiritual Zionism, competing with one another. Though it is easy to admire the idealism of the proponents of spiritual Zionism, the horrors of World War II and the Holocaust made the strategies and approaches of the political Zionists seem far more appropriate. Jews were being slaughtered. They needed to be saved. Instinctively the Jewish people went into Exodus mode, engaging themselves in the task of bringing a beleaguered remnant from slavery to freedom. There was no time to debate the extent to which one or another element of the Yishuv (pre-state Israel) was consistent with the highest ideals of Sinai consciousness.

Many in Israel continue to argue that the principles of spiritual Zionism need to be more fully heeded. In fact there are numerous examples of how Israeli society has tried to live by core Jewish values and principles. Yet most would admit that such concerns are virtually always relegated to secondary status, taking a back seat to concerns about Israel's safety and security. It would be admirable if the Jewish people could live in the world solely as the people of Sinai, but for as long as the world poses dangers to Jewish survival, history seems to demand that Jews continue to be a people of the Exodus as well.

The contemporary philosopher Rabbi David Hartman points to this tension in the Jewish condition when he writes:

> Sinai permanently exposes the Jewish people to prophetic aspirations and judgments.... Sinai requires of the Jew that he believe in the possibility of integrating the moral seriousness of the prophet with the realism and political judgment of the statesman. Politics and morality were united when Israel was born as a nation at Sinai.... The prophets taught us that the state has only instrumental value for the purpose of embodying the covenantal demands of Judaism. When nationalism becomes an absolute value for Jews, and political and military judgments are not related to the larger spiritual and moral purpose of our national renaissance, we can no longer claim to continue the Judaic tradition.[6]

While the tension that Hartman highlights has existed throughout Jewish history, it became more acute when the Jewish people established the state of Israel. Being situated in a region where it was surrounded by nations sworn to its destruction, the Jewish state has been willing to use every means at its disposal to defend itself, even in the face of world condemnation. Still, rarely does a day go by in modern Israel when Jewish voices don't call out for the government to find a way to uphold the moral vision of Sinai and act with compassion, even toward those who might intend harm to the state. Indeed, this Sinai consciousness is embedded in the Declaration of the Establishment of the State of Israel:

"The state of Israel ... will be based on freedom, justice and peace as envisaged by the prophets of Israel."

The Psychology of Jewish Survival

The Exodus-Sinai continuum provides a theoretical framework that helps to explain not only the way that the sages of the Jewish tradition interpreted sacred texts, but also Jewish collective behavior through the course of history. This continuum is the prism through which I shall analyze both the sacred texts and the contemporary history that is the focus of this book. To some extent, the Exodus-Sinai continuum I suggest here parallels more familiar frameworks that have been used to interpret Judaism and the history of the Jewish community, such as particularism/universalism or conservatism/liberalism. Yet those continua tend toward dualism. A particular interpretation or communal action is seen as particular or universal, conservative or liberal. By applying the Exodus-Sinai analysis to Judaism and to the Jewish community, one can see how both elements are often at play at the same time. The thesis proposed here leads to a more accurate understanding of the factors that influence both Judaism and the actions of the Jewish community.

The complementary nature of the Exodus-Sinai continuum is illustrated by the fact that each pole on the continuum contains elements of the other. Even as I shall use the term Exodus consciousness to describe the way Jews and the Jewish community might act in a fashion that is defensive and protective of group self-interest because the Exodus experience is at the core of Jewish political consciousness, the Exodus biblical narrative also contains one of the phrases that is the cornerstone for Jewish universalism: "You shall not oppress the stranger for you were strangers in the land of Egypt" (Exod. 23:9). Even into the present day, the tendency of Jews to identify with those who are most weak and vulnerable can be understood as the historical conditioning of a people born in slavery.

Sinai consciousness is no less complex. Even as I use the term Sinai consciousness to describe the way that Jews aspire to altruistic, other-directed behavior in accordance with a pursuit of justice and a sense of sacred purpose, the holiness inherent in Sinai contains a strong impulse for the Jewish people to remain a people apart. The life of holiness entails many customs that reinforce the distinctiveness of the Jewish people, a prerequisite for the Jewish people to be bearers of a prophetic heritage to the world. While social justice initiatives are usually aligned with the Sinai impulse of Jewish tradition, without a healthy dose of the Exodus impulse, the Jewish people would have disappeared long ago. With regard to Israel, it is instructive that a prayer written after the state of Israel was established, now widely accepted and recited by Jews, blesses Israel as "the first promise of our redemption." It implicitly recognizes that the current Jewish state may aspire to manifest the highest ideals of Sinai, but that it has yet to attain it.

Each impulse, Exodus and Sinai, is meant to be a corrective on the other (see chart at the end of this chapter). As we will see in Parts III and IV of this book, each tendency suggests a different course of action for the Jewish community. I shall use the Exodus-Sinai framework as a way to better understand and explain social justice in the context of Jewish values, community, and identity.

○
—————
○

Leo Baeck said that "Man lives within the universe and within history" and that the Jewish people's existence testifies to the fact that both are part of a larger "oneness."[7] Sinai represents the Jewish people's encounter with the universe, with a moral calling, and with God. The consequences of that encounter—essentially the teachings of Judaism—are written all over the face of Jewish history. Exodus represents the Jewish people's experience with their history, moving again and again from a situation of persecution, oppression, and annihilation to a place of liberation and freedom. The Jewish people are shaped by Sinai consciousness just as Judaism is shaped by the Exodus impulse. Both are part of a larger oneness. Judaism and the Jewish people are best served when the twin impulses are integrated and are in balance. History has not always allowed this ideal integration to exist, but our understanding of the Jewish tradition and of the Jewish community is informed by it.

Twin Impulses in Jewish Consciousness

	EXODUS	SINAI
Dimension	Political/ethnic	Spiritual/religious
Impulse	Survival	Sacred purpose
Ideal modality	State of Israel	Messianic (*olam habah*)
Motivation	Group self-interest	Torah/God's word/holiness
Psychology	Defensive	Altruistic/other-directed
Characterization	Members of the tribe	Members of the covenant

I will turn now to an examination of the classical texts of Judaism, both biblical and rabbinic canons, to see how the concept of justice developed and how it was applied.

II SINAI

3

Genesis

Abraham and "the Call"

The Torah identifies Abraham as the original ancestor of the Jewish people. Simply put, he was the first Jew, and we are his descendents—spiritually, if not genetically—and the heirs to the legacy that he established.

Sometimes it is hard, however, to recognize what of Abraham's legacy remains present in today's Judaism. A great deal has changed. For one thing, Abraham's chief form of religious observance was the offering of animal sacrifices. And his cultural practices—among them slavery and polygamy—were very different from ours. So it is worth asking: How did Abraham shape the Jewish tradition that we inherit today? What is it about Abraham's legacy that defines both him and us as Jews?

The Torah suggests that Abraham's selection as the emissary who would bear witness to the one God in the world is related to his willingness "to do what is right and just" (Gen. 18:19). The word for righteousness in the Torah is *tzedakah*. The word for justice is *mishpat*. This is God's call to Abraham: to live a life of righteousness and justice. If Abraham heeds this divine call, the Jewish people—Abraham's spiritual offspring—will bring blessing into the world. With Abraham, God begins to build a covenantal relationship with one family, a family that becomes the Jewish nation. If one family can respond to God's call "to do what is right and just," perhaps the world can come to live that way as well. Perhaps the Jewish people can become, in the prophet Isaiah's famous words, "a light of the nations" (Isa. 42:6).

Abraham is also important because he was the first monotheist, the first believer in only one God. Both Islam and Christianity, as monotheistic faiths, also view Abraham as their ancestor. Abraham's call, therefore, resonates deeply within those faith traditions as well. Some who despair of the tribal, national, and political grievances that have pitted these faith communities one against the other in the modern world have begun to talk about "the Abrahamist tradition," as if trying to create a new grouping that evokes the original, pure, ethical call of God to a common ancestor.

A Test

In the Torah's first book—Genesis, or *B'reishit*—an argument over the fate of two cities becomes the occasion for Abraham to demonstrate his worthiness to be the ancestor of the Jewish people.

The narrative relates that God has determined to destroy Sodom and Gomorrah, cities of total wickedness. In response to God's plan, Abraham lodges the first human-rights complaint in Jewish history. He challenges God's plan based precisely on the value that God professes to hold dearest: "Will you sweep away the innocent with the guilty?" he asks. "It would be a desecration for You to do such a thing.... Shall the Judge of the whole earth not do justice?" (Gen. 18:23–25). Abraham challenges God's command by citing to God the very call for "justice" that was God's charge to him just verses earlier. The strategy works. Abraham succeeds in winning from God broader promises of mercy for the residents of Sodom and Gomorrah. First he gets God to agree that he will spare the city if fifty righteous people can be found. Not resting on his early negotiating success, Abraham pushes the deal until he gets God to agree to spare the city even if he can only find ten righteous people. Abraham wins a moral victory. And he passes a test.

Abraham heeds the divine call in his advocacy on behalf of the doomed residents of Sodom and Gomorrah even as it pits him against God. Abraham's status as ancestor of the Jewish people depends upon his sense of moral responsibility. For generations to follow, rabbinic commentators would cite this episode as the epitome of righteous behavior. Many rabbinic commentators compare Noah, who saved his family from the flood and allowed the rest of the world to perish in the flood, with Abraham, who seeks to save the lives of the people of Sodom and Gomorrah. Abraham models the individual whose concern does not begin and end with himself, his family, and his tribe. He feels a moral obligation for all people, even when they are not part of his tribe, even when they might be wicked. The Jewish people are born when Abraham sets an example of righteousness and justice for his descendents, who will be called, in turn, to bring righteousness and justice into the world.

The importance that Judaism places on doing what is right and just—*tzedakah* and *mishpat*—is indicated by the frequency with which the Jewish tradition pairs those values and sets them as a yardstick for expected behavior. The prophet Jeremiah said:

> Let not the wise glory in their wisdom; let not the strong glory in their strength; let not the rich glory in their riches. Take glory in this alone: in knowing Me well, that I am the Lord Who does kindness, and righteousness and justice throughout the land; for in these I delight (Jer. 9:22–23)

In the Talmud, King David is also an exemplar of one who acts in accordance with these two values, particularly as they relate to judicial matters that come before him. Justice married to righteousness, the teaching goes, yields compromise. The passage goes on to recount that the way King David fulfilled both mandates was that when a poor person committed a crime and the just penalty would be a fine that he could not afford, David would find him guilty and then pay the fine out of his own pocket. In this way, both justice and righteousness could be served.[1]

Advocacy and Responsibility

Throughout their history, Jews have taken it for granted that Abraham's example with Sodom and Gomorrah was not to be considered the exception, but rather the rule. Ever since Abraham questioned God's moral judgment, there has been a longstanding Jewish tradition of advocacy on behalf of justice. Jews believe that morality and truth are the business of human beings, and not the exclusive province of God. Jews believe that their greatest responsibility is speaking truth and acting justly, no matter who—or Who—says otherwise. Jews have always assumed that the moral imperatives of our tradition apply to everybody equally, even to God.

In the Torah, there are many instances of prophets criticizing God's behavior toward the Jewish people: "Do not give God a quiet moment," the prophet Isaiah urges, "until God rebuilds Jerusalem" (Isa. 62:7). In the Talmud, we find audacious spokespeople, like the miracle worker Honi, chastising God for failing to show the qualities demanded by the Jewish moral tradition: "I swear by Your great name that I will not move from here until You show mercy to your children."[2] The Jewish practice of confronting God manifests itself often in subsequent generations. The great Hasidic master Levi Yitzchak of Berditchev tried to force God's hand and end the exile of the Jewish people: "I am coming to You in a legal manner concerning Your people Israel. What do You want of Israel?… I shall not go hence, nor budge from my place, until there be an end of exile."[3]

The Birth of the Sinai Impulse in Judaism

Abraham is a man whose belief in God drives him to abandon home and country, to set himself apart from other nations and other faiths. In Abraham's first encounter with God, he is commanded: "Go forth from your land, and your birthplace, and your father's house, to the land that I will show you. And I will make you a great nation" (Gen. 12:1–2). Following God's command, Abraham journeys to Canaan where he becomes a stranger in a foreign land. But ethnic and political separatism is not what makes Abraham the first Jew.

The Torah tells us that Abraham truly became the father of the Jewish people when he heeded God's call to adopt a sacred purpose, spreading righteousness and justice in the world. The Jewish people would not be merely a people apart, a separate ethnic and political unit. Instead, they would be a people bound to a higher calling. According to God's covenant with Abraham, every Jew is called upon not simply to believe in the values of righteousness and justice, but to act on them: motivated by moral responsibility, to advocate—as Abraham did—on behalf of the vulnerable of all nations. Abraham lived in Canaan as "a stranger and a sojourner" (Gen. 23:4), but his sense of separateness and apartness did not prevent him from heeding a universalistic moral call

—from behaving with altruistic compassion toward the people of Sodom and Gomorrah.

This sense of a higher calling—an altruistic urge to bring righteousness and justice into the world—is the Jewish legacy from Abraham. It is what I call in this book the "Sinai impulse." Interpretations of this calling, of course, have changed dramatically. It is interesting that modern Jews seem disinclined from using the term "calling," as if uncomfortable with the suggestion that we have received some message that might guide our lives from a transcendent source. Christians, of course, use the term with great frequency, a fact that makes many Jews all the more uncomfortable with it. And yet, this is precisely what our legacy from Abraham is. God's call to Abraham, to which Abraham responds, challenges the first Jew to extend the boundaries of righteousness and justice in the world. This calling takes on more specific, legal form at Sinai, making it easier to pass down through the generations, but it starts with Abraham.

Over time, the Jewish understanding of "calling" evolves. It is the genius of the rabbinic tradition that it takes the broad categories of righteousness and justice and redefines those concepts based on changing circumstances. Genesis, the first book in the Torah, tells the story of how Abraham and his family came to heed God's call. The second book in the Torah, Exodus, describes the evolution of Judaism from the faith of a single isolated family into the ethical tradition of an entire nation.

4
Exodus

Embracing the Covenant

Abraham's calling was not forced upon him. He accepted it willingly. The Book of Genesis gives a word to Abraham's voluntary commitment to his moral and ethical responsibilities: *brit,* or sacred covenant. A covenant, as commonly understood, is an agreement between people, an expression of mutual obligation. But *brit* has always meant something special to the Jewish people.

The Bible tells the story of how one man's call to justice became the commitment of an entire people. The most important moment in this transformation came at Mount Sinai, when Abraham's descendents forged a *brit* of their own. At Sinai, Abraham's call was democratized, as an entire nation bound itself to God's revelation as conveyed by Moses. The obligations of the covenant were not meant to be fulfilled by one prophet or priest, nor by a class of prophets or priests. They were to be the obligations incumbent upon all Jews, for all time.

Exodus 19 reinforces how closely tied are the concepts of Exodus and Sinai. Chapter 13 of the Book of Exodus already tells of Pharaoh giving permission to the children of Israel to leave Egypt, having suffered through a series of plagues culminating with the death of all the firstborn of the Egyptians. The retelling in Exodus 19 provides an important textual spin. According to verse 4, the children of Israel are not simply brought from one geographical locale (Egypt) to another (the wilderness en route to the land of Israel). They are brought closer to God ("to Me"). These few verses underscore that the purpose of the Exodus is not just an escape from slavery and political freedom but also a journey to a sacred way of life. The children of Israel were brought out of Egypt to renew a covenant that was first forged between Abraham and God. Now it will be a covenant with Abraham's descendants, the children of Israel. The acceptance of the covenant is what leads God to call the Jewish people "a kingdom of priests and a holy nation" (Exod. 19:6).

The Sinai moment symbolizes the Jewish people's commitment to a higher moral purpose. The nation's natural instinct for tribal cohesion and survival had to be counterbalanced by a commitment to work for a messianic world in which the principles of righteousness and justice will obtain for all peoples. This is the meaning of Sinai. This is the implication of being a covenanted people (Isa. 42:6). It binds the Jewish people to God. And it binds the Jewish people to a moral and ethical calling.

From Exodus to Sinai

It is Sinai that separates the Jewish people from all the other nations on earth. Even for those who do not believe literally in the Torah's account of God's appearance on Sinai, it is not difficult to appreciate the importance of Sinai to the Jewish mind. Sinai is the moment when the Jewish people had a shared experience that added a sacred purpose to the people's liberation from Egypt. Sinai was the birth of the Jewish sense of obligation to each other and to the world. It introduced to the world the idea of human interdependence and social responsibility, also known as ethical monotheism. Sinai is the root of the Jewish understanding that freedom begins with responsibility.

Since Sinai, Jews have thought of their covenantal responsibilities in terms of mitzvot. Mitzvot literally means "commandments." The mitzvot are specific moral obligations, the essential elements of the Jewish people's national call. The Ten Commandments contain some of the most famous, and most fundamental, of these mitzvot: "You shall not murder"; "You shall not commit adultery"; "You shall not bear false witness" (Exod. 20:13). But the Ten Commandments hardly tell the whole story. Tradition counts 613 commandments in the Torah. As the sages of the Talmud strove to explain and amplify these commandments, they formulated many more obligations. We can think of mitzvot as the concrete expressions, or the practical applications, of Jewish values.

The genius of Judaism is that every generation searches for its own understanding of what it means to heed the national covenant entered into at Sinai, to do what is right and just. The revelation at Sinai was more than a moment in history; it is a continuous revelation that can inform the ethical and moral choices of Jews in every generation. Rabbinic sages, from the earliest history of the Jewish people up until the present, have taken the seminal verses from the Torah and adapted them to instruct the Jews of their generation regarding how they might faithfully abide by the covenant of Sinai. Thus the commandments of the Torah do not represent the totality of our commitment to the covenant. They are only the beginning.

A People with a Mission

The Jewish people have always understood themselves to be charged with a special mission. Isaiah's language for this is "a covenanted people" (*brit am*).

> I, the Lord, have called you to righteousness; I have taken you
> by the hand; I have shaped you; I have appointed you as a
> covenanted people, a light of the nations. To open blind eyes,
> to release captives from prison and from the dungeon, those
> who sit in darkness (Isa. 42:6–7).

The covenant at Sinai commits the Jewish people, as individuals and as a community, to a higher calling. It is an agreement that demands the pursuit of justice. Judaism teaches that its adherents are not holy because of who they are, but because of what they do. Some Jews believe that they have a special relationship with God, but they understand that relationship in terms of a special responsibility. The blessing recited over the Torah reading expresses it perfectly: "Blessed are You... Who chose us from among all the nations, and gave us Your Torah." What does it mean to be "chosen?" To embrace the Torah and its commandments, and the ethical values expressed through them.

What about those who do not believe that God literally "chose" the Jewish people? Does that lessen the power of the covenant? The covenant is not simply with God. It binds everyone in the community to each other and to a shared sense of the same calling. It is as powerful a bond as land and language, the more conventional elements of national identity. It explains how it is that after the Jewish people lost their national sovereignty in the land of Israel in the year 70 CE, they could still retain a sense of group consciousness, even as Jews were dispersed throughout the world.

There is a Jewish teaching that the soul of every Jew, past and present, stood at Sinai to hear the Ten Commandments. Whether this is understood literally or figuratively, the meaning is clear. The covenant at Sinai transcends generations. It unites Jews across the world and throughout time. Exodus reminds the Jewish people of how they came to be a free people. Sinai reminds the Jewish people of their ethical obligations to the world.

Genesis teaches how Abraham's calling to act justly was the essence of his Jewishness. It was the substance of his covenant. Exodus teaches how the Jewish people renewed that covenant at Sinai, embracing Abraham's sense of moral purpose even as it amplified and adapted Abraham's calling. As the Jews became a nation, the covenant became the unifying commitment that bound them together in mutual responsibility. But, as with Abraham's altruistic advocacy for the residents of Sodom and Gomorrah, the Jewish covenant was never only about protecting the interests of other Jews. We turn to the Torah's third book, Leviticus, to study in greater depth the imperative of altruistic compassion—the sense of moral purpose, born with Abraham's covenant and developed at Sinai—that has always defined the Jewish people.

5

Leviticus

Roadmap to a More Perfect World

It seems fitting that the Torah's third book, Leviticus, which contains so many of Judaism's commandments, carries the Hebrew name *Vayikra,* "God called." The book contains the cardinal principles that guide Jewish behavior and consciousness for the rest of history. While all commandments are important, not all commandments are equal. From the vast body of Jewish law, developed over millennia, some commandments jump out as essential expressions of the Jewish commitment to the cardinal virtues of righteousness and justice. These are the fundamental Jewish values—*klallim,* "core Jewish values," which are the essential moral principles that define what it means to be a Jew.

So what are these *klallim?* Which among them are most important? How are they central to the Jewish sense of justice?

The Holiness Code

The centerpiece of Leviticus is the Holiness Code, which is announced by the verse: "You shall be holy" (Lev. 19:2). The Holiness Code is our most remarkable collection of *klallim,* rivaling the Ten Commandments as the most ancient and the most lasting expression of Judaism's moral core.

What does the Torah mean when it asks us to be "holy"? In Judaism, holiness is neither vague nor abstract. Specifics are given in abundance. One part of the holiness equation deals with what Jewish tradition calls "commandments between a person and God" (*beyn adam l'makom*), essentially ritual practices. Such commandments would include ritualized behavior such as dietary laws (*kashrut*) and keeping the Sabbath. The other part of the holiness equation defines the character of interpersonal relations (*beyn adam l'chavero*), ethical laws that regulate the relationship between individuals and the societies in which they live. Judaism does not privilege one category of commandments over the other; both are required of the observant, conscientious Jew.

The ritual laws set Jews apart from the societies in which they find themselves. The ethical laws, however, call upon Jews to be fully engaged with that very society. The fact that those Jews who are most committed to Jewish ritual tend to be least engaged with general society and those Jews who are most engaged with society are least likely to be highly observant of Jewish rituals underscores the challenge of doing both.

To the extent that this book's focus is on the issue of social justice, I will look more closely at the ethical laws of Judaism, though doing so is not to suggest that they are more important than Judaism's ritual laws. In fact, holiness is very much tied up with the notion of the Jewish people being "a people apart" as discussed in Chapter 1. Yet it is the aspect of the Holiness Code that deals with the Jewish people's relationship with other nations of the world that will provide the best insight into the foundations for a social justice ethic in Judaism.

Most of the commandments enumerated in the Holiness Code address obligations between people and among members of a community. These are the most basic rules for establishing a just society—charity, business ethics, and guidelines for interpersonal respect. Among these rules are: the commandment to leave the corner of one's field for the poor to glean (Lev. 19:10); the commandment to treat a laborer fairly and pay fair wages in a timely way (Lev. 19:13); and the commandment to render fair and just decisions, neither favoring the poor nor deferring to the rich (Lev. 19:15).

Perhaps the most pregnant and vexing of all ideas in the Holiness Code is the verse: "You shall love your neighbor as yourself" (Lev. 19:18). Rabbi Akiva, one of the greatest sages of the Talmud, declared it the most important principle (*klal*) in the Torah. Unlike most of the other verses in the Holiness Code, this verse does not explicitly mandate any particular course of action. Instead, it calls for an attitude, a way of thinking about other people. If we love other people as ourselves, then presumably it will only be natural to treat them as we would like to be treated. Those three Hebrew words—*v'ahavta l'reacha kamocha*—provide the rationale for a universe of moral behavior. If this *klal* is the most important rule in the Torah, as Rabbi Akiva believed, then Judaism is a religion that cherishes, above all else, treating other people well. According to Rabbi Akiva, then, compassion for the other is at the heart of Judaism.

Judaism is not a naïve religion. In an ideal world, everyone would love everyone else. But is it really possible to care about other people as much as we care about ourselves? What about people we've never met? Jewish thinkers have recognized that it is very difficult to live our lives by this principle. We may not truly love strangers as we love ourselves, but this verse implies that we must act as if we do. The great sage Hillel interpreted this principle in a very practical way: "What is hateful to you, do not do to others. This is the whole Torah. The rest is commentary: now go and study" (Babylonian Talmud, *Shabbat* 31a). According to Hillel's interpretation, it would be unjust to treat another person—even an enemy—in a way that we would not like to be treated.

The Image of God

Everyone agrees that loving your neighbor as you would love yourself is a central principle of Judaism. But not everyone agrees with Rabbi Akiva that it is the "most important" Jewish value.

In the Jerusalem Talmud we read the following:

> Rabbi Akiva taught: "Love your neighbor as yourself." This is the most important rule in the Torah. Ben Azzai says: "Man was created in the image of God." That is an even greater principle (Jerusalem Talmud, *Nedarim* 9:4).

Ben Azzai here takes issue with Rabbi Akiva and suggests that the implication of the verse "Man was created in the image of God" (*b'tzelem Elohim barah oto* Gen. 1:27) has greater ramifications, and therefore greater significance, than the principle "love your neighbor as yourself." The Akiva principle presupposes love, first of oneself, and then of the other. It is a difficult thing to legislate. But once we accept the premise that all human beings are images of the Divine, there is a basis for arguing that we must treat others with justice and kindness. It speaks to the fundamental equality of all people. To say that everyone is created in God's image is to say that everyone deserves respect. It recognizes that we might not always love other people, but Judaism insists that no matter how we feel, we need to treat all people with dignity. Though the verse from Leviticus—love your neighbor as yourself—is held aloft in Jewish teaching, it is the principle of Ben Azzai that is enshrined in America's Declaration of Independence:

> We hold these truths to be self-evident: That all men are created equal; that they are endowed by their Creator with certain unalienable rights; that among these are life, liberty, and the pursuit of happiness.

The difference of opinion between Akiva and Ben Azzai is far more than theoretical. Because we do not know the limits of the phrase "you shall love your neighbor as yourself," we are left to wonder, who is "our neighbor"? Are we called to love only those people who are physically near to us? Or perhaps "neighbor" should be read less literally. Perhaps it refers to those who are emotionally near to us, wherever they may live. Are all other Jews our "neighbors"? What about non-Jews? Is any American citizen a "neighbor"? What do we owe people who live far away, people we've never met and never will meet? In a time when electronic media has made the world into a "global village," is every living person our "neighbor"? And does that mean that we have the same moral obligations to every person in the world that we do to our actual neighbors?

Ben Azzai's "image of God" principle suggests that our obligations extend to all people, regardless of religion or nationality. It is a universalist perspective. In contrast, Rabbi Akiva may be saying that our moral obligations depend on our personal relationships and our communal memberships. Most Americans, for instance, believe that we have a stronger responsibility to the American poor than to the African poor. Similarly, many Jews believe that we have a stronger responsibility to the Jewish poor than to the non-Jewish poor; or, that we have a stronger responsibility to advocate for Israel's security than we do to advocate for the security of another country at risk. "Love your neighbor as yourself" could easily yield this more particularist understanding of ethical obligation. In fact most rabbinic commentators interpret the intent of the Hebrew word *reacha* (neighbor) to refer to other Jews, even though most modern readers would instinctively read the verse to mean "all people."

Finding a Balance

One can be a particularist and still believe that we have moral responsibilities toward non-Jews. Particularists, however, might be inclined to more readily prioritize the needs of those people who are close to them. Similarly, universalism is not really the argument that we have the same exact moral obligations to all people. Even the most committed universalists would tend to agree, for instance, that parents have a special moral obligation to their own children.

The Jewish community's response to contemporary issues often reveals the divide between particularistic and universalistic tendencies within the community. This is not a new phenomenon. Rabbinic literature is filled with examples on both ends of this spectrum. An objective reading of the Jewish tradition will reveal passages that seem discriminatory toward non-Jews. It will reveal, as well, passages that embrace the universalist spirit of Ben Azzai.

The Rabbis were products of their historical context. It should not be surprising to read a particularistic passage written at a time and in a place where the Jewish people were under extraordinary pressure from hostile neighbors and host countries. Given the Jewish historical experience, it should be more surprising to find as many passages as we do that reflect a sense that all human beings are part of the human family, created by God, and deserving of compassion and respect.

Jews are products of both Exodus and of Sinai. The Exodus impulse has helped Jews remain a distinct nation culturally, ethnically, and politically. This particularist impulse of Jews—prioritizing Jewish needs and Jewish interests—has helped the Jewish people survive. But the Jewish calling extends beyond physical survival and self-defense. Jews are also the people of Sinai, bound by a national covenant to a higher calling, an altruistic sense of moral responsibility toward all humankind. The Jewish people's universalist impulse grows out of this sense of moral responsibility. Just as the particularistic and self-interested impulse preserves Jews physically, the universalistic and altruistic impulse preserves Jews spiritually, helping Jews survive as a nation with a special purpose and keeping alive their higher calling.

The Jewish people have been trying to define "who is our neighbor?" ever since they received the commandment to "love your neighbor." Even today, periods of conflict and uncertainty make us more willing to suspect the outsider, those who are potentially our enemy or adversary. We may advocate for an ethic that would have us treat every human being as if they were made in the image of God, but history and common sense beckon us to be cautious. History is filled with individuals and groups that sought to persecute or kill the Jews. It has conditioned Jews to be suspicious of outsiders and it has reinforced the solidarity of the Jewish community, which understands that there is strength and comfort in numbers.

It may well be that the spirit of Ben Azzai's teaching epitomizes Sinai consciousness, seeing every person as equal in the eyes of God and requiring equal treatment and respect. But Akiva's preference for "loving your neighbor," with its implicit national, ethnic, and religious boundaries, may be the teaching that is more closely in accord with the historical experience of the Jewish people. Steering a course between these two paths is one of the great challenges that has faced the Jewish people throughout history. Critical to the ability of Jews to navigate this course were prophets, a role introduced in the Book of Numbers.

6

Numbers

From Wilderness to Prophecy

Our lives are different from the lives of our biblical ancestors. God does not appear to us in fire and smoke. We've never witnessed rivers turned to blood or seas split in two. We inherited the Torah, but it was given to us by our parents and our teachers, not by God on Sinai. Over the generations, there have been few common experiences of redemption to unify the Jewish people. For many Jews, Judaism has no single source of authority to reinforce our moral calling. God does not speak directly to us as a people. Most modern Jews connect to the legacy of Judaism via Jewish tradition, the body of laws, customs, and beliefs shaped over the centuries.

During the earliest, formative stage of Judaism, it was the prophets who interpreted what God wanted from the Jewish people. It was the prophets who kept the Jewish people true to the covenant. Much of the Bible is the record of prophecy, which includes some of the greatest poems and the most powerful moral teachings that have ever been written. Prophets like Isaiah, Jeremiah, and Micah—most living in Judea more than 2,500 years ago—became the lasting moral and ethical voice of Judaism. They reminded the Jewish people of the Torah's core values, sometimes in the harshest of tones. At the same time, the prophets preached new core values, expanding on the central commitment of the Jewish people to righteousness and justice. And, most importantly, the Torah's prophets developed the vision that has sustained the Jewish people over millennia, an image of a world healed through justice and holiness.

The First Prophet

B'midbar, the fourth book of the Torah, is usually rendered as Numbers. But a literal translation is "in the wilderness." Numbers tells of the Jewish people's legendary forty years of wandering through a harsh desert. Furious at their faithlessness, God withdraws from them. It is Moses's responsibility to lead the Israelites through the years of doubt and suffering, from the Exodus from Egypt until they arrive at the entrance to the Promised Land.

An important part of Moses's job was transmitting God's word to the Jewish people. In Numbers chapter 11, Moses is overwhelmed at the responsibility of being the primary intermediary between God and the children of Israel. The Israelites, born in slavery, cannot shed their slave mentality. They do not fully appreciate the gift of freedom. They focus on what they once had, and what they lacked, rather than on what redemption has made possible. The covenant at Sinai seems less important to them than a good meal. And so they complain again and again to God's messenger, Moses. Just as Moses is about to give up, asking God to kill him so as to spare him the ongoing burden of dealing with the ungrateful Israelites (11:15), God suggests an alternative. God tells Moses to bring seventy elders of Israel and God will invest them with the same "spirit of God" that Moses has been given. Then they will share the burden of leadership with Moses.

Just as the Book of Exodus takes the notion of covenant from one individual (Abraham) and invests it onto a larger group (the children of Israel), so, too, does Numbers take the notion of leadership and interpreting the word of God from Moses and invests it onto a larger representative group of tribal elders. This development is more than a managerial innovation to deal with an unruly work force. It represents the Jewish tradition's understanding of how the Jewish people are to become "a nation of priests and a holy nation."

In Jewish tradition, Moses is considered the first of the prophets, a messenger of God. But a prophet is not simply a messenger or a channel. In Abraham Joshua Heschel's classic study of the prophets, he says, "Above all, the prophets remind us of the moral state of the people: Few are guilty but all are responsible."[1] Just as Moses presents God's teachings to the Jewish people, we also find him arguing the people's case before God. In this, he is the heir of Abraham, who first challenged God's judgment over Sodom and Gomorrah. In the Book of Numbers, God tells Moses that the Jewish people will need other leaders, prophets to share the burden and to guide the Jewish people when Moses is gone. This is the beginning of the Jewish tradition of prophecy. The prophets who arise after Moses will shape themselves in his image.

Moses is the memory of the Jewish people, reminding them of their covenant. He is the Jewish people's conscience, rebuking them when they stray from the commandments. Finally, Moses offers the people a vision, inspiring them with what is possible. The prophet makes the present respond to the demands of the past and the promise of the future. These three roles—memory, conscience, vision—become the defining characteristics of the Jewish prophet.[2]

Memory

The prophets come to remind the Jewish people of Judaism's core values. The prophet never forgets the commitment to justice that is at the heart of Judaism. The prophet Isaiah exclaimed: "Stop doing wrong and learn to live right. Devote yourself to justice. Uphold the rights of the orphan, defend the cause of the widow" (Isa. 1:17). The prophet is that messenger who interprets to his generation a message that was first conveyed to Abraham, renewed and expanded to the Jewish people at Sinai, and is able to reframe it in the context of contemporary circumstance.

Of course, the prophets do not simply repeat the words of the covenant. Memory doesn't mean repetition. Prophets also interpret. They reshape the Jewish calling in the way that seems most powerful to them, at the time. The prophecies they deliver are the response to the questions: What is the essence of the Torah for our time? What does God want from us? Their formulations are the source of some of the most profound wisdom bequeathed to civilization. Evidence this classic formulation of Micah: "He has told you, O man, what is good and what God requires of you: Only to do justice, to love goodness, and to walk modestly with your God. Then will your name achieve wisdom" (Mic. 6:8–9).

A prophet is not someone who sees the future. A prophet is one who best remembers the past and knows how to convey its meaning to a new generation.

The Prophetic Conscience

The biblical prophet is often reluctant. Moses did not feel equal to God's charge that he challenge Pharoah. Jonah did everything possible to avoid his task of giving warning to the people of Nineveh. "I do not know how to speak," the prophet Jeremiah protests, when he first receives his calling, "I am only a boy" (Jer. 1:6). But just like Moses and Jonah, Jeremiah conquers his fear. Prophets learn that they have a certain power and it is acquired by being channels for God's truth. Whether or not prophets actually hear God speak to them, they are certainly the embodiment of one of humanity's finest qualities—moral judgment, the ability to distinguish between right and wrong.

History proved Jeremiah's reluctance well founded. Jeremiah's prophetic career spanned the traumatic years before the destruction of the First Temple in 586 BCE. Though hopeful for the long-term survival of Judaism and the Jewish people, Jeremiah was a realist. He knew that Jerusalem would fall to the more powerful Chaldean empire and her residents would be taken into exile. Jeremiah's foreboding prophecies were not well received. He was imprisoned for a long time. In the end he was kidnapped by Judean refugees fleeing the Babylonians and he died in captivity. In fact, many of the Bible's prophets met sorry ends. Practically all were unpopular. But even when they were afraid of the consequences, they were not silenced by fear.

Imagine the reaction that greeted these words of Jeremiah when he preached them in Jerusalem's holy Temple to the Israelites who came there for their daily offerings:

> Thus saith the Lord of Hosts, the God of Israel: Mend your
> ways and your actions and I will let you dwell in this place....
> If you really mend your ways and your actions; if you execute
> justice between one man and another; if you do not oppress

the stranger, the orphan and the widow; if you do not follow other Gods to your own hurt; then only will I let you dwell in this place, in the land which I gave to your fathers for all time (Jer. 7:3–7).

The unpopular part of the prophet's job is chastising the people for their wrongdoing. Prophets don't simply lay out a vision of what is good. They seek to correct what is bad. They live in obedience to the Torah's principle: *hocheach tocheach et amitecha,* "you shall surely rebuke your friend" (Lev. 19:17). This principle mandates a response to injustice. At the same time, the Torah says clearly that someone who deserves criticism is still "your friend." That is, sin doesn't necessarily corrupt the sinner. For all of their criticisms and laments, Jewish prophets have always been optimists at heart. When they criticize, it is with the belief that righteousness is possible and justice is achievable. The world can be repaired.

The Prophetic Vision

The stereotype of a prophet today is a bearded man standing on a street corner. He holds a sign that says, "Repent! The End Is Near!" Judaism's prophets certainly call for repentance, a return to doing good. But Jewish prophecy is much less about telling the future or predicting a gloomy end in fire and brimstone than it is about goading society in the direction of peace, justice, and redemption.

The prophet reminds the people of who they are—members of a nation redeemed from slavery, witnesses to revelation, party to an unbreakable covenant. And the prophet offers a vision of what the Jewish people might be—a nation that leads the way toward a better world. The prophet Amos says: "Seek good and not evil, so that you may live.... Hate evil and love good. Establish justice in the gates" (Amos 5:14–15). The prophet offers a promise that redemption is not only something that happened to our ancestors. It is something that can happen again should our generation mend its ways and live righteously. In this sense, the prophet is not necessarily someone who can "tell the future" as it will be. Instead, the prophet has a vision of the future as it should be, and as it might be, if the people align their behavior with the ethical precepts of the covenant.

Isaiah, speaking in God's name, says: "Observe what is right and do what is just. For soon My salvation will come and My justice will be revealed" (Isa. 56:1). From the principles of the Torah, the Bible's prophets developed powerful and compelling visions of a world governed by righteousness and justice. It is a messianic vision meant to motivate and inspire each generation of Jews to do its part to bring about that reality. One passage from Isaiah chapter 2 resonated so powerfully that when the United Nations was established and built after World War II, with near-messianic expectations of the kind of world such an institution might bring about, part of this prophecy was inscribed on the wall of the U.N. Plaza:

> In the days to come, the Lord's house shall stand firm above
> the mountains and tower above the hills. And all the nations
> shall gaze upon it with joy. Many people shall go and shall say:
> "Come, let us go up to the mount of the Lord, to the House of
> the God of Jacob, that He may instruct us in His ways and that
> we may walk in His paths." For instruction shall come forth
> from Zion, the word of the Lord from Jerusalem. Thus He will
> judge among the nations and arbitrate for the many peoples.
> And they shall beat their swords into plowshares and their
> spears into pruning hooks. Nation shall not take up sword
> against nation; neither shall they learn war anymore (Isa.
> 2:2–4).

Despite the fact that this prophecy has not yet been fulfilled, people of faith have been inspired by these words for centuries to work for a world of justice and peace. It is the power of the prophetic vision. While many people might stake a claim to speaking in God's name in our time, the measure of the true prophetic voice is the extent to which it is consistent with the prophetic vision of these words from the Bible. A prophet is that rare individual in our own time who has the courage to distinguish between justice and injustice and is willing to speak out about it, even when it means challenging those in power. In holding aloft the memory of the covenant with God, serving as the conscience of a generation, and offering a vision for a better future, prophets are rarely popular. Often it remains for history to judge who among us has been prophetic. Such was the case with Martin Luther King, Jr., who was a controversial figure in his time but who is now honored for the prophetic voice with which he challenged racial injustice in America.

Prophets speak on behalf of the weak, the powerless, and the oppressed. They vex the strong, the powerful, and the oppressors. They shape what has been called "prophetic Judaism." Prophets serve as messengers from God. The Book of Deuteronomy will provide some insight as to what "a message from God" might mean.

7

Deuteronomy

How Central Is God?

For most of Jewish history, the Jewish pursuit of righteousness and justice has been rooted in the belief that there is a God and that God cares about how we live our lives. It has been an article of faith that the commandments are God-given, a divine blueprint for the life of holiness.

But in the modern era, things have changed. Many Jews continue to cherish Judaism's ancient beliefs: that God exists, that the Torah and its commandments are of divine origin, and therefore that our moral responsibilities come from God. But other Jews find it difficult to believe these things. Surveys consistently find that Jews are the most likely segment of the American population to doubt the existence of God. Some are atheists, denying the existence of an otherworldly God. Many more are agnostic, unsure whether they believe in God.

So it is important to ask the questions: Does the covenant (*brit*) have any meaning for those who question God's existence? What, in the absence of God, would be the status of the Torah's commandments and its moral obligations? What authority would stand behind the Jewish people's special calling, the millennial responsibility to righteousness and justice?

Is God Dead?

For more than a hundred years, our understanding of religion has been challenged by the nineteenth-century German philosopher Friedrich Nietzsche's infamous aphorism: "God is dead." Nietzsche didn't kill God. He was merely announcing what many people already believed to be true—that the idea of God as an infallible, transcendent being has no meaning in a world of science and reason.

Before the modern era, Jews—like gentiles—tended to take the existence of God for granted. It was generally believed that God gave the Torah, or at least part of it, to Moses on Sinai. It was further believed that the Talmud, as part of the revelation at Sinai, was also imbued with divine authority. The moral and ethical foundations of Judaism, therefore, were understood to be crafted by God. Our commitment to righteousness and justice was, first and foremost, a matter of obeying the word of God.

But modernity chipped away at faith. Biblical scholarship began to bring forth convincing evidence that the Torah was written not by a perfect God, but by fallible people. Darwin was one of many scientists whose work undermined a belief in God as the creator of all things. As science unveiled more and more about the workings and origins of the world, fewer people were drawn to the idea of God as an omnipotent master of all things.

Notwithstanding the challenge of modern science and reason, most people are drawn to some type of faith and most believe that there is a power or force in the universe greater than themselves. That sentiment is often expressed as "faith in God." America is a strange paradox in that it represents one of the most secularized societies in the world and yet more Americans claim to believe in God than anywhere else in the industrialized world.

A 2003 poll[1] revealed that more than 80 percent of Americans profess a belief in God. The breakdown, however, is revealing because Protestants answered 90 percent in the affirmative, Catholics 79 percent, and Jews only 48 percent. Jews are also less likely than other Americans to believe in God as the author of the Bible. It seems ironic that God's "chosen people" are more skeptical than other Americans that there even is a "chooser." While some would speculate that such differences can be explained by the educational level of Jews relative to other Americans, or geographic differences between industrial, urban America and the Bible

Belt, it is worth exploring how the structure of Judaism itself may contribute to this phenomenon.

The Practical Faith

In the Book of Deuteronomy, the Jewish people prepare to enter the land of Israel and Moses reviews their history in the desert. Moses knows that he will not enter Canaan. His part of the story is coming to an end. Moses has been the strongest connection between the Jewish people and God. How will the Jews survive Moses's death? As the book draws to a close, the Torah offers a valuable reflection on its own authority, one that has guided Jews for millennia as they confront the question of how to fulfill God's covenant without direct revelation or an intermediary like Moses, who was able to speak on God's behalf.

> Thus God says to the Israelites: This teaching which I enjoin upon you this day is not hidden from you, nor is it beyond your reach. It [the commandments] is not in the heavens that you should say, "Who among us can go up to the heavens and get it for us and impart it to us that we may observe it?" Neither is it beyond the sea that you should say, "Who among us can cross to the other side of the sea and get it for us and impart it to us that we may observe it?" No, the thing is very close to you, in your mouth and in your heart, to observe it (Deut. 30:12–14).

It is a most remarkable passage. Whereas many ancient religions invest an elite body of clergy or master teachers with the authority to interpret religious codes of behavior and practice to the faithful, this Torah passage suggests that the interpretation of the Torah is within reach of every member of the children of Israel. It is the confirmation of a status first mentioned in the Book of Exodus when the Israelites were called "a kingdom of priests and a holy nation" (Exod. 19:6). Certainly the Torah takes for granted that the commandments come from the heavens—that is, from God. But just as the covenant expanded from Abraham to all of Israel, and leadership expanded from Moses to the seventy elders, so, too, do the commandments now become the responsibility of the people to learn, interpret, and obey. The passage seems to suggest that the Torah does not belong to God any longer. It is in the mouth and hearts of the people Israel (Deut. 30:14). The value of the laws is to be judged, the Torah suggests, less by their origin than by what they mean and what they can bring to the world.

One of the central themes of Jewish thought, and one that we keep encountering in our exploration of righteousness and justice in Judaism, is the importance of making a difference here and now, of healing our world. It is not hard to see that the core values expressed in the Holiness Code, especially those in the realm of rules governing the behavior between people (*beyn adam l'chavero*), remain relevant even if God's existence is challenged. The truth and importance of Isaiah's moral imperatives do not depend on Isaiah's hearing them from God's mouth.

Judaism is, in many ways, a very practical religion. Certainly there are elements of our tradition that talk about paradise and the world to come. But much more prevalent in our tradition is talk about acting ethically in this world. Even as traditional Judaism holds as central the notion that the legitimacy of the Torah derives from the belief that it was God-given, there are hints in the classical literature of a more human-centered approach to the demands that Judaism places on its adherents:

> Rav Huna and Rav Jeremiah said in the name of Rav Hiyyah b. Abba: It is written, "They have forsaken me and have not kept My law" (Jer. 16:11). This means: "would that they had forsaken Me but kept My law, since by occupying themselves with it, the light it contains would have led them back to Me" (Prologue to *Lamentations Rabbah*).

This rabbinic exchange suggests that even if one were to have doubts about God, a person must live a life faithful to the commandments. There seems to be the confidence that such a lifestyle will lead a Jew back to faith in God. An even more remarkable passage from the Talmud provides a glimpse of a rabbinic debate over the meaning of the verse from Deuteronomy 30 that says the law "is not in the heavens."

> On that day, Rabbi Eliezer put forward all the arguments in the world, but the sages did not accept them.
> Finally he said: "If the law is according to me, let that carob tree prove it."
> He pointed to a nearby carob tree, which then moved from its place a hundred cubits; and some say, four hundred cubits.

They said to him: "One cannot bring a proof from the moving of a carob tree."

Said Rabbi Eliezer: "If the law is according to me, may that stream of water prove it."

The stream of water then turned and flowed in the opposite direction.

They said to him: "One cannot bring a proof from the behavior of a stream of water."

Said Rabbi Eliezer: "If the law is according to me, may the walls of the House of Study prove it."

The walls of the House of Study began to bend inward. Rabbi Joshua then stood up and rebuked the walls of the House of Study: "If the students of the wise argue with one another in matters of Jewish law," he said, "what right have you to interfere?"

In honor of Rabbi Joshua, the walls ceased to bend inward; but in honor of Rabbi Eliezer, they did not straighten up, and they remain bent to this day.

Then said Rabbi Eliezer to the Sages: "If the law is according to me, may a proof come from Heaven."

Then a heavenly voice went forth and said: "What would you interfere with Rabbi Eliezer? The law is according to him in every instance."

Then Rabbi Joshua rose up on his feet, and said: "It is not in the heavens."

What did he mean by this?

Said Rabbi Jeremiah: "He meant that since the Torah has already been given on Mount Sinai, we do not pay attention to a heavenly voice; for God has written in the Torah, 'Decide according to the majority.'"

Rabbi Nathan met the prophet Elijah, who was on a mission down from heaven. He asked him: "What was the Holy One, blessed be God, doing in that hour?"

Said Elijah: "God was laughing and saying 'My children have defeated me, my children have defeated me.'"

BABYLONIAN TALMUD, *BAVA METZIA* 59B

The rabbis of the Talmud certainly understood the Torah to be a divine inheritance. But they also cherished its teachings as a uniquely human possession. Post-biblical Judaism places great value on the power of each generation of Jews to interpret God's law in accordance with the needs of the generation. In this passage, Rabbi Eliezer's attempt to recruit God to validate his position is rebuffed by his contemporaries. Rabbi Joshua declares audaciously that no answer can come from heaven (God). Rabbi Jeremiah cites God as the authority for the actual practice of rabbinic sages negotiating a difference of opinion—majority rules. Judaism, as a practical and humanistic religion, has evolved from the stage of revelation to the stage of rabbinic deliberation. What is right in Judaism is that which wins the consent and agreement of those charged with interpreting the covenant anew for each generation.

Judaism is a religion that values practice more than belief. In Judaism, a good person is not necessarily someone who believes the right things. A good person is someone who does the right things. Jewish sacred texts have inspired and taught wisdom to hundreds of generations of Jews. The Torah has shown Jews how to lead a better life. Traditional Jews have an unshakable belief that the Torah is the word of God. But should Jews who question the Torah's origin automatically dismiss the content of that covenant? It is unfortunate that many modern Jews do just that, seeing Judaism as an all-or-nothing proposition. What is critical is to cultivate a language that allows modern Jews to see the Jewish tradition beyond such a stark, either/or proposition.

Beyond Either/Or

The Jewish tradition identifies God as the Creator of the world, the Redeemer from Egyptian bondage, the Author of the covenant at Sinai, the One who brought the Jewish people into the promised land, fulfilling a promise first made to Abraham. The first of the Ten Commandments proclaims God's centrality to the Jewish story: "I am the Lord your God, who brought you out of the Land of Egypt" (Exod. 20:2). One could make the case that the fulfillment of every commandment is an affirmation of the One who issued the commandment.

The contemporary Jew is torn between a world of science and rationalism and a tradition that makes God central to Jewish history. Some see it as an either/or proposition. Either you believe in God and dismiss, or at least compartmentalize, the world of science and reason, or you embrace science and reason and reject the notion of God. Many non-Jews who are people of faith look to the Bible and to their own religious teachings for inspiration and direction when thinking about their personal conduct and the stewardship of the society in which they live. Often Jews feel uncomfortable with those who use theological and religious language as an impetus for their actions in the realm of social justice. Part of this feeling is driven by an instinctive reaction against an approach made popular by the Christian right, whose positions are often anathema to Jews. In addition, many Jews feel that they come to their values via the universal values embraced by Western civilization, not aware that many of those values derive from the Bible and are ascribed to God's teachings. For many Jews, rejecting God also requires rejecting Judaism because they cannot separate belief in God from the imperative to adhere to Jewish tradition.

It is sad that some Jews abandon Judaism because they see themselves as too sophisticated to believe in the miraculous Bible stories. What makes it sad is that it is avoidable. There is a rich literature of Jewish theology that takes us far beyond the either/or equation. There are many theological options available to the person who cannot accept a literalist reading of the Bible or believe in an all-powerful, all-knowing God.

Abraham Joshua Heschel, descendant of a long line of Hasidic rabbis, was born and educated in Europe. Eventually he became a professor at the Jewish Theological Seminary in New York. To Heschel, there was no doubt about God's existence, nor about God's centrality to the universe. And yet Heschel saw the Bible, and all of Judaism, as far more concerned about human beings than about God. He taught that we live in a world bordering on absurdity and mystery, in danger of meaninglessness. To affirm God is to see meaning beyond the mystery, to encounter the world with a sense of awe and wonder, or what he called "radical amazement."

Heschel left behind a legacy of a life deeply committed to social justice and a body of writing that encouraged Jews to find holiness and sanctity in life. To Heschel, the Bible is not so much a history of the Jewish people as it is a record of God's quest for righteous people. Heschel taught, in the spirit of his Hasidic ancestors, that God does not dwell in or beyond the sky, but in every heart that is willing to accept the divine.[2]

A generation later, one of Heschel's students, Rabbi Arthur Green, built on Heschel's teachings and began to create a theology that joined mystical, rational, and Hasidic thought. He calls it Jewish mystical humanism. An accomplished scholar and teacher who also served for a time as the president of the Reconstructionist Rabbinical College, Green has tried to move Jews past the "vertical metaphor" in the divine-human relationship, the suggestion that God dwells in heaven while humans are "down below" on earth. While he recognizes that traditional texts and liturgy reinforce the vertical metaphor, Green urges people to understand God as "the innermost heart of reality." There is a hidden God, buried deep within every person, longing to be discovered. The God within points to a single, universal truth that underlies all religions, even though the symbolic language and practice of each faith makes religions appear different and even competitive in the real world.[3]

In Relationship

It is clear that it is difficult to make any statement about God that will achieve wide agreement or consensus in a pluralistic Jewish world. We are simply too diverse a people to be of one mind on the God question.

Perhaps, however, we can say that Jews and the Jewish people are in relationship with God, however we understand that word, from Abraham until the present day. Abraham is called by God, or believes that he is, and acts accordingly. Inspired by his example, we are his heirs in pursuing righteousness and justice. The Hebrews are redeemed by God from Egypt, or believe that they are, and act accordingly. We use that historical lesson as an inspiration for how we relate to other oppressed minorities. The children of Israel enter into a covenant with God at Sinai, or believe that they do. As a result, we are a people who place tremendous value on law, in good deeds, and in building societies that uphold justice.

It may well be that, despite our theological differences, we do not need to say any more than this.

8

Sinai Applied

Seven Core Values of the Rabbinic Tradition

The centuries that followed the close of the biblical canon challenged the Jewish people to find a way to do just what Deuteronomy chapter 30 suggested—take the laws revealed to the Jewish people at Sinai and translate them into a set of values that could guide a nation throughout history. The loss of national sovereignty in the year 70 CE confronted the Jewish people with the challenge of adapting the laws of the Torah for their lives in a diaspora. It was the rabbinic sages of the Jewish tradition who began to shape the legal and ethical principles that have guided Jews until the present day. The voluminous literature that the rabbinic sages created is still read and interpreted and stands as a testament to rabbinic genius and the desire of at least some Jews to have their lives guided by classical Jewish values.

What follows are seven Jewish values that are at the core of Jewish teachings about social justice. When I use the term Sinai impulse or Sinai consciousness as descriptive of certain behaviors of Jews or of the Jewish community, these are the values that define that standard. It goes without saying that this list is far from comprehensive. It does, however, provide a language that can be used to articulate Judaism's historic commitment to social justice.

Chesed—Lovingkindness

Torah/Teaching

Simeon the Righteous used to say: "On three things does the world stand: Torah, service (to God), and acts of lovingkindness."

ETHICS OF THE ANCESTORS 1:2

In Chapter 5, we learned that Rabbi Akiva advanced the primacy of the principle to "love your neighbor as yourself," *v'ahavta l'reacha kamocha* (Jerusalem Talmud, *Nedarim* 9:4). *Chesed*, a word that is sometimes rendered as "lovingkindness" and sometimes as "compassion," derives from Akiva's principle to extend the love of self to others.

The Jewish tradition recognizes the difficulty—perhaps the impossibility—of loving all people. Rabbi Ovadiah Sforno, a sixteenth-century Jewish commentator on the Torah, sums up an important strain in the Jewish tradition when he comments on the practical implications of the biblical imperative to "love your neighbor as yourself": "That is to say, try to do for your neighbor what you would want for yourself, if you were in your neighbor's place." Even if we do not love everyone, it is possible to act toward every person with *chesed*, lovingkindness. *Chesed* means always asking ourselves how we would behave if we cared about every person at least as much as we care about ourselves. *Chesed* is perhaps the purest expression of the altruistic impulse in Judaism, the impulse that was exemplified by Abraham's advocacy for the people of Sodom and Gemorrah and that, at Sinai, became the central moral purpose of Judaism. A true act of *chesed* is a good deed done with no expectation of reward. *Chesed* is an act of compassion extended without a motive of self-interest. In the words of the prophet Zechariah: "Let your judgments be guided by truth [*emet*] and compassion [*chesed*], and may mercy [*rachamim*] guide your dealings with all people" (Zech. 7:9).

The behaviors that fall under the heading of *chesed* span the range of human interaction. The scholar and philosopher Maimonides, in his encyclopedic compendium of Jewish laws, the *Mishneh Torah*, lists just a few:

> It is a positive commandment to visit the sick, and comfort
> mourners, and bury the dead, and celebrate a wedding....
> These commandments are implied in the commandment "Love
> your neighbor as yourself" (*Yad,* "Laws of Mourning" 14:1–2).

Maimonides teaches that acting with lovingkindness means more than giving of our resources and our time. It means giving of ourselves, sharing the full range of human emotion, from joy in a time of celebration, to sorrow in a time of mourning. Part of what drives *chesed,* then, is empathy.

Everyone has material needs. And so, every Jew is obligated to give charity. But everyone has spiritual and emotional needs, too. "Deeds of lovingkindness," taught the Talmud's Rabbi Eliezer, "are greater even than charity. Charity is only towards the poor; but lovingkindness can be directed towards anyone" (Babylonian Talmud, *Sukkot* 49b). And while Judaism forbids Jews from giving so much charity that the givers themselves are reduced to poverty, Maimonides explains that "there is no prescribed measure" for the boundless obligation of *chesed.*

The Rabbis did not want to leave the definition of *chesed* to human intuition. Having already suggested in our theme passage, *Ethics of the Ancestors* 1:2, that *chesed* is one of the pillars on which the world stands, the Rabbis set about to define it. Using a verse from the Bible in which God is described as *rav chesed,* "full of compassion" (Exod. 34:6), the Talmud goes on to explore God's actions, as recorded in the Bible, to determine what it might mean for human beings to be "full of compassion." Thus we have the following:

> "You shall walk after Lord your God," this means that you
> should imitate God's virtues. Just as God clothed the naked, so,
> too, should you clothe the naked. Just as the Holy One visited
> the sick, so, too, should you visit the sick. Just as the Holy One
> comforted mourners, so, too, should you comfort mourners.
> Just as the Holy One buried the dead, so, too, should you bury
> the dead (Babylonian Talmud, *Sotah* 14a).

The behaviors cited in the passage from the Talmud typify the kinds of actions that fall under the definition of *chesed.* Implicit in the passage is the rabbinic view that, just as God extends compassion to all humanity, so, too, must Jews practice *chesed* in every human interaction.

Kavod Habriot—Dignity of All Creatures

Torah/Teaching

The fundamental dignity of all creation is very precious to God. There is no value more precious than it.

RABBI MENACHEM BEN SOLOMON HAMEIRI, 13TH CENTURY
SCHOLAR, IN HIS COMMENTARY ON THE BABYLONIAN TALMUD,
BERACHOT 19B

Kavod habriot is the Jewish principle that requires that we accord every one of God's creatures a level of dignity. Traditionally, this principle has been applied to all human beings, although some have extended it to the animal kingdom as well. Long before Western society embraced the concept of universal human rights, Judaism taught that every person—Jew and gentile, male and female, rich and poor—deserves to be treated with respect.

The centrality of the principle of *kavod habriot* is underscored in a Talmudic citation that teaches that any rabbinic ordinance may be set aside for the purpose of preserving *kavod habriot* (*Berachot* 19b). This is because *kavod habriot* is a principle that supersedes other, more specific legal obligations. Rabbi Abraham Isaac Kook, the first chief rabbi of the Yishuv, the prestate settlement of Jews in Palestine, said:

> Protecting [the respect] one rightfully deserves is not a matter of arrogance. On the contrary, there is a *mitzvah* to do so. The opinion of the *halakhic* decisors is that it is prohibited to relinquish *kavod habriot* even in the case of a *mitzva*" (*Mussar Avikha,* p. 73).

Jews must carry themselves in a dignified way and society must never function in such a way as to deny a person's dignity, regardless of the circumstances.

In Chapter 5, we learned that the Talmud's Ben Azzai believed that Judaism's most important principle is *b'tzelem Elohim,* treating all human beings with the dignity appropriate to a creature made in the image of God. The principle derives from the story of creation, which culminates in the creation of Adam and Eve: "God created humankind in the divine image" (Gen. 1:26). When we treat others with dignity, Judaism teaches, we are indirectly paying our respect to God. The converse is also true, as the Mishnah says: "All people are beloved for they are created in the image of God" (*Ethics of the Ancestors* 3:18).

It is instructive that the Jewish tradition speaks of *kavod habriot*—literally "respect for all creation"—and not *kavod ha'adam,* "respect for humankind." Jewish tradition reminds us that human beings were the last of God's creations. "The Lord is good to all," sings the psalmist, "and God's mercy extends to all creation" (Ps. 145:9). There is an important place within Judaism for both environmentalism and advocacy for humane treatment of animals. The Jewish concern for the dignity of the nonhuman world owes something to the principle of *kavod habriot.*

The protection of the natural environment (*haganat hatevah*) also has deep roots in the Jewish tradition. The natural environment is owed the respect and dignity due all of God's creation. A *midrash* tells of God charging the first man with a responsibility to preserve the environment:

> When God created Adam, God led him around the Garden of Eden and said to him: Behold my works! See how beautiful they are!... See to it that you do not spoil and destroy my world; for if you do, there will be no one after you to repair it (*Ecclesiastes Rabbah* 7:13).

Judaism also embraces the idea that animals must be treated respectfully. The prohibition against cruelty to any living creature (*tza'ar ba'alei chaim*) is implicit in the Ten Commandments, where we are told that even beasts of burden must rest on the Sabbath (Exod. 20:10). The Torah and the Talmud return repeatedly to the basic kindnesses that humans owe to animals under our charge. Jewish tradition even played a pioneering role in the development of the concept of animal rights. Centuries ago, Maimonides, the great medieval legal authority, explained that in some circumstances, "There is no difference between the pain of man and the pain of other living beings" (*The Guide for the Perplexed* 3:48).

Kavod habriot is an attitude that must be translated into behaviors. It is intended to guide the behavior of Jews not only with other human beings, but also with animals and with the natural world. It also needs to inform the public policies of the societies in which we live. A society that implements a law or practice that results in diminishing, in any way, the dignity of one group of its citizens violates the principle of *kavod habriot,* and citizens of conscience are duty bound to do all in their power to oppose or reverse such a policy. "All commandments between man and his fellow man," taught the twentieth-century Talmudic scholar Joseph Soloveitchik, "are based on *kavod habriot.*"

Bakesh Shalom—Seek Peace

Torah/Teaching

Shun evil and do good:
Seek peace, and pursue it.

PSALMS 34:15

Bakesh shalom, implores the psalmist: "seek peace." As if that were not enough, the psalmist goes a step further: "and pursue it" (*v'rodfeihu*). Wishing for peace will not get the job done. Nor will thinking good thoughts. Judaism's call is to dedicated action, the tireless pursuit of peace. It is interesting that the challenge, "pursue it," added as a device to underscore the imperative, is also used to emphasize the importance of pursing justice as in "Justice, justice shall you pursue" (Deut. 16:20).

In the Jewish liturgy, God is "maker of peace" (*oseh hashalom*) and "ruler of peace" (*adon hashalom*). In the midrash, Rabbi Judan ben Yosi is quoted as saying, "Great is peace because God's name is peace" (*Vayikra Rabbah* 9:9). Jerusalem, the name of Judaism's holiest city, has in it the word *shalem,* which is also the root of the Hebrew word *shalom. Shalem* means "whole," "complete." *Shalom* means "peace." The fact that Jerusalem may be the most contested piece of real estate in history makes the idealized notion of a "city of peace" all the more compelling.

Shalom is probably the Hebrew word that people are most likely to know. In Hebrew, *shalom* means not just "peace" but also "hello" and "goodbye." It seems fitting that almost any conversation in Hebrew begins or ends with *shalom.* For thousands of years—from the Torah's prophets to the teachings of the Talmudic rabbis, and on to today—the pursuit of peace has been one of Judaism's core principles.

The importance that Judaism places on pursuing peace is rooted in Judaism's extraordinary reverence for human life. Taking a single life, according to the Mishnah, is like "annihilating an entire world" (*Sanhedrin* 4:5). Killing a person destroys a world of potential.

Conversely, saving a life—through the pursuit of peace—is as important as saving an entire world. In the modern era, when nuclear war poses a real threat to the entire world's survival, the Mishnah's metaphor carries added weight. At the very least, this passage forces a person of conscience to weigh very carefully a decision to go to war, recognizing how easily lives are lost on the battlefield.

Still there is a recognition in the Jewish tradition that wars often begin when one nation or people feels wronged. "The sword comes into the world," teaches the Mishnah, "because of justice delayed and justice denied" (*Ethics of the Ancestors* 5:8). Isaiah offers the flip side of the same idea with: "For the work of the righteous will be peace and the effect of righteousness will be calm and security forever" (Isa. 32:17). It has long been recognized that ongoing oppression of a given group is a recipe for violence and war, often only waiting for the opportunity to express itself.

The Book of Ecclesiastes offers: "There is a time for everything, a time for every experience under heaven.... A time for loving and a time for hating; a time for war, and a time for peace" (Eccles. 3:1–8). On the one hand, Judaism is the religion of Isaiah, whose prophecies contain the most famous antiwar lines of all: "And they shall beat their swords into plowshares and their spears into pruning hooks. Nation shall not take up sword against nation; neither shall they learn war anymore" (Isa. 2:4). On the other hand, Judaism is also the religion of the prophet Joel. Hundreds of years before the Common Era, Joel turned Isaiah's famous phrasing on its head, framing a prophecy to prepare the people for war: "Prepare for battle! Wake the warriors! Let all the fighters come and draw near! Beat your plowshares into swords, and your pruning hooks into spears" (Joel 4:9–10). Neither Joel nor Isaiah expresses the entire message of the Jewish tradition. Isaiah is speaking of an ideal world, a world of peace that we must work to bring about; Joel is speaking of the world in which he lived, where war is sometimes a tragic necessity. It is painful to consider that Joel's prophecy may be the more prudent for our own day.

Judaism justifies the use of force to prevent an aggressor from taking innocent lives. In cases of self-defense or in defending the lives of those who are powerless to defend themselves, Jews are not just permitted, but in fact obligated to use force. Because every life is precious, Judaism teaches that we cannot allow aggressors to take human life. The name that our tradition gives to a war that is morally necessary is *milchemet mitzvah*. A *milchemet mitzvah*, then, is a war that is a mitzvah—a war of obligation, in fulfillment of our commitment to the preservation of human life.

Since a *milchemet mitzvah* is regarded as a necessary evil, Judaism is very wary of glorifying war and violence. The Torah tells us that King David, Jewish tradition's greatest warrior, was forbidden from building the Temple—Judaism's holiest site—because he had shed blood. Jewish legend also records the distress of Jacob—Abraham's grandson—when he realized that, in defending himself against attack, he might be forced to kill: "Jacob feared that he might be killed, and was greatly distressed that he might have to kill others" (*Genesis Rabbah* 76:2). Killing in self-defense, as the story of Jacob reminds us, is almost as terrible as it is necessary. From the time of Jacob to the modern Israeli army, Jews have always been reluctant warriors.

Jewish tradition teaches that defensive war, entered into as a last resort, should be conducted with as much respect and care for human life as possible. Long before Western societies agreed on laws of moral warfare, the Torah forbade the killing of noncombatants (Deut. 20:14). The Torah considers it unacceptable for an army fighting in enemy territory to pursue a so-called scorched earth policy, destroying fields and fruit-bearing trees (Deut. 20:19). And, finally, according to the Talmudic sages, the Torah outlaws siege warfare, the practice of starving civilian populations and enemy combatants indiscriminately (*Sifre Deuteronomy* 203).

Jewish tradition struggles to balance *bakesh shalom,* seeking peace, with the obligation to protect ourselves and save lives by recourse to a defensive war. "Who is a true hero?" asks *Avot d'Rabbi Natan,* an ancient moral treatise. "One who can turn an enemy into a friend." Thus the Torah teaches that before every war must come earnest attempts to make peace.

Lo Ta'amod—You Shall Not Stand Idly By

Torah/Teaching

You shall not stand idly by the blood of your neighbor: I am the Lord.

LEVITICUS 19:16

Three verses before the Book of Leviticus offers up the famous maxim "Love your neighbor as yourself," there is a verse that puts forth a commandment that might have even wider ramifications. Verse 16 seems to anticipate the human tendency to ignore injustice. The Jewish value *lo ta'amod al dam reacha,* the prohibition to not stand idly by while the blood of your neighbor is being shed, makes it an obligation to try to stop a crime, an injustice, or an atrocity. The choice to go about one's daily affairs as if there were no moral obligation to act is a violation of this biblical commandment.

Lo ta'amod extends the right and obligation of self-defense—rooted as it is in our Exodus impulse toward self-preservation—to the altruistic effort to protect other people's lives, an effort rooted in Judaism's Sinai impulse. Motivated by this value, Jews bear the responsibility to protect other people's right to live free of aggression and injustice.

Judaism understands that sometimes the failure to use force in defense of life will only lead to further violence and aggression, and ultimately more loss of life: "If someone comes to kill you," taught the rabbis of the Talmud, "you kill them first" (Babylonian Talmud, *Sanhedrin* 72a). The individual who represents the threat is called in Hebrew a *rodef,* literally, "a pursuer." When one has evidence of a pursuer's intentions, Judaism sanctions killing that person before he or she kills you first. The Talmud connects this principle to *lo ta'amod:*

> From where do we learn that if someone pursues his friend
> with the intent to kill, one is obligated to intervene, even if
> that means taking the murderer's life? The Torah says, "You
> shall not stand idly by the blood of your neighbor" (Babylonian
> Talmud, *Sanhedrin* 73a).

The experience of the Jewish people during World War II heightened Jewish consciousness about the application of the principle *lo ta'amod.* Historians have brought to light how much information was available by the early 1940s about Hitler's plans to exterminate the Jews of Europe and his ability and willingness to do it. Arthur Morse's book *While Six Million Died* and David Wyman's *The Abandonment of the Jews* provide painful details of a world violating this very principle, sitting idly by while the blood of others was being shed. It was in light of that historical experience that, after the war, Jews became leaders in campaigns for human rights and were in the leadership of many human rights organizations (an issue that will be explored at greater length in Chapter 11).

The entire field of human rights attempts to balance the right of countries to run their own affairs, free from outside interference, against the danger posed if a country begins to persecute and/or kill some subset of people within its borders. The often-quoted phrase "Never Again" was supposed to mean that, given the horrors of the Holocaust, the world would never again let genocide take place. The failure of the world to heed that call is underscored by numerous genocides since the end of World War II, most recently the "ethnic cleansing" in the Balkans in the early 1990s, the genocide in Rwanda in 1994, and the genocide in the Darfur region of Sudan in the first decade of the twenty-first century. In each case, the nations of the world reacted slowly and inadequately, making possible the massacre of millions of innocent people. The record of religious communities in response to such atrocities is not much better than that of the United Nations or the industrialized nations of the world. The moral principle of *lo ta'amod* has hardly become standard practice in the post-Holocaust world.

According to many traditional and modern Jewish authorities, the value of *lo ta'amod* extends much further than intervention in defense of human life. Jews have a powerful responsibility to take action on behalf of vulnerable people in general, when help is possible. The Rabbis take *lo ta'amod* as a commandment to protect not only the lives of others, but also their property (Ridbaz on *Choshen Mishpat*, 426). The Rabbis of the Talmudic era further extended *lo ta'amod* to require speaking out when silence would lead to injustice:

> From where do we know that if you are in a position to offer testimony on a person's behalf, you are not permitted to remain silent? From, "You shall not stand idly by the blood of your neighbor" (*Sifra Leviticus* on Lev. 19:16).

Withholding testimony in a court, or failing to come forward when your testimony might advance the cause of justice, is a violation of this Jewish principle.

It is rare that we are called on to serve as witnesses in court, but we may be in other situations when we can act on behalf or in defense of others. Voting, one might argue, is a way of offering testimony, as is lobbying public officials on an issue that affects the health and welfare of society.

Coming to a public demonstration that raises awareness about a cause—be it decrying gun violence, protesting hate crimes, or demanding higher wages for underpaid workers—are all examples of the application of the principle *lo ta'amod.* The principle at work points in the direction of civic engagement and social responsibility for the society in which we live.

Here, *lo ta'amod* is complemented by another important Jewish value, *lo tuchal l'hitalem:* "You cannot turn away" (Deut. 22:3). The Torah introduces *lo tuchal l'hitalem* in the context of the moral imperative to return a lost object to its owner, but the value has much broader implications. *Lo tuchal* can be seen as expressing the obligation to assist whenever people are in need and cannot help themselves. Notice carefully the Torah's language. We are not told that we "shall not turn away" but rather that we "cannot." Helping someone in need, the Torah implies, ought to be instinctive. So deep-seated is our moral responsibility that it ought to seem physically impossible to "turn away."

Darchei Shalom—The Ways of Peace

Torah/Teaching

We support the non-Jewish poor together with Jewish poor, and we visit the non-Jewish sick alongside Jewish sick, and we bury non-Jewish dead alongside Jewish dead, all for the sake of the ways of peace.

BABYLONIAN TALMUD, *GITTIN* 61A

One of the abiding tensions in Jewish ethics is how Jews are supposed to relate to non-Jews. There exist in the Jewish tradition some fairly shocking passages about non-Jews that would offend modern sensibilities, such as Shimon bar Yochai's statement that even the best of the gentiles should be killed (Jerusalem Talmud, *Kiddushin* 66b)! Yet such statements are more than balanced by other texts that cast gentiles in a more sympathetic light, as with the sage Samuel's observation that God will make no distinction between Jews and non-Jews on the day of judgment (Jerusalem Talmud, *Rosh Hashana* 57a).

The contrasting examples provide evidence of the dangers of taking quotes out of context. A full and fair survey of classical Jewish texts will reveal that the historical circumstance conditions the attitude of a given sage. Thus Shimon bar Yochai uttered his indelicate comment after he witnessed his teacher, Rabbi Akiva, tortured to death by the Romans. Conversely, Samuel lived in the Babylonian exile during which Jews enjoyed excellent relations with their hosts and were able to develop a communal life that was actually intellectually and materially superior to the one experienced by their counterparts in Palestine. His kind comment about gentiles needs to be understood against that backdrop.[1]

It is in this context that we must understand the principle of *darchei shalom,* the ways of peace. In this formulation, *shalom* is not referring to the absence of war but rather to peaceful social relations between Jews and non-Jews. The quote from *Gittin* 61a calls upon Jews to provide for the non-Jewish poor just as they would provide for the poor among the Jews. The Talmud goes on in the same passage to list other acts of compassion, like tending to the sick and burying unclaimed bodies. This suggests that such acts of compassion should have no national, ethnic, or religious boundaries.

There is perhaps no area of ethical concern that reflects greater inconsistency in the thinking of rabbinic sages than that of relations with gentiles. Much of the anti-gentile sentiment and legislation in rabbinic Judaism was influenced by the Bible's aversion to idolatry. Judaism begins with Abraham's rejection of the idolatrous ways of his father and his culture. In the Talmud, idolatry joined incest and murder as one of the three cardinal sins that Jews must avoid, even at the risk of death. One rabbinic teaching suggests that the practice of idolatry is tantamount to denying the entire Torah (*Sifre* Deuteronomy 54). Motivating some of the harshest rulings, like not needing to return the lost property of a gentile (*Baba Kama* 38a), had to do with categorizing gentiles as idolaters. Since the goal of monotheism is to root out idolatry from the world, it should not be surprising to find many rabbinic sages who regarded gentiles as unworthy of fair and equal treatment.

By the Middle Ages, despite the fact that gentile treatment of Jews during this period had not much improved, prominent rabbis issued decisive rulings to correct any impression given by earlier rulings that gentiles could be treated unfairly. Maimonides, living in twelfth-century Egypt, still believed that Christians were idolaters, yet he wrote:

> It is forbidden to defraud or deceive any person in business.
> Jew and non-Jew are to be treated alike. If the vendor knows
> that his merchandise is defective, he must so inform the pur-

chaser. It is wrong to deceive any person in words, even without causing him a pecuniary loss (*Yad, Mekirah,* xviii:1).

In his Mishnaic commentary Maimonides remarked: "What some people imagine, that it is permissible to cheat a gentile, is an error, and based on ignorance." Within a generation, Rabbi Menachem Meiri (1249–1316), in his commentary (*Bet Bekhira*) on the Talmudic tractate *Avodah Zara,* Idol Worship, would issue a definitive ruling declaring that neither Christians nor Muslims should be considered idolaters. As such, longstanding restrictions on commerce and social relations between Jews and gentiles were eliminated. Subsequent rabbinic sages repeated and reaffirmed the position that Jews must comply with the highest standards of justice and fairness in their dealings with gentiles.

Sefer Hasidim, an ethical treatise dating from late twelfth-century Germany, maintained that Jews must continue to have strict boundaries in their dealings with gentiles. At the same time, it exhorted Jews to be ethically scrupulous in their dealings with gentiles, provided that these non-Jews lived according to the seven Noachide laws. This principle, established early in the rabbinic tradition, says that gentiles can attain the ultimate reward of a share in the world to come provided they observe the universal moral laws set forth in the biblical Book of Noah concerning murder, stealing, and the like. Jews, on the other hand, are required to observe all 613 commandments of the Torah to merit the same ultimate reward. Perhaps the most remarkable passage in *Sefer Hasidim* is the one that holds up a noble act by a Christian as worthy of emulation by Jews (No. 58).

By the nineteenth century, when there already existed the possibility for Jews to live among gentiles on more or less equal terms, rabbinic authorities gave even greater emphasis to the way Jews behaved among gentiles. Rabbi Samuel Raphael Hirsch, one of the leaders of neo-Orthodoxy in Germany, said that the conduct of Jews needed to be exemplary so that non-Jews would come to know that the Torah was about truth, justice, and love. Conversely, he claimed that injustices committed by Jews against non-Jews were worse than those committed against Jews because such acts would bring the entire religion of Judaism into disrepute.[2]

Although the phrase *darchei shalom* does not appear in the Bible, this rabbinic principle becomes an important Jewish guidepost for behavior. It points to a consciousness about how Jews are viewed by others and an acute sensitivity that the welfare of the Jewish community depended on the good graces of those in power. Here, too, one can find a range of attitudes from defensive to altruistic. Thus, in some places, Jews are urged to act in a respectful and fair manner with gentiles so as to "avoid enmity" (*Avodah Zarah* 26a). The Hebrew expression used is *meshum aivah*. In other places the texts warn Jews against bad behavior toward gentiles because it will "profane God's name" (*Baba Kama* 113b), what is known in Hebrew as a *chillul hashem*. This notion suggests that the reputation of the God of the Jewish people is tied up with the reputation of the Jews themselves and vice versa. The opposite idea is *kiddush hashem,* Jews acting in such a way as to bring honor to God's name. Throughout history, acts of Jewish martyrdom, when Jews allowed themselves to be killed rather than abandon their faith and Jewish practice under duress, reinforced the linkage between the behavior of Jews and how God was perceived in the world.

Darchei shalom, acting properly for the "ways of peace," is the most altruistic of these three rationales given for acting kindly toward the gentiles. On one level, the end result is no different from the rationales "to avoid enmity" and "so as not to profane God's name." In all three cases, Jews try to avoid shameful behavior and the trouble that might result because of that behavior (since others have power over them). On another level, one can also read *darchei shalom* as motivated by more than just wanting to avoid more persecution or another pogrom. It can be read as a sincere desire to create harmonious relations with other ethnic and religious groups. Given the fact that society still falls short of this level of intergroup respect and tolerance in the twenty-first century, the expression of this value in premodern Jewish texts is fairly significant.

Ahavat Ger—Loving the Stranger

Torah/Teaching

You shall love the stranger, for you were strangers in the land of Egypt.

DEUTERONOMY 10:19

No commandment is repeated as often in the Torah as that of protecting the stranger. The Rabbis enumerate thirty-six separate injunctions that underscore the centrality of the principle in Jewish tradition. The core teaching from Deuteronomy 10:19 makes this commandment anything but theoretical. The verse invokes the Jewish people's historical experience of being strangers. While many commandments of the Torah require faith—we act in a certain way because God commands us—the value of protecting the stranger is historically intuitive. Jews identify with the outsider because they themselves have been outsiders.

In the Bible, the word *ger* refers to gentiles who live among Jews. Such outsiders require special protection. They are alone, without ties of religion, nation, or culture and, therefore, vulnerable. In the prophetic literature, the *ger* is associated with the widow and the orphan. Treatment of the stranger emerges as a category that is more than a legal designation, as it is in the earlier stages of Israelite history. It is a euphemism for the weak outsider who needs protection. The *ger* has no natural allies. It is, therefore, the obligation of every Jew to protect him or her.

When the Israelites took possession of the land of Israel, the earliest ethical impulses of the Jewish people acquired legal status. It is therefore telling that among the first laws established in the land of Israel was the defining of the status of *gerim* (literally "foreigners" who attached themselves to the Israelites and resided among them). Since the land was apportioned among the Israelites, the *gerim* were essentially day laborers or artisans. In an agrarian society, this virtually assured their dependency on the kindness of the landowners. That is what makes the biblical command so significant. The Israelites must treat the strangers in their midst as "equal before the law" (Deut. 1:16). Equally significant is the fact that the Bible mandates a form of welfare for the strangers in the land, instructing all landowners that the corners of their field and the fallen grain was to be left for the poor and the stranger (Lev. 19:10). Both are mentioned in the same verse, suggesting that poverty was commonplace among those who were outsiders.

What begins as the directive not to oppress the stranger evolves into treating the stranger fairly and providing her or him with sustenance and support. But the Bible does not stop there. In the same chapter that introduces the phrase "You shall love your neighbor as yourself" (Lev. 19:18), we read: "The stranger who shall reside with you shall be to you as one of your citizens; you shall love him as yourself for you were strangers in the land of Egypt. I am the Lord your God" (Lev. 19:34).

Whatever ambiguity might have existed about the intended meaning of "love your neighbor,"—that is, only Jews or those beyond the tribal circle?—is now gone. Verse 34 says explicitly that the love you feel for yourself and your kin must also be extended to the stranger, the outsider.[3]

This is the implication of the verses that tell us that God loves the stranger (Deut. 10:19), God protects the stranger (Ps. 146:9), and God considers those who oppress the stranger in the same category as adulterers and those who bear false witness (Mal. 3:5). The Jewish tradition is making the case that God is on the side of the stranger, and by extension, Jews understand that it is to the stranger's side that Jews must rally. If loving the stranger did not quite make it into the "top ten" commandments, the verse from Malachi seems to be trying to add an amendment. Adultery and false witness are both part of the Ten Commandments, and the prophet is saying that one who does not protect the stranger is no better than one who violates the core covenant from Sinai.

This clearly seems to be the intent of the prophet Jeremiah when he says that the land of Israel is reserved for people who follow a certain ethical course of action in their lives:

> If you execute justice between one person and another, if you
> do not oppress the stranger, the orphan and the widow, if you
> do not shed the blood of the innocent, if you do not follow
> other Gods ... then will I let you dwell in the land which I
> gave to your fathers for all time (Jer. 7:5–8).

Similarly, the prophet Zechariah uses this "vulnerability ethic" as a centerpiece for what is required for Jews to merit God's reward of living in the Promised Land: "Execute true justice, deal loyally and compassionately with each other, do not defraud the widow, the orphan, the stranger, and the poor, and do not plot evil against one another...." (Zech. 7:9–10). Again we find the invocation of the ethic of compassion, and it is not restricted to the *ger*. Rather the *ger* becomes symbolic of all outsiders, all who are victimized by the forces of oppression.

The historical experience of oppression makes it impossible for Jews to ignore the Torah's commandment to protect the vulnerable. The modern nation-state has become accustomed to gaps between privileged and underprivileged classes. It is often justified by the economic, political, and/or religious ideology of the ruling elite. Jews have been on both sides of that divide. It is easy to act with sympathy to the outsider when that is your status as well. It is much harder when you begin to have a taste of privilege. In the last century, Jews have begun to experience increasing levels of privilege, both in the diaspora and in their own state. The measure of how committed Jews are to the Sinai ethic is the extent to which Jewish people ally with those who are as oppressed as Jews once were.

Emet—Truth

Torah/Teaching

These are the things you must do: speak the truth to one another, render true and perfect justice in your gates.

ZECHARIAH 8:16

The best way to convey the centrality of *emet,* "truth," to Judaism's value system is to note that the Bible often speaks of God as "the God of truth" (Jer. 10:10; Ps. 31:6). A passage from the Book of Exodus, which was later codified as one of the thirteen attributes of God, ends with God being described as "abundant in compassion and truth," *rav chesed v'emet* (Exod. 34:6). In rabbinic thought, humanity is meant to emulate these attributes of God. The commandment to "speak the truth" is about much more than avoiding lies. *Emet* mandates an attitude of moral honesty and spiritual integrity. Truth, in Judaism, is not merely what is not false. It is what we know on the deepest level to be ethically correct. To "speak the truth" is to advocate on behalf of what is morally true.

Emet also implies integrity, both outer and inner. The outer integrity is the avoidance of hypocrisy, when someone says one thing but believes or does something else. "The Holy One hates people who say one thing in their mouths and another in their hearts" (*Pesachim* 113b). The standard for inner integrity is even higher. The Talmud tells the story of a scholar named Rab Safra, who was a merchant but who was approached by a customer while praying the *Shma*. The customer, unaware that Safra was forbidden to speak during the solemn prayer, raised his initial price offer for the item he wanted to buy. Safra heard the initial price and was prepared to accept it. Feeling that taking the higher price would violate the principle of *emet,* Safra finished his prayer and told the customer that he had already consummated the transaction in his mind at the lower price and that should stand as the price (*Makot* 23a).

Another perspective on *emet* emerges from a fascinating juxtaposition of two verses in the *Ethics of the Ancestors*. This book of the Mishnah opens with the dictum of Simeon the Righteous: "On three things does the world stand: Torah, service (to God), and acts of lovingkindness" (1:2). At the end of the first chapter, a similar maxim is attributed to a later sage, Shimon ben Gamliel: "The world survives because of three things: fairness, truth, and peace" (1:18).

It is of course possible to understand the two statements as representing conflicting worldviews. With such a reading, ben Gamliel set "fairness, truth, and peace" (*din, emet,* and *shalom*) above Simeon's "Torah, service, and acts of lovingkindness" (*Torah, avodah,* and *gemilut chasadim*). In one of the classical commentaries on the Mishnah dating from the seventeenth century, Ovadiah of Bartenura reconciles the two passages. The Bartenura suggests that we read the first Mishnah as: "the world would not have been created but for these three things." In other words, humanity was brought into the world to engage in study (*Torah*), to become spiritually grounded by "serving God" (*avodah*), and to engage in personal acts of lovingkindness (*gemilut chasadim*). These values are at the core of any individual's moral contract. The Bartenura reads the second Mishnah as: "civilization is sustained by these three things." That is to say, the health of society depends on fairness, truth, and peace. Indeed, the history of civilization gives evidence that when these latter qualities are lacking, major conflict between tribes, peoples, and nations ensues. When these elements, cornerstones of what we call the "social contract," are lacking, societies are often plunged into conflict that puts the very future of the world at risk. Humanity, according to these texts, is worth creating if individuals can be trained to live by the moral contract. But human fidelity to study, service, and acts of kind-·ness is not sufficient to sustain society. Only through engagement with society and working to establish justice, truth, and peace can the world endure.

Sometimes truth hurts. At other times truth can be dangerous. Judaism tries to offer some advice on both. On a personal level Jews are instructed by the verse: "Do not hate your brother in your heart. You must surely rebuke your friend, so that you will not share in his guilt" (Lev. 19:17). The first part of the verse suggests the danger of having a strong negative feeling toward another person and not expressing it so as to avoid conflict. The verse anticipates some of the insights of modern therapy, which helps people talk through some of the anger felt toward a spouse, a friend, or a professional colleague in a way that might smooth out the relationship. Failure to do so inevitably leads to more conflict in the future. The second part of the verse teaches a collective responsibility of all those who share in God's covenant. A Jew who truly loves his or her neighbor will help that neighbor live in accordance with the expectations of the Torah. "All love that does not include some criticism," said the sage Yossi ben Chaninah, "is not true love" (*Genesis Rabbah* 54). Ben Chaninah seems to be teaching that rebuke, when called for, is the essence of good friendship, and good citizenship is an extension of the concept of *emet.*

It seems then that the rabbis felt that *emet* could sometimes be tempered in the cause of a higher value. The Talmud records a debate between Hillel and Shammai on whether the truth must be told if a wedding guest simply does not believe that the bride looks beautiful. Truth is so important, answers Shammai, that a guest who thinks the bride unattractive simply cannot tell her otherwise. Hillel, however, argues that kindness ought sometimes to outweigh strict sincerity: a guest should tell the bride that she looks "beautiful and graceful" (Babylonian Talmud, *Ketubot* 17a). The Talmud accepts Hillel's view as authoritative, ruling that the spirit of kindness outweighs the need to deliver unvarnished truth.

No such allowance, however, existed for truth or rebuke when the welfare of society or the standards of righteousness and justice were at stake. Following Leviticus 19:14 about the necessity of rebuke, the Talmud says: "If one can stop the whole world from sinning, and does not, he is held responsible for the sins of the whole world" (*Shabbat* 54b). This principle of *hocheach tocheach,* bringing forward the harshest truth to society in the name of God, is the spirit of the biblical prophetic tradition that we explored in Chapter 6. The prophets—Isaiah, Jeremiah, Ezekiel, Amos, and others—are exemplars of *emet,* speaking truth to power, even at great risk to themselves. Their objective was to get the behavior of individuals and society to align with the highest standards of righteousness and justice that began with Abraham's call from God.

This is the kind of prophetic witness that Judaism expects from every generation. It often comes from the most unlikely places. History suggests that the closer one gets to power, the harder it is to respond to the call that Abraham heard so clearly in the solitude of the desert. Yet, as hard as it might be, Judaism has a messianic disposition. Sinai can live in the heart of every and any Jew, from the most religiously observant to the most skeptical nonbeliever. This messianic belief is suggested by a verse from the Book of Psalms that reconciles attributes that often seem to exist in conflict. It reads: "[One day] compassion and truth will meet, righteousness and peace will kiss; truth will well up out of the ground and justice will rain down from the heavens" (Ps. 85:10–12).

In a similar way, Jews throughout history have often been pulled between Exodus and Sinai impulses. As we now turn to the contemporary history of the American Jewish community, we shall explore how these tendencies have played themselves out and how they might be reconciled akin to the verse from the Book of Psalms.

III EXODUS AND SINAI IN AMERICA

9

The American Jewish Community and the Public Square

America's first Jews were the descendents of Jews expelled from Spain and Portugal. In 1654 they founded the country's first synagogue, Congregation Shearith Israel, in New Amsterdam (now known as Manhattan). America seemed to offer a new kind of freedom, a place where they could live with pride as Jews. When the United States was born, its new president, George Washington, justified their hope in a famous 1790 letter to the Hebrew Congregation of Newport, Rhode Island, promising that "the Government of the United States, which gives to bigotry no sanction, to persecution no assistance, requires only that they who live under its protection should demean themselves as good citizens." From the very beginning, Jews had faith that the American experience would be different.

Jews enjoyed unprecedented freedom and opportunity in America, but for a long time, they remained outsiders in this country. In the face of religious, cultural, and economic barriers, Jewish immigrants clung to one another for support. For centuries, the ancestors of America's Jewish immigrants built strong communities that provided for the religious, social, and economic needs of Europe's Jews. This tradition of self-governing communal institutions was reestablished in the New World, and it helped Jews adapt to their new life in America.

America was a country of immigrants, ruled by a government that, by European standards, made few demands on the everyday lives of its citizens. American public life was defined by a tendency of individuals to meet their needs by banding together in voluntary organizations. Jews were well suited to thrive in this environment. Jews came from a culture that put a high value on communal organization, and the free and open American setting facilitated their efforts to organize themselves to meet their group needs. Synagogues were organized and quickly emerged as the retail outlet for Jewish association, providing for Jews' religious, educational, and pastoral needs. Community-wide institutions were created to provide for an array of social services. Jewish burial societies were created to tend to the ritual requirements at the end of life. Finally, Jews set up national and local public affairs agencies to take responsibility for the way they interacted with American society, public officials, and the world—the world of the "public square."

It was these Jewish public affairs agencies that created the most interesting synthesis between the Exodus consciousness and Sinai consciousness of American Jews. As these agencies were initially set up to defend the life and liberty of Jews at home and abroad, their work was "survival" writ large. At the same time, these "defense agencies," which came into existence to protect the rights of Jews, quickly defined their agenda more broadly, seeking to advance the principles of liberty, justice, and fairness that would allow America to live up to the ideals of its founding fathers. The Jewish community, through its public affairs agencies, wanted to bring a bit of Sinai to America.

National Defense Agencies

The first years of the twentieth century saw a dangerous rise in Russian anti-Semitism. The czar supported a series of vicious pogroms against Russian Jews. Many Russian Jewish refugees fled to the United States. Until that point, American Jews had no national lobbying group and it became clear that only government-to-government pressure could help European Jewry. In 1906, a group of Jewish philanthropists who, because of their wealth, enjoyed access to American public officials, founded the American Jewish Committee (AJCommittee) to represent the interests of the American Jewish community.

The Anti-Defamation League (ADL) was founded in 1913 as a department of B'nai Brith to combat anti-Semitism and discrimination in American society. As if to underscore the need for the organization, two years after its founding, a Jew named Leo Frank living in Georgia was unjustly convicted of rape and murder and then was dragged from his prison cell and lynched by a gang fired up by anti-Semitic propaganda. The ADL eventually outgrew its B'nai Brith roots, became independent, and focused its mission on combating prejudice and discrimination against any ethnic group and defending and protecting the rights of Jews all around the world.

The third major Jewish defense agency created in the early twentieth century was the American Jewish Congress (AJCongress), founded in 1918. In the aftermath of World War I, there was a need for an umbrella group to address the plight of Jews in Europe, and the AJCongress took on that mandate. But what began as a task-specific organization soon took on a life of its own under the leadership of the charismatic Reform rabbi Stephen Wise. The AJCongress became an outlet of expression for recent Jewish arrivals from eastern Europe who sought an organizational vehicle for their concerns. While the AJCommittee was led primarily by wealthy German Jews who favored quiet, behind-the-scenes contacts with public officials, the AJCongress represented a more populist approach. Wise shaped the AJCongress in the image of his Zionist passions, and his assertive public response to the rise of Nazism led his organization to take the lead in organizing a boycott of German goods in the United States. The AJCongress was an early proponent of Zionism, years before the AJCommittee came to support the effort to create a Jewish state.

All three of these national agencies grew in scope over time, taking on a more diverse agenda driven by the interests of their respective memberships. These organizations did not limit themselves to defending Jewish interests, even though that was the impetus behind the founding of each. Their respective mandates encompassed most of the critical social issues facing American society. The AJCommittee sponsored research, published *Commentary* magazine, and became a major force in intergroup relations and international affairs. The AJCongress became a leading force on a variety of civil liberty issues, most notably church-state separation, doing some of the most cutting-edge legal work in the country on an issue that defined American democracy and the protection of minority rights. The ADL took up many cases of discrimination that affected both Jews and non-Jews, combated prejudice, and today sponsors the World of Difference program, one of the largest educational programs in the country promoting diversity, tolerance, and intergroup understanding.

Essentially the defense agencies, created by American Jews, were making two statements through their work. First, their very activity made the case that Jews were not going to disappear in the melting pot of America. Jews had group interests and it was they, perhaps more than any other immigrant group in America, who pushed American democracy to sanction cultural pluralism, a theory that meant that ethnic groups did not have to give up their distinctiveness to be good American citizens. None other than Louis Brandeis, a Boston lawyer who was known for his advocacy on behalf of poor working people and the first Jew appointed (in 1916) to the U.S. Supreme Court, articulated this very principle:

> The new nationalism adopted by America proclaims that each race or people, like each individual, has the right and duty to develop, and that only through such differentiated development will high civilization be attained. Not until these principles of nationalism, like those of democracy, are generally accepted will liberty be fully attained and minorities be secure in their rights. Not until then can the foundation be laid for a lasting peace among the nations.[1]

The second point that came through the wide-ranging work of Jewish defense agencies and communal umbrella agencies was that there was no conflict between protecting Jewish rights and working to make America into a more just and fair society. Once again, it was Louis Brandeis who articulated the consistency between Jewish aspirations and American ideals, thus justifying the ongoing strong communal identity of American Jews. He later extended this principle to justify his avid public support for the cause of Zionism, well before this was a widely held or popular position, even among Jews:

> There is no inconsistency between loyalty to America and loyalty to Jewry. The Jewish spirit, the product of our religion and

experiences, is essentially modern and essentially American. Not since the destruction of the Temple have the Jews in spirit and in ideals been so fully in harmony with the noblest aspirations of the country in which they lived.[2]

Throughout the twentieth century, Jewish thinkers expanded on these ideas: Horace Kallen, as the intellectual expositor of cultural pluralism in the early twentieth century; Rabbi Mordecai Kaplan, whose philosophy of Judaism was based on a synthesis of the best values of Judaism and the best values of American democracy; and finally Milton Konvitz, a noted legal scholar whose contributions to the field of constitutional rights and civil liberties made all the more compelling his book, *Judaism and the American Idea,* which described how Jewish values shaped American law and politics. These scholars and others made the case that Judaism and the Jewish community could contribute to American culture, just as American culture could enhance Jews and Judaism.[3] This was the spirit in which the Jewish community engaged in the American public square.

In the Aftermath of the Holocaust

The end of the Holocaust in 1945 found the Jewish world in a state of crisis. Six million European Jews had been murdered. The American Jewish community had been singularly incapable of effective intervention on behalf of their European coreligionists with American public officials.[4] The Soviet Union was turning inward, essentially imprisoning two million-plus Soviet Jews in its anti-Semitic empire. And the ancient longing for a Jewish homeland had become a bona fide political movement that would see its fulfillment in 1948 with the birth of the state of Israel. The American Jewish community needed to find a better way to advance its interests in the public square.

It was against this backdrop that several new organizations emerged to give Jews a more powerful collective voice on issues of concern to the Jewish community. By the early twentieth century, the Jewish community established a philanthropic network to fund local needs under the aegis of the United Jewish Appeal and, later, the Jewish federation network. Among the local agencies that were established were community relations councils (CRCs) charged with handling the local Jewish community's interactions with the larger society. In 1944, a national organization called the National (Jewish)

Community Relations Advisory Council (NJCRAC) was created to coordinate the work of these local CRCs.[5]

The NJCRAC was charged with developing coherent policy directions for CRCs nationwide and coordinating that deliberative process with the national Jewish defense agencies that responded to their respective constituencies. Though the NJCRAC could not force its views on the national agencies, and there were many examples when one or more agencies dissented from a NJCRAC initiative, the umbrella did provide an important forum for shaping an American Jewish approach to public policy issues. By shaping policy statements on issues as varied as church-state separation, welfare reform, education, human rights, health care, immigration, and the environment—not to mention the security of Jews at home and abroad—the NJCRAC was able to speak on behalf of the American Jewish community to public officials and leaders of other interest groups. Today, the Jewish Council for Public Affairs (JCPA), as it was recently renamed, represents more than a hundred local CRCs and thirteen national Jewish public affairs organizations.

While the development of NJCRAC was driven by internal needs and interests, the impetus for the creation of the Conference of Presidents of Major American Jewish Organizations (known as the Presidents Conference) came from the U.S. State Department. In 1955, as tensions built up in the Middle East in the months that led up to the 1956 war between Israel and Egypt, the State Department was overwhelmed by the number of Jewish individuals and organizations lobbying on behalf of the nascent Jewish state. The State Department requested that the Jewish community consolidate its lobbying on behalf of Israel. The Presidents Conference became that agency. Today, under the umbrella of the Presidents Conference, the leaders of more than fifty national Jewish organizations—from synagogue groups to Zionist organizations to the national Jewish defense agencies—formulate consensus positions on the Middle East and other international issues and present them to the American government. The Presidents Conference has become a central address in the Jewish community on matters of international affairs, with considerable access to both the State Department and the White House.

In its efforts on behalf of Israel, the Presidents Conference was joined in the early 1950s by the American Israel Public Affairs Committee (AIPAC), a registered lobby that seeks to create a strong

U.S.-Israel relationship.[6] Though other Zionist groups, including Hadassah and the Zionist Organization of America, were active on behalf of Israel, even before 1948, no organization rivals AIPAC in terms of its ability to influence American public officials in ways that benefit Israel. By the 1980s other national Jewish organizations began to defer to AIPAC on Israel-related issues in Washington.[7] With a national network of wealthy, politically active donors who work hard to cultivate relationships with elected officials, AIPAC has helped to ensure record levels of foreign aid flowing to the Jewish state from the United States, forged collaborative relationships, facilitated arms transfers between the respective military establishments of the two countries, and ensured that both Republican and Democratic administrations remain sympathetic with, and favorable toward, Israel in the Middle East conflict. In the past decade, AIPAC is regularly cited as one of Capitol Hill's most important, effective, and powerful lobby groups on any issue.[8]

In the years since George Washington sent his letter to the Hebrew Congregation of Newport, Rhode Island, the American Jewish community evolved from a vulnerable immigrant community, primarily concerned with protecting its own rights at home and the safety of Jews overseas, to a political powerhouse, weighing in on not only a wide array of issues that affected the Jews, but also the broader quality of life in America and in the world. In the first part of the twentieth century, rabbis and the national rabbinical unions like the Rabbinical Assembly of America (Conservative movement) and the Central Conference of American Rabbis (Reform movement) gave Jewish voice to issues of moral and ethical concern, including the rights of workers and the issue of war and peace. However significant such clergy leadership was on broad issues of social justice—especially in the way it connected advocacy on such issues to the teachings of the Jewish tradition—the American Jewish community increasingly vested responsibility for public affairs work to the secular umbrella agencies of the community. They had the expertise and staff time that the rabbis lacked to work on public issues.

The political maturation of the community accelerated considerably in the years following World War II.[9] In broad strokes, the Jewish community was first motivated to engage in the public square to fight anti-Semitism and discrimination at home and the danger to Jews overseas. In the post-war years, the agenda came to include support for the state of Israel and the rescue of endangered Jewish communities around the world, most prominently Soviet Jews.

In the 1960s, Jews began to better understand a core principle of community relations—minorities need allies, and allies work on each other's issues. In other words, the ability of a minority group to advance a particular agenda in the public square is largely determined by the extent to which it can attract other groups to its cause. Of course such arrangements are often reciprocal. Group A supports group B on an issue in return for the support that group B provides to A. Because of this fact of American political life, some have argued that Jewish involvement in the civil rights movement was motivated by Jewish self-interest. To the extent that there were discriminatory practices in schools, in hiring in the private sector, and in government contracting, Jews had a vested interest in working to eradicate such barriers. All minorities, Jews included, would benefit. But Jews were also instinctively sympathetic to the plight of African-Americans, given Jewish teachings about justice as well as the history of Jewish persecution through the ages, which made Jews instinctively sympathetic to victims of injustice. The Jewish public agenda came to include promoting intergroup relations, advocacy for civil rights, economic opportunity, and a host of progressive social policy concerns.[10]

Jewish leaders learned to frame issues affecting Jews in the broadest possible way so that the desired solution would be seen as benefiting a wide cross-section of Americans. Ensuring that Jewish children in public schools were not subjected to Christian prayer resulted in the Jewish community playing a leading role in creating appropriate legal safeguards to the First Amendment's establishment clause. Concern over the difficulty Jews had gaining permission to immigrate to the United States brought about Jewish leadership in the coalition that lobbied for a major expansion of American immigration quotas. Similarly, Jewish organizations often make the case that America should support Israel because it is the only democratic country in the Middle East that can be a trusted and reliable ally.

To those who understand the way that coalitions between disparate groups come to shape American public policy, the strategy makes perfect sense. It has allowed the Jewish community to build allies across the spectrum of issues. It has made the Jewish community a critical player on issues dealing with the quality of life in America and the way America engages with the international community. But if we look past the pragmatism of the approach, we come to understand that the motivation and the passion that run so deep among American Jews on these issues also has to do with their desire to bring a piece of Sinai to American shores. The very values that shaped Jewish life, community, and identity for centuries (and that were explored in Parts I and II) are the driving force that animates Jewish civic engagement in America.

Jews and Politics

Parallel to the emergence of the Jewish community as a force to be reckoned with in the American public square is the phenomenon of Jews becoming increasingly prominent in American politics. As with other ethnic communities in America, the entry into public life represented an increased level of acculturation for Jews. Jews were no longer guests in a strange land, but rather full partners in the American democratic endeavor. For most American ethnic groups, like the Irish and the Italians, the acculturation that paved the way for participation in American civic life coincided with a commensurate decline in ethnic communal strength. Not so with the Jews. The Jewish community continued to enjoy vigorous communal solidarity, even as individual American Jews rose to prominence in the American political realm.

The coming of age for Jews in American politics can be dated to President Franklin Roosevelt's New Deal. Credited with helping bring America through the Depression, the New Deal substantially expanded the scope of the federal government. At a time when Jewish professionals found doors closed to them in the private sector, in academia, and even because of the discriminatory administration of federal contracts, Washington was eager for lawyers, economists, and policy analysts of talent. It was the first opportunity for Jews to enter into public service. Even though most of the positions were in behind-the-scenes civil service posts, the New Deal opened the door to more prominent positions of authority in the decades to follow. Among the Jews who came to Washington to serve President Roosevelt during the New Deal were: Felix Frankfurter, later to be appointed to the Supreme Court; Benjamin Cohen, who drafted much of the New Deal legislation; and Henry Morgenthau, Jr., who became Secretary of Treasury and then the national chairman of the United Jewish Appeal.

Jews would not remain behind the scenes for long. In the post-war years, with their increasing affluence and social status, Jews were increasingly prominent in the American political arena. The public debate over civil rights and the Vietnam War in the 1960s gave rise to a culture of political activism at the grassroots level in America. It also led to a significant growth in the number of public interest groups that organized the American public around issues of civic importance. Jews played prominent roles, both as board members and as professional leaders, in many of these groups and causes. Joseph Rauh and Arnie Aronson were in the forefront of the Leadership Conference on Civil Rights (LCCR). Norman Dorsen and Ira Glasser were among the leaders of the American Civil Liberties Union (ACLU). In the front lines of the feminist movement was Betty Friedan, who served as the first president of the National Organization for Women (NOW), along with Bella Abzug, Phyllis Chesler, and Letty Cottin Pogrebin. Human Rights Watch (originally Helsinki Watch), which played a leading role in monitoring human rights abuses around the world, was founded by the New York publisher Robert Bernstein. Norman Lear, the pioneering television producer of *All in the Family,* used his fame and fortune to found People for the American Way, an organization that worked to counter the influence of the Christian Right and to secure the principles of American pluralism and tolerance. David Cohen and Fred Wertheimer served as successive presidents of Common Cause, an organization committed to good government and equitable campaign financing. With many of these groups headquartered in Washington, and the work often involving interaction with elected officials and their staffs, Jews quickly became key players at the center of American political life.

The Jews who rose to national prominence as organizers and political activists in the American public were only the tip of the iceberg. Behind them were thousands of Jews who were active in an array of organizations committed to creating a more just and equitable America. These Jews had varying levels of Jewish knowledge and identity. Some, like Sidney Hillman—who became a national leader in the labor movement as the first president of the Amalgamated Clothing Workers of America—came from an Orthodox background and were educated in parochial schools (*yeshivot*). Others had a perfunctory exposure to Judaism as children. Most were not particularly identified with the organized Jewish community. What they all seemed to share, however, was a deep belief in the ability to bring positive social change to America and to the world. John Gardner, a non-Jew who served as the Secretary of Health, Education, and Welfare under President Lyndon Johnson and was one of the chief architects of Johnson's Great Society programs (he went on to found both Common Cause and Independent Sector), once commented that Jews were holding together the social fabric of American civic life all across the country. He cited their leadership in social services, as well as their generosity as manifested in Jewish philanthropy leadership in United Way campaigns throughout the country.[11]

By the 1980s, Jewish involvement in American politics became even more visible as Jews began to run, and win, races for public office at the local, state, and federal level. The disproportionate Jewish involvement in this sphere was made evident by the fact that by the year 1992, there were a record ten Jews in the U.S. Senate and thirty-three Jewish members of the House of Representatives. This was at a time when the percentage of Jews in America was under 3 percent. More significantly, Jews were being elected from jurisdictions with very few Jews. Dan Glickman, a Jew who was elected to Congress from Kansas's fourth district in 1977 (and later went on to serve in President Clinton's cabinet as Secretary of Agriculture), used to joke that he could barely find a *minyan* of Jews (ten) in his entire district. The profile of Jews in public life has also been enhanced by the seven Jews who have served on the U.S. Supreme Court, from Louis Brandeis at the beginning of the twentieth century to Ruth Bader Ginsburg and Stephen Breyer in the early twenty-first century.

Indeed, Jews became so active in the political sphere that there emerged two new organizations to better organize Jewish influence and fundraising on behalf of the two major political parties. In 1985 the National Jewish Coalition was formed to bring more Jews into positions of prominence in the Republican Party. It was telling that the word "Republican" was left out of the organization's name, an indication that such an effort would be going against the tide of Jewish political sympathies at the time. By 1999 the organization changed its name to the Republican Jewish Coalition (RJC), signifying that a Jewish Republican was no longer the anomaly it once was in the community. A counterpart organization, the National Jewish Democratic Council (NJDC), was founded in 1990.

Of course, the ticket to political influence in contemporary America is money, and enough Jews both have it and have used it to result in the election of many candidates sympathetic to Jewish interests and concerns. In the post-Watergate era, a change in campaign finance laws limited the amount of money individuals could give to candidates for public office but permitted the creation of political action committees (PACs) that could "bundle" money to give to candidates. PACs essentially provided a way to circumvent the limits of personal contributions to candidates. The Jewish community was quick to take advantage of this provision, and soon there were more than sixty pro-Israel PACs funneling close to $5 million per cycle to mostly pro-Israel candidates for Congress. Some estimates suggest that Jews may have been responsible for as much as 50 percent of the funding of the Gore-Lieberman presidential ticket in 2000 and one-third of the funding for the Bush-Cheney ticket in that same race.[12]

At least part of the influence that AIPAC, the pro-Israel lobby based in Washington, enjoys with Congress owes to the fact that its members are significant contributors to incumbents or candidates who are friendly to Israel. Their financial support results in AIPAC's having unparalleled access when it wants to speak to a member of Congress on an issue of concern to the Jewish community. One recent report revealed that AIPAC board members gave an average of $72,000 in political contributions, to both Republicans and Democrats, in the four years since the election of 2000.[13] This kind of money, and the willingness to contribute it to candidates who face increasingly expensive, media-oriented campaigns, insures that Jewish voices will be heard and that Jewish individuals will become increasingly prominent in the political arena.

There are Jews who are not so comfortable with the rise of Jewish financial and political clout. For them, it conjures up fears of longstanding stereotypes about Jews having undue and pernicious influence over world events. One of the most widely distributed anti-Semitic tracts in history is *The Protocols of the Elders of Zion,* a book of canards authored in the nineteenth century that portrays Jews as conspiring to seek global dominance. Similarly, American-based racist groups in this last century have frequently leveled accusations against Jews for controlling both banks and public officials. Nonetheless, most Jews feel no need to apologize for proactive and lawful Jewish involvement in American politics. This confidence is one of the signs of a minority group growing more comfortable with its status in American society.

If the Jewish community needed a symbol for its coming of age in American politics, they could find none better than the choice of Joe Lieberman as the vice-presidential running mate of Al Gore in the 2000 presidential election. At the time of his selection, Lieberman was a Democratic senator serving the state of Connecticut. Not only was he Jewish, but he was an observant Orthodox Jew married to a woman named Hadassah, whose family survived the Holocaust. The Jewish community met the news with a mixture of delight and anxiety. Delight because it signaled that no door was closed to Jewish advancement in American society. Anxiety because it raised the concern that Lieberman would be a lightning rod for anti-Semitism, if not worse. While the Gore-Lieberman ticket did not win the White House,[14] the campaign was remarkable for the fact that Lieberman's Jewishness was taken in stride by the American electorate. Not only did it not stir up any anti-Jewish action or comment, but the consensus was that Americans admired this Jew who took his faith so seriously.

Politics as Creed

Senator Lieberman was extremely conscious of and articulate about what his candidacy meant to Jews and to America. Here is how he framed his experience in one observation:

> Although politics was not exactly a Jewish profession in the early days of the republic, individual Jews did throw themselves into the democratic process. Some were traditional politicians, such as Judah Benjamin, who represented Louisiana in the Senate before serving in the cabinet of Confederate President Jefferson Davis. Others entered politics as machine politicians. Many more, such as Emma Goldman and the radicals of the early 20th century, were inspired by the ideal that they had a duty to repair the world.
>
> Some of these people took the route of elected or appointive office through the major political parties. Individuals such as Oscar Strauss, the first Jew to serve in a president's cabinet, were at the center of the reform tradition in American politics. Many others entered public life as outsiders. They fought for equal rights for the working class, for equal rights for their co-religionists abroad, for abolition of slavery, and for voting

rights for women. But whether as establishment politicians or as radicals, these Jewish Americans seemed to have been influenced (consciously or unconsciously) by Scripture's mandate: "Justice, justice shalt thou pursue."[15]

Lieberman saw a connection between Jewish social revolutionaries like Emma Goldman and one of the first Jewish American public officials, Judah Benjamin (Lieberman's own life and career are more clearly in line with the latter). In his mind, both shared a commitment to bring about a more just society as envisioned by the legacy of the biblical passage "justice, justice shall you pursue" (Deut. 16:20). Judaism puts forth a vision of an ideal society in which the "lion shall lie down with the lamb" (Isa. 11:6), "nation shall not lift up sword against nation" (Isa. 2:4), and in which the "stranger, widow and orphan will find protection" (Zech. 7:10). This messianic vision is deeply embedded in the consciousness of the Jewish people.

Because historical circumstances rarely put Jews in positions of power where they could bring about such a messianic vision, much of that impulse was directed toward the religious realm. The traditional Jewish liturgy contained glimpses of an ideal world that Jews prayed for. Rabbis upheld this ideal through their preaching and teaching. Talmudic references to "the next world" gave Jews a sense that, though the messianic ideal may be remote, it was at the very least worth striving for in the present. The ethic of the Jewish tradition was always to try to create a world in which peace and justice prevail. Here, in the land that allowed Jews to fulfill the prophetic obligation to speak truth to power, America provided an unparalleled opportunity to effect this messianic vision through politics.

Not only was America free of many of the political disabilities that condemned Jews to second-class status in Europe, but the very language of the founders was replete with biblical and theological imagery. America was described as the "Promised Land." Americans were seen as the beneficiaries of God's election and fulfilling God's will in the New World. Jews may be among the most secularized of America's faith communities, but in many ways the realm of politics has been their temple. Given the emphasis in Jewish texts on social responsibility, politics provided a vehicle through which Jews could fulfill the most cherished mandates of the Jewish tradition for equality, justice, and peace. Of course, most Jews were hardly aware of those teachings in any specific way. But even as many Jews distanced themselves from traditional Jewish learning and practice, the central values of compassion, good deeds, and charity became part of a secularized Jewish ethic.

The stories of the Bible and the Jewish holidays served as touchstones for those who sought to bring about ethical solutions to society's problems. One such example was Herbert Lehman, who served as governor of New York in the 1930s and then, later, in the U.S. Senate.

> My Jewish heritage has unquestionably affected my political and social thinking. All through my years of public life I have felt strongly the importance of keeping faith with the ethics of Judaism, and its basic concept that "creed without deed" is meaningless. As a Jew and a human being I have accepted no boundaries except those of justice, righteousness, humility and charity.... In a very real sense the aims and ideals of the Jewish religion are identical with the purposes of Democracy.... In these difficult days of declining liberalism, it is important for us as Americans and Jews to try to regain the moral perspectives first charged by our Jewish heritage. Our mission is to fight against injustice when practiced against any minority, anywhere in the world. We Americans of Jewish heritage have a special obligation consistent with our ancient heritage to be messengers of peace.[16]

Lehman's sentiments are illustrative of how otherwise-secular Jews were shaped in their political consciousness by Jewish history and tradition.

Not everyone looks upon this phenomenon so kindly. The neoconservative commentator Irving Kristol, for example, believes that equating Judaism and social justice is ill conceived and injurious to Jewish interests. He notes how much religious fervor exists behind the Jewish commitment to liberal social solutions to contemporary policy dilemmas and identifies it as a consequence of the Jewish embrace of secular humanism. He defines secular humanism as a form of atheism that denies God's existence and, in its place, affirms humanity's ability to bring about the vision of prophetic Judaism through the instruments of the nation-state. Kristol believes that it is "unJewish" to replace God with the secular state. Furthermore, he believes that with humanistic democratic socialism discredited in the world today, Jewish liberalism will become less and less tenable once Jews come to their senses.[17]

While Kristol and his neoconservative colleagues have their detractors, it is interesting how he, too, sees politics as a deep creedal commitment of Jews. Somehow, Jews are playing out their deepest-held values and their self-perception as American Jews in the realm of politics. Whether one looks at the percentages of Jews who are registered and voting in elections, the cluster of Jews in key metropolitan media markets and states with relatively high electoral votes, the preponderance of Jews in public interest groups that work to effect policy, or the disproportionate numbers of Jews who are now members of Congress, Jews do have an influence on American politics that far outstrips their relative numbers of the American population. Equally interesting is how American Jews wield that political influence.

Understanding Jewish Political Behavior

Over the past fifty years, American Jews have consistently exhibited liberal ideas and liberal voting patterns. In so doing, Jews defy the tendency for groups to vote their economic interests. In general, the higher the socioeconomic class, the more likely a group will exhibit conservative attitudes and voting patterns. The more economically disadvantaged a group, the more likely that group will manifest liberal attitudes and voting patterns. Nevertheless, Jews have remained overwhelmingly committed to the Democratic Party ever since the presidency of Franklin Roosevelt. In the last four presidential elections (1992: Clinton-Bush; 1996: Clinton-Dole; 2000: Bush-Gore; 2004: Bush-Kerry), Jews cast 80 percent, 78 percent, 79 percent, and 75 percent of their votes for the Democratic ticket, respectively. In congressional and state-wide elections, Jews tend to vote two to three times more often for Democratic candidates than for Republicans. This voting pattern led the noted American Jewish political commentator Milton Himmelfarb to observe that "the Jews earn like Episcopalians and vote like Puerto Ricans."

The Jewish Public Opinion Survey,[18] conducted in 2000, found that 49 percent of Jews identified themselves as Democrats, compared to only 10 percent who identified as Republicans. Thirty-five percent of Jews called themselves "liberal," compared with only 8 percent who called themselves "conservative." This breakdown has been consistent over the past several decades. When comparing the attitudes of Jews to those of comparable white, college-educated, urban samples, Jews remain an anomaly. The non-Jewish groups are considerably more conservative than comparable groups of Jews. Among the issues that most distinguish Jews from their non-Jewish counterparts are their support for abortion rights, gay rights, and separation of church and state and their sympathy for the economically disadvantaged.[19] Jews also stand apart from their non-Jewish counterparts on issues of foreign affairs. When asked whether the United States should send troops to a foreign country to intervene on behalf of a persecuted minority, Jews were 2–1 in favor of intervention, compared to non-Jewish Americans, who were 2–1 against it.[20]

It is far easier to quantify attitudes than it is to explain them. Neither high income nor advanced education is sufficient to explain Jewish distinctiveness in their political tendencies because Jews at every level stand apart from non-Jewish Americans who mirror their income and educational level. A much more compelling explanation goes back to Sinai and historical consciousness. Even as American Jews become less religiously observant, less knowledgeable about Jewish teachings, and increasingly secular in their outlook, their engagement in American public affairs has been shaped by the Jewish historical experience. It is the Jewish communal ethos, honed as much by historical experience as through knowledge of sacred texts, extended to the realm of public affairs.

Typical of the way that many Jews think about issues of broader societal concern was a speech delivered at the 1989 annual conference of the National Jewish Community Relations Advisory Council (later JCPA) by its chairman, Michael Pelavin. In the address, Pelavin invoked the memory of his parents, who came to America from Europe in the early twentieth century, and of his grandparents, who eked out a living as peddlers. Noting the success that American Jews had come to enjoy in the space of just two generations, he explained why it would be unconscionable for Jews to simply "vote their pocketbook":

> Two thousand years of Jewish experience ... has ingrained in us an understanding that conditions threatening to the fundamental rights of any individual in society jeopardize the rights of all.... We remember that the freedoms embodied in the Bill of Rights—of speech, assembly, press, worship and the right to petition the government—must always be protected, for they are the very bedrock of the society in which we have flourished.[21]

What has characterized Jewish engagement in American political affairs at its best is the ability to balance the Exodus and Sinai impulses of Jewish life. It is not surprising when a community acts in the political arena to protect its group self-interest. The Jewish community has done that, and done it well. What is more remarkable is the fact that the Jewish community has found a way to frame issues of concern to its own constituency in a much more universal way, understanding the broader implications of specific policies that it has advocated. On one level, this can be understood as a wise community-relations strategy. A minority group in America needs to be conscious of advancing an argument on any given issue in the broadest possible terms in order to appeal to a wide cross-section of the electorate and of elected officials. In addition, allying with other groups on issues of concern to them will likely earn that group's loyalty in return.

Perhaps the best example of this on the national level is the Congressional Black Caucus (CBC), which has an extraordinarily solid pro-Israel voting record. Starting in the 1970s, the CBC produced alternatives to the federal budget as a way of highlighting the fact that federal budget priorities continued to ignore the poorest and most vulnerable Americans. The CBC budget was heavily weighted against defense spending and international expenditures, proposing instead massive investments in education, in health care, and in urban America. Yet, year after year, the CBC budget retained the $3 billion of foreign aid earmarked for Israel. This sympathy for a core Jewish concern among leaders of the CBC can be explained, at least in part, by the fact that the Jewish community was a loyal supporter of legislative initiatives of importance to the black community.

One of the American Jewish community's most veteran political activists, Hyman Bookbinder, served as the American Jewish Committee's Washington representative for more than twenty years. He wrote in a 1984 *New York Times* op-ed about the way the Jewish community tries to balance group self-interest with the interests of the general society:

> In carrying out my responsibilities as a representative of an
> American Jewish organization, I never forget this central truth:
> "The Jewish interest cannot be pursued except in the context of
> the general interest." On the domestic front, the fight against

anti-Semitism and for Jewish participation in all aspects of American life is inseparable from the general struggles for civil rights and equal opportunity. The commitment to a secure Israel ... depends upon a strong America, economically and militarily, and on a credible foreign policy that commands the confidence of the free world.[22]

But Jewish political behavior cannot be understood exclusively in these pragmatic terms. The language of Jewish public discourse invokes history and reflects Sinai consciousness again and again, balancing the community's natural Exodus instinct for group survival with an impulse to create a more just and peaceful world for all. Typical of this heritage-laden understanding of the importance of political education for the American Jew was Joseph Lieberman's explanation of the meaning of his vice-presidential candidacy in 2000:

> Today, Jewish Americans are broadly represented in all aspects of American civic life. They have been elected to public office in historic numbers and serve in high appointive office, as members of the president's cabinet, as ambassadors, and as judges at all levels of the federal and state judiciaries. Jews have gained prominence as political journalists, political pundits, political theorists (of the right, the left, and the center), civil servants, community activists, campaign consultants, staff to elected officials, as well as sources of campaign contributions.... We all have a stake in the health of this unique, free, pluralistic country. And America needs the commitment to justice, spirituality, and the communitarian ethic of Jewish tradition.[23]

Lieberman was articulating an article of faith of American Jewry's civic creed that explains a range of Jewish activity in the American public square over the past half-century. The next three chapters will look at three issues in which this creed played itself out.

10

Jews and the Struggle for Civil Rights

There is a certain mythic quality to the story of Jewish involvement in the civil rights movement in America in the middle of the twentieth century. Several generations of Jews were raised being told about how Jews were the primary allies of blacks during the struggle. The photograph of Rabbi Abraham Joshua Heschel walking shoulder to shoulder with Dr. Martin Luther King, Jr., on the march from Selma to Montgomery in 1965 has become iconic and a symbol of the alliance between blacks and Jews. The murder of civil rights workers Andrew Goodman, Michael Schwerner, and James Chaney (two Jews and a black) during Freedom Summer of 1964 enshrined in martyrdom representatives of the two communities who gave their lives for the cause of freedom. In 1994, Hugh Price, the president of the National Urban League, testified to the historic alliance between Jews and blacks when he said in a speech, "Many whites of good will have accompanied us on our long journey for racial, social and economic justice. None has matched the Jewish community as long-distance runners in the civil rights movement."[1]

More recently, though, historians have argued that the black-Jewish alliance was one driven by mutual self-interest and that when the respective interests of each community diverged, the alliance dissolved.[2] There are elements of truth in both of these characterizations. The history of

Jewish involvement in the civil rights movement illustrates many of the themes of Jewish community and Jewish identity that would recur during the second half of the twentieth century.

It is easy to forget that at mid-century, even as America was engaged in a war to defeat Nazism in Europe, Jews experienced significant discrimination at home. A 1942 survey of employment advertisements in the *New York Herald* and *New York Times* revealed that a third of businesses only wanted Christian applicants. The most prestigious law and medical schools had quotas to keep down Jewish admissions. A 1944 public opinion poll indicated that one-third of Americans would either join or be sympathetic to an anti-Semitic political campaign.[3] Thus it was not only out of any sense of noblesse oblige or high-minded moralism that Jews joined with blacks at mid-century to fight prejudice and discrimination in America. Jews and blacks faced similar obstacles in their attempts to realize the American dream of socioeconomic advancement and prosperity.

In 1946, at a plenary session of the National Community Relations Advisory Council (NCRAC), a representative from B'nai Brith argued against an overt partnership with the black community, suggesting that such a relationship would not be in the best interests of Jews. Fearing that Jews and their interests would be lost in a partnership, given that blacks so outnumbered Jews in America, the delegate favored a "go-it-alone approach." It was Rabbi Stephen Wise, then the president of the American Jewish Congress and one of the most respected figures in American Jewry, who carried the day with a counterargument that an alliance of the two ethnic groups would maximize the chances for remedies to existing discrimination and open the door to legislation that would ensure equal opportunity for all Americans.[4]

The Jewish Connection

By 1950 blacks and Jews were already working together in the struggle to create a permanent national commission to safeguard fair employment practices. President Roosevelt set up a Presidential Commission on Fair Employment Practices (FEPC) in 1941 to head off a threatened march being organized by A. Philip Randolph, founder of the Brotherhood of Sleeping Car Porters. Roy Wilkins, who later became the leader of the National Association for the Advancement of Colored

People (NAACP), joined Randolph's effort, as did Arnold Aronson, a Jew who served on the staff of the NCRAC in New York. While the trio did not succeed in their effort to launch a permanent FEPC, what did emerge instead was the Leadership Conference on Civil Rights (LCCR), with this threesome as the cofounders. Over the next three decades, the Washington-based LCCR was the single most effective civil rights organization in the country, spearheading the Civil Rights Acts of 1957, 1960, and 1964, the Voting Rights Act of 1965, and the Fair Housing Act of 1968. Aronson was the critical link between black leaders of the civil rights movement and the organized Jewish community. In fact, though Aronson's NCRAC office was in New York, he regularly spent part of every week in Washington doing the staff work of the LCCR, and he had an instrumental role in the historic 1963 March on Washington.

Aronson was not alone. In fact, it is hard to overstate the Jewish engagement in the civil rights movement. At the LCCR itself, Marvin Caplan was the Washington director, William Taylor headed up its civil rights enforcement division, and nationally prominent attorney Joseph Rauh served as general counsel. All were Jewish. The Religious Action Center of Reform Judaism in Washington provided office space to the LCCR, and it was around their conference table that much of the groundbreaking civil rights legislation of the era was first drafted. But Jewish sympathy and mobilization for American blacks dates back to even before the LCCR. From 1910 to 1940, the Chicago-based president of Sears, Roebuck, Julius Rosenwald, personally underwrote the building and development of more than 2,000 primary and secondary schools serving black children and twenty black colleges in the South. It is estimated that prior to school desegregation, 40 percent of southern blacks were educated at one of these institutions. Joel Spingarn, the New York-born son of Austrian immigrants, left a promising academic career to become one of the founders of the NAACP, serving as its chairman from 1913 to 1919. At the height of the civil rights era, another Jew, Boston businessman Kivie Kaplan, also chaired the NAACP (1966–1975).

Nor was it just individual Jews who were driven by their sympathies and consciences to help blacks. Jewish national defense agencies played critical roles in pushing America in the direction of fulfilling the motto "equal justice for all." In the early 1950s, the American Jewish Committee commissioned black psychologist Kenneth Clark to do a study on the impact of segregation on black children. The findings were later cited in the historic 1954 Supreme Court decision *Brown v. Board of Education,* which led to the desegregation of America's schools. The Anti-Defamation League conducted massive educational programs aimed at racial and religious intolerance using films, display cards, radio, and television. The legal department of the American Jewish Congress led the effort that resulted in legislative remedies for employment discrimination in twenty states, covering some 60 percent of the nation's population.

Jewish involvement in the civil rights struggle also went deep. It is estimated that thousands of Jewish students made their way to the South during the 1960s, joining efforts being coordinated by a variety of organizations to arrange sit-ins and marches to desegregate transportation and schools and to register voters. One-third to one-half of the Freedom Riders in the summer of 1961 were Jewish, and a similar percentage of Jews took part in the Mississippi Freedom Summer in 1964 (during which Goodman, Schwerner, and Chaney were murdered).[5] Harder to measure, but clearly affecting thousands of more Jews growing up in this era, was the widespread sympathy Jews felt for the civil rights struggle. Rabbis preached about civil rights from their pulpits. Jewish periodicals carried articles about the justice of the cause. Many of the activists interviewed for this book trace their earliest feelings for social justice to hearing their parents talk about Martin Luther King, Jr., and the movement for civil rights as a moral calling. In 1963, Rabbi Joachim Prinz, the president of the American Jewish Congress and a refugee from Nazi Germany, was one of the speakers who addressed 250,000 people at the March on Washington. It was the same stage from which, minutes later, Martin Luther King, Jr., would deliver his historic "I Have a Dream" speech. To the extent that one of the great accomplishments of the civil rights movement was making de facto discrimination illegal, the organized Jewish community threw all of its political muscle behind the passage of the era's two most important pieces of civil rights legislation—the Civil Rights Act of 1964 and the Voting Rights Act of 1965.

Jewish Identity

One question that was not discussed much during the 1950s and 1960s was: What was Jewish about what Jews and the Jewish community did within the civil rights movement? According to most of the people who have studied the period and who have spoken to the participants, the answer is: Not very much. The writer and social commentator Charles Silberman argues that those involved in the movement lacked Jewish commitment and those Jews who were most committed to Judaism were rarely personally involved in the struggle. Judith Weinstein Klein, a clinical social worker who counseled numerous civil rights workers, found that Jewish activists seemed far more involved in other people's search for identity than in their own relationship to Judaism. Many Jewish young people who went south to join the struggle were children of affluence who were embarrassed about the gap between their privileged lifestyles and their liberal values, which articulated a concern for the poor and the downtrodden. To the extent that suburban synagogues of this era symbolized the Jewish desire to display their newfound affluence to their gentile neighbors, many Jews who were committed to social equality and aware of "the other America" consciously rejected their Jewish ties. Michael Schwerner identified himself as an atheist who believed in humanity instead of God. He declined to become a bar mitzvah and later declared that he was not a Jew, but a man. His funeral was held at the Community Church in New York. Funeral services for Andrew Goodman were held at the Ethical Culture Hall without any religious ritual at all.[6]

In her book on Jewish women who went south to work in the civil rights movement, Debra Schultz probed the Jewish identity of her subjects. Not surprisingly, she found a good deal of ambivalence. Some of her subjects wondered whether they could consider themselves Jewish if they were not religious. Some were angry at even being identified as Jewish because of their personal disagreements with what they perceived to be the political, cultural, or religious views of mainstream American Jewry. Still others were fiercely proud to link their political activism to their Jewish identity. At the same time, Schultz found that even the most secular of the women activists identified with some form of Jewish cultural identity.[7]

Lest we judge these activists too harshly, it needs to be remembered that two factors militated against such activists identifying with Judaism in a more confident and overt way. First, the tenor of the 1950s, in which these young civil rights activists were raised, was one of conformity. From tract housing in the suburbs to styles of dress and hair, there was a certain image of what good, middle-class Americans were supposed to look like and how they were supposed to act. William Whyte's *The Organization Man*, published in 1956, described the era as populated by people who left their souls at home when they entered the corporations and organizations of America, surrendering their personal identities to some larger social ethic not of their own making. Americans of this era conformed to these expectations because, they believed, it would ensure prosperity, acceptance, and success.

The second factor that contributed to low levels of Jewish identification by activists relates to where the Jewish community was in its process of accommodating to American life. Still somewhat insecure about their status in American society, Jews wanted nothing so much as to be more American. It simply wasn't considered acceptable to make an issue about your ethnicity or faith. The cultural shift toward more assertive ethnic identity was still a few years off.

For many, therefore, engagement in the civil rights movement was a surrogate religion. It stirred passion, it provided a sense of working toward a noble goal, and it offered a feeling of solidarity and community with fellow travelers committed to a common ideal. Few civil rights activists felt themselves spiritually fed in this way by Judaism. For that reason, Abraham Joshua Heschel was an anomaly. He spoke of the struggle in terms of the biblical imagery of the Exodus, not unlike Dr. King, with whom he established a close and abiding friendship. In the manner of the biblical prophets, Heschel often rebuked white Americans, Jews included, for their silence and complicity in the face of America's deep-seated racism. For this reason, he more than once identified American whites (and Jews) with Pharaoh. Many Jews took pride in the fact that in the front of newsworthy marches and demonstrations for civil rights stood a rabbi who looked the part of a biblical prophet and whose stirring language matched his physical appearance. Yet few Jews at that time resonated with the Jewish depth of Heschel's vision.

After his return from the Selma-Montgomery march in 1965, Heschel wrote in his diary about his disappointment with the Jewish community:

> I felt again what I have been thinking about for years—that Jewish religious institutions have again missed a great opportunity, namely, to interpret a civil-rights movement in terms of Judaism. The vast majority of Jews participating actively in it

are totally unaware of what the movement means in terms of the prophetic traditions.[8]

Rabbi Arthur Hertzberg, who had a combined career as a congregational rabbi and an activist and was at one point president of the American Jewish Congress, noted in 1963 that liberal politics took the place of Jewish activity for most Jewish youth.[9] The civil rights movement was a universe of meaning that would not so much reinforce Jewish identity as it would take its place.

Jewish religious institutions were not totally insensitive to the struggle and its religious implications. At the convention of the Conservative movement's Rabbinical Assembly in the spring of 1963—during deliberations over the establishment of an institute to document the heroism of Christians who risked their lives to save Jews during the Holocaust—one rabbi challenged his colleagues. That very morning's newspaper carried pictures of police in the South letting dogs loose on demonstrating blacks. "We too will be condemned for doing nothing," he said, underscoring the irony of talking about the Holocaust while ignoring the moral challenge of the moment. What resulted was the Birmingham Resolution, which asked rabbis to volunteer in Birmingham as representatives of the organization to the civil rights struggle. Nineteen rabbis volunteered.[10]

The Reform movement was even more public in its support for the civil rights movement. Rabbi Maurice Eisendrath assumed the presidency of the Reform umbrella organization, the Union of American Hebrew Congregations (UAHC), in 1943 and by the mid-1950s was already shaping a program that sought to engage Reform Jews in real-world social action consistent with Reform's longstanding ideological alignment with the prophetic teachings of Judaism. When Reform rabbis started traveling south in the 1960s, it was not only in the context of the politics of the situation, but as a matter of religious witness. Sixteen Reform rabbis were arrested for praying in an integrated group in front of a restaurant in St. Augustine, Florida, in June 1964. In a letter written from their cell, the rabbis spoke of the religious motivations for their actions. "We came in the hope that the God of us all would accept our small involvement as partial atonement for the many things we wish we had done before and often." Invoking the memory of humanity's inaction in the face of the Holocaust, the letter closed with a blessing from the traditional Jewish liturgy: "Blessed are Thou, O Lord, who freest the captives."[11]

Al Vorspan, then staffing the Commission on Social Action of the UAHC, was sent to Mississippi during Freedom Summer of 1964 by the Union in an official capacity and was joined by several dozen Reform rabbis. Still, he recalls how lonely it was to be an identified Jew in the environment of the civil rights movement. He confirms that the vast majority of Jewish volunteers in the South during these years were there without Jewish ties or connections. Worried about the risks of being too bold, and fearful of the repercussions that might affect the Jews in the South, no other Jewish organizations mobilized their memberships to travel south.[12] Indeed, Jews in the South were mostly mortified by the high profile of Jews who traveled to their communities to engage in activism during the civil rights struggle. They had worked hard to be good citizens and good neighbors. They were certain that the Jewish presence marching and demonstrating alongside blacks would only result in anti-Semitism. Illustrative of this attitude, the president of the Conservative synagogue in St. Augustine came to the prison where the Reform rabbis were being held and chastised them for acting so irresponsibly. Even the UAHC was pressured by many of its congregations in the South and by some major financial supporters to lower its profile on the issue.

Jewish Self-Interest

By the late 1960s the respective interests of blacks and Jews began to diverge. Jews entered the civil rights movement out of a desire for justice and to rid America of all barriers to economic advancement and social integration. Jews were already making major strides in terms of their socioeconomic success. Not so with American blacks. The evidence that, even with legal barriers falling, blacks were stuck at the bottom of America's socioeconomic ladder led to pressure for remedial measures. These included demands for financial reparations for the consequences of slavery, racial balance in certain fields of employment, and programs to increase the number of blacks in universities and professional schools. One of the more publicized examples of the clashing interests of the respective communities took place during the 1967–1968 school year. An attempt to seize local control of the school board by blacks in the

Ocean Hill-Brownsville section of Brooklyn led to the firing of thirteen Jewish teachers and a headline-grabbing confrontation between blacks in the community and Albert Shanker, the Jewish president of the American Federation of Teachers.

But the cracks in the black-Jewish alliance appeared even earlier. The Student Nonviolent Coordinating Committee (SNCC), which was created in 1960 with the support of Dr. King's Southern Christian Leadership Conference (SCLC), became increasingly radicalized. By 1965 many of SNCC's leaders began to question the effectiveness of King's nonviolent philosophy. In the early 1960s, Malcolm X was coming into greater prominence as a key leader of the Nation of Islam, preaching separation rather than integration for American blacks. In one speech, Malcolm X declared that blacks would be better off facing a white racist sheriff in Selma than continuing to work in alliance with Jewish liberals. The sheriff, he said, was a wolf, but the Jews were like foxes. With a wolf, at least you knew where you stood.[13]

While only a minority of blacks aligned themselves with Malcolm X, alliances with whites, however well-meaning those whites may have been, were falling out of favor in the civil rights movement. In the summer of 1964 looting and burning broke out in Harlem after an incident with police. The violence soon spread nationwide. Between 1964 and 1968 there were 329 race riots in 257 cities across America, the result of the anger and resentment of blacks living in urban slums coming to a head. Small retail stores located close to black neighborhoods were often the targets during the riots. Many of these shops were owned by Jews who had populated these neighborhoods just one generation earlier. James Baldwin's *The Fire Next Time,* published in 1962, both captured the frustration of blacks who had not seen their lives improve from the early efforts of the civil rights movement and shaped black consciousness about the need for blacks to control their own destiny. As early as 1960 the National Jewish Community Relations Advisory Council reported on the troubling rise of anti-white feeling in the black community, including demands being made to institute quotas guaranteeing slots for blacks and vandalism that was affecting Jewish storeowners in black neighborhoods.

Herein lay the great divide between Jewish students, whose idealism and commitment led them to travel south to help blacks achieve equality, and the organized Jewish community, which had a responsibility to protect the growing threat to Jewish interests. A 1962 American Jewish Committee survey found that 80 percent of Jews supported desegregation but 52 percent were opposed to having "Negroes" move into their neighborhoods. In his landmark 1963 essay published in *Commentary*, "My Negro Problem—and Ours," Norman Podhoretz, *Commentary*'s editor, set a tone that neoconservatives would follow for decades to come. Describing himself as someone who went from liberalism to radicalism, Podhoretz became the preeminent spokesman for Jews who "saw the light" and ridiculed Jewish middle-class liberals who did not understand what was in their best self-interest. In his experience growing up in Brooklyn, it was the blacks who were the oppressors, not the oppressed. It became commonplace for people to later describe neoconservatives as "Jewish liberals who had been mugged." It described more than a few American Jews.

In a perspective that would foreshadow future debates about the appropriate scope of Jewish organizations, Eli Ginzburg, a professor at Columbia University and the son of the eminent rabbinics scholar Louis Ginzburg, mocked the invitation that came to him by the American Jewish Congress to address its convention on the state of the American Negro. Though Ginzburg was personally involved in the issue of civil rights, he believed that Jewish organizations should restrict themselves to issues that directly affected Jews.[14]

In the 1960s America still had not remedied its unfortunate legacy of racism. The Jewish community was split between two camps. One camp was passionately concerned about the fate of blacks and other people of color who suffered from ongoing discrimination in America. The other camp was made up of Jews who felt that the interests of the Jewish community needed to be a Jew's first priority. This polarization was paralleled in the black community as well. At the extremes of each community lay the Black Panthers, who rallied under a banner emblazoned with a fist, and the Jewish Defense League of Meir Kahane, which resorted to vigilantism to protect poor Jews victimized by thugs, often black, in the inner city. Between those extremes there continued to be real collaboration between the two communities, but also real differences.

While Jewish community groups supported affirmative action programs as early as 1965, there has been an increasing sense in the Jewish community that special consideration for black candidates, in education and in hiring, will inevitably lead to decreased opportunities for Jews.

Most Jewish groups support the principle of affirmative action, but oppose quotas and set-asides for minority applicants. Many African-Americans do not appreciate these nuances and believe that Jews have been unwilling to risk their privileged status in America to create more opportunities for African-Americans. Jews, who have benefited from an American society that provides greater opportunity based on merit, have not been willing to support a system that provides opportunities based on class or race. Jews have also felt betrayed by the evidence of African-American anti-Semitism and by a tendency among more radical African-American groups to portray Israel as an oppressor of another disadvantaged nation of color, the Palestinians. When anti-Jewish comments were made by Jesse Jackson in the 1980s and by Louis Farrakhan in the 1990s, African-Americans rallied around their leaders. They resented the calls from Jewish organizations for Jackson, and later Farrakhan, to be reprimanded or sanctioned.[15]

On the other side of the ledger, the Jewish community continues to be closely aligned with the African-American community on many issues, including education, health care, affordable housing, and a more equitable tax code. The annual program plan of the Jewish Council for Public Affairs for the past thirty years has endorsed the better part of the domestic agenda of most African-American public interest groups. As a result, African-American members of Congress have been loyal supporters of key issues on the American Jewish agenda, such as aid to Israel.

In several cities around the country programs have been created to bring African-American and Jewish youth together to better understand each other's cultures and histories.[16] Many synagogues still partner with African-American churches to do joint programs on Martin Luther King, Jr.'s birthday and/or for joint Passover seders. The Foundation for Ethnic Understanding, founded in 1989 by Orthodox rabbi Marc Schneier and co-chaired by black hip-hop mogul Russell Simmons, continues to celebrate the common vision of the two communities and promotes programs and activities that celebrate it. There is even an annual event at the Israel Embassy in Washington, held on Martin Luther King, Jr.'s birthday, that gives out an award to a black and a Jew who have made the greatest contribution to civil rights. Remarkably, not only have programs that tie the two communities together survived periods of major intergroup strife and conflict, but new programs continue to be created. It speaks to a bond that reveals much about the identity and communal psychology of both groups.

Sinai Consciousness

Given the great disparity in the socioeconomic levels of the black and Jewish communities, the programs and institutions they share strike some as strange. The phenomenon is even more baffling considering the ongoing disagreement about strategies to bring about greater equality for people of color in American society. While it is true that the Jewish community shares an interest in breaking down legal and social barriers to full social equality in America, that motivation does not explain why thousands of Jews demonstrated, marched, lobbied, and risked their lives to go south during the civil rights movement. That explanation lies much deeper in the psyche of American Jews.

It is undoubtedly true that few of the Jewish civil rights activists, with the exception of a handful of rabbis, were motivated by the religious principles of the Torah. Yet the social justice principles that I have identified with the Sinai impulse are often internalized by Jews, whether or not they ever sat at the feet of a Jewish educator. For Jews, the principle of *din,* justice and fairness, became part of their folk culture, conveyed by parents to their children in the way they saw and experienced the world. Jews who devoted themselves (and in some cases, gave their lives) to the cause of civil rights identified with the outsider status of American blacks because they themselves did not yet fully feel a part of the mainstream of American life. As such, their activism was a manifestation of the Jewish value of *ahavat ger* (loving the stranger). To the extent that most white Americans were not willing to confront the reality of American racism and discrimination against blacks until the civil rights movement put the issue onto the front pages of American newspapers, activist Jews were among a small minority of whites who were committed "not to stand idly by" while their neighbor's blood was being shed, the value of *lo ta'amod al dam re'echa* (*Sanhedrin* 73a).

Few, if any, Jewish activists used this language at the time. Even the rabbis involved in the struggle spoke about their religious witness in the most general of terms. But most American Jews had a personal story in which persecution and oppression were not more than a generation behind them. The appeal to Jews of the struggle for equality on the part of American blacks had little to do with Jewish concerns about discrimination in the workplace. Rather, it had to do with a cultural instinct for acting on a situation that was morally reprehensible and patently unjust. A generation earlier it manifested itself in Jewish involvement in the American labor movement. At the turn of the century in Europe, Jews embraced socialism as a way to effect greater social equality, an ideology later apparent in America as well. Just a few years after the height of the civil rights movement, this passion for justice presented itself in the anti-war movement and the feminist movement. In all of these struggles for social change, Jews played leadership roles far disproportionate to their numbers, a phenomenon best understood as Jews, whether religious or secular, acting on a Sinai consciousness that was passed down through the generations.

The neoconservative reaction against Jewish involvement in the civil rights movement, and concerns about the way that Jewish interests might be at risk, had an intensity that is hard for many Jews to understand with the passage of time. It is worth remembering, however, that Jews in the 1950s and early 1960s still saw themselves as new arrivals in America, with a history of persecution, on probation in a land of great opportunity. It was inevitable that, in response to Jewish activists who were abandoning their Jewish ties to engage fully with a movement for the liberation of American blacks, Jewish voices and the organizations charged with ensuring Jewish group survival would push back. With the emergence of black consciousness, which sometimes included a call for black separatism, concerns about Jewish security and group self-interest spilled beyond the confines of a handful of neoconservative intellectuals. This is a story that will be explored at greater length in Chapter 13.

Jews can take rightful pride in their seminal contributions to one of the great social justice movements in American history. The 1960s was a decade during which many Jews and Jewish organizations allied with another minority group with whose oppression they could empathize. Even as some voices in the Jewish community argued that the interests of Jews and blacks were far less coincident than liberals suggested, this was an era when the messianic Sinai instincts of Jews ran strong. King and Heschel seemed to echo biblical prophetic voices challenging the leaders of society to protect the poor and the vulnerable.

As for those voices that called on Jews to be more mindful of their particular group interests, within a few years they would be challenged when young Jews would begin a campaign for the rights of their own sisters and brothers.

11

Soviet Jewry

A Cause of Our Own

The emergence of Soviet Jewry as a cause for American Jews in the 1960s revealed a significant shift in the mood of a maturing Jewish community. It also represented a new chapter in the way Jews understood what was necessary to pursue justice in the world. From the time Jews entered the mainstream of Western society upon their political emancipation in late eighteenth-century Europe, significant Jewish energy went into social and political movements that benefited the disadvantaged or disenfranchised. While Jews were among those oppressed peoples, the ideologies that Jewish activists embraced were mostly universalist, if not utopian. Not only was this true of Jewish communists and socialists in eastern Europe in the late nineteenth and early twentieth centuries, it was also true of the Jewish leadership of the American labor movement in the early twentieth century. With the exception of the Zionist movement—which represented a revolutionary solution to the problem facing Jews in a world of emerging nationalisms—the goal of most crusades for social justice in which Jews played prominent roles was not to address the problem of Jews as Jews. It was to advance a vision of a new order in which all people would experience equality, freedom, and dignity, Jews among them.

The civil rights movement was a classic example of this kind of Jewish crusade for justice. While Jews would benefit from an America that no longer discriminated against anyone on the basis of race, creed, or ethnic origin, few of the Jews who assumed leadership roles in the civil rights struggle were invested in the way Jews might cultivate their own religious or ethnic identity in America. But just as the black leaders of the civil rights movement became more assertive about their own ethnic uniqueness—a consciousness that made Jews increasingly unwelcome among the movement's leadership (as discussed in the previous chapter)—Jews began to assert themselves and their own identity in a way that surprised even the leadership of the organized Jewish community. The cause of Soviet Jewry was thus both a justice cause around which Jews could rally and, simultaneously, a vehicle for a newfound Jewish ethnic consciousness.

The Crisis of Soviet Jewry

The Soviet Union was a vast empire that, by the mid-twentieth century, included between two and three million Jews, the third largest Jewish community in the world. The power of the Communist Party that dominated the Soviet Union was made possible by its ability to control nearly all aspects of public and private life, including media, education, culture, and religion. An important element of the Soviet government's program was strict limitation on emigration. The myth of the so-called worker's paradise, the perfect republic of economic and social equality, depended on a totalitarian political system and a police state that had little regard for the rights of its citizens. The infamous "iron curtain" separated the Soviet Union from the outside world as the Communist Party did its best to ensure that Soviet citizens could not compare the material prosperity and political freedoms of the democratic West with their own relative poverty and lack of such liberties.

For centuries, Jews lived in areas that would later be ruled by the Soviet Union. In the nineteenth century, the Russian Empire—ancestor of the Soviet Union—was home to the largest Jewish community in the world. Because the ruling czarist regime subjected its Jewish citizens to severe discrimination and deadly violence, hundreds of thousands of Russian Jews immigrated to America from 1880 to 1920. This circumstance also drove a much smaller number of Jews to begin the first of several waves of immigration to Palestine in the nascent Zionist movement. It was thus not surprising that, at the beginning of the twentieth century, many Jews aligned themselves with the revolutionary Communist Party, which succeeded in toppling the czarist government in 1917. Jews were attracted by Communism's promise of equality, freedom, and an end to discrimination. But it was not too long before the hopes of Jewish Communists were dashed. Far from protecting Jewish freedom, the new Soviet government began to repress all religion. Over time, the mix of Communist ideology and historically ingrained Russian anti-Semitism became disastrous for the Jews.

By the 1960s, Soviet Jewry had reached a point of crisis. The brutal reign of Joseph Stalin, in the years after World War II, had seen the summary execution or imprisonment of many of the Soviet Union's most important Jewish cultural figures. Stalin's successor, Nikita Khrushchev, proved a less savage but more systematic anti-Semite. The age-old stereotype of the Jew as a voracious capitalist was revived, and capitalists were portrayed as the worst enemies of the Soviet Union. Jews were then cast as disloyal citizens and enemies of the Soviet people.

While the state-sponsored media shaped public opinion through anti-Semitic rhetoric, the Soviet government launched a coordinated campaign of oppression against its Jewish citizens. Synagogues were closed. It became illegal to train and ordain rabbis. Communications with Jewish communities in the diaspora and in Israel were strictly monitored. Jews were prevented from entering certain schools or professions. Jewish activists and leaders were imprisoned and even executed, charged with vaguely defined offenses like "parasitism," "hooliganism," and "economic crimes." Despite official claims that the Soviet Union allowed freedom of thought and expression, Jews who protested against the repressive and anti-Semitic dictatorship were jailed or exiled to remote parts of the empire. Emigration was forbidden to Jews. Attempts to clandestinely leave the country put Jews at risk of capital prosecution.

After Israel's victory in the 1967 Six-Day War, Soviet Jews experienced an upsurge of Jewish identity and many began to apply for visas to immigrate to Israel. Not only did the Soviet government reject these applications, but it also subjected the applicants to harsh consequences, including expulsion from schools and jobs. These "refuseniks" became ever more committed to their Jewish identity, organizing "underground" groups to study Hebrew, Jewish history, and Jewish literature. They were subjected to constant harassment and occasionally to fabricated legal charges that could lead to arrest and imprisonment. The Soviets also became the primary sponsor and source of anti-Zionist and anti-Semitic propaganda in the world, allying themselves with the Arab states that were sworn to Israel's destruction. It became increasingly difficult for Soviet Jews to survive as Jews. Soviet Jews were cut off from the community of world Jewry and from the state of Israel. Forbidden from engaging in Jewish education, persecuted in their attempts to forge a communal life, and barred from emigrating, Soviet Jews were in danger of disappearing.

The Jewish Response

It is instructive to note that the Israelis were working on behalf of Soviet Jews a full decade before American Jewry rallied to the cause. In 1952 Nehemia Levanon set up the clandestine "office without a name" in Israel to both support the effort of Soviet Jews to retain their Jewish identity and to encourage their immigration to the state of Israel. Later, this office became the obscurely named Liaison Bureau (*Lishkat Hakesher* in Hebrew). To the extent that information about the plight of Soviet Jewry was known, Jewish leaders around the world believed that quiet diplomacy was the best way to bring some relief for Jews living in the most powerful totalitarian regime in the world, fearing that more public protests would put Soviet Jews at risk.

The first crack in the wall of quiet diplomacy came when Abraham Joshua Heschel gave a speech at a 1963 conference held at the Jewish Theological Seminary on the moral implications of the rabbinate. Rabbi Heschel urged his audience to act on behalf of their Soviet coreligionists: "Russian Jewry is the last remnant of a people destroyed in extermination camps, the last remnant of a spiritual glory that is no more."[1] Within a month, leaders of the Presidents Conference, NJCRAC, the Synagogue Council of America, and the American Jewish Committee began discussing how to launch a national campaign to save Soviet Jewry. Around the same time, the two Jewish members of the U.S. Senate, Jacob Javits (R-NY) and Abraham Ribicoff (D-CT), and Supreme Court Justice Arthur Goldberg raised the issue of Soviet Jewry with President John Kennedy.[2] Kennedy agreed to bring up the topic in political and business contacts with the Soviets. By April 1964, the growing sentiment for more activism on the Soviet Jewry issue resulted in twenty-four American Jewish organizations coming together in

Washington to create the American Jewish Conference on Soviet Jewry (later renamed the National Conference on Soviet Jewry [NCSJ]). Looming over the gathering was the shadow of the inability of Western Jews to save European Jewry during the Holocaust. History was providing Western Jewry with a second chance.

But more than anything else, it was the activist consciousness of the Vietnam War and the civil rights movement that changed the strategy of the Soviet Jewry movement from one of quiet diplomacy to one of aggressive struggle. The push came from young people. The catalyst for the creation of what would become the Student Struggle for Soviet Jewry (SSSJ) was Jacob Birnbaum, a German-born British citizen. Birnbaum was the grandson of Nathan Birnbaum, one of the founders of the Zionist movement and the man credited with coining the term "Zionism." Jacob Birnbaum had traveled through Europe, North Africa, and Israel, engaging in and leading a variety of causes to help Jews. When he came to New York in 1963, he displayed a knack for attracting young, committed Jews to mobilize on behalf of Soviet Jews. Among his early recruits were: Rabbi Shlomo Riskin, who would become the first chairman of SSSJ; Malcolm Hoenlein, who was later chosen to lead the Greater New York Conference on Soviet Jewry and eventually became the professional head of the Conference of Presidents of Major American Jewish Organizations; Rabbi Irving Greenberg, who became one of the founders of CLAL, the Center for Jewish Leadership and Learning; and Glenn Richter, who became the national coordinator of SSSJ. Richter had volunteered in the civil rights movement with SNCC, and the entire atmosphere of the time was charged with a spirit of political activism designed to highlight injustice.

It was Birnbaum who began to galvanize legions of students, first heavily concentrated in the yeshiva world of New York but later spreading across the denominational spectrum and the country, to take up the call to march and protest to save Soviet Jews. On May 1, 1964, the Soviet Union's Independence Day, SSSJ mounted the first of hundreds of rallies it would sponsor over the next twenty-five years. The organization succeeded in bringing a thousand young Jewish students to stand in silence in front of the Soviet Mission to the U.N., symbolizing the silence imposed on Jews by Soviet authorities.

The meeting that hatched the plan to call a May Day demonstration for Soviet Jewry took place on the campus of Columbia University, and it was attended by about 200 students. One student led a song that he composed on the spot called "History Shall Not Repeat." Remarkably, the meeting took place only four days before May 1. The desire to attract media coverage for the cause by having the demonstration on a symbolic day drove the decision to act quickly and decisively. Characteristic of the enthusiasm of the students and their sense of urgency, the students' spontaneity stood in stark contrast to the much slower and deliberative approach of the organized Jewish community, which the students found so unacceptable. In the pamphlet distributed throughout New York to announce the demonstration, Birnbaum articulated the twin motivations for the struggle:

> Just as we, as human beings and as Jews, are conscious of the wrongs suffered by the Negro and we fight for his betterment, so must we come to feel in ourselves the silent, strangulated pain of so many of our Russian brethren.... We who condemn silence and inaction during the Nazi Holocaust, dare we keep silent now?[3]

Quiet diplomacy versus activism became a theme for the Soviet Jewry movement, and it was a subtext for some of the tension that existed between the various factions of the campaign. The National Conference for Soviet Jewry (NCSJ) was the vehicle of the organized Jewish community. For seven years, working first under the name of the American Jewish Conference, the NCSJ was not well-funded. It was also somewhat hampered by serving as an umbrella group to constituent Jewish organizations from which the Conference needed to forge a consensus. Furthermore the NCSJ found itself partially constrained by the Liaison Office in Israel, which tended to withhold a lot of information from the Americans and was resistant to the idea of making Soviet Jewry into a very public campaign. Still the NCSJ succeeded in organizing rallies in twenty-five cities in the summer of 1964 and coordinated a rally of 10,000 Jews from more than 100 cities in Lafayette Park, across from the White House, in September 1965. Furthermore, it was the NCSJ that could take most of the credit for getting Soviet Jewry on the agenda of the U.S. State Department in the early 1970s, a breakthrough that eventually led to the full engagement of the U.S. Congress and the White House in the cause over the next twenty years.

On the more activist end of the spectrum was the Union of Councils for Soviet Jewry (UCSJ), a grassroots movement that began in Cleveland and eventually grew to twenty-two affiliated groups across North America. The UCSJ shared with the SSSJ a disdain for the establishment, which they felt was too timid on the issue. Both the SSSJ and the UCSJ tended to be more closely aligned with the refuseniks themselves and their calls to take a hardline posture vis-à-vis the Soviet government. The more established groups, led by the NCSJ, often weighed their strategy based on political considerations emanating from Washington, Moscow, and Jerusalem. The fact that leaders of the Jewish establishment groups succeeded in having high-level dialogues with Soviet officials on the issue of Soviet Jewry incensed the refuseniks, who felt that they needed to be part of such conversations, or at least consulted about them. By 1970, the Jewish Defense League (JDL), led by Orthodox rabbi Meir Kahane, came into the mix and began to push the limits of civil dissent, justifying the group's harassment of Soviet officials, and later its violence, in the name of saving Jewish lives. A JDL ad in the *New York Times* (March 26, 1970), picturing spilled blood, began: "The Shame of American Jewry! Our silence helps to shed this blood!"

A key turning point in the struggle to raise the profile of the Soviet Jewry movement in the Jewish community and in the world was Elie Wiesel's book *The Jews of Silence*. The book challenged American Jewry with Wiesel's assertion that, in the absence of active intervention on behalf of Soviet Jewry, Jews would face an accusatory finger of silent complicity for a second time within the same generation. Wiesel already had an international reputation as an author, having published in 1958 *Night,* a widely hailed memoir of his experiences at the Auschwitz concentration camp. As a personal witness to the Holocaust and someone who emerged as a voice to speak for those who perished, Wiesel had a stature that gave him enormous credibility. As a result, his book recounting his meetings with Soviet Jews during the Jewish High Holy Day season of 1965 received immediate and wide attention when published in the United States a year later. The title of the book made poignant use of the double meaning of "Jews of silence." The Soviet Jews were widely understood to have been silenced by the communist government under which they lived. But it was the silence of world Jewry that Wiesel intended to highlight and shame.

Wiesel recounted two conversations with Soviet Jews:

> In Kiev a Jew said to me, "I hope you will not have cause to
> regret that you have abandoned us." And in Moscow a religious
> Jew said, "The preservation of human life takes precedence over
> all six hundred thirteen commandments. Don't you know that?
> Don't our cries reach you?"

Wiesel ended his book with the following:

> I believe with all my soul that despite the suffering, the hard-
> ship and the fear, the Jews of Russia will withstand the pressure
> and emerge victorious.... I returned from the Soviet Union dis-
> heartened and depressed. But what torments me most is not
> the Jews of silence I met in Russia, but the silence of the Jews I
> live among today.[4]

Wiesel's call to action did not fall on deaf ears.

Jews, Coming of Age

The Holocaust was the single most powerful symbol in the consciousness of American Jewry. Among the lessons learned from the Holocaust
were the price of silence and the unintended complicity of those who
failed to act when they had a chance to stop an injustice. The student
activists of SSSJ demonstrated their understanding of this lesson early
on. Wiesel's book conveyed the lesson to a much broader cross-section
of American Jews. In the twenty-five years that followed the publication
of *The Jews of Silence,* the Soviet Jewry movement galvanized American
Jewry.

Synagogues put signs saying "Free Soviet Jewry" or "Let My People
Go" on their front lawns. Bar and bat mitzvah students were twinned
with young people their age in the Soviet Union who were not able to
have that Jewish rite of passage because the Soviets did not permit Jews
to receive a Jewish education. Many Jews wore bracelets with the names
of "prisoners of conscience," Soviet Jews who were being held in jails
because of their Jewish activities. Names like Vladimir Slepak, Anatoly
Sharansky, Ida Nudel, Yosef Begun, and Yuli Edelstein became contemporary Jewish heroes for the courage they displayed in pursuing their

Jewish activities and pressing their case for emigration in the face of Soviet harassment, intimidation, and the threat of imprisonment. Jewish organizations, especially youth groups, began their meetings by writing letters of support to Soviet Jewish activists and to those who were in prison. Jewish organizations recruited hundreds of Jews to travel to the Soviet Union as "tourists," and the briefings that prepared them were all about how to contact Jewish refuseniks. During these trips, Jews brought materials that were not available inside the country to sustain Soviet Jews. The contraband—which could get the tourists or the recipients arrested—included Bibles, Russian-Hebrew dictionaries, books like Leon Uris's *Exodus,* information about Israel, prayer books, and religious articles. More than anything else, the "tourists" brought the Soviet Jews hope and a promise that they would not be forgotten by their fellow Jews around the world.

While differences in strategy between the various organizations making up the Soviet Jewry movement would sometimes lead to friction and bad blood between the activists, in retrospect, each wing of the movement served a distinct and important role. Groups like the SSSJ and UCSJ helped raise the consciousness of hundreds of thousands of American Jews to the cause of Soviet Jewry through their headline-grabbing demonstrations and public campaigns, while the NCSJ ushered in an era when Jewish organizational representatives were able to engage with the highest levels of Washington officialdom on matters of foreign policy. In 1974 the Jackson-Vanik amendment passed Congress as an amendment to a trade bill. Essentially, the bill made economic trade and the investment and technology that is a byproduct of such trade—something the Soviets desperately needed to shore up their failing economy—contingent on the easing of Soviet emigration restrictions. The Nixon administration, eager to establish closer ties with the Soviet government, opposed the bill, arguing that it would undermine efforts to pursue detente with the Soviets. It was the UCSJ, following the lead of the refuseniks, and somewhat to the chagrin of the less confrontational leadership of the NCSJ, that pushed the amendment.

Never before had the Jewish community gone head to head with a sitting American president, a move made even riskier given the importance of Nixon's support for Israel. Just one year earlier, Nixon intervened on Israel's behalf during the 1973 Yom Kippur War by ordering an emergency airlift of arms when Israel's supplies ran dangerously low after Egypt's surprise attack in the Sinai. Nevertheless, Jewish leadership held firm, the bill passed, and for the next few decades it became a key element of American foreign policy that put extraordinary pressure on the Soviet Union. In the years immediately following the passage of the bill, it resulted in the Soviet Union allowing between 13,000 and 50,000 Jews to emigrate from the Soviet Union per year, most of them going to Israel. Jackson-Vanik was a watershed mark in the political maturation of the Jewish community. It was engineered by congressional staffers who were Jewish, working in close collaboration with Jewish organizational leadership and garnering broad support from the American public and many non-Jewish public officials. It was a formula that would work with increasing effectiveness in the years to come, mostly on Israel-related issues.[5]

The Soviet Jewry movement reached its climax on Sunday, December 6, 1987. What came to be called the Summit Rally for Soviet Jewry was organized to take place the day before Soviet premier Mikhail Gorbachev met with President Ronald Reagan. On that occasion, 250,000 people, mostly Jews but some non-Jews as well, gathered in the shadow of the U.S. Capitol to proclaim their support for the cause of Soviet Jewry. It was by far the largest pro-Jewish demonstration in U.S. history, made all the more remarkable by the fact that it happened outside of New York, where it was always easier to mobilize large numbers because of the heavy concentration of Jews in the metropolitan area. Further electrifying the crowd was the presence of former prisoner of Zion, Anatoly Sharansky—now Natan Sharansky—the single most recognizable Soviet Jew, who became the darling of the Western press for his ability to face down and embarrass the Soviet Union during his years of activism and imprisonment.

The next day, President Reagan showed Gorbachev the headlines to underscore the popular American support for his hardline stance against the Soviets. Soon afterward, as part of his promotion of "glasnost" (openness) in Soviet society, Gorbachev began to relax the restrictions on Jewish emigration. It did not take long for the trickle of immigration to become a torrent, reaching a high of 185,000 Jewish Soviet emigrants in 1990. By 1991, when the Soviet Union dissolved into a number of independent republics, there were no legal barriers left to emigration. In total, about one million Jews left the Soviet Union in the decade after the Summit Rally, many of them choosing to make a new home in Israel.

Jewish Identity

The success of the Soviet Jewry movement has no parallel in Jewish history. It marked a political coming of age for American Jewry in its dealings with the American government. It put a Jewish issue of justice on the world stage and drew the sympathy and support of thousands of non-Jews. It made Jews who stood up against Communist totalitarians into moral heroes. It validated Zionism in the court of world opinion, as it represented the hope and refuge for hundreds of thousands of Jews who wanted nothing more than to "return to their homeland" even though they had never been there before.

More than anything else, the Soviet Jewry movement led Jews to become less apologetic about their Judaism, less concerned about blending into the American social fabric, and proud to publicly proclaim their Jewish identity and Jewish loyalties. A large part of this change can be attributed to Israel's remarkable victory in the 1967 Six-Day War. The combination of concern about Israel's possible annihilation by surrounding Arab armies in the weeks leading up to the war and relief and jubilation at the overwhelming Israeli military victory ended a millennial Jewish complex about the Jew as a weak victim. Coming at a moment when blacks and women were also asserting their group identities, the time was ripe for Jews to find their own ethnic voice and a cause of their own. One study of the leadership of the Soviet Jewry movement showed that 51 percent were also involved in the antiwar movement, 28 percent in the civil rights movement, and 26 percent in campus activism.[6] In an age of intense political activity, Jews were not lacking causes. What they did lack was a language of "liberation" of the sort that inspired and mobilized blacks and feminists during an age of assertive group identity.

Stepping into that void was a handful of young Jews whose voices were somewhat threatening to Jewish establishment figures but who nonetheless played an important role in strengthening Jewish pride and identity. One was Aviva Cantor Zuckoff, the editor of the New York-based *Jewish Liberation Journal.* Zuckoff argued that Jews had been conditioned into a psychologically submissive state, "paralyzed by fear for their own survival and unable to think beyond it." This condition led to an inability on the part of Jews and Jewish groups to stand up for other Jews. She wrote in 1970:

> Try to imagine, if you can, a group of Jews demanding repara-
> tions from the Church or some other oppressive institution for
> 2,000 years of oppression. Of course, it's a complete wild fanta-
> sy. We wouldn't do it. We would tell ourselves we're above all
> that. The truth is, Jews are terrified of asserting their power in
> this manner. One of the main roots of so much antagonism to
> the black power movement is Jews' jealousy of blacks for not
> being afraid to do this.[7]

Today the passage is a tad ironic given the fact that in the last decade, the Jewish community has, in fact, secured tens of millions of dollars in reparations from German, French, and Swiss officials for Jewish proper-ty confiscated during the Holocaust. At the time of Zuckoff's piece, however, such Jewish communal assertiveness was unheard of.

The theme of Jews being jealous of blacks struck an ironic chord given that many American Jews carried an inflated sense that they had "made it" whereas blacks had not. The decade-long alliance between the two groups made analogies between them ever more poignant. Perhaps the classic essay of this genre of assertive Jewish identity came from the pen of M. J. Rosenberg, a college student who later enjoyed a successful career on Capitol Hill with AIPAC and as a commentator on Jewish and Israeli affairs. Published in the *Village Voice* in 1969, the piece was called "To Uncle Tom and Other Such Jews." Rosenberg ridiculed the Jews who joined black nationalist groups, not as Jews, but as whites. The rejection of white leadership in those organizations was to be expected because "why would they want Jewish Toms," "Toms" being a reference to blacks who tried to deny their ethnic origins to gain acceptance in white society. Declaring his own liberation as a proud Jew, Rosenberg declared:

> And thus from this point on, I shall join no movement that
> does not accept and support my people's struggle. If I must
> choose between the Jewish cause and the progressive, anti-Israel
> SDS [Students for a Democratic Society, the most prominent
> leftist student group of the time], I shall choose the Jewish
> cause.

He ended with an accusation aimed at his contemporaries and the lead-ership of the Jewish community: "Thirty years after the Holocaust, you have learned nothing and forgotten everything. Ghetto Jew, you'd better do some fast thinking."[8]

Along the same lines, Yaakov Kirschen, the cartoonist for the *Jewish Liberation Journal,* drew a cartoon in which he portrayed a young black man with an afro saying to a bespectacled Jew with long sideburns desperate to join the struggle, "Your brothers in the Soviet Union are being cruelly oppressed. Have you ever demonstrated in support of them?" To which the Jew replies: "Well … with all my activities on behalf of the Vietnamese, the blacks, the Chicanos, Indians, etc., there isn't much time." The black then calls the Jew "pig," the classic insult of the era to describe hopelessly unliberated people. Unfazed, the Jew asks, "Can I still make a donation to your cause?"[9]

There was a similar dawning of consciousness among many of the Jews in the Soviet Union at almost the exact same time, perhaps explaining the soulful connections felt between Jewish activists in America and the Jews whose names filled their placards and their bracelets. Anatoly Sharansky introduces his autobiography *Fear No Evil*—published upon his release from prison in 1986—by saying:

> For the activist Jews of my generation, our movement represented the exact opposite of what our parents had gone through when they were young. But we saw what happened to their dreams, and we understood that the path to liberation could not be found in denying our own roots while pursuing universal goals. On the contrary; we had to deepen our commitment, because only he who understands his own identity and has already become a free person can work effectively for the human rights of others.[10]

The Soviet Jewry movement was the Jewish community's liberation movement. It enabled Jews to rally around a cause that would support fellow Jews. Significantly, the Soviet Jewry movement also paved the way for Jewish involvement in the emerging human rights movement. It serves as a classic example of how the Jewish community could both champion an issue that was a direct threat to Jewish survival—the Exodus impulse—and also use its hard-won political influence to ally with non-Jewish victims of oppression around the world—a manifestation of Sinai consciousness.

From Soviet Jewry to Human Rights

The Soviet Jewry movement marked the first sustained and successful human rights campaign in history, and it led to campaigns on behalf of oppressed people all around the world by a growing number of human rights organizations. While the Universal Declaration of Human Rights had been passed by the United Nations in 1948, that document, and the additional treaties and conventions that followed in its spirit, rarely affected the actions of nations because the U.N. had no enforcement mechanism. There was no tradition of public campaigns to embarrass and bring pressure to bear on governments that acted in violation of international human rights accords.

But two things changed this reality. The first was the Soviet Jewry movement, which mounted just such a public campaign. Coming on the heels of the creation of Amnesty International in 1961, the Soviet Jewry movement made headlines with its high-profile demonstrations in New York and Washington. The second was Jimmy Carter, elected in 1976, who became the first U.S. president ever to make human rights a key factor in determining U.S. relations with foreign countries. In 1978 there were only three organizations in the world dedicated to human rights. Ten years later there were hundreds, and many took their cues from the strategies and tactics employed by the Soviet Jewry movement.[11]

This credit notwithstanding, the Soviet Jewry movement was not of one mind regarding how broadly it would cast its efforts in the context of human rights. All parties in the movement agreed that the priority was to help secure freedom for Jews to immigrate to Israel. But it was more complicated than that. Should the movement press for greater freedom for Jewish religious and cultural life within the Soviet Union, assuming some number of Jews would never emigrate? Should the movement support Soviet Jews who wanted to move to countries other than Israel? To the extent that the Soviet Jewry movement cast itself as a human rights campaign seeking broad international support for its cause, the answer to both questions needed to be yes. But to the extent that the movement was a Jewish identity effort with a Zionist bias, the answer to both questions from the mainstream Soviet Jewry movement would be no. There was tension between the American Jewish community and the Israelis on the issue of Soviet Jewish émigrés using their visas to Israel to exit the Soviet Union, only later to change their destination to other countries in the West. It would precipitate one of the first major confrontations between American Jewish leadership and the Israelis.[12]

Even more telling was the extent to which the Soviet Jewry movement was going to allow the agenda of Jewish emigration to be tied to the issue of political dissent in the Soviet Union. Anatoly Sharansky precipitated this dilemma when he allied himself, in the early 1970s, with political dissidents Andrei Sakharov and Yuri Orlov, helping these non-Jews in their effort to force the Soviet Union to comply with international standards of human rights. Many believed that Sharansky's arrest in 1977 and harsh thirteen-year sentence was the way the Soviets punished him for his alliance with those who were seen as enemies of the entire Communist system. Because the Israelis saw the Soviet Jewry issue as primarily one to facilitate Jewish immigration to Israel, they were not interested in being drawn into a broader campaign to hold the Soviets accountable for other human rights abuses within the country.

The National Conference for Soviet Jewry, which tended to follow the lead of the Israelis, also shied away from this linkage on strategic grounds. It would be far easier for the Soviets to accede to a program of national repatriation of Jews to Israel—a face-saving euphemism used by the Communist regime to describe Soviet Jewish emigration—than to appear to be caving in to demands from the West to reform their entire political system. According to this view, linking the Soviet Jewry cause with that of political dissidents would only threaten the success of a movement that needed disciplined and focused objectives. Only the Union of Councils for Soviet Jewry held to the position that the Soviet Jewry movement needed to frame its cause in the context of a wider human rights campaign even as its main strategic objective was freedom for Soviet Jews. The UCSJ believed that the cause was far better served in the court of world opinion if the Soviet Jewry movement were seen as one that involved human rights concerns that affected more than just Jews.[13]

Despite the differences in strategy, it seems clear that the movement's success in winning the sympathy of the public and of public officials was due to the fact that a parochial effort was framed as a humanitarian issue with broader implications. This was the essence of the community relations approach of the entire organized Jewish community during the decades following World War II. Interestingly, by the 1970s and 1980s, the Jewish community was using the same tactics that were enjoying success in the Soviet Jewry struggle to advocate on behalf of Jews in Arab countries and in Ethiopia as well. The challenge was to combine the energy of a movement driven by Jews asserting their solidarity with fellow Jews around the world with the more politically sophisticated strategy of linking such efforts to the interest in human rights around the world. Not surprisingly, it was Elie Wiesel who was a critical figure in making this connection.

Wiesel's odyssey took him from Holocaust survivor and witness to spokesperson for Soviet Jewry to world humanitarian. He came to understand that the most important lesson of the Holocaust was acting on the Jewish value "not to stand idly by" (*lo ta'amod al dam re'echa*) when similar persecution was taking place against any group, anywhere in the world. For this he was awarded the Nobel Peace Prize in 1986. In his acceptance speech he said the following:

> Of course, since I am a Jew profoundly rooted in my people's memory and tradition, my first response is to Jewish fears, Jewish needs, Jewish crises. For I belong to a traumatized generation, one that experienced the abandonment and solitude of our people. It would be unnatural for me not to make Jewish priorities my own: Israel, Soviet Jewry, Jews in Arab lands....
> But others are important to me. Apartheid is, in my view, as abhorrent as anti-Semitism. To me, Andrei Sakharov's isolation is as much a disgrace as Joseph Begun's imprisonment and Ida Nudel's exile. As is the denial of Solidarity and its leader Lech Walesa's right to dissent. And Nelson Mandela's interminable imprisonment....
> ... Human rights are being violated on every continent. More people are oppressed than free. How can one not be sensitive to their plight? Human suffering anywhere concerns men and women everywhere.[14]

The last line was a knowing paraphrase of Martin Luther King, Jr.'s famous line, "Injustice anywhere is a threat to justice everywhere." In that same year, 1986, Wiesel penned a call to the Jewish community to mobilize against apartheid. It appeared in the annual joint program plan of the National Jewish Community Relations Advisory Council (NJCRAC) and was called "The Shame of Apartheid." The most renowned voice of

Jewish suffering during the Holocaust was calling on Jews to look past their sense of victimhood to bring their political clout to bear on another humanitarian horror affecting blacks in South Africa. While the NJCRAC had registered its strong denunciation of apartheid as early as 1966, and then again in its 1979 program plan, the Jewish community now seemed to have enough confidence in its own place in American public life to take on an international humanitarian issue on moral grounds. Beginning in the late 1980s one could find Jewish organizations actually mobilizing on the issue of apartheid by their advocacy for trade sanctions against South Africa's government as well as in public demonstrations in front of the South African Embassy in Washington. Advocacy for blacks in South Africa was a natural corollary to the Jewish community's advocacy for Jews in the Soviet Union.

A similar trajectory—from particular to universal concern—characterized the way that the Jewish community approached the issue of Holocaust remembrance and genocide. In the late 1970s, NBC televised a miniseries called *Holocaust*. Though the tragedy of the Holocaust was well documented by historians and writers for at least two decades, the appearance of the docudrama on commercial television heightened interest in the topic. One direct outcome of the media attention was that the domestic affairs advisor to President Jimmy Carter, a committed Jew named Stuart Eizenstat, succeeded in getting Carter to appoint a President's Commission on the Holocaust. Established in 1978, Elie Wiesel was chosen to chair the commission. After many months of deliberating the best way to memorialize the Holocaust, the commission made several recommendations. The primary recommendations were: (1) to create a national museum about the Holocaust in Washington, D.C.; (2) to have a national day of remembrance for the Holocaust; and (3) to create a Committee on Conscience to serve as a first alert against future genocides anywhere in the world.

The commission's final report did note the uniqueness of the Jewish tragedy of the Holocaust: "While not all victims were Jews, all Jews were victims, destined for annihilation solely because they were born Jewish." It therefore found it appropriate for the museum to primarily focus on the story of the Nazi program to exterminate the Jews of Europe. At the same time, the members of the commission felt that among the chief lessons to be learned from the Holocaust was that persecution of any group of people, anywhere in the world, must be protested early and in the most vigorous fashion so as to avoid future holocausts. Thus the Committee on Conscience was designed to "receive reports of genocide (actual or potential) anywhere in the world." Its mandate would then be to access the highest levels of the U.S. government so as to stimulate worldwide action to stop such humanitarian crimes.[15]

This universalizing of the lessons of the Holocaust was underscored twice by Wiesel as he invoked contemporary plights of potential genocide as a spokesman for the Commission on the Holocaust. In September 1979, when Wiesel delivered the report of the President's Commission to Jimmy Carter, he spoke of the plight of the Southeast Asia boat people who were trying to escape Cambodia and he urged American intervention to avert a humanitarian tragedy. A second, more public call to conscience took place in 1993, when the U.S. Holocaust Memorial Museum was dedicated in Washington, D.C. In a speech in front of more than a thousand guests—including several heads of European states sitting on the stage—Wiesel referred to the tragedy unfolding in the Balkans, where Bosnian Muslims were being systematically slaughtered by Serbs. Using the museum as both prop and prod, Wiesel looked directly at President Bill Clinton and urged him to intervene to stop the slaughter.[16] While Wiesel was not an official spokesman for the Jewish community, he embodied the suffering of the Jewish people by virtue of being a Holocaust survivor and chronicler of that tragedy. Now he served as the conscience of the Jewish community, trying to find the right words and symbols to spur those in power into action on behalf of defenseless victims of oppression.

In retrospect, it seems fitting that, between the establishment of the President's Commission on the Holocaust and the opening of the Holocaust Museum, the U.S. Congress finally ratified the Genocide Treaty in 1986. The treaty was passed by the U.N. in 1949, in the wake of the Holocaust, to declare genocide an international crime that the community of nations would act to prevent and/or punish. The idea for the treaty—and the word "genocide" itself—was the brainchild and lifelong crusade of a Polish-Jewish lawyer named Raphael Lemkin, who lost his entire family in the Holocaust. The United States was among the last nations to ratify the treaty even though it was submitted to the Senate for ratification in 1949 by President Harry Truman. Opponents of the treaty worried that it would subject U.S. actions to the politically motivated scrutiny of members of the international community. For more than thirty-five years there existed an ad hoc committee for the ratification of the Genocide Treaty, made up of more than sixty organizations, Jewish organizations prominently among them. The leadership of the coalition at the time of the treaty's adoption included Hyman Bookbinder, who served as the Washington representative for the American Jewish Committee, and Arthur Goldberg, former U.S. Supreme Court justice and U.S. ambassador to the U.N., who served as the coalition's chairman. On February 19, 1986, the day the Senate Foreign Relations Committee finally approved the treaty, setting the stage for eventual passage by Congress and signing by President Ronald Reagan, the sole witness testifying on behalf of the treaty was Elie Wiesel.[17]

The way that Jewish communal advocacy for Soviet Jewry led inexorably to activism on human rights and the way that memorialization of the Holocaust led to a Committee on Conscience and ultimate ratification of the Genocide Treaty exemplify the way that Jews and the Jewish community have approached the public affairs agenda. Elie Wiesel emerged as a symbol of how the Jews acted with appropriate care and concern for their own while also extending their growing communal clout to other groups, both at home and abroad. The expansion of the Jewish communal agenda in the public square also represented something else. It illustrated how the Jewish community balanced its Exodus agenda and its Sinai consciousness.

History taught the Jews the dangers of letting down their guard against those who might do them harm. Indeed, the Jewish community continued to be fully prepared to respond to threats against Jews anywhere in the world and threats to the state of Israel. But the Soviet Jewry movement marked a significant point of maturation for the American Jewish community. Jewish leaders could sit with top government officials in Washington, Helsinki, or Moscow and, without apology, advocate for the rights of Jews. Overt expressions of Jewish identity were met with admiration by an American public that respected both religion and liberty. American Jews could still be motivated by reminders of their failure to intercede effectively on behalf of their coreligionists during the Holocaust. But the community was not so traumatized by that tragedy that it could not see past the protection and defense of its own people around the world to become advocates for other victims of oppression and persecution. Jewish activity on both fronts proved that it was possible to merge Exodus consciousness and Sinai consciousness.

12

Protecting and Defending the State of Israel

If there is one issue that serves as the yardstick of how the American Jewish community has evolved over the last fifty years and of the challenges that arise in trying to balance its Exodus and Sinai tendencies, it is the relationship between American Jewry and the state of Israel. In the early years of the state, Jews had not yet found their political voice, and there was little overt advocacy for the state of Israel. This approach was consistent with the ambivalence of Jews about their Jewish identity in post-war America. Jews were enjoying their newfound affluence and moving into the suburbs mushrooming around the metropolitan areas where Jews resided. Jews were eager to blend into this American milieu and resisted overt displays of their ethnicity. Bold advocacy on behalf of a foreign country was not in the cards. After the Six-Day War in 1967 there was an upsurge of Jewish ethnic pride and Israel took a more prominent place on the agenda of the organized Jewish community. By the mid-1980s, the "Israel lobby," a creation of the Jewish community, was the envy of the political world in terms of its ability to deliver American support for the state of Israel. But the very strength of the Jewish community's advocacy for Israel also created a dilemma for those who dissented from the community's party line, and the divisions that emerged would have long-term implications for the way that Jews identified with Israel and with the Jewish community itself.

Israel and American Jewish Identity

President Harry Truman's decision to recognize Israel after it declared its independence in May 1948 was influenced both by his long-term friendship with a Jewish Zionist, Eddie Jacobson, and by his desire to win Jewish votes in his upcoming election bid. From that moment forward, elected officials paid increasing attention to the growing strength of the Jewish vote, the Jewish purse, and the Jewish voice. Throughout these early years, the Jewish community worked to improve America's relationship with Israel. In 1951, the Zionist activist Si Kenen, who had become Washington's first official lobbyist for American aid to Israel, worked with sympathetic lawmakers to secure $65 million to help Israel resettle its huge influx of immigrants. The following year, this aid package rose to $73 million. In 1959, Kenen's small lobbying outfit took the name AIPAC, the American Israel Public Affairs Committee. Together with the newly created Conference of Presidents of Major American Jewish Organizations, AIPAC formed the base of a Jewish foreign policy establishment that eventually became one of the most powerful lobbies in Washington. But prior to 1967 this effort was hardly a blip on the political radar screen.

A confluence of factors made 1967 the turning point in American Jewry's relationship with Israel. First, activism was in the air. From civil rights to the antiwar movement to women's liberation, American society was filled with the winds of political change. Second, these social change movements gave birth to a surge of ethnic pride that would change the character of America forever. Suddenly it was less American to blend in than it was to declare one's ethnic roots. Third, and perhaps most decisively, there was a belief within world Jewry that Israel was on the brink of destruction.

The weeks leading up to the Six-Day War were an ominous time for Jews all over the world. Egypt was provoking Israel with a blockade of its southern shipping port and hostile Arab armies were amassing at Israel's borders, promising to push Israel into the sea upon the declaration of hostilities. There was no reason to expect that Israel could hold out against armies that had an overwhelming advantage in terms of equipment and troops. Jews suddenly faced the possibility of a second Holocaust in one generation. When Israel scored a decisive victory in just six days, it seemed nothing short of miraculous to world Jewry, and it gave birth to a deep sense of Jewish pride and an emotional connection to Israel on the part of Jews that was unthinkable just months earlier.

One measure of this emerging connection was the financial contributions of American Jewry to Israel through the organized structures of the Jewish community. The United Jewish Appeal (UJA), serving as the primary conduit of contributions to Israel, increased its fundraising from $136 million in 1966 to $317 million in 1967. The purchase of Israel Bonds, which provided a longer-term investment vehicle for diaspora Jews to help the state of Israel develop its infrastructure, increased from $76 million in 1966 to $190 million in 1967. Another indicator of the visceral reaction of American Jews to the threat faced by Israel prior to the Six-Day War was the fact that 7,500 Jews went over to Israel in June 1967 to take over civilian jobs of Israelis who were being called up for military duty.[1] In fact, since 1967, whenever Israel faced a crisis, there was an upsurge of both moral and financial support for Israel on the part of American Jews. This took place in the wake of the Yom Kippur War in 1973, when tens of thousands of Russian Jews began to immigrate to Israel in the early 1990s, and when Israel conducted a dramatic airlift of Ethiopian Jews to Israel in 1991.

The security and survival of the state of Israel became central to the consciousness and culture of the American Jewish community. The entire communal apparatus was engaged to ensure Jewish survival, and it rose to the level of a civil religious ethic that united the American Jewish community.[2] It included federation leadership development programs that imparted the norms of the civil religion, annual events like fundraising dinners, telethons, and national conventions like the General Assembly, sponsored by the Council of Jewish Federations. Many of these gatherings rivaled Jewish holidays as significant times in the yearly calendar. Missions to Israel, sponsored by Jewish federations around the country, gave American Jews both a political education as well as a deeper emotional tie to the Jewish homeland. Many Jews were powerfully affected by such missions, resulting in unprecedented levels of financial generosity and commitment to communal voluntarism. The fact that so many Jews came to feel deep concern over the welfare of the state of Israel made the communal fundraising mechanisms among the most effective of any non-profit enterprise in America. Indeed, though the annual communal fundraising campaigns also raised dollars for a host of local agencies serving the needs of the Jewish community, Israel is what motivated most Jews to be generous in their financial donations. Safeguarding Israel was the engine that drove American Jewish fundraising.

Similarly, American synagogues made support for Israel a centerpiece of their programs. Israel Independence Day took on a ritualized form and was observed in synagogues. Congregations recruited their members for community-sponsored walks, parades, and festivals for Israel. Many synagogues set aside some prime time during the High Holy Day season, when more American Jews were gathered in one place than at any other time of the year, to conduct a fundraising campaign for Israel Bonds. American Jewish identity was shaped by the lessons of history and the heroic profile of Jews in the young state of Israel. In the decades that followed 1967, American Jews were inspired by the narrative of a Jewish state emerging out of the ashes of the Holocaust and persevering, against all odds, to create a democratic society in the Middle East. Jewish communal organizations channeled this shared sense of identity into a sense of civic obligation to the Jewish polity that connected Jews throughout the world. This historical, communal, and political arena became American Jewry's sacred space. One could argue that the UJA slogan "We Are One" was a more fully embraced creed of American Jewry than any particular commandment from the Jewish religious tradition.

Not everyone thought that such a singular focus on Israel in the mind of American Jewry was healthy. Arthur Hertzberg, a rabbi active on a host of public Jewish issues through the American Jewish Congress, observed the irony of Israel becoming the religion of American Jewry when he said, "One can no longer be excommunicated in modern America for not believing in God, for living totally outside of the tradition or even for marrying out. Indeed, none of these formerly excommunicable offenses debar one today from occupying high offices in positions of Jewish leadership." Hertzberg concluded by saying that what would keep a Jew from being accepted in Jewish communal life, certainly in a leadership capacity, would be lack of loyalty to Israel and Zionism.[3] Leonard Fein, a writer and Jewish activist, observed eloquently in his book *Where Are We? The Inner Life of America's Jews* that the state of Israel is all that kept Jews from collapsing in despair after the tragedy of the Holocaust. Yet his entire book, published in 1988, was a plea for Jews to create a Jewish identity that does not exclusively revolve around the Holocaust and the state of Israel.[4]

Still, in the realm of politics, singular focus is a good thing. As Jews became more prominent in American politics and society in the second half of the twentieth century, their opinions grew more influential in the corridors of power. Any public official who wanted to cultivate financial or political support from the Jewish community had to be solidly supportive of Israel. Key to the Jewish community's advocacy for Israel during this period was its ability to make the case that America's national interests and values dictated a strong and enduring partnership with the state of Israel.

The following excerpt from the annual program plan of the National Jewish Community Relations Advisory Council (NJCRAC) in 1981/82 is characteristic of the case made for Israel on both Jewish and American terms:

> For Jews—in America and throughout the world—Israel has special and poignant significance: religious, historical, emotional. It is the biblical homeland of the Jewish people, for which Jews have yearned and prayed over the centuries, now restored to them after so long in exile. It is the place in which Jews fleeing persecution and death have found welcome and refuge. It is a symbol of nationhood to Jews so long and in so many lands denied the status that nationality implies. It is a land peopled by Jews, with whom Jews everywhere share a rich heritage of history, culture and traditions, generating a profound sense of affinity.
>
> For the United States, too, Israel has had a place of special importance, not only as a military ally but, ever since U.S. recognition of the infant State upon its proclamation, as an outpost of democracy, Western in orientation and value system in a politically unstable region of autocratic governments, some still not far from feudalism. In the three decades since Israel's creation, the bonds between her and the U.S. have steadily grown stronger.

It would be these twin sentiments, the former driving Jewish commitment, the latter making the case to American public officials, that would set the stage for an unprecedented display of Jewish political strength in the closing decades of the twentieth century.

The Israel Lobby

Several events combined to strengthen Israel's position in Washington in the second half of the twentieth century. The first happened on the heels of the 1973 Yom Kippur War. Israel found itself perilously at risk after Egypt launched a surprise attack on the holiest day of the Jewish year. Were it not for an emergency airlift of arms ordered by President Richard Nixon, the outcome of that war would have been very much in question. After the Yom Kippur War, Congress approved the largest aid package to Israel in the history of the bilateral relationship—$2.2 billion (which included a significant amount of arms sales). Jews lobbying Congress for aid to Israel stressed the fact that the two countries shared a commitment to democracy and Western values. It was an argument with significant appeal to American Jews because it bolstered pride in their own Jewish identity. Yet the United States' expenditure of such massive levels of foreign aid was not motivated purely by sympathy for shared values. Public officials think in terms of protecting national interests. America was looking for a way to counterbalance the Soviet Union's growing influence in the Middle East. Israel, a Western-style democracy, was the obvious choice to become America's ally in the region.

The second event that strengthened Israel's standing in Washington was the battle over the sale of sophisticated surveillance planes, called AWACS, from the United States to Saudi Arabia in 1981. Even though the United States considered the Saudis to be its allies, Israel considered them to be its sworn enemies. Jews greatly feared that the Saudi government would use the AWACS to spy on Israel and provide Arab states with an advantage in a future military conflict. The entire Jewish community, including AIPAC, the Presidents Conference, and NJCRAC, mobilized against the sale. Arrayed against the Jewish community was newly elected president Ronald Reagan, big business, and the paid lobbyists of Arab states who were promoting the sale. Ironically, though the Jewish community failed to stop the sale, the lobbying effort organized by AIPAC under its new executive director, Tom Dine, revealed an aggressiveness and sophistication that left Washington duly impressed.

Tom Dine was not a product of the Jewish community and its organizational establishment. He was a veteran of Capitol Hill, having worked on the staffs of liberal Democratic senators Ted Kennedy and Frank Church. Convinced that votes were won or lost at the grassroots level, Dine came to AIPAC in 1980 and set out to build a national membership base that could influence local members of Congress. Understanding that elected officials were dependent on those who could help finance expensive campaigns, AIPAC educated its membership about the importance of political fundraising. AIPAC also began to cultivate relationships with highly placed officials in the executive branch of government that could lead to increased bilateral relations with Israel, especially in trade, commerce, and defense. Finally, by expanding AIPAC's executive committee, Dine was able to become increasingly independent of the leadership of the national Jewish community based in New York. Within a decade, AIPAC was *the* Israel lobby. Whereas once AIPAC worked with other national Jewish organizations to coordinate a uniform approach to Israel-related issues, by the mid-1980s AIPAC was going it alone. AIPAC had the support of its membership, a growing following in official Washington, and an enviable reputation of being virtually unstoppable. In the dozen years that Dine presided over AIPAC, its membership grew fivefold and its budget tenfold.[5]

AIPAC's rise was not hurt by the presidency of Ronald Reagan. Even though it was Ronald Reagan who pushed through the AWACS sale in 1981 against the wishes of AIPAC, Reagan outdistanced all of his predecessors in terms of his support of the Jewish state. As with President Nixon, Reagan was driven by his commitment to defeat Soviet Communism in the world. The Middle East was one of the most visible fronts in the cold war, and Israel was America's strongest ally in a region of Soviet client states. The Reagan administration also quickly learned that AIPAC was a great ally to have on Capitol Hill. AIPAC lobbyists helped deliver critical Democratic votes—on Reagan's foreign aid packages, on weapon sales, and on other key congressional votes—because AIPAC successfully made the argument that all of these positions would be beneficial for Israel. In turn, the Reagan administration rewarded Israel. It kept pushing up the level of foreign aid given to Israel until it reached $3 billion a year, by far the largest recipient of U.S. foreign aid of any country in the world. It signed a formal military pact with Israel. There was a sharing of scientific and technological intelligence enjoyed by no other country in the world. Even while much of the Jewish community fought Ronald Reagan on his domestic agenda—American Jews actually gave him less support in his reelection bid in 1984 (33 percent) than they had in the 1980 election (40 percent)—U.S. support for Israel rose to an all-time high.

As a single-issue organization, AIPAC bore no responsibility for the broader agenda of the organized Jewish community. In cultivating its relationship with public officials in the administration and in Congress, AIPAC helped to secure Israel's "special relationship" with the United States. Nowhere is this phenomenon more evident than at the annual AIPAC Policy Conference. Monday night of the conference is designated as the Congressional Dinner. Somewhere between one- to two-thirds of both the House and the Senate show up in person, a turnout that no other lobby group even comes close to matching. After the formal program, many members of Congress attend private receptions, eager to spend face time with the people who helped to get them elected and whose support they will need if they choose to run for reelection. Indicative of how closely the U.S. government followed the lead of AIPAC in crafting its policy in the Middle East was the appointment of Martin Indyk as U.S. ambassador to Israel in 1995. Indyk previously served for eight years as the founding director of the Washington Institute for Near East Policy, a think tank set up and funded by AIPAC supporters. Nor did it escape the notice of insiders that by the 1990s, a large percentage of the U.S. administration's Middle East policy planning team was Jewish: Dennis Ross, Dan Kurtzer, Aaron Miller, and Richard Haass.

AIPAC's activity did not only take place in high-profile Washington settings. Beginning in the 1980s, AIPAC developed an extensive network of college students who were trained in Israel advocacy. Every year hundreds of these students would join with the adult leadership of AIPAC at its annual Policy Conference. By the early 2000s, when Israel was again in crisis due to the second intifada, AIPAC had identified sixty campuses where it did its most intensive work. These campuses were either hotbeds of anti-Israel propaganda or campuses with strategic importance in terms of future Jewish and political leadership. AIPAC partnered with Hillel and other organizations on another 240 campuses. AIPAC estimates that it reaches about 5,000 students a year through its advocacy trainings. One sign of the intense interest in AIPAC on campus is that 1,800 students applied to attend the 2003 Policy

Conference. In the end AIPAC selected 850 to come, with at least one student from every one of the fifty states in the country. Not only has AIPAC's attention to young people paid off in terms of cultivating future Israel activists, it has also had considerable impact on the Jewish identity of tens of thousands of Jewish college students.

So effectively did AIPAC and the rest of the Jewish community make its case for Israel that U.S. support for the Jewish state seemed immune, even from an increasingly partisan Washington. The staunch support of Ronald Reagan continued in the administration of his successor, George H. W. Bush, despite the well-publicized flap in 1991 when Bush tried to pressure Israel to stop using U.S. loan guarantees to expand its settlements in the West Bank. Democrat Bill Clinton was deeply committed to promoting the peace process that began in Oslo and took on that name. He successfully got Israeli premier Yitzhak Rabin and Palestine Liberation Organization (PLO) Chairman Yasser Arafat to sign an accord on the White House lawn in September 1993 that led to the creation of the Palestinian Authority. During Clinton's two terms, even though the United States was publicly committed to taking an "even-handed approach" to the Middle East conflict, leaving it up to the parties to negotiate their own final treaty, the United States never lessened its level of economic, military, and political support for Israel. By the summer of 2000, when Yasser Arafat refused to sign an agreement brokered at Camp David by Bill Clinton—an agreement that would have given the Palestinian Authority an independent state in more than 90 percent of the territories controlled by Israel since the Six-Day War in return for a final peace agreement—all U.S. attempts at even-handedness ended. In early 2001 the new Republican administration of George W. Bush took office and totally isolated Arafat, identifying him as an obstacle to peace. Meanwhile, the United States came to feel even closer to the Jewish state as both countries became the target of Islamic fundamentalism. Israel suffered several years of suicide bombings from Palestinian extremist groups and the United States was shocked as Middle East terrorism came to its shores in the attacks of September 11, 2001.

Not surprisingly, American Jewish grassroots support for Israel was affected by political events. In general, during the 1990s, most national Jewish defense agencies headquartered in New York reduced their number of staff devoted to Israel concerns because the action was increasingly taking place in Washington. Local community relations councils also became less engaged in Israel issues as hawks and doves debated the advisability of Israel trading land for peace and how it might do so. It was far easier to mobilize the community when Israel was facing international condemnation or was fighting for survival than it was to build consensus around an elusive peace process. In fact, it was the issue of how to bring peace to the Middle East that revealed growing rifts between the Jews whom we might identify as "Exodus Jews" and those who might be termed "Sinai Jews."

Israel: From Darling to Dilemma

In the decades that followed the Six-Day War some American Jews grew increasingly uncomfortable with the way Israel handled the territories it captured in 1967. The symbol of Israel being in control of more than a million Arabs in these territories created a public relations nightmare for Israel and, by extension, for world Jewry, whose self-image was now quite tied up with Israel's fate. The election of Menachem Begin in 1977, the first member of the rightist Likud party to win the premiership of Israel, made matters worse. Begin opened the door for massive Jewish settlement of the West Bank, territory he insisted on calling by its biblical name of Judea and Samaria, signaling Israel's intention to retain this biblically promised inheritance forever. Liberal voices in the American Jewish community were torn between their desire to be supportive of Israel at a time when the press and parts of the public and political establishments were critical of Israeli policy and their impulse to speak their conscience.

What started as occasional critiques of Israeli policies in Jewish periodicals and in conversations at formal and informal Jewish gatherings took organizational form just after the conclusion of the Yom Kippur War (in December 1973) with the launch of Breira, the Hebrew word for "alternative." In its first public statement, Breira called for Israel to make "territorial concessions," and to "recognize the legitimacy of the national aspirations of the Palestinians" so as to pave the way to a lasting peace in the region. More telling than these positions, which were by no means new ideas in Jewish circles, was the motivation for creating the organization. In the founding statement the organizers said, "We deplore those pressures in American Jewish life which make open discussion of these and other vital issues virtually synonymous with heresy." Breira hoped that having a critical mass of voices under one organizational umbrella might buffer some of the criticism that was inevitable, given the challenge such critiques posed to the Jewish establishment. By 1974 Breira had organized an Advisory Council of 250 people that was chaired by Rabbi Arnold Jacob Wolf, the director of Yale University Hillel, and included about 100 Conservative and Reform rabbis. The founding group included some high-profile names in the Jewish community like: Rabbi David Wolf Silverman, a professor at the Jewish Theological Seminary in New York; Rabbi Balfour Brickner, who was working for the Reform movement but would soon become the senior rabbi of the Stephen Wise Free Synagogue in New York; and John Ruskay, who was then a Jewish educator and later would become executive director of the New York Jewish Federation. Other prominent Jewish liberals refused to join because of their ties to the Israeli Labor Party, which was in power in Israel at the time and which was clearly implicated in Breira's critiques.

By 1976 Breira's activities were getting noticed. The *Washington Post* ran a story under the headline "U.S. Jews Beginning to Go Public in Criticism of Israel." In June of that year, the Presidents Conference had a debate on the limits of permissible dissent in the American Jewish community. In November, several Jews active with Breira participated in a meeting in Washington, D.C., with two Arabs who had ties to the PLO. Within days of the story hitting the *Jerusalem Post* (authored by Wolf Blitzer, later of CNN fame), virtually every mainstream Jewish organization and leader was condemning Breira. The president of the Reform rabbinate, Rabbi Arthur Lelyveld, who had marched with Martin Luther King, Jr., proclaimed that groups like Breira "give aid and comfort ... to those who would cut aid to Israel and leave it defenseless before murderers and terrorists." The public censure drove many in Breira to resign, and in 1977 the organization disbanded.[6]

But criticism of Israel was also coming from more mainstream groups, and some of those voices were not so easy to dismiss and discredit. Typical of this trend of thought was a statement from the Social Action Commission of Reform Judaism, which criticized Israel's settlement policy as "irresponsible" and "provocative." Rabbi Henry Siegman, then executive director of the Synagogue Council of America and soon to assume the professional leadership of the American Jewish Congress, published an article in *Moment* magazine in 1976, even before Begin's election, in which he criticized Israel for its failure to deal appropriately with the administered territories captured during the Six-Day War and with the Palestinians living in those territories. The organized Jewish community, recognizing the breakdown of consensus on this issue, neither endorsed nor condemned the settlements, saying instead that they could be dealt with if and when an Arab peace partner came forward.[7]

In the early 1980s tension increased between Jewish communal organizations that were working to increase support for Israel in the United States and Jewish individuals and groups that felt an obligation to hold Israel to a high moral standard. In response to attacks on northern villages in Israel from the PLO in southern Lebanon, the Israeli army launched a military operation into Lebanon to drive the PLO out. Unlike Israeli's usual surgical strikes into areas harboring terrorists, Israeli troops and their surrogates, Christian Phalangists, who also wanted to oust the PLO from southern Lebanon, became caught up in a prolonged campaign. When the Phalangists entered the Palestinian refugee camps of Sabra and Shatila and massacred hundreds of Muslim civilians, Israel was assigned a large part of the blame in the international community. Even though the Israeli government convened a commission (the Kahan Commission) that later assigned indirect responsibility to the Israelis and recommended the dismissal of two top Israeli commanders serving in the area at the time, it was not enough to quell the concern by Jews that Israel was no longer following the moral high road.[8] Many American Jews, who once celebrated Israel as the sole democracy in the Middle East that persevered against tremendous odds, now grew increasingly disenchanted with the policies its government was pursuing. While only a small minority sought organizational channels to express their concern and critique of Israel publicly, these events marked the beginning of a trend that caused large portions of the American Jewish community to distance themselves from Israel.

Characterizing the disquiet in the American Jewish community over Israeli actions, Bennett Yanowitz, the national chairman of the National Jewish Community Relations Advisory Council, said the following at the group's 1983 convention:

> Our responsibility to preserve the Jewish state encompasses responsibility to preserve those values that we believe have enriched Jewish life and permitted us to view ourselves as a

light unto the nations. This vision of Israel as a light unto the nations, our deep affection for the country, our historic ties to the land of Zion, all of these, as well as other considerations may give rise to feelings of uncertainty or unhappiness with specific Israeli actions from time to time.

But Yanowitz went on to say, "Dissent, broadcast nationally through the media, contributes to undermining ... the national climate of support for Israel." Given that there did exist discreet channels to communicate American Jewish concerns to Israeli officials, Yanowitz concluded that Jews should desist from taking their criticism into the public square, as it would undermine the unity of the Jewish community and jeopardize U.S. support of the Jewish state.[9]

Yanowitz was articulating a nuanced position. While Jews could raise concerns about Israeli policy and even express such concerns to Israeli officials, community discipline was critical so as not to undermine American support of Israel. The argument made perfect sense—to an insider. It was next to impossible to impose such discipline on American Jews who answered to no hierarchy and at a time when any person could hang up a shingle and start a new organization. Notwithstanding the singular influence of AIPAC in Washington, in the final two decades of the twentieth century, Jewish organizations with a specific perspective on the Middle East conflict were a cottage industry. On the left were organizations like Americans for Peace Now, the Israel Policy Forum, and the New Jewish Agenda, the last of which included some of the same activists who had launched Breira in 1973. *Tikkun* magazine became an intellectual forum for much of the discussion on how to preserve a secure Israel and, simultaneously, recognize the legitimate national aspirations of the Palestinian people. *Tikkun* even organized several Washington conferences designed to lobby public officials with its proposed solutions to the conflict.

On the right was a coalition that included the vast majority of the Orthodox community, the Jewish War Veterans, and a newly invigorated Zionist Organization of America led by activist Morton Klein. Most Orthodox Jews were sympathetic to Israeli government efforts to settle territories captured in the Six-Day War, largely because these areas were part of the biblical land of Israel promised by God to the Jewish people. American Orthodox Jews also made up a significant percentage of those

Jews who moved to these controversial new settlements. Many of these settlers were Orthodox Jews who had made *aliyah* from the United States. Thus, even in the face of growing criticism of Israeli policies from some quarters of American Jewry, Israel was being staunchly defended from the pulpits of Orthodox and not a few Conservative synagogues, while the ZOA and others were making the case on Capitol Hill to support Israeli policies on the basis of geopolitical realities.

In such an environment, it was virtually impossible to enforce the communal discipline that had long provided a strategic advantage to American Jewish lobby efforts on behalf of Israel. While AIPAC still set the tone, there were now Jewish voices on both the right and the left that challenged AIPAC's claim to be the sole American Jewish voice on Israel. Then, in 1992, the entire controversy got turned on its head when the Labor Party recaptured the premiership of Israel. Newly elected premier Yitzhak Rabin came to the United States and criticized the leadership of AIPAC and the Presidents Conference for suppressing dissent for so long. Rabin interpreted their position as an attempt to silence a view that was in accord with Labor Party policy and to favor the policies of Israel's Likud Party.

After Yitzhak Rabin and Yasser Arafat signed the Oslo Accords in Washington in 1993, the American Jewish community was challenged to adjust its longstanding opposition to the Palestinian leader. Suddenly, Israel and the Palestinian Authority (PA)—the new quasi-state led by Yasser Arafat—were peace partners. At one point, Jewish organizations even put together a day when Jews lobbied Congress to pass a bill that would extend a financial aid package to the fledgling PA, a most bizarre experience for many who had spent their whole career making the case that Arafat was a terrorist who could not be trusted. To the distress and dismay of public officials supportive of Israel, suddenly there was a cacophony of competing voices coming from the Jewish community, all weighing in on the right course of action. Right-wing Jews lobbied Congress to prevent the aid package to the new PA. Some even advocated cutting off aid to Egypt, Israel's first peace partner. Left-wing Jews wanted full American engagement to support the painful concessions that Israel would likely have to make in any final agreement with the PA. J. J. Goldberg, in his book *Jewish Power*, argues that centrist Jewish organizations were hesitant to offer Rabin the full support they once offered to Likud prime ministers Menachem Begin and Yitzhak Shamir because they were concerned about the recriminations that might occur when a Likud government came back into power. The support for the more conciliatory, liberal position seemed to carry a price, even during the administration of an Israeli Labor government. When Likud returned to power with the election of Benjamin Netanyahu in 1996, the lobbying work of the Jewish communal establishment was more straightforward. It was easier to make a public case for an embattled Israel holding out against antidemocratic and terrorist Arab forces than it was to negotiate the nuances of a peace agreement around which there seemed to be little clear consensus, either in Israel or in the American Jewish community.[10]

The sociologist Steven M. Cohen outlined the parameters of American Jewry's disunity over Israel when he labeled the three camps amoral Zionists, moralizing universalists, and conditional doves.[11] The descriptions and motivations of these competing camps have not changed much, even to the present day. The amoral Zionists, represented by the neoconservatives who published their opinions in the pages of major daily newspapers and periodicals like *Commentary* magazine, argued that Jews have superior historical claims to the land of Israel, that Jews have too long been the victims of persecution (with the Holocaust being the most recent painful example), and that the Arabs are bent on a campaign to delegitimize any claim of Jews for a Jewish homeland in the Middle East. This line of argument is the one most easily embraced by the organized Jewish community as it seeks to raise money from Jews for Israel and to cultivate U.S. political support for the Jewish state. According to this position, any liberal weakness shown by Jews could easily be seized upon by Israel's enemies and lead to Israel's demise.

The moralizing universalists are best represented by *Tikkun* magazine and the prominent Jews who every so often take out full-page ads in the *New York Times* that challenge Israeli policies or advocate a more conciliatory policy toward the Palestinians. Often invoking teachings about peace and justice in the Jewish tradition, this camp believes that it represents the prophetic voice of our time, rebuking Israel for its moral callousness and recoiling at harsh Israeli military actions that it considers "so unJewish." It would have Israel take more risks for peace, arguing that, given Israel's military dominance in the region, it should remove itself from a circumstance in which it is seen as an unwelcome occupier ruling over Arab lands and people.

Between these two extremes, Cohen found that most American Jews were conditional doves. What he meant by that is that they share some of the concerns of the universalists about Israeli actions but they also suspect the integrity and true intentions of the Palestinians. Recognizing the danger posed by Israeli concessions in exchange for peace that is not later honored by Palestinian leadership, most American Jews are willing to defer to the policy judgments made by Israel and by the American Jewish organizations that work in close collaboration with the Israelis. That is what explains polls conducted by Cohen before the start of the Oslo peace process in which 69 percent of American Jews felt that Israel should talk with the PLO, a position that the Israeli government was not willing to follow at the time of the survey. At the same time, even larger percentages of Jews responded affirmatively to statements about the lack of trustworthiness of the PLO and a belief that that organization would destroy Israel if given the chance.

This profile of American Jews who find themselves caught between the stridency of both right and left helps explain why most Jews simply defer to the experts. Even as the American Jewish community continues to effectively cultivate U.S. political support for Israel, Jews themselves have become far more ambivalent about the Jewish state. In surveys conducted in the 1980s, about 75 percent of Jews considered Israel to be an important part of their Jewish identity. Almost two-thirds of American Jews said that the destruction of Israel would represent one of the great personal tragedies of their lives.[12] But in a 2003 survey by the American Jewish Committee, only 6 percent of respondents said that Israel was the most important part of their Jewish identity. Being part of the Jewish people scored highest with 41 percent, and a commitment to social justice ranked second at 19 percent.[13] This finding was consistent with the study conducted for the book *The Jew Within*, published in 2000. That survey found that American Jews rated Israel much lower as a component of their Jewish identity than Torah, the High Holy Days, the Jewish people, the Jewish family, and the Holocaust.[14] Raising even greater concern among the leadership of the organized Jewish community is the disparity of attachment to Israel when compared to other generations. The 2000 National Jewish Population Survey found that 68 percent of Jews ages 55–64 felt "very" or "somewhat" emotionally attached to Israel. By contrast, Jews ages 35–44 scored 56 percent on that question and college students were at 36 percent.[15]

The reasons for this decline are open to speculation. Israel's invasion of Lebanon coupled with the expansion of its settlement activity in the West Bank during the 1980s resulted in widespread criticism of Israel in the Western media. Israel was as likely to be a cause for discomfort to Jews as it once was a source of pride. In the face of these criticisms being leveled at Israel, it was hard to teach about Israel in Jewish schools, camps, and youth groups the way it was done ten years earlier—the heroic, small Israeli David overcoming the evil, Arab Goliath. Israel was now a regional superpower, and there were serious questions being raised about how Israel was using its newfound military and political might. Many institutions simply stopped addressing the topic of Israel at all, seeing that the issues were too tied up in geopolitics that were well beyond the expertise of the typical Jewish educator.

Adding to the ambivalence about Israel was the controversy over the "Who is a Jew?" issue. Non-Orthodox Jewish denominations in America became extremely critical of Israel when, as a result of the political influence exerted by Orthodox parties in the Israeli government, the status of non-Orthodox weddings, divorces, and conversions came to be challenged. The decision of Israel's Ministry of the Interior effectively discounted the legitimacy of the vast majority of diaspora Jews. These factors combined to erode American Jewry's love affair with Israel. Over time, Israel became less central to the identity of American Jews, a trend that was even more pronounced among younger Jews.[16]

During the 1990s this trend continued, as Israel seemed to be on the road to peace and American Jewish support no longer seemed to be as essential to Israel's survival. When Prime Minister Yitzhak Rabin and his foreign minister, Yossi Beilin, began giving interviews saying that Israel no longer needed the money of American Jews and that the funds would be better spent on enhancing the Jewish identity of American Jewish youth, leaders of the organized Jewish community reacted with shock and horror. The Israelis were undermining the most compelling appeal of American Jewish fundraising. Now the Israelis were saying that they were no longer the poor cousin. With a thriving economy and peace at hand, the relationship between diaspora Jewry and Israel had to change.

Israel returned to crisis mode in 2000. The Oslo peace process was in shambles and the country was under assault from an epidemic of suicide bombings. With America clearly in Israel's corner and with Islamic fundamentalism identified as the common enemy, American Jews once again were quick to come to the barricades to help Israel. The United

Jewish Communities—the umbrella agency for the Jewish community resulting from the merger of the United Jewish Appeal with the Council of Jewish Federations—launched another one of their special fundraising drives, this time called the Israel Emergency Campaign. The campaign raised tens of millions of dollars to fund after-school and summer programs for Israeli children, armored buses, medical and trauma centers, bullet-proof vests, security personnel, and medical and financial aid for victims of terror. Communities sponsored solidarity missions to Israel, bringing over Jewish tourists to fill empty hotels and help an ailing Israeli economy. Finally, AIPAC could barely accommodate the increased number of Jews who wanted to come to its annual Policy Conference, and the organization enjoyed a swelling of its membership and of its financial contributions. National Hillel worked closely with AIPAC to mobilize college students, forming the Israel on Campus Coalition, made up of a wide array of Jewish organizations from the left to the right. This was particularly important, since the campus became a focal point for anti-Israel propaganda and mobilization.

Still, for every Jewish college student now energized to work on Israel's behalf, there were at least as many who felt themselves disconnected from the Jewish state. Some felt that Israel was overly aggressive in its retaliations against terrorist incidents. Some faulted Israel for decades of occupation of the West Bank. While terrorist behavior was not excused, there was overwhelming evidence that the occupation was at least partially responsible for the deep-seated hatred of Israel by Palestinians. A broad cross-section of American Jews found the whole Middle East situation hopelessly complex and, perhaps, insoluble. They resisted the oversimplified attempts of Jewish organizations to portray the situation as Israel being the good guys and the Palestinians, the bad guys. While some number of these Jews joined peace-oriented organizations, both Jewish and interfaith, most simply pulled back from deep emotional connections with Israel, hopelessly ambivalent about what was the right and just course of action.[17]

Leonard Fein has described this ambivalence in the following way:

> There are two kinds of Jews in the world. There is the kind of Jew who detests war and violence, who believes that fighting is not "the Jewish way," who willingly accepts that Jews have their own and higher standards of behavior. And not just that we

have them, but that those standards are our lifeblood, are what we are about. And there is the kind of Jew who is convinced that it is time to strike back at our enemies, to reject once and for all the role of victim, who willingly accepts that Jews cannot depend on favors, that we must be tough and strong. And the trouble is, most of us are both kinds of Jew.[18]

Between Conscience and Solidarity

The fact that the place of Israel in the mind of American Jews transitioned from a source of great pride to one of excruciating moral dilemma in the space of just twenty years relates directly to our understanding of Jewish historical consciousness. Jews are driven by their twin impulses to survive as a people (Exodus) and to help the world be ordered in accordance with a higher moral standard (Sinai). When confronted by the difficult reality that these twin objectives might be in conflict, as was the case in the decades following the Six-Day War, Jews went in two different directions. Some Jews rallied to Israel's support and redoubled their efforts to protect and defend Israel. Other Jews, no less concerned about Israel's survival, nevertheless attempted to hold successive Israeli governments accountable for any actions that might be interpreted as an abuse of power or an obstacle to eventual peaceful coexistence in the region. The gap in the perceptions of the respective camps, Exodus and Sinai, was enormous.

The Exodus perception of the Middle East conflict by American Jews was that Israel was subjected to an unfair double standard in the court of world opinion. Motivated by a sense of historical justice, Exodus Jews would claim that the Jews had but one state in the Middle East where Arabs claimed more than twenty. The Jewish state was a haven for Jews surviving the Holocaust and fleeing persecution in the years since the end of World War II. Israel fought its wars to defend itself against Arab aggression, not to capture more territory. There were numerous examples of Arab rejectionism, such as the PLO's Cairo resolution of 1974, which advanced the idea that Palestinians should accept any offer of territory from Israel with the intention of using it as a forward base to destroy the state of Israel. However much Israelis and Jews the world over took hope in the Oslo peace process that promised some normalization of relations between Israel and the Palestinians, that effort unraveled when Yasser Arafat refused to accept the deal offered to him at Camp David in the summer of 2000 by Israeli Prime Minister Ehud Barak. Subsequently, the areas controlled by the Palestinian Authority again became a source of terrorist activity that targeted Israeli men, women, and children.

So voluminous is the support for this Exodus interpretation of the history of the Middle East that the famed American Jewish attorney Alan Dershowitz wrote an entire book, *The Case for Israel*, that cites one incident after another of Arab duplicity and Israel's noble intentions to live in peaceful coexistence with its Arab neighbors that date back to the British mandate over Palestine in the early twentieth century. The book was widely circulated throughout the Jewish community, and particularly on college campuses to help Jewish students defend Israel in the face of other student groups—some including substantial numbers of Jews—that were much more sympathetic to the cause of the Palestinians.

One example of how Israel is often unjustly accused of wrongdoing in the court of world opinion is the Israeli invasion of Jenin in April 2002. Located in territories captured by Israel in 1967, Jenin was an Arab town that had come to be known in Palestinian circles during the second intifada as "the martyr's capital." More than twenty suicide bombers who successfully infiltrated Israel between September 2000 and April 2002 were traced to Jenin. After the Israel Defense Forces took action against Jenin, Palestinian leaders accused the Israelis of massacring hundreds of Palestinian civilians and burying them in mass graves. Every major media outlet in the world prominently featured stories of this alleged Israeli atrocity. After the U.N. and other human rights organizations had a chance to investigate, it turned out that, in fact, fifty-four Palestinian bodies were found. No mass graves were discovered. Further investigation revealed that Israel lost twenty-three soldiers in the action, mostly because the Israelis chose not to strafe bomb the town, but rather to go from house to house to find the terrorists and bombmaking facilities. The Israeli command specifically made a decision to put their soldiers at greater risk so as to limit Palestinian civilian injury and death.[19] Israelis point out, with bitterness and not a little irony, how many massacres have been perpetuated by Arab regimes against their own citizens that the U.N. has never even bothered to investigate. Nonetheless, this pattern of Israel being judged by a double standard has become a constant in its history. In response, the more Israel was criticized in the media and in the world, the stronger the organizations that defended Israel in the American Jewish community (such as AIPAC, the Presidents Conference, and the national Jewish defense agencies) grew.

There is, of course, another perception of the Middle East conflict. Quite apart from those critics of Israel who are from outside the Jewish community (and there are many), there are numerous Jewish organizations that have criticized selected actions of the Israeli government or trends in Israeli society. They are based in Israel, the United States, and throughout the rest of the world. Some are human rights groups like B'tzelem, an Israeli group that reports on allegations of Israeli human rights violations. Some are groups working to advance dialogue and understanding between Israeli Jews and Arabs, such as the U.S.-based Seeds of Peace and the Israeli-based Givat Haviva, which won the UNESCO prize for peace education in 2003. Still others operate in the U.S. political arena, attempting to offer an alternative Jewish voice on Middle East peace, such as Americans for Peace Now and Brit Tzedek v'Shalom. These groups are not unconcerned about threats to Israel's survival, but they are primarily motivated by the Sinai impulse of Jewish identity. They expect the Jewish state to be guided by the values of righteousness and justice that have guided Jews since the dawn of history. They expect the Jewish state to live up to the aspirations expressed in the Declaration of the Establishment of the State of Israel, and to be a country "based on freedom, justice and peace as envisaged by the prophets of Israel." They expect that a people so long oppressed would look into the eyes of their Palestinian neighbors, identify with their plight, and act with sympathy and compassion.

In terms of Israel-related Jewish organizations, the relationship between the more pragmatic Exodus camp and the more idealistic Sinai camp is often uneasy. The former certainly is far better organized and represents the predominant perspective of the organized Jewish community. The latter often feels itself unheard and disenfranchised by those who have the ear of public officials as representatives of the organized Jewish community. When Israel faces a crisis, as it did with the second intifada, Jewish individuals or groups that are not in step with the communal party line find themselves facing ostracism, if not worse.

Ironically, it seems that the sympathies of American Jews may be moving in the direction of the Sinai camp. The latest study conducted by Steven Cohen in early 2005 showed that two-thirds of American Jews "are sometimes disturbed by Israel's policies and actions." The number of American Jews who said that "Israel is an important part of my Jewish identity" was 57 percent, down from 75 percent in the 1980s.[20] Many

Jewish students on college campuses cannot find a place where they can express support for Israel in a nuanced and critical way, especially when they believe in the right of the Palestinians to have a state of their own in the Middle East.[21]

Indications are that the divide between the Exodus and Sinai perspectives on Israel and the Middle East are more acute in America than in Israel. Even before the death of Yasser Arafat in 2004, the ideological lines between the Israeli left and right were shifting. In reaction to the campaign of terrorism aimed at Israeli civilians during the second intifada, the Israeli left more or less acquiesced to the erection of a massive security barrier between Israel and centers of Palestinian population. To the vast majority of Israelis, this barrier proved effective in dramatically cutting down on terrorist incursions into Israel, even though the notion of separation had long been an anathema to Israeli liberals committed to peaceful coexistence. Conversely, by 2005, Likud Prime Minister Ariel Sharon and his deputy prime minister, Ehud Olmert, who would succeed him in the post, began to argue that Israel must end its "occupation" of Palestinian areas to pave the way to a two-state solution to the Middle East conflict. They were driven by the demographic reality that the rapid growth of the population in Palestinian areas would soon create an Arab majority in the state of Israel. It was with this argument that Sharon convinced his cabinet to support an Israeli withdrawal from Gaza in June 2006. Ironically, this had been the rationale and the policy advanced by the Israeli left for the previous thirty years.

It is the job of American-based Jewish groups charged with defending the state of Israel to advance the most compelling case to public officials of why Israel needs aid and support in the face of threats to its survival. In a public policy universe of competing interests, it is not always the easiest sell, which explains why AIPAC and the organized American Jewish community find contrary opinions emerging from alternative Jewish groups not only troublesome, but even dangerous to Israel's future. Yet just as Rabin's overture to the PLO in the early 1990s created sudden shifts in the attitudes and policies of American Jewish organizations, so, too, did Ariel Sharon, as the duly elected leader of Israel, cause a realignment of policy, almost overnight, when he chose a more conciliatory approach to the Arab-Israeli conflict after the death of Yasser Arafat. And just as an Israeli peace overture can alter a strategic direction taken by Israel's Jewish defenders in the United States, so, too, can the actions of Islamic terrorists give pause to those American Jewish groups that are inclined to shine a bright and critical spotlight on the moral conduct of Israeli policy.

It needs to be pointed out that the Sinai impulse is not just an American Jewish phenomenon. Within Israel's thriving democracy, a day does not go by when Israeli policies are not subject to even harsher critique from Israeli Jews. Time and again Israel gives evidence that the Sinai impulse is deeply embedded in its own culture. There are numerous examples of social justice consciousness in Israel. While a full treatment goes beyond the scope of this book, two such examples are the decision during the second intifada to mount in the corridors of the Knesset a photo exhibition on Israeli military mistreatment of Palestinian civilians[22] and the Israeli Supreme Court decision in June 2004 to force the Sharon government to move the security barrier so as to minimize the violation of property rights and freedom of movement of Palestinians. Both examples illustrate how Israeli Jews attempt to balance their real security needs with their commitment to the prophetic Jewish values of compassion and the pursuit of peace.

The effort to protect and defend the state of Israel has long been the focal point for some of the most intense divisions in the Jewish world between Exodus and Sinai impulses. That is because Israel is not only the worldly reminder of the Jewish people's near-demise during the Holocaust but it also symbolizes the Jewish people's fondest hopes for a bright future. Israeli society seems to make more room for the expression of dissent about government policies regarding Palestinians, security, and the attempts to find an acceptable resolution to the Middle East conflict than does the American Jewish community. This is the result of ongoing anxiety on the part of the American Jewish community about how dissent within the community might compromise its ability to influence policy makers on matters of critical concern to Israel's survival. It puts into bold relief the tension that a minority group feels between political effectiveness and what some view as high-minded but naïve moralizing. In fact, it was largely around the issue of Israel that the organized American Jewish community began to rethink its commitment to social justice as a centerpiece of communal policy.

IV A New Era

13

What Is a Jewish Issue?

The three case studies in Part III help illustrate how American Jews balanced their Exodus instincts for group survival with their Sinai impulse to bring about a more just and equitable world. Those two goals were not always at odds. In fact, for a time during the middle of the twentieth century, many Jews saw the two goals as quite complementary. An America that guaranteed the rights of its minorities would be good for Jews. An America that challenged its political nemesis, the Soviet Union, for that country's persecution of Jews and other political dissidents would help the plight of Soviet Jews. An America that fortified its support for the only democracy in an otherwise undemocratic Middle East would benefit the state of Israel. But the balance between Exodus and Sinai strategies was hardly a static formula. Over the course of the second half of the twentieth century, circumstances changed dramatically in ways that would affect the public profile of the Jewish community and its understanding of what was in its best interests. The adaptations of the community to these changes, and the reactions to those adaptations, would shape the Jewish identity of future generations of American Jews.

A Changing Political Landscape

The primary concern of national Jewish organizations in the first half of the twentieth century was defending Jewish rights, at home and abroad. National Jewish organizations stood up against anti-Jewish discrimination in the United States and also raised their voices to protect endangered coreligionists abroad. After World War II the Jewish community engaged in a public program of much greater breadth. The Jewish community was convinced that the First Amendment protections against undue entanglement of church and state and its protection of individual liberties were essential ingredients in assuring the full and successful integration of Jews into American society. The community also acted on its historical experience that blatant social inequality posed threats to the very stability of that society. Social unrest, generated by those in a society who had the least to lose, often led to the scapegoating of Jews. Thus, even as Jews were climbing the ladder to higher socioeconomic status in America, a key part of the communal agenda was to ensure that public officials addressed the needs of those who were not sharing in America's prosperity. Because of the wide scope of this agenda, the Jewish community found itself at the center of numerous social causes and in coalition with a host of other groups that shared similar interests.

There is some debate among observers of American Jewish life about whether the Jewish communal embrace of issues like First Amendment freedoms, civil rights, health care, quality education, immigrant rights, and so forth was driven by the community's self-interest or by some larger, altruistic commitment to help those who were most vulnerable and disadvantaged. In fact, an understanding of the interplay between Exodus and Sinai impulses in Jewish life suggests that the motivation cannot be attributed to one or the other, but rather to the subtle combination of both. By the 1980s, however, it was clear that it was the need to advance group self-interest that had become the primary impetus behind Jewish organizational behavior. Those who advocated for a less parochial and more universal approach to policy issues found themselves on the defensive.

The seeds of this change in the American political landscape were sown even earlier. It can be traced to the very civil rights struggle that American Jews, to this day, point to with pride as an example of Jewish compassion and political solidarity. Jews played prominent leadership roles in the early years of the civil rights movement, but by the early 1960s there were examples of Jews being pushed out of leadership positions in a variety of civil rights organizations as blacks sought greater control over the movement that directly affected their rights. For Jews, such actions seemed a betrayal not only of the personal bonds of solidarity between members of two minority groups that had worked side by side for the expansion of civil rights in America, but also of the very ideals of equality and integration that had characterized the movement. The fact that Jews had provided much of the financial support for the civil rights movement only further condemned them in the eyes of increasingly militant black leaders who experienced such support as white paternalism. Jewish appeals to a common history of oppression fell on deaf ears. Jews were driven by a desire to create an America in which all citizens, regardless of race, religion, or ethnic origin, were accorded equal treatment. While this vision of the future was one shared by Dr. Martin Luther King, Jr., the nonviolent strategy that King advocated was gradually overtaken by the more militant strategy of black power advocated by the likes of Malcolm X, Eldridge Cleaver, Stokely Carmichael, and Bobby Seale.[1]

The parting of ways in terms of long-term civil rights strategy was more than an ideological debate. Black leaders became more assertive, arguing that the solution to the legacy of American racism lay in compensatory entitlements for the entire black community. There was less and less sympathy for the approach that asked that blacks be treated the same as whites. There was talk about exacting financial reparations for decades of oppression against blacks in America, about creating guaranteed slots for blacks in certain trades, universities, and professional schools, and about the need for greater control of the schools that educated black children. All of these strategies pitted black interests against Jewish interests.

In the early years of the civil rights movement, northern Jewish activists criticized their southern coreligionists for their tepid response to the great justice cause of the era. In turn, southern Jews felt vulnerable and exposed as northern Jews shuttled back and forth for actions that stirred up anxiety, rage, and resentment among southern whites. In the late 1950s, bombs were set off at Beth El Congregation in Miami and at The Temple in Atlanta. Explosives were also found in half a dozen other southern synagogues during this time, and rabbis who preached in favor of civil rights were the recipients of subtle and not-so-subtle threats to stop their agitation. A 1961 poll showed that 40 percent of southern Jews considered the Supreme Court's 1954 *Brown v. Board of Education* decision striking down "separate but equal" schooling "unfortunate," as compared with 97 percent of northern Jews who viewed the same decision favorably. A majority of southern Jews during this period, anxious about their standing in heavily white, conservative, and Christian communities, felt that desegregation was moving way too fast.[2]

As the tenor of the civil rights movement began to change in the mid-1960s, even northern Jews began to question whether the struggle for equal rights that had galvanized so many was in the best interests of the Jewish community. One flashpoint was the prospect of busing programs to help desegregate urban schools. In a 1964 editorial, *Congress Bi-Weekly*, the journal of one of the most liberal Jewish groups, the American Jewish Congress, noted sadly that more and more Jews were becoming advocates for "separate but equal" out of concern for the future quality of the schools that their children attended. The executive of the St. Louis Jewish Federation, Herman Kaplow, seeking to guide his community toward a rational communal policy, stated: "It is not the responsibility of a Jewish agency to meet Negro needs unless it also serves the total general community."[3] As if to underscore the evolution of views about how far Jews should go to protect the rights of others, especially when it compromised their own interests, Rabbi Harold Schulweis, a leading Conservative rabbi who was known for his liberal views, published an article entitled "Jewish Liberals, Alas!" in which he argued that Judaism itself was being betrayed by those Jews who put the interests of other groups above the needs of their own community.[4]

Perhaps the most famous incident that pitted blacks against Jews was during the 1967–1968 school year, when the local school board in the predominantly black section of Brooklyn called Ocean Hill-Brownsville sought greater control over the schools in its neighborhood. Not only were there calls for a more Afrocentric curriculum to bolster the pride of the black children of the school, but that curriculum would also require the hiring of more black teachers. On the other side of the controversy was the teacher's union—the United Federation of Teachers (UFT)—which was led by a Jew, Albert Shanker, and whose membership in and around New York was disproportionately Jewish. The union wanted to protect the jobs of teachers with seniority in the system, mostly white and Jewish. The union feared that the local school board would summarily dismiss these teachers in favor of black teachers. When ten teachers were in fact fired by the local school board for sabotaging the experimental new curriculum, the UFT staged a thirty-six-day walkout, effectively shutting down the schools.[5]

As if the conflict between black and Jewish group interests was not bad enough, the controversy took on even more incendiary overtones in September 1968 when, upon the desk of a Jewish teacher in the same school district, a pamphlet appeared that read:

> If Afro-American history and culture is to be taught to our black children it must be done by Afro-Americans who identify with and who understand the problem. It is impossible for the Middle East murderers of colored people to possibly bring this important task the insight, the concern, the expanding of the truth that is a must if the years of brainwashing and self-hatred that has been taught to our black children by these bloodsucking exploiters and murderers is to be overcome.[6]

The characterizing of American Jewish teachers as "Middle East murderers of colored people" connected the fraying of the black-Jewish alliance with the second major political development that changed the self-perception of American Jews for at least the next generation. At virtually the same time as tensions in Ocean Hill-Brownsville were effecting a shift in attitudes in America about race, intergroup relations, and political liberalism, war broke out in the Middle East. In the weeks leading up to the June 1967 war, Egyptian President Gamal Abdel Nasser orchestrated a series of provocative actions against Israel, including dismissing the U.N. forces in the Sinai Peninsula, which separated Israeli and Egyptian troops, and blocking the Straits of Tiran, which effectively shut down Israel's sole southern shipping port of Eilat. A torrent of broadcasts from Arab radio stations predicting the imminent destruction of the state of Israel accompanied Jordanian troop movements on Israel's eastern border and Syrian mobilization on Israel's northern border. Jews, both in Israel and around the world, feared a second Holocaust, as there was little confidence that Israel could successfully defend itself in a three-front war.

With the benefit of a preemptive strike against the Egyptian air force on June 5, Israel turned disaster into one of the most remarkable military victories in modern warfare. Meeting little resistance, Israel captured the entire Sinai from Egypt, all the territory up to the Jordan River from Jordan, including the old city of Jerusalem, and the strategic Golan Heights from Syria. Only a U.N.-imposed cease fire prevented the war from extending past six days when Israel was in a position to occupy even more Arab land. It was a defining moment, not only for Israel, but for American Jewry as well, and three lessons cast an indelible imprint on the American Jewish psyche.

First, interest and pride in Israel surpassed anything that American Jewry had experienced before. The national fundraising arm of the Jewish community, the United Jewish Appeal (UJA), launched an emergency appeal for Israel. American Jews, anxious for tangible ways of helping the beleaguered Jewish state, literally cleaned out their bank accounts to make extraordinary gifts. In six months the UJA raised $307 million, more than twice what it raised the entire previous year. Second, so great was the identification with the state of Israel that it sparked a movement of Jewish pride that was consistent with the new era of ethnic pride sweeping the United States. Suddenly Jews started wearing Stars of David around their necks and *kippot* (headcoverings) on their heads, and pressure built on college campuses to launch courses and programs in Jewish studies.

The third lesson was, perhaps, the most profound. American Jews were struck by how alone they were at their moment of greatest need. Not only were nations the world over silent in the face of overt military aggression against Israel by Arab nations, but a host of American subgroups with whom the Jewish community had allied for several decades on issues of common concern—Catholic and Protestant churches, liberal advocacy groups, the black community—failed to rally to Israel's side despite desperate pleas from American Jewish organizations. In the years that followed the Six-Day War, these same groups would become among Israel's harshest critics. They would accuse Israel of becoming an occupying power and of denying the newly emerging Palestinian people their territory and political sovereignty.

In 1968, historian Arthur Morse published his classic work *While Six Million Died: A Chronicle of American Apathy.* It told the story of how America, and the rest of the world, failed to act on behalf of the European Jews who faced genocide at the hands of the Nazis. Even though Jews threw themselves wholeheartedly into the enterprise of being good Americans and allies of other oppressed groups, little had changed since World War II. The lesson seemed clear—few would mobilize to save Jewish lives or to rally around Jewish interests. Jews could only rely on themselves to protect Jewish interests, not on the goodwill of others.[7]

These were among the changes in the American political landscape that help explain the American Jewish engagement in the struggle for Soviet Jewry (see Chapter 11) and its advocacy for the state of Israel (see Chapter 12). But to fully understand the American Jewish community's evolving approach to issues of social justice, we need to look at some additional changes in the American political context. With the election of Ronald Reagan as president of the United States in 1980, social conservatives made an all-out assault on the proposition that massive government spending could alleviate poverty. President Reagan's election signaled a growing national consensus around less government, reversing a fifty-year trend—from FDR's New Deal to Lyndon Johnson's Great Society—that government programs could solve major social problems in America. Some critics, among them black conservatives, challenged the belief that affirmative action programs or busing would bring about social and economic progress for the black community. The Christian right found its political voice and began to challenge the notion that the public square should be stripped of all manifestations of religion. Jesse Jackson, who declared himself a candidate for president in 1983, and later, Reverend Louis Farrakhan of the Nation of Islam—two of the most visible leaders in the black community—each made comments offensive to Jews. One study showed that the higher the level of education, the more likely it was that blacks would hold anti-Semitic attitudes.[8]

Against this backdrop, and framed by President Reagan's strong support of Israel and championing of the issue of Soviet Jewry, the Jewish community began to reassess how it engaged in the public square. No ideological dogma, liberal or otherwise, was going to dictate Jewish policy. The civil rights struggle had gone from one of moral clarity and high principle, around which Jews and the Jewish community could rally, to one of debatable strategies, around which Jews could not totally agree. No clarion issue took its place. The publication of the National Jewish Population Study of 1990 sent shivers down the spine of Jewish communal leaders with reports of intermarriage rates above 50 percent accompanied by data showing dramatic declines in the commitment of Jews to the Jewish community. The Jewish community slowly, but decisively, began to narrow its focus from one that sought to frame its agenda in a broad societal context to one that was much more focused on issues of Jewish survival—threats to Jews abroad and signs of communal weakness at home. Single-issue groups emerged to focus on elements of this Jewish survival agenda, whether focused on Israel, fighting anti-Semitism, or rescuing Soviet Jews. The Jewish community, increasingly affluent and politically savvy, seemed less inclined to work with undependable allies to advance communal interests. It had the resources and the organizational clout to advance its own agenda.

Adding to the crisis facing the field of Jewish community relations were indications that there was little ideological consensus within the community itself. The Orthodox community grew in numbers and in self-confidence in the last two decades of the twentieth century. In 1999 the Orthodox Union opened its own public affairs office in Washington, D.C., the Institute for Public Affairs, signaling its desire to bring the voices of more than 1,000 modern Orthodox congregations into the public policy arena. Their politics were consistently more conservative than that of the rest of American Jewry. The fact that large segments of the Orthodox community sent their children to day schools raised the question of why the organized Jewish community continued to oppose some form of federal assistance for parochial education, especially when an argument could be made that the graduates of Jewish day schools were the key to the Jewish community's future vitality. The organized Jewish community's longstanding commitment to strict separation of church and state seemed to carry more than a hint of secular bias, keeping the public square free of any religious influences. In communities around the country, Orthodox groups arranged with local officials for public displays of menorahs during the winter holiday season, often alongside a Christmas scene. More than once, the organized Jewish community found itself in the uncomfortable position of opposing both Christian and Jewish displays, a position of principled consistency to be sure, yet an action that alienated highly committed Jews in the process.

Even the Jewish community's instinctive opposition to the Christian right and its socially conservative agenda was challenged from within the Jewish community. During the 1980s and 1990s, the mainstream organizations of the Jewish community, represented by the Jewish Council for Public Affairs (JCPA), consistently advocated in favor of a woman's right to reproductive choice. Just as consistently, the Union of Orthodox

Jewish Congregations registered their dissent from this policy (as was their right in the JCPA process). Orthodox interpretations of Jewish law were much less likely to sanction abortion than the rulings of non-Orthodox religious authorities. The Orthodox Union opposed legislative formulations that were overly permissive with regard to making abortions widely available and affordable as a matter of government policy. Their preference was to leave such decisions in the hands of a woman and her rabbi. The Orthodox position on abortion was far more nuanced than that of either the staunchly "pro-life" Catholic Church or the evangelical Christian right. Still, there was substantial sympathy from the Orthodox community for religious voices that placed a higher value on "reverence for life" than on "choice."

The attitude to evangelical Christians was further complicated by their avid support for the state of Israel. At a time when mainline Christian denominations would heap criticism on Israel's treatment of Palestinians and Israel's occupation of land claimed by Arabs, evangelical Christians were among Israel's most reliable political allies. Evangelical Christians raised millions of dollars for Israel and filled tour bus after tour bus with Christian pilgrims going to the Holy Land, even when Jews stayed away during times of increased violence in the region.

In 1983, Rabbi Yechiel Eckstein, a Chicago-based Orthodox rabbi, created the International Fellowship of Christians and Jews (IFCJ) to help mobilize support among evangelical Christians for Jews and for Israel. To date, the IFCJ has raised close to $100 million from Christians to support Jewish immigration and resettlement of Jewish refugees in Israel, social welfare programs in Israel, and services to Jews in the former Soviet Union. In 2002, in the midst of the second intifada in Israel that brought an epidemic of suicide bombings throughout Israel, the IFCJ launched Stand for Israel to mobilize support for the Jewish state. On the first day of prayer and solidarity sponsored by the IFCJ, fifteen million Christians were mobilized in 16,000 churches across the country to pray for Israel. At a time when Jews and Israel felt so isolated in the world, this kind of non-Jewish support could not be easily dismissed.

In 1993 another Orthodox rabbi, Daniel Lapin, based in Mercer Island, Washington, founded an organization called Toward Tradition to galvanize greater support for the alliance between Jews and the Christian right. The agenda of Toward Tradition was about as far as could be imagined from that of mainstream Jewish organizations, and it included support for limited government, a strong military, and a moral public culture. Through publications and occasional Washington conferences, Toward Tradition contributed to the breakdown of what had been a longstanding consensus that aligned the Jewish community with a liberal, social justice domestic agenda.

Neither Rabbis Eckstein nor Lapin were mainstream Orthodox leaders. Nor did their views carry a lot of influence in the Jewish community. Yet their organizations represented part of a broader trend that amounted to a breakdown in the ideological consensus of American Jewry with regard to social policy. If one were to read the resolutions of the Reform movement's biennial conventions or the program plans of the Jewish Council for Public Affairs (JCPA) at the end of the twentieth century, one might conclude that there was no retreat from the broad social justice agenda that had characterized Jewish communal advocacy for some forty years. The published JCPA public affairs agenda for 2000–2001 included thirteen pages on equal opportunity and social justice issues including poverty, healthcare, affordable childcare, race relations, public education, immigrant rights, and reproductive choice. Another thirteen pages were devoted to church-state issues and the Bill of Rights, and twelve pages focused on environmental issues. Twelve pages were devoted to Israel and international concerns such as human rights and Jews in other countries.

Yet a study conducted in the year 2000 comparing the attitudes of the general Jewish public with the national leadership of the JCPA suggested that the leadership was seriously out of step with its constituency. The study found that 17 percent of Jews opposed the death penalty compared with 66 percent of the JCPA leadership. Sixty-five percent of the Jewish public was opposed to affirmative action while 70 percent of the JCPA leadership endorsed it. As for religious symbols on public property, 43 percent of the Jewish public was supportive of a Christmas manger scene on city property and 47 percent of that same sample supported a Chanukah menorah in the same place. In contrast, only 5 percent of the Jewish leaders sampled would support the manger scene and 7 percent would be in favor of the Chanukah menorah.[9]

In addition to the changing political climate in America in the second half of the twentieth century, the liberal biases of the Jewish community were also facing an ideological challenge. Since the 1967 Six-Day War, *Commentary* magazine had waged an intellectually serious and sustained campaign to convince the Jewish community that neoconservatism, and not liberalism, was in the best interests of the Jewish community. Sponsored by the venerable American Jewish Committee and under the editorship of Norman Podhoretz, *Commentary* writers like Milton Himmelfarb, Midge Decter, and Irving Kristol questioned historic ethnic alliances, challenged the left for its anti-Israel posture, and encouraged America to strengthen its military capabilities and challenge the Soviet Union in the world. When Jeanne Kirkpatrick, longtime *Commentary* contributor and professor of political science at Georgetown University, was appointed by President Ronald Reagan to be the U.S. ambassador to the United Nations in 1980, the influence of *Commentary* on shaping American public policy was lost on no one. In a symposium appearing in the January 1980 issue of *Commentary* magazine, "Liberalism and the Jews," many of the fifty-two rabbis and intellectuals invited to contribute questioned whether an uncritical alignment between Jews and the liberal orthodoxies of the time continued to be good for American Jewry. The balance between Exodus and Sinai impulses in the organized Jewish community was undergoing realignment.

Anti-Semitism: Real and Imagined

The comedians who played the Borscht Belt in the Catskill Mountains in the post–World War II era knew that the best way to get a quick laugh was to make a joke about Jewish insecurity. It was a vein that ran deep in the Jewish psyche. Jewish history was a long litany that ran from the enslavement in Egypt, to expulsion from the land of Israel, to the ghettos and pogroms of the Middle Ages. The Holocaust was simply the final piece of evidence that the modern era would not bring about the eradication of anti-Semitism. Germany was a paragon of an industrialized and educated nation, yet its citizens were as susceptible to the poisonous hatred of Jews as were the peasants of White Russia.

There is substantial evidence that America was different. There were some notable anti-Semitic individuals in the early part of the twentieth century, like Henry Ford and the radio personality Father Charles Coughlin, both of whom were able to tap into significant public sympathy for their bigotry. At mid-century there were Jewish quotas in place in certain American universities, and there was still exclusionary behavior in both social and business settings, a phenomenon portrayed in the

1947 movie *Gentleman's Agreement* with Gregory Peck. But by the end of the twentieth century, the periodic expressions of anti-Semitism that occurred found little, if any, resonance in America. As Jews entered the top tiers of business, science, media, academia, the arts, medicine, and politics, there seemed to be no more barriers to Jewish achievement and no backlash from gentile America. A major study of anti-Semitism in America in the mid-1990s reported that both behavioral and attitudinal anti-Semitism were at all-time lows.[10]

Yet American Jewish perception of anti-Semitism seems to defy logic or evidence. A 1989 study of American Jewry by Steven M. Cohen, sponsored by the American Jewish Committee, found that 57 percent believed that one day American Jews could face severe anti-Semitic persecution. Forty-one percent believed that Jews were widely disliked by gentile America. Just over a quarter of the sample agreed with the statement: "As a Jew, I don't feel totally safe in America."[11] A 1998 study, also by the American Jewish Committee, found that an overwhelming majority of American Jews (95 percent) saw anti-Semitism as a problem in America, and 42 percent questioned whether, in fact, all positions of influence are open to Jews.[12]

There was a huge perception gap between what Jews believed to be true and what was actually true. In a 2000 sampling, 70 percent of Jews who held leadership positions in the Jewish community believed that "virtually all positions of influence in America are open to Jews." Only 30 percent of the general Jewish sample agreed with that same statement.[13] The comparison of Jewish attitudes with that of gentiles is even more striking. A 1982 study by Daniel Yankelovitch asked Jews whether they thought that non-Jews would react negatively if their political party nominated a Jew to be their candidate for the presidency of the United States. Seventy-eight percent of Jews believed that they would. But when a gentile sample was asked if they would be troubled by such a decision by their political party, only 28 percent said that they would.[14]

When Jonathan Pollard, an American Jew who was a U.S. Navy intelligence officer, was arrested for passing classified U.S. secrets to Israel in 1986, it raised the worst fears imaginable for American Jews. For years, the America versus Israel dual-loyalty dilemma was a hypothetical discussion topic at Jewish youth groups and camps—What would you do? Which country would you favor? After the Pollard arrest and his eventual life sentence, there was widespread sentiment among

Jews that Jewish loyalty to America would now and forever be questioned. But here, too, Jewish fears turned out to be exaggerated. Just five years after the trial, an overwhelming majority of Jews remained concerned about the repercussions of the Pollard affair, while most Americans did not remember who Jonathan Pollard was, and those who did, could not recall for whom he was spying.

Thus there appeared to be two distinct narratives of American Jewish history. One narrative—an Exodus narrative—could draw a straight line from 2,000 years of persecution in the Jewish diaspora to the abandonment of Israel during the Six-Day War and the spurning of Jewish efforts to advance a social justice agenda in America. Such a narrative reinforced anxieties about the place of Jews in the world, with no exception made for America. As argued by the *Commentary* crowd and others who followed this line of reasoning, Jews needed to keep their focus on those matters that bore directly on Jewish group interests. It supported the Exodus impulse in Jewish life, and it explains the strength and tenacity of the defense agenda of the American Jewish community.

The second narrative of American Jewish history would suggest that America is different. This line of thinking would suggest that fears of anti-Semitism run far deeper than the American reality warranted. It would support a Jewish communal agenda that was broadly defined and that extended beyond those issues that focused on Jewish self-interest. This more optimistic—though others would argue naïve—view bespoke a faith in America, its institutions, and the fair-mindedness of the American people. American Jewish solidarity with progressive social justice causes would certainly be rewarded with important allies on the issues of greatest concern to the Jewish community. Typifying this Sinai approach to Jewish life was Leonard Fein's 1988 book, *Where Are We? The Inner Life of America's Jews.* In it he made the case that too much of Jewish life was focused around the memory of the Holocaust and the protection of the state of Israel. This "obsession with survival" did not befit a prophetic people, he argued, and the singular focus on our external enemies distracted us from finding the true meaning and purpose of Jewish existence.[15]

Fein was not alone. A similar view was conveyed by Edgar Bronfman, the heir to the Seagram's liquor fortune whose standing in the business community, philanthropy, and outspokenness made him one of the most visible Jewish leaders in the world. Since 1979 he had served as the president of the World Jewish Congress (WJC) and provided the lion's share of that organization's funding. Bronfman had impeccable credentials as a defender of Jewish interests. Not only did the WJC protect Jewish interests all around the world, but Bronfman also used his seat on the board of DuPont to block a deal with Conoco, an oil business arrangement that was just a bit too favorable to Saudi Arabia, a sworn enemy of Israel.

In Bronfman's keynote address at the 1994 General Assembly of the Council of Jewish Federations, the annual gathering of the communal and philanthropic elite of the Jewish community, with several thousand attendees, he cited the progress in the peace talks between Israel and her Arab neighbors, predicting that, without an Israel in crisis, American Jewry was in danger of losing its central organizing principle. He ridiculed the number of Jewish organizations that tripped over each other to defend Israel and fight anti-Semitism. He urged the leadership of the community to rally around an agenda that would better ensure the Jewish identity of the next generation—Jewish education, summer camps, strengthening Jewish life on college campuses, subsidized day schools, and free identity-enhancing trips to Israel for young people.[16]

Bronfman was among the growing chorus of voices that spoke out about how the agenda of the Jewish community was changing. At the time of his speech, Israel did seem to be on the road to peace. The disintegration of the Soviet Union in 1989 signaled the beginning of a mass exodus of Soviet Jews to Israel and to the West. Even more significantly, the Jews who remained behind in the third largest concentration of Jews in the world were now out from under a Communist regime hostile to Jews. They set about developing the schools and infrastructure necessary to become a self-sustaining Jewish community. Even the issue of Holocaust commemoration reached a crossroads with the 1993 opening of the U.S. Holocaust Museum in the shadow of Washington's Jefferson Memorial. The museum's dedication, attended by several heads of state of European countries where Jews had been slaughtered, seemed to mark a moment in history when the world finally was saying to the Jews, "We are sorry. This victimization of Jews will never happen again." Suddenly, the three focal points of the Jewish defense agenda—remembering the Holocaust, protecting the state of Israel, and saving Soviet Jewry—seemed outdated, primarily because the primary Jewish objectives of each had been largely achieved.

Indeed, in the community there were indications that a new agenda was coming to replace the defense/survival one. The buzzword in the community became "continuity," meaning survival not in the most basic sense of Jews not being persecuted or killed, but in the creation of a sustained community imbued with Jewish knowledge and commitment. For too long the Jewish community had lived the prediction of Jewish philosopher Simon Rawidowicz, who called Israel "the ever-dying people," surviving only because Jews were too stubborn to be annihilated by their enemies. Now it was time to revisit the content of Jewish values and wisdom and make that the *raison d'etre* of Jewish life.

In the last two decades of the twentieth century, there was indeed a renaissance in American Jewish life that focused on an agenda beyond defense and survival. There was a burst of energy in the realm of Jewish education, with day school enrollment soaring and new schools opening up around the country virtually every year. The Partnership for Excellence in Jewish Education (PEJE) was founded in 1997 to support this trend. Jewish organizations put a high priority on seeing to it that their professionals and lay leaders were more conversant with Judaism. CLAL (the Center for Learning and Leadership), founded in 1974, emerged as a highly-valued educational resource to meet that need. The Wexner Heritage Program began to offer intensive Jewish education to some of the most promising up-and-coming leaders all around the country, planting seeds for a committed and informed Jewish leadership pool for years to come. It has reached some 2,000 Jews in over thirty communities since its inception in 1984. By the turn of this past century, some 5,000 Jews engaged in Jewish learning every week through the Florence Melton Adult Mini-School, which has grown to some sixty communal affiliates since its founding in 1986. Attendance at the courses of the Department of Continuing Education at the University of Judaism in Los Angeles exceeded 12,000.

A similar ferment could be found in the realm of Jewish religion and spirituality. As America itself awoke to its most intense engagement with spirituality in its history, Jews began to look beyond their parents' synagogues to find the riches of Jewish spirituality. Hundreds of books appeared to feed the Jewish search for greater spirituality in life. The authors of the books were sought-after teachers at newly created retreat centers like Elat Chayyim in New York and Metivta: A Center for Contemplative Judaism in Los Angeles. Rabbis and synagogues woke up to the spiritual hunger of American Jewry, and organizations like Synagogue 2000 and STAR (Synagogues: Transformation and Renewal) were created to help synagogues redesign their programs to better address the needs of the community. A handful of synagogues around the country pioneered new models of community, prayer, and governance to support the interest of Jews in a more spiritually compelling Judaism.[17] By the end of the century, Jewish identity had become a lot more than defense and survival.

The New Anti-Semitism

But the new millennium was not kind to those who declared the defense/survival agenda dead and buried and who trumpeted an era of Jewish renaissance. Three events, in relatively close sequence—the second intifada in the Middle East, the U.N. Conference on Racism in Durban, South Africa, and the September 11 terrorist acts in New York and Washington, D.C.—brought about a resurgence of the Jewish community's worst fears and anxieties. These events triggered the community's Exodus impulse, an impulse that some had felt was of decreasing urgency ever since the 1989 collapse of the Soviet Union, long the sponsor and patron of anti-Israel and anti-Semitic activity in the world.

In the summer of 2000, the Oslo peace process, which had held out the promise of a peaceful settlement of the Middle East conflict between Israel and the Palestinian Authority (PA), came to a screeching halt. Yasser Arafat rejected a generous land-for-peace offer from Israeli Prime Minister Ehud Barak at a Camp David meeting convened by U.S. President Bill Clinton. In September, a wave of suicide bombings sponsored by several Palestinian terrorist organizations claimed the lives of dozens of Israeli civilians in pizza shops, on public buses, and in open-air markets. This campaign of terror continued for several years, with the Israelis blaming Yasser Arafat and the PA for not doing enough to rein in the web of terrorist groups operating freely in PA territory. By 2004, more than 1,000 Israelis, mostly civilians, had been murdered by terrorist actions, and thousands more were maimed and wounded. The Israelis, retaliating after almost every incident, targeted terrorist cells in the West Bank and Gaza and tried to disable the groups by assassinating their leaders. Finally, with no end in sight to the cycle of violence, Israel began to construct a barrier to separate Israel from the densest concentrations of Palestinian villages. While the barrier proved effective in stopping most of the terrorist incursions, Israel came under heavy criticism by the international community. In July 2004, the International Court of Justice actually rendered a nonbinding opinion that Israel was in violation of international law by constructing the barrier on occupied land. Soon thereafter the Presbyterian Church (USA) passed a resolution calling for selective divestment of all church funds from corporations doing business with Israel, the National Council of Churches issued a booklet detailing the human rights violations associated with the barrier, and Israel was again the subject of international condemnation and isolation.

The second event that provided a rude wake-up call to Jews was a U.N.-sponsored World Conference on Racism in Durban, South Africa, in early September 2001. Notwithstanding the evidence of dozens of totalitarian countries around the world engaged in the most ruthless practices against ethnic minorities and political opponents, the overriding focus of the proceedings was on the human rights excesses of the state of Israel. Though many Jewish organizations chose to boycott the conference, aware from the preliminary drafts that the conference was going to become a forum for the most virulent expressions of anti-Semitic and anti-Zionist sentiments, some Jews did attend. Israeli cabinet member Rabbi Michael Melchior's stirring defense of Israel and critique of the hypocrisy of the gathering read in part:

> Barely a decade after the UN repealed the infamous "Zionism is Racism" resolution, which Secretary-General Kofi Annan described, with characteristic understatement, as a "low point" in the history of the United Nations, a group of states for whom the terms "racism," "discrimination," and even "human rights" simply do not appear in their domestic lexicon, have hijacked this Conference and plunged us to even greater depths. Can there be a greater irony than the fact that a conference convened to combat the scourge of racism should give rise to the most racist declaration in a major international organization since the Second World War?[18]

Melchior's presentation, though valiant, did little to stem the tide, as the Durban conference gave both increased visibility and a certain legitimacy to the new anti-Semitism. Within the next few years, *Wall Street Journal* reporter Daniel Pearl was kidnapped by Islamic extremists and forced to say that he was a Jew from a Zionist family. His captors decapitated him and circulated a video of his murder on the Internet. Egyptian state television produced a miniseries that repeated the canards of the classic anti-Semitic tract *The Protocols of the Elders of Zion,* one of the favorite texts of Nazi ideologues. The Palestinian Authority produced for use in their schools a textbook that claimed that the Holocaust was a myth fabricated by Jews to rally world sympathy for the Zionist design to take land that rightfully belongs to Palestinians. Even America was not immune to the new wave of hatred, as signs at "peace rallies" protesting America's invasion of Iraq read "Death to the Jews" and posters appeared in college dorms that said "Jews=Nazis."[19]

The third incident, coming only days after the conclusion of the Durban conference, was the hijacking of four planes on September 11, 2001, and the devastation to the World Trade Center and the Pentagon, resulting in the death of more than 3,000 individuals. It brought home to America the terror and insecurity that had been so much part of the experience of Israelis for decades. The American Jewish community, while mourning this loss of life and the loss of American innocence as Islamic terrorism finally came to American shores, also recognized this as a moment when the full might and power of the United States might be brought to bear against an enemy that Israel and America now had in common. President George W. Bush committed his administration to do whatever was necessary to fight the international war on terrorism. While victory was not to be achieved in any near term, there was some sense of comfort on the part of the American Jewish community that America saw its fate linked with that of Israel, Jews, and Western civilization against the forces of Islamic fundamentalism.

The Jewish community did not sit on its hands. The organized community was nothing if not a well-oiled machine that was more than equipped to mobilize appropriate responses to these new threats to Israel and the Jewish people. As mentioned previously, the United Jewish Communities launched an Israel Emergency Campaign and raised $350 million over the course of two years, underwriting after-school programs, security personnel to keep children out of harm's way, and trauma counseling centers in Israel. AIPAC redoubled its efforts to marshal the support of Congress and the administration during this time of crisis in Israel. Tapping into the desire of American Jewry to be of assistance to Israel, AIPAC's membership soared to 90,000 (it had been 55,000 until the outbreak of the second intifada), and attendance at its annual policy conference went from 800 in 1994 to some 5,000 in 2004. Perhaps the most impressive example of how the Jewish community mobilized on behalf of Israel during this time was an Israel Solidarity Rally in front of the U.S. Capitol on April 15, 2002. The rally was organized by the Conference of Presidents after a suicide bombing during a Passover seder at a hotel in Netanya, Israel. In less than a week's time, 100,000 Jews descended on the nation's capital to express their support for Israel.

Such mobilizations do not come without a price. Just as with the debate in the 1970s over whether it was appropriate for Jews to publicly criticize Israeli settlement policies at a time when the Jewish community was trying to rally public support for Israel, so, too, during the second intifada the Jewish community was not always tolerant of dissenting opinions. Committed doves like Michael Lerner, who criticized Israeli policies toward the Palestinians both in his *Tikkun* magazine and beyond, was ostracized by the mainstream Jewish community. Lerner reported receiving death threats from self-identifying "defenders of Israel and the Jewish people." Various Jewish groups that attempted to march in Israel solidarity rallies with signs calling for a "just peace" between Israel and the Palestinians found themselves facing hostile receptions if not being prevented outright from marching with other Jewish groups. When Paul Wolfowitz, a senior official in the Bush administration who was both Jewish and one of the architects of a policy that was determined to fight terrorism all around the world, spoke at the solidarity rally on Capitol Hill in April 2002, he was roundly booed when he expressed sympathy for innocent Palestinian civilians who were killed in the rising cycle of violence in the Middle East. Wolfowitz's Sinai-like sentiment found little resonance in the ranks of Jews who were rallying to defend an Israel under siege.

Some would argue that the Jewish community, which for decades—operating out of the community's Exodus impulse—did its job of defending Jewish interests, had simply amassed more power than what was in its own best interests. A longtime Democratic staffer on Capitol Hill reported that members of Congress who are privately in favor of an even-handed peace settlement to the conflict in the Middle East, requiring concessions from both Israel and the Palestinians, feel constrained from publicly advancing such a position out of fear of retribution from the Jewish community. Jews involved in organizations that have been on record as critical of certain Israeli policies, such as Israel Policy Forum, Americans for Peace Now, and Brit Tzedek v'Shalom, generally feel that the organized Jewish community is not particularly hospitable to their views or their involvement at the communal table. At gatherings of college students, there are as many students who feel disenfranchised by the mobilization on behalf of Israel that leaves little room for criticism of Israel as there are those who have been energized to work with AIPAC and other pro-Israel efforts.[20]

If there were alternate American Jewish narratives, one feeding the Exodus impulse and the other feeding the Sinai impulse, the events at the dawn of the twenty-first century pushed the pendulum decisively in the direction of the more defensive/survival mentality.

Jewish Priorities Reexamined

Two recent histories of Jewish liberalism in twentieth-century America conclude that the Jewish community was never quite as liberal as it believed itself to be. Marc Dollinger, in his *Quest for Inclusion: Jews and Liberalism in Modern America,*[21] argues that the Jewish community was primarily driven by a desire to advance its own acculturation in America. When a liberal cause, like civil rights, advanced that acculturation agenda, Jews joined it. When the cause did not advance that agenda, Jews parted company with it. Michael Staub in *Torn at the Roots: The Crisis of Liberalism in Postwar America* chronicles how a variety of liberal social justice efforts emerging from within the Jewish community were delegitimized and undermined by the organized Jewish community's propensity to raise the specter of the Holocaust and Jewish survival concerns.[22]

The best way to understand the complex picture of Jewish engagement with a range of social justice concerns is to appreciate the contours of the debate over competing Jewish priorities. During the administration of Ronald Reagan, Marshall Breger was the White House liaison to the Jewish community. He tells the story of setting up a meeting for several Jewish organizational representatives with White House chief of staff Donald Regan. The first forty minutes of the meeting were taken up with the Jewish representatives pressing the administration on its policy over aid to families with dependent children (AFDC in legislative parlance). It was not what Regan expected and, in retrospect, Breger uses the story to chide the Jewish community for having its priorities all confused.[23]

The story helps reveal the tension in American Jewish life and politics. The fact that the Jewish organizational representatives were at a meeting with the most senior official in the White House and used precious time to speak about an issue that had little to do with Jewish interests—because the AFDC program primarily benefits low-income households—but everything to do with Jewish values indicates how determined the Jewish community was to balance its Exodus instincts with its Sinai commitments. On the other hand, Breger uses the story to suggest how wrongheaded such an approach is, arguing that the representatives were not doing the job that they were hired to do—protecting Jewish interests. Breger goes on to suggest that Jewish organizations' primary responsibility is to speak to those issues that affect Jews as a group or to those issues that affect many Jews. Aware that the Jewish community has a history of working in coalition with a wide array of groups on issues that transcend narrowly defined self-interest, he argues that such coalitions require the Jewish community to make concessions that are not in its long-term interest. Nor does he believe that there is evidence that such coalitions "pay off" down the road in terms of reciprocal support for Jewish issues.[24]

What might have been a theoretical argument about Jewish priorities a decade earlier took on more practical and immediate relevance during the Reagan administration. Here was a president who was a staunch defender of the state of Israel, willing to challenge Soviet totalitarianism around the world, and committed to keeping the struggle of Soviet Jews on the front burner in negotiations with the Soviet Union. Many would ask: Was it really in the Jewish community's interests to challenge the president on his domestic agenda just because it did not accord with the liberal tendencies of American Jews? In fact, the Jewish community did continue to play both cards simultaneously during the two terms of Ronald Reagan's presidency.

Al Chernin, who served as the professional head of the Jewish Council for Public Affairs (JCPA) during the Reagan years,[25] defended that approach by saying that enlightened self-interest requires taking a much longer view than simply what is best for the Jews at a given moment in time.

The self-interests of the Jewish community have been shaped
by the Jewish ethos. That humanistic ethos, which has driven
Jews in modern history, has evolved from 2000 years of Jewish
Diaspora history ... and [from] the social justice imperatives of
Judaism.... Happily for the Jewish community, America's
enlightened self-interest in an open, economically healthy, pluralistic society coincides with Jewish self-interest and the Jewish
ethos. We should reject those false prophets who urge us to
turn away from these social justice imperatives.[26]

The challenge to Chernin's view was summarized by Murray
Friedman, longtime director of the Philadelphia chapter of the American
Jewish Committee. Friedman argued that Chernin and the organized
Jewish community were overly tied to the orthodoxies of American liberalism. He believed that the Jewish community would do well to reex-
amine its positions on racial equality, abortion, and separation of church
and state. On each of these fronts, Friedman believed that Jewish self-
interest suggested an approach quite different than the one that was still
characterizing the public pronouncements of the JCPA.[27]

Indeed, if one were to follow the annual deliberations of the JCPA
since 1980 or track the voting behavior of Jews right through the 2004
elections, there is substantial evidence that the Jewish community has
not retreated from its embrace of social justice as a communal ethos. The
JCPA continued to issue statements in support of advancing opportunities for underprivileged Americans, for gay and lesbian rights, for
woman's rights, for improving educational opportunities in the nation's
cities, for protecting the environment, for expanding access to health
care and day care, for protecting human rights around the world, and so
forth. American Jews continued to vote in the 75–80 percent range for
Democratic candidates for president. National organizations like the
Reform movement's Religious Action Center and the National Council
of Jewish Women continued to participate in many of the coalitions that
advocate for progressive causes.

But closer scrutiny of the field of Jewish communal relations in the
last two decades reveals a decisive move away from the broad-based liberal agenda of mid-century to a more narrow, self-interested agenda akin
to the one proposed by Marshall Breger. Not only did the Reagan presidency complicate the calculation about who were the Jewish community's real allies on social and political issues, but there were also changes

afoot in the priorities of the Jewish federation system that funded the national JCPA and its affiliates all around the country. The federation system was becoming increasingly focused on internal concerns. On top of the communal agenda was the defense of Israel. The next major priority was concern about Jewish continuity raised by the findings of the 1990 National Jewish Population Study. At a time when the demographics showed that the American Jewish community was at risk as a result of rising intermarriage and assimilation, communal policy suggested that communally funded Jewish organizations should stay focused on those issues that would clearly advance Jewish group interests. In the view of many leaders in the federation system, those issues did not include the broad domestic agenda championed by the likes of Al Chernin.

Throughout the 1980s and 1990s local affiliates of JCPA were having their budgets cut by their parent federation bodies, and pressure mounted on JCPA to restrict itself to issues around which there was communal consensus. Whereas the focus of Jewish advocacy had once galvanized around issues of broad societal concern, now the greatest energy in the domestic arena focused on seeing to it that the Jewish community got its fair share of government funding for its own social service agencies. Many local Jewish communities hired lobbyists to work state capitols for the growing amount of government dollars being made available for social service delivery. Here was a pocketbook issue for the Jewish community because of its many agencies providing just such social services, and not just to Jews. In interviews with ten Jewish community relations professionals working around the United States, only one felt that her agency's commitment to social justice issues was at a level equal to or greater than what it was fifteen years ago. All the others reported a major retreat from a social justice agenda.[28] One professional, bemoaning the decreased willingness of the Jewish community to take leadership on a central domestic social justice issue, contrasted the Jewish community's willingness to challenge President Reagan's tax cuts and domestic spending cuts in the 1980s and the refusal of the federation system to mount a similar challenge to President Bush's similar policy direction in the early 2000s.[29]

Larry Rubin, who served as the executive vice-chairman of the JCPA from 1990 to 2000, often found himself on the defensive with leaders of the federation system over his agency's inclination to address itself to broader issues of American life. One example was JCPA's official opposition to the

1994 balanced budget amendment pending in Congress. Opposition to this amendment was consistent with JCPA's longstanding advocacy to support social programs that could help poor Americans. However, with the leadership of the federation system becoming increasingly conservative, and in many cases Republican, JCPA was constrained from taking any action on the position that had been approved by its national convention.[30]

In 1999 a long-simmering conflict between the liberal-leaning JCPA and federation leadership went public. The JCPA was challenged by some of the wealthy leaders of the federation system, a system that provided JCPA's funding, to use communal dollars for issues that represented clear Jewish needs. According to one news report, those concerns did not include the environment, gay rights, or campaign finance reform.[31] This trend was a blow to those Jews who were long committed to balancing the Jewish communal Exodus agenda with a more universal Sinai agenda. In his final address to the national convention of the JCPA in 2000, before he resigned as its executive vice-president, Larry Rubin lamented the fact that even as there was an increasing need for the Jewish community to lead the charge on advancing a justice agenda, both at home and abroad, the community had turned decisively inward.[32]

It was in this context that those Jews who were as attuned to the Sinai vision of Judaism as they were to the Exodus vision began to find alternate avenues to advance the Jewish values and priorities they cherished.

14

Beyond Self-Interest

It has become commonplace in the Jewish community to cite the central role that Jews played in the civil rights movement as evidence of the Jewish community's commitment to social justice. Chapter 10 provided many examples of such involvement, and these examples, such as Rabbi Heschel's relationship with Martin Luther King, Jr., are often pointed to with pride by Jews, some of whom were not even alive back then. It is easy to forget that Dr. King and the civil rights movement were extremely controversial at the time. As is so often the case with prophets, it is easier to confer such lofty labels after the passage of several decades, when history itself has weighed in on the justice of the cause. Dr. King and Rabbi Heschel took risks for what they believed was morally right and religiously imperative. They more than earned the admiration, even awe, that the passage of time has bestowed upon them.

Yet the commitment of a religious community to social justice cannot rest on the shoulders of a few activists in the past. In the case of the Jews in America, there is not a decade that has passed when Jews were not in the forefront of efforts to bring about a more just society—to paraphrase the biblical mandate: healing the sick, clothing the naked, and providing shelter for the destitute. The references in Chapter 9 to some of the giants of social reform and social justice whose primary locus of activity was general American society hardly scratch the surface of Jewish involvement. The list and record of such individuals is deserving of its own treatment, but that is beyond the purview of this book. Here I shall look at how the Sinai impulse for justice has found expression through an increasingly diverse array of Jewish organizations that formed outside of the orbit of the organized Jewish community. In most cases, these efforts were the result of efforts by a handful of individuals with near-missionary zeal to take on a social justice cause under Jewish auspices. Some of these organizations were national and some were local. What is most interesting is that the activity of the independent organizations increased just as the zeal of the organized Jewish community to pursue this mandate waned, suggesting something very important about the nature of American Jewish identity.

Justice, Justice Shall You Pursue

The civil rights movement went a long way toward eliminating legal barriers against people of color in America. Yet it would be naïve to think that the legal and legislative accomplishments of that movement eradicated major inequities in American society. African-Americans and Hispanics still lag far behind white Americans in every conceivable measure of socioeconomic achievement. Heavily concentrated in America's inner cities, African-American and Hispanic youth often grow up in communities characterized by high levels of crime, violence, teenage pregnancy, and substance abuse. Substandard housing, schools, and recreational facilities add to a social environment that too often perpetuates poverty and hopelessness.

In contrast, starting in the second half of the twentieth century, Jews have enjoyed unparalleled prosperity. Second- and third-generation American Jews took their place as part of America's professional elite—lawyers, doctors, accountants, and business owners. They were disproportionately represented in the halls of Congress, in the boardrooms of America's largest corporations, and on the best college campuses as both students and faculty members. Jews left the urban areas that were home to their immigrant parents and grandparents and moved to affluent suburbs. Meanwhile, poor ethnic Americans moved into the very same urban neighborhoods where Jews once lived.

Forty years after President Lyndon Johnson declared "war on poverty" and unveiled his Great Society programs, America had a larger gap between rich and poor than at any time in its history. In 2002, the bottom 20 percent of Americans earned 4 percent of the gross national income. The top 5 percent earned 21 percent of that income. From 1970 to 2000 the income gap between rich and poor doubled in size. In the wealthiest country on earth, thirty-five million people live in poverty, a number that includes one in four (12.2 million) American children. The government-set "poverty line" is defined as earning less than $18,104 a year for a family of four. A single mother, working full-time at minimum wage ($5.15/hour), makes $1,157 under the poverty line.[1] The more children a single mother needs to support, the greater the financial burden. Living in poverty often means making painful choices between shelter, food, and health care. The poor have no choice but to forgo what many middle-class Americans would consider basic necessities of life. It is this reality that has led most advocates for the poor to identify social and economic issues as the new frontier of the civil rights movement.

There is evidence to support those who would criticize the Jewish community's insularity from the problems of America's urban poor and the more general phenomenon of socioeconomic injustice in America. Some Jews do not understand why African-Americans and Hispanics need special treatment if other ethnic groups, like the Jews, succeeded in moving from immigrant poor status to middle and upper class in a matter of two or three generations. There is physical distance between where Jews now live and where the urban poor live, and the psychological distance between the two communities is even greater. In the absence of regular personal contact between the groups, there is a growing lack of understanding of the forces that lead to the persistence of urban poverty.

Faith communities in America have long been one of the major providers of support to the needy. In the Catholic and Protestant communities these efforts are usually organized under church sponsorship. The Jewish community's larger efforts to promote social justice have tended to come from independent organizations, outside the rubric of religious denominations, though congregations increasingly have become sponsors of targeted social action programming.

In fact, some of the most sustained and creative efforts of the Jewish community to support social justice efforts in America over the past fifty years have taken place not through the large umbrella agencies of the organized Jewish community, but rather through new organizations that were formed by Jews committed to a specifically Jewish approach to social justice. Some of the Jews behind the creation of these organizations were deeply committed to Jewish life and wanted to make an explicit connection between their understanding of Jewish teachings and engaging in social justice work in the world. Others had more tenuous ties to the Jewish tradition, but their ethnic ties were sufficiently strong that they wanted to pursue their particular political and social passions under a Jewish banner. In most cases, these new organizations were narrowly focused, using one particular strategy, or they were efforts that focused on one particular community. By the 1980s, such focus underscored a growing realization that the solution to the country's most systemic injustices would not be ameliorated through congressionally mandated federal programs. In the face of growing public antipathy to such programs, especially when they carried a price tag of higher taxes, both Republican and Democratic administrations grew less inclined to have the federal government involved in major social reengineering.

Such Jewish organizational efforts represent dazzling creativity and dogged determination even though the nature of the efforts rarely leads to final claims of "success—job accomplished." First I will highlight two of the earliest examples of community-based social justice initiatives in the Jewish community. I will then focus on the explosion of new national Jewish organizations devoted to social justice efforts in the 1980s. Finally, I will seek to explain why these independent groups and initiatives have proliferated and what they signify.

The Jewish Council for Urban Affairs (JCUA), Chicago

The pioneer in the field of local Jewish community organizing for social/economic justice, the Jewish Council for Urban Affairs (JCUA), was founded in 1964 when legendary activist Saul Alinsky secured a $15,000 gift from Kivie Kaplan to seed a Chicago-based Jewish effort to fight poverty and racism. The money was given to Rabbi Robert Marx, who served as the lay head and religious spokesman for the group. He, in turn, hired a young organizer named Lew Kreinberg to engage in the work of community organizing.

The JCUA quickly earned attention and legitimacy by becoming immersed in the fate of Lawndale, one of the poorest urban ghettos in the country, located on Chicago's west side. In 1945 Lawndale was 95 percent Jewish. Ten years later, the Jews had moved farther out to the suburbs and Lawndale was a decaying neighborhood, predominantly African-American. This was a pattern that was repeating itself throughout the country and would later sow the seeds of intergroup tensions. Jews often retained ownership of properties in the neighborhoods they once inhabited, renting them out to the ethnic groups that were now moving in. Many Jews were upstanding and responsible landlords, but when black nationalism turned more militant and separatist in the late 1960s, there were many accusations made against Jewish business owners ("slumlords") who were profiting at the expense of poor people of color.

President Lyndon Johnson's Model City program was making millions of dollars of federal funds available to communities like Lawndale, but the program was top down; nobody was listening to the people living in the communities in question. When it came to light that the federal money coming to Chicago would turn Lawndale into a middle-class neighborhood built around a golf course, it gave credence to the line that comedian Dick Gregory often used: "Urban renewal is negro removal." JCUA was committed to empowering local residents to shape the future of their own neighborhood, and it led to the creation in 1967 of the Westside Federation, headed by a local African-American minister. By hiring outside urban planners and strategically using the media to publicize details of the plan, the Westside Federation, with the help of JCUA, got an alternate plan approved for their community that brought in a state-of-the-art high school, a community-based bank, and a thorough renovation of Douglas Park at the center of the neighborhood.[2]

Using similar organizing strategies, JCUA went on to engage in other poor neighborhoods in and around Chicago. In each effort, they fought discriminatory policies of banks and real estate companies, blocked evictions of residents, worked to shape urban renewal policies that would help residents rather than enrich business interests, and created job training programs and economic development plans that would help poor people. In the 1980s, as homelessness across America reached crisis proportions due to new federal policies that deinstitutionalized thousands of mentally ill Americans and cuts in federally subsidized housing, JCUA was at the forefront of efforts to respond to the challenge. JCUA was instrumental in founding the Chicago Coalition for the Homeless, and it established food pantries and vegetable gardens throughout the city to help feed the hungry. JCUA also worked to educate the Jewish community of Chicago about the relationship between Judaism and the issues it was working on. One such example was a "Judaism and Urban Poverty" curriculum that was used in congregational schools throughout the Chicago area.

One of JCUA's most creative initiatives was its Community Venture Program (CVP), started in 1991. Using the longstanding Jewish communal principle of no-interest loans, CVP raised money from Jews to provide loans for community redevelopment projects in at-risk neighborhoods. This "first money" is often hard, if not impossible, to come by in poor neighborhoods. The $4 million raised since 1991 under the CVP program has leveraged more than $100 million in additional bank loans for housing projects that have produced some 2,400 units for poor people. The program still exists and continues to grow.

JCUA is currently led by executive director Jane Ramsey, who came to the organization in 1979 and is considered one of the pioneers in the field of local Jewish social justice organizing. Raised in a Reform Jewish household in the suburbs of Chicago in the 1960s, she was deeply influenced by two of her childhood rabbis at North Shore Congregation Israel in Glencoe. Rabbi Edgar Siskin was the senior rabbi, who would give fiery, impassioned sermons about the need to mobilize for civil rights. The assistant rabbi, Harold Kudan, was a much more low-key presence, and yet his vital role in organizing a summer camp for inner-city kids under the auspices of the congregation was not lost on Ramsey, who worked as a counselor at the camp. After receiving a graduate degree in social policy from the University of Chicago, Ramsey worked with juvenile offenders and then at Chicago's City Hall. She then sought out a place where she could combine her passion for justice with her personal Jewish commitments.[3] That place was JCUA, and under Ramsey's leadership the organization has grown to have a budget of more than $1 million and a staff of nineteen professionals.

Bet Tzedek, Los Angeles

A second example of an independent, local social justice effort that has touched the lives of thousands is the Los Angeles-based Bet Tzedek, "house of justice." Founded in 1974 by a small group of lawyers, rabbis, and community activists seeking to act on the central tenet of Jewish law and tradition, *tzedek, tzedek tirdof,* "justice, justice shall you pursue" (Deut. 16:20), Bet Tzedek was established to provide free legal services to needy people throughout Los Angeles County. The vast majority of the people served by Bet Tzedek are non-Jews, though the organization also sponsors a program that works with elderly Holocaust survivors to help them secure reparation payments from Germany and other European countries.

Bet Tzedek has a multifaceted program that has become more ambitious as the organization has grown in scope. Its Housing Law Project represents low-income tenants facing wrongful evictions and files class action lawsuits on behalf of tenants living in slum and substandard housing conditions. Its Kinship Care Program helps children who live with relatives other than their parents, providing legal services and education to help these surrogate parents secure appropriate health care, education, and insurance for the children in their care. Low-income senior citizens, often easy targets for scam artists who trick the elderly into signing unfair loan papers (thus putting their homes at risk of repossession), can find legal recourse through Bet Tzedek's Consumer and Home Equity Fraud Task Force. The Home Caregiver Project helps poor people acquire the resources to care for aging relatives in their homes, avoiding costly and impersonal institutional alternatives such as nursing homes.

A good example of the way Bet Tzedek directly addresses issues of economic justice is its Employment Rights Project. Low-income workers are often paid below the federal minimum wage. It is not uncommon for employers to withhold or delay a paycheck, an action that has devastating consequences to poor families living so close to the margins of poverty. This problem is compounded when the workers are undocumented immigrants. Scared of being deported, most of these immigrants wouldn't dream of challenging their employers in court, even if they knew how to do it. Furthermore, federally funded legal service agencies are prohibited from providing undocumented immigrants legal assistance. Bet Tzedek takes on dozens of such cases every year.

Today Bet Tzedek has three locations as well as representatives at some thirty senior centers in Los Angeles County. It has a budget of $8.2 million and a staff of 55 full-time lawyers supported by an additional 300 attorneys who provide pro bono work for the organization. Bet Tzedek now serves more than 10,000 poor people every year, from every conceivable racial and religious background.

An Alternate Organizational Universe

In addition to these two pioneering efforts established at the local level, no less than nine new national organizations blending Judaism and social justice burst onto the American Jewish scene in the late 1970s and the ensuing decade. Compared to the large, multi-issue organizations like the Religious Action Center, the American Jewish Committee, and the Jewish Council for Public Affairs—which had long dominated the field of Jewish public affairs—these organizations were more modest, identifying a specific niche for themselves. They were the catalyst for a level of ferment around Jewish social justice activity that was unprecedented in the history of the American Jewish community. Each organization demonstrated an ability to attract constituencies and funding. Collectively, these organizations signaled a new stage in the maturation of the American Jewish community, and the scope of their activities represents an impressive commitment on the part of American Jews to social justice activity.

The organizations included:

- **New Israel Fund** (1979). Founded as a vehicle to help support democratic and social justice initiatives in the state of Israel, by 2003 the New Israel Fund had granted over $120 million to more than 700 organizations in Israel, specifically supporting organizations dedicated to safeguarding civil and human rights, bridging social and economic gaps, and fostering tolerance and religious pluralism. Its contributor base reached a high of 20,000 in the mid-1990s.
- **Shalom Center** (1983). Founded by Rabbi Arthur Waskow as a resource center with an initial focus on nuclear disarmament, the Shalom Center's agenda later broadened to include peace in the Middle East, environmental justice, race, civil liberties, gender, and globalization.
- **Jewish Fund for Justice** (1984). Designed to raise money from the Jewish community for poverty and justice-related causes around the United States, primarily beyond the boundaries of the Jewish community, the Jewish Fund for Justice now also engages in programs of education and fosters grassroots social action in the Jewish community.
- **American Jewish World Service** (1985). Raising money from the Jewish community for projects in the third world, includ-

ing special appeals for disaster relief, the American Jewish World Service also sponsors service missions for Jewish groups to underdeveloped regions around the world.

- **MAZON: A Jewish Response to Hunger** (1985). Founded by writer/activist Leonard Fein, MAZON now raises more than $3 million for allocation to agencies in the United States that either feed hungry people or that work on hunger advocacy.
- *Tikkun* (1986). A magazine founded by Rabbi Michael Lerner focusing on social justice and spirituality with a subscriber base of more than 20,000. Its advocacy arm is called the *Tikkun* Community and it sponsors periodic national conferences and political advocacy, with particular attention given to the Israel-Palestinian conflict.
- **Shomrei Adamah** (1988). Literally "guardians of the earth," Shomrei Adamah was founded by Ellen Bernstein to raise consciousness in the Jewish community about ecology. It published *Let the Earth Teach You Torah* and *Judaism and Ecology,* along with other educational resources, and signed up some 400 synagogue affiliates across the country.
- **PANIM: The Institute for Jewish Leadership and Values** (1988). A Washington-based educational foundation founded by Rabbi Sid Schwarz, PANIM sponsors leadership seminars and produces educational materials that integrate Jewish learning, values, and social responsibility. It serves more than 100 communities around the country.
- **Shefa Fund** (1988). A Philadelphia-based organization founded by Jeffrey Dekro, the Shefa Fund promotes socially responsible investing of Jewish communal assets and serves as a clearing house for progressive grant making by Jewish foundations.

What brought about this emergence of new organizations? What did it signify? These questions will be addressed at the end of this chapter, but first I will look more closely at several of these groups to better understand them and the trend they represented.

The Shalom Center

The idea for the Shalom Center emerged from a conversation between Arthur Waskow and the president of the Reconstructionist Rabbinical

College (RRC), Ira Silverman, in 1983. They believed that there needed to be a uniquely Jewish organizational voice that would speak to the issue of the global arms race being driven by the superpower struggle between the United States and the Soviet Union. The Shalom Center was set up to be that voice. Waskow was no stranger to political activism. From 1963 to 1977 he was a resident fellow of the Institute for Policy Studies, a left-leaning Washington, D.C.–based think tank on governmental policy and social change. He wrote several books on issues of nuclear strategy, disarmament, racial conflict, and nonviolent social change, and he was active in the movement to end the Vietnam War. In the early 1980s he moved to Philadelphia and he was invited to join the faculty of the RRC.

Waskow has emerged as one of the most prolific and provocative figures in the Jewish social justice movement, and his "conversion" from antiwar activist to one of the *rebbes* of the movement has taken on a mythic quality. As he tells it, the moment occurred when he was part of a committee meeting of the Jewish Community Council in Washington in 1968. It was a time of turmoil and unrest. Dr. King had been assassinated. Cities around the country, Washington included, went up in flames in the ensuing riots. Protesters were descending on Washington to lend their voice to King's "Poor People's Campaign," and their presence became national news as they set up tents on the Mall facing the U.S. Capitol in what came to be dubbed "Resurrection City." Word reached the Council meeting that a new group of arrivals could not be accommodated on the Mall. A local Catholic Church had offered to let them sleep in its facility for the night but there were no showers. A request came to the downtown Jewish Community Center to allow the protesters to shower. When the request was denied by the Center, members of the Council committee decided to organize a takeover of the Center at 5 p.m. that very day. The executive director of the Council tried to head off the provocative action that was certain to lead to bad press. When he asked why it had to be that very day at 5 p.m., one member of the group, Arnold Sternberg, replied, "Because *maariv* [the evening prayer service] is at 5:30 p.m. and I intend to *davven* it in the lobby of the JCC!" Not only did the JCC relent and open up its showers to the protesters, but Waskow had a revelation. He got a glimpse of the powerful synthesis of Judaism and radical politics.[4]

A year later, Waskow published *The Freedom Seder* and helped to convene a public Passover seder in Washington, D.C., at which the new liturgy was first used. The Passover haggadah, which would become a classic of radical Jewish literature, integrated the symbols of the Jewish story of oppression in Egypt with the modern oppressions in American society of racism, the war in Vietnam, the greed of American corporations, and the degradation of the environment. The seder took place on April 4, 1969, the first anniversary of the assassination of Martin Luther King, Jr.

When Waskow found his Judaism, he jumped in with both feet, first founding the Shalom Center in 1983 and eventually acquiring private ordination from Rabbi Zalman Schachter-Shalomi. When the Soviet Union fell in 1989, the Shalom Center shifted its focus from nuclear disarmament to a more eclectic range of social justice issues. Through its periodic newsletter—sent to about 14,000 subscribers—and books, the Shalom Center has produced some of the most creative resources and liturgies popular in Jewish social activist circles.

Waskow has not lost his talent for the type of guerilla theater that became popular in the antiwar movement, although now his public demonstrations are deeply Jewish. In 1997 Waskow organized a Tu B'Shvat (the Jewish new year of trees) seder in the redwood forests of California to bring attention to the planned clear-cutting of that treasured natural resource by the Jewish-owned Maxxam Corporation. In 1998 he organized a service for Hoshannah Rabbah (a fall festival that has water as a central symbol) on the banks of the Hudson River in upstate New York, just downstream from a General Electric plant that was dumping PCB chemicals into the river. In April 2004 Waskow revived his Freedom Seder at the Riverside Church in Manhattan, where Dr. King and Rabbi Heschel jointly appeared in 1967. Once again, the date was April 4, the anniversary of King's assassination. With his prophetic temperament, poetic soul, and willingness to challenge institutions, both within and beyond the Jewish community, Waskow is one of the pioneers of Jewish social justice in the American Jewish community.

MAZON

Founded in 1985, MAZON, the Hebrew word for "sustenance," is the only national Jewish organization devoted exclusively to addressing the problem of hunger. One of the ways that MAZON highlights the reality of hunger in the midst of plenty is to encourage Jewish families celebrating weddings, *b'nai/b'not mitzvah,* and other occasions to contribute 3 percent of the cost of the event to MAZON. They urge the hosts to highlight that fact with note cards on each table as a way to raise the consciousness of invited guests. Though a small percentage of grants (under 10 percent) are allocated for overseas hunger relief, the vast majority of MAZON grantees are based in the United States. The idea for MAZON emerged in a conversation between Harold Schulweis, rabbi of one of the leading Conservative congregations in Los Angeles, Valley Beth Shalom, and Leonard Fein, then the editor of *Moment* magazine. Fein floated the idea in the pages of his magazine and soon thereafter was instrumental in setting up the independent organization in Los Angeles.

MAZON's beneficiaries fall into four program categories. The Advocacy/Education/Research program supports local, state, and national anti-hunger coalitions that seek to shape public opinion and influence public policy as it relates to government food-assistance programs. This program includes organizations that are trying to minimize the impact of welfare reform on poor people. The Emergency/Direct Food Assistance program provides support for meal programs for the needy, as well as soup kitchens and meals for frail and elderly people. The Food Bank program supports warehouses that collect foodstuffs for further distribution to feeding programs. Finally, the Multi-Service grant program supports organizations that provide an array of services to foster self-reliance among hungry and low-income people such as job training, case management, medical care, and housing assistance. The vast majority of the beneficiaries of MAZON's grants are poor non-Jews.

Endorsed by more than 800 synagogues from across the denominational spectrum and supported by more than 85,000 individual donors, MAZON currently distributes approximately $3 million each year to some 260 organizations, mostly in grants ranging from $10,000 to $20,000. Since its founding, MAZON has provided more than $30 million in grants to combat hunger. Of all the organizations mentioned in this chapter, MAZON has by far the highest name recognition in the Jewish community and the largest donor base. This can be attributed in part to the fact that, from its inception, MAZON sought and received organizational buy-in from synagogues across the denominational spectrum. Additionally, for a community whose affluence was manifest in increasingly expensive and lavish life cycle celebrations, the self-tax encouraged by MAZON provided an obvious and not so onerous way to bring to the fore the selfless value of *tzedakah* to family and friends during the festivities. Finally, many Jews who might have given philanthropic dollars to general anti-hunger organizations like Oxfam felt good about having a Jewish organizational vehicle as the conduit for their charitable dollars to vulnerable populations.

Tikkun

In the mid-1980s, Michael Lerner began showing up at Jewish conventions and gatherings and telling people that he was going to launch an alternative to *Commentary* magazine to provide a progressive vision of Judaism and contemporary issues. He made good on his promise. *Tikkun* magazine was launched in 1986 as a "quarterly Jewish critique of politics, culture and society." Within a decade of its launch, *Tikkun* could boast a circulation that was on par with *Commentary,* about 20,000. Unlike *Commentary,* however, *Tikkun* never was satisfied with just producing a magazine. It was determined to launch a movement.

Michael Lerner was inspired in his youth by the teachings of Abraham Joshua Heschel. Identifying as a political radical while he studied philosophy at UC Berkeley in the 1960s, Lerner ultimately decided that the liberal and progressive movements were defeating themselves because they were not addressing the ethical and spiritual dimensions of the human experience. He went on to get a second PhD in clinical psychology and founded the Institute for Labor and Mental Health where, as a psychotherapist, he realized that many working-class people were "moving to the right because the liberals didn't seem to understand or address the alienation and meaninglessness fostered by the 'me-firstism' of the market economy." Lerner cites feminism, the civil rights movement, peace and ecological activists, and Christian social justice thinkers as his ideological inspirations. Like Arthur Waskow, Lerner received private ordination from Rabbi Zalman Schachter-Shalomi, and now, in addition to his work with *Tikkun,* he serves as the rabbi of a congregation in the San Francisco Bay area.[5]

It is clear that Lerner has succeeded in tapping into some of the alienation of a certain segment of American Jewry. In his inaugural editorial, Lerner criticized the American Jewish community as a microcosm of American society—overly secular, assimilationist, and obsessed with wealth. The pages of the magazine have attracted some of the most notable thinkers, both within and beyond the Jewish community, offering a vision for a society committed to spirituality, ecological sensitivity, justice for the oppressed people of the world, and a just and lasting settlement to the Middle East conflict. The attraction of *Tikkun's* alternative vision for the Jewish community has been most obvious in the periodic conferences it has sponsored. *Tikkun's* largest gathering was a Summit on Politics, Spirituality, Ethics and Meaning held in Washington, D.C., in April 1996 that attracted 1,800 people. But numbers do not tell the whole story. The Jews drawn to *Tikkun* gatherings are mostly those who do not feel that the organized Jewish community represents them. Michael Lerner has tapped into a constituency of marginally affiliated, mostly younger American Jews who have few other outlets for their political aspirations under Jewish auspices.

In January 2002 *Tikkun* announced the creation of the *Tikkun* Community, which would undertake education, engage in coalitions, and participate in national campaigns on public policy issues. Michael Lerner always wanted *Tikkun* to be more than just a journal of opinion, and the *Tikkun* Community gave that vision an organizational rubric and actively sought members. Lerner used the tragedy of September 11, 2001, as the springboard for this new stage of his vision. The five objectives of the *Tikkun* Community were: interdependence and ecological sanity; making economic and social institutions more socially responsible; support for struggles for social justice and peace; peace and justice in Israel and Palestine; and a growing spiritual consciousness in the world. While most of the individuals who agreed to serve on the national advisory board were Jewish religious and communal leaders, they did include some notables from beyond the Jewish community, like African-American writer and activist Cornel West, filmmaker Michael Moore, and new-age thinker and writer Ken Wilber.[6]

In 2003 the *Tikkun* Community hosted a Teach-In to Congress for Middle East Peace, hoping to challenge AIPAC's status as the defining voice of the Jewish community on Israel-related matters. Among the speakers at the conference were: Ohio Congressman Dennis Kucinich, who, at the time, was seeking the Democratic nomination for the U.S. presidency; Susannah Heschel, daughter of Abraham Joshua Heschel and herself a respected scholar/activist for progressive causes; and Dr.

Ziad Asali, president of the American-Arab Anti-Discrimination Committee. Addressing the "road map," which stood as America's approach to Middle East peace at the time, the conference offered an alternative plan that included: (1) a return by Israel of all territories occupied in the 1967 war, with minor adjustments; (2) a viable Palestinian state in the West Bank and Gaza Strip; and (3) a commitment to end extremism and the teaching of hatred by both sides in the conflict. Lerner reported after the conference that many congressional staffers indicated that their bosses, elected members of Congress, would be sympathetic with the content of the *Tikkun* peace plan, though they would likely stop short of signing onto it for fear of criticism from the powerful AIPAC and pro-Ariel Sharon lobbies.[7]

Michael Lerner and *Tikkun* are both magnets for many alienated Jews and lightning rods for criticism. The criticism is mostly directed at *Tikkun*'s persistent critique of Israeli human rights abuses and settlement policy. It also needs to be noted that the very eclecticism of the magazine—that seems to serve it well as a magazine—may be far less suitable for its organizing strategies, which have had several false starts. Still, *Tikkun* has clearly established itself as the journal of record for progressive Jewish social justice activists and a beacon to Jews hungering for an integration of Judaism, progressive politics, and spirituality.

An Emerging Culture of Service

To fully appreciate the extent to which American Jews have sought avenues to reach out beyond their own community to help heal the world, one must look at the growing phenomenon of community service. The first organization to offer such an opportunity was the American Jewish Society for Service (AJSS). Established in 1950, AJSS places Jewish high school students in disadvantaged American communities each summer to work on some kind of construction project that will improve the quality of life for that community. In 1969 the New Jersey region of the National Federation of Temple Youth (NFTY), Reform Judaism's youth movement, started a summer Urban Mitzvah Corps for high school students in the New Brunswick area, also engaging them in community service to help an underprivileged neighborhood. Several other regions of NFTY have recently replicated this program.

But community service became a much more prominent feature of

American Jewish life in the 1990s. The reason is clear. Ethnic groups in America do best when a behavior they want to encourage can be tied to a trend in the larger society. In 1990 the Clinton administration pushed through Congress the National and Community Service Act to promote a new culture of service in America, akin to the ethic created by John Kennedy's Peace Corps and Vista programs in the 1960s. With the passage of the bill in 1990, there emerged a host of governmental and nongovernmental agencies that encouraged, provided seed funding for, and produced educational materials to support the growth of community service. High schools across the country began to make a certain number of hours of service a prerequisite for graduation. A study by Independent Sector showed that by the mid-1990s, youth service had reached its highest level in five decades, with close to 70 percent of high school students reporting participation in some form of community service. The study also found that patterns of service established during the teen years carried through to the adult years in terms of high levels of civic engagement.

There was little question that Jews were highly, if not disproportionately, represented in the practice of community service. But whereas a previous generation might have been satisfied with large numbers of Jews engaging in "good works," the ethic of the Jewish community had changed. It was now important to understand the Judaic roots of the activity, whether it was advocacy for a piece of social justice legislation or working in a soup kitchen. In 1994 PANIM published a curriculum entitled *Jewish Civics: A Tikkun Olam/World Repair Manual,* designed to provide just such a resource in the Jewish community. PANIM then launched its Jewish Civics Initiative, a yearlong Judaically framed community service and learning program that, in ten years, grew to more than twenty communities.[8]

But this was only the tip of the iceberg. American Jewish World Service (AJWS), which was established in 1985 primarily as a conduit for philanthropy from the Jewish community to the third world, began to grow its volunteer service programs in the mid-1990s. It launched a Jewish Volunteer Corps for adults prepared to spend up to a year in a third world country, lending expertise and guidance. Soon thereafter AJWS launched shorter-term overseas programs for college youth through an International Jewish College Corps, an Alternative Spring Break program, and a delegations program for Jewish institutions wanting to put together service missions of varying size and for different ages. In the Jewish social justice universe, no organization has grown as rapidly as AJWS. From 1998 to 2006 its budget grew from $2 million to $21 million. Much of that growth can be attributed to the fact that AJWS became a vehicle for Jewish contributions for disaster relief around the world—the December 2004 tsunami in southeast Asia alone added 40,000 donors to the AJWS previous donor base of 10,000. Even more significant has been the dynamic leadership of Ruth Messinger, who took the helm of the organization in 1998 after serving as Manhattan borough president and losing a bid to become mayor of New York City. During her tenure at AJWS, Messinger emerged as the single most recognized face of Jewish social justice in the Jewish and general community. It was also due to Messinger's efforts that the Jewish community took leadership on the Save Darfur: Rally to End Genocide in Washington, D.C., in April 2006.

During the 1990s, national Hillel, serving Jewish students on college campuses, launched a *Tzedek* Hillel program, engaging college students in meaningful community service in the areas surrounding their universities. In 1998 Rabbi David Rosenn launched Avodah: The Jewish Service Corps, modeled after the Jesuit Volunteer Corps, which placed Catholic college graduates in houses in urban areas around the country to live, volunteer, and explore their faith for a year. Avodah, committed to the integration of Judaism and social activism, opened its first house in New York and by 2004 had two houses in Washington, D.C., with plans to expand to Chicago and other cities in the future.

Perhaps the most ambitious service undertaking in the Jewish community to date is the National Jewish Coalition for Literacy (NJCL), launched in 1997 by the ever-creative Leonard Fein. NJCL was designed to mobilize volunteer tutors from the Jewish community to serve as reading partners for at-risk children in grades K–3. NJCL parlayed the Jews' love of books and the written word into a major effort to fight illiteracy in America. Since its launch, NJCL has spread to fifty communities and boasts approximately 12,000 weekly volunteers, ranging in age from fifteen to ninety.[9] The plethora of Jewish organizations focusing increasingly on getting Jews engaged in volunteer service led to the founding of the Jewish Coalition for Service (JCS) in 2001. JCS is both an umbrella group for those organizations sponsoring service opportunities that run for a week or more and an agency whose direct mission is to expand such opportunities for the Jewish community across the country. As of 2004, it counted fifty programs and organizations as affiliates.

It is interesting that about thirty-five out of the fifty affiliates of the NJCL are housed in the community relations councils of local Jewish federations. It would not have been the kind of activity that these agencies would have sponsored twenty years earlier. In fact, directors of these agencies around the country report that, with the exception of efforts related to Israel advocacy, most of the social justice energy in their communities is tapped through volunteer service efforts, much of which is sponsored by local synagogues, rather than through centralized efforts around political advocacy. Mitzvah days have become extremely popular in synagogues, providing a time when whole families can come out on a Sunday and engage in several hours of volunteer work that both helps someone or some agency and provides immediate gratification for the volunteer. There has also been a significant increase in synagogue-based programs that place people in soup kitchens, food pantries, literacy work, and Habitat for Humanity-like housing projects and that engage them in some form of environmental activism.

One of the more ambitious synagogue-based social action projects that illustrates how large numbers of Jews can be galvanized around a cause that transcends group self-interest is a program called Out of the Cold, based in Toronto. The program started in the late 1980s when some nuns began to provide food and lodging to the homeless at several downtown Catholic churches. As the numbers of people served began to grow, Jews, some of whom were members of Holy Blossom Temple (Reform), were among those who volunteered to keep the program going. It wasn't long before these very volunteers began to lobby their temple to start a similar program. Although there were concerns expressed from the neighbors as well as from constituencies within the congregation about property values, bad elements doing damage to the building, health concerns, and potential violence, there was ample evidence from the churches already involved in the program that precautions could be taken to minimize such risks. After the board of Holy Blossom Temple approved the program in 1994, it took off. More than a decade into the experiment, Holy Blossom sponsors a shelter in its building one day per week for the twenty-two weeks of the winter, feeding about 100 people and sleeping about fifty on mattresses in the social hall and foyer area.

What is most significant about this undertaking is how it affected the congregation. Organizers of Out of the Cold at Holy Blossom count about 100 volunteers per week and 450 volunteers overall who do everything from shopping for food, to meal preparation, to staying overnight to staff the facility. Approximately $35,000 is raised each year to underwrite the costs of the program. Both the rabbi at that time, Dov Marmur, and his predecessor, rabbi emeritus Gunther Plaut, spoke in favor of the program to the board and were regular attendees on shelter nights, sharing meals with the homeless and often offering some public words to those who gather so as to provide a spiritual framework to the experience for the homeless as well as for the volunteers. Many teens in the community continue to volunteer on shelter nights, finding in the activity a tangible way to connect to the ethical mission of the congregation. Adult volunteers express pride that their congregation lives out the lofty ideals of the Jewish prophetic tradition. Since Holy Blossom enlisted in the Out of the Cold program, four other Toronto area synagogues have joined the twenty-five churches in the program.[10]

Toronto is not alone in such a social action undertaking, although it may be the largest such Jewish-sponsored homeless program in terms of people served and volunteers in North America. Congregations like Rodeph Sholom (Reform) in Manhattan and Germantown Jewish Centre (Conservative) in Philadelphia similarly open their doors to allow homeless people to sleep during cold winter nights. Other congregations, like B'nai Jeshurun (Conservative) in New York City, Central Reform Congregation (Reform) in St. Louis, Mishkan Shalom (Reconstructionist) in Philadelphia, and IKAR (Independent) in Los Angeles, have acquired reputations for their cutting-edge social action programming. All have attracted unaffiliated Jews, drawn by the social justice orientation that is held up as a central tenet of Jewish communal life by the respective rabbis.

Another example of how ready American Jews are to be engaged in hands-on social justice work can be found at a modest-sized Reform temple in New Jersey. Rabbi Joel Soffin of Temple Shalom in Succasunna, New Jersey, has time and again shown an ability to mobilize large numbers of congregants for social justice projects. He has led groups of fifteen to twenty congregants on trips to Argentina, Ukraine, Ethiopia, and El Salvador over the past several years. With each trip, he has launched a supplementary project that has mobilized large numbers of members from his congregation of 500 families. For El Salvador, he invited families to buy chickens at $5 each to help Salvadorans feed their families. Following a trip to Ethiopia, he committed to raising one million quarters after he found out that a quarter was enough to pay for a meal in Ethiopia. Soffin was also the impetus behind an Adult Mitzvah Corps program sponsored by the Union of Reform Judaism, which brings twenty-five to forty adults and teens each summer on a weeklong house "blitz build" in conjunction with Habitat for Humanity. Woven into the week is the opportunity for Jewish learning and worship. Soffin observes that Jews today are far less interested in politics than they are in hands-on ways to bring aid and comfort directly to those in need.[11]

Numerous congregations of every denomination across the country have found ways of connecting with underprivileged populations to provide support and aid. Rabbi David Saperstein, who as the head of the Reform movement's Religious Action Center is in regular contact with congregations throughout the country (within and beyond the Reform movement), believes that social action activity on the congregational level is many times greater today than it was in the 1960s, which is the time that most people think of as the golden age of Jewish social justice.[12] One indication of the extent to which social justice has become a central value of Jewish education is that some kind of *tikkun olam* (world repair) activity is increasingly becoming an expectation required of bar and bat mitzvah teens by their congregations prior to their ceremonies. Irving Greenberg, a leading thinker and activist in the American Jewish community and an Orthodox rabbi, has commented on the emerging culture of service in the Jewish world by saying: "The time has come to articulate the obligation for personal service to others as a fundamental obligation of a human being, according to Judaism.... Service must be upheld as a norm expected of Jews."[13]

○
——
○

Several interrelated reasons can be cited for the emergence of these many new Jewish organizations and so much new activity committed to some form of "repairing the world" within a short period of time. First, the Jewish community, from its origins in America, was one based on voluntarism. In other words, any group of like-minded individuals could begin an organization just as they could start a new synagogue. There was no hierarchy in the community that was required to charter a new organization. All that was required was a critical mass of believers dedicated to the mission of a given organization and a source of funding.

There obviously were enough Jews in America who were passionate about justice work in a Jewish key to support these new endeavors.

Second, the growing affluence of the Jewish community made it easier to start new organizations. More and more Jews with significant resources and/or family foundations were willing to make grants outside of the federation system. In fact, the growth of a universe of new justice-related institutions coincided with the emergence of a trend in which Jewish family foundations were determined to chart their own course in philanthropy instead of giving the lion's share of their "Jewish" gift to the federation campaign. As the trend in philanthropic circles moved away from large, central fundraising and allocation systems, new organizations had a greater chance to identify sources of support. Innovative new organizations in the orbit of Jewish social justice succeeded in finding their share of patrons. Many of these fledgling organizations received significant support from The Nathan Cummings Foundation, which began to operate in 1990. The Jewish Life program of the Cummings Foundation, under the direction of Rabbi Rachel Cowan, became the first stop of most Jewish social justice organizations seeking support. With total Cummings grants in the social justice area ranging from $300,000 to $800,000 per year, an organization could often leverage that grant to attract other foundations and individual donors.

Yet while these factors help us to understand the context that made it easier for new organizations to be formed, it does not fully explain why so much of this new activity was in the realm of justice. For that we must return to the themes of Exodus and Sinai. It is no coincidence that at the very time the organized Jewish community became more focused on matters of communal self-interest in its public agenda, there was an explosion of new energy in the realm of Jewish social justice. It was as if there was a certain threshold of communal energy that felt an obligation to pursue issues of justice, not only as it might relate to the welfare and safety of the Jewish people but as it might relate to a larger circle of humanity, both at home and abroad. This Sinai impulse reasserted itself through the organizations profiled in this chapter and others precisely because it was being denied in the national agencies charged with representing the interests of the organized Jewish community. Fair-minded people could disagree on the wisdom of the organized Jewish community's narrowing its focus so as to expend more energy and resources on the survival needs of the Jewish people, but, in a sense, Jews voted with their feet. The supporters of these organizations combined with those Jews who participate in some form of social action activity in synagogues across the country represent hundreds of thousands of Jews. It is hard to ignore the coincidence of so many new Jewish social justice organizations coming into existence at the very time that the organized Jewish community was turning inward. The Jewish people's Sinai impulse would not be denied.

It needs to be added that Exodus and Sinai were not mutually exclusive choices. Many of the Jews who participated in and contributed to new Jewish social justice organizations and activities were the same Jews who supported the mainstream organizations of Jewish life. One thing that the organized Jewish community did with great skill was to cultivate a philanthropic instinct among Jews. New Jewish organizations would be foolish not to seek out the support of the very Jews who were the pillars of the organized Jewish community. Not only did the engagement of such mainstream supporters confer legitimacy on the new organizations, but the fledgling organizations would soon also learn that it was not so easy to replicate the fundraising success of the mainstream Jewish community among those who were never trained in that organizational culture. Furthermore, Jews who had avoided all affiliations with the organized Jewish community were not so easy to find. Unaffiliated Jews found secular organizations through which they could advance their social justice passions, both as volunteers and as contributors.

Jews had a choice. As an ethnic group, they were sufficiently integrated into the American setting so that if they wanted to engage in organizations with no Jewish sponsorship that worked for human rights, the environment, worker rights, poor families, and so on, they could easily do so. Indeed, tens of thousands of Jews did just that, just as they had done since they first arrived in America. It is worth noting, however, that the leaders of these new Jewish social justice initiatives report that they have had success attracting to their organizations a significant number of people who were, at best, marginally connected to the organized Jewish community. Demographic studies of the Jewish community on both the local and national levels over the past thirty years give evidence of sharp declines in levels of affiliation. While the organized Jewish community's decreasing attention to social justice issues was not the only factor behind the distancing of Jews from the organized Jewish community, it certainly is among the contributing causes. A recent study gave evidence of a trend among younger Jews to reject the parochial tendencies of the organized Jewish community. They are not supportive of the argument that Jews, and by extension, the Jewish community, owe a greater obligation to needy Jews over non-Jews in need. In particular, these younger Jews exhibit much ambivalence over the most potent symbols of contemporary Jewish tribalism—the Holocaust, Israel, and organized Jewry.[14]

It is ironic that the very concerns over Jewish survival and Jewish identity that led to a more narrowly framed Jewish public agenda (the Exodus impulse) may have accelerated the disenchantment of Jews with the organized Jewish community. While to insiders it made sense to focus Jewish communal resources and energies in directions that bore direct benefit to particular Jewish survival concerns, it resulted in a communal profile that was ever less attractive to younger American Jews who were becoming assimilated into American culture. This phenomenon explains the appeal of Jewish organizations that pursued a uniquely social justice agenda. A 2000 study bears out that even as Jews continue to rank at the top of the socioeconomic scale, a trend that almost always predicts more conservative attitudes on social issues, Jews continue to harbor attitudes significantly more liberal than their non-Jewish counterparts on matters like compassion toward the disadvantaged, welfare programs, abortion, and church-state separation.[15]

This trend speaks to the tenacity of the Jewish values ethos that I have identified as the Sinai impulse. Thus it should not be surprising that the Jewish organizations that seek to advance a Sinai agenda report an ability to attract large numbers of Jews who would otherwise have little, if anything, to do with the organized Jewish community. This interplay between younger Jewish activists and the leadership of the organized Jewish community got even more interesting as social justice organizations began to take root in selected communities around the country, a phenomenon that we will explore at greater length in the next chapter.

15

Social Justice Takes Root

In the evolution of the American Jewish community, the 1980s represented a tipping point in the creation of a network of new and innovative national organizations that focused on Jewish social justice or community service. Collectively, the organizations profiled in the previous chapter began to touch the minds and hearts of hundreds of thousands of Jews with the message that social justice was a fundamental part of what it means to be a Jew. But if in the 1980s these national organizations fertilized the field of Jewish social justice, the harvest began in earnest in the 1990s as Jewish social justice activity started to take root in communities across the United States.

This chapter will look at the creation of local Jewish social justice organizations in four communities—Washington, D.C., Los Angeles, Minneapolis, and Boston—drawing from those examples some observations about the changing face of the Jewish community and of Jewish identity. But even though the organizations I shall look at date from the 1990s, the spirit hovering over these efforts goes back to a Jewish radical social reformer born in Chicago almost 100 years earlier.

Saul David Alinsky was born in 1909 to Orthodox Jewish parents, and his early education was in a traditional yeshiva. Alinsky grew up in the ethnic neighborhoods of Chicago where he was part of vicious gang wars between Polish and Jewish teens. At the age of eleven, he was picked up by the police when he and some Jewish friends were beating up a Polish kid in retaliation for a previous attack on one of their Jewish friends by Poles. His mother was so mortified when she came to retrieve Alinsky from the police station that she took him straight to the rabbi. Alinsky told the rabbi what had happened, sure that the wise elder would understand that what was great about America was that Jews were allowed to fight back when attacked. Instead the rabbi looked intently at Alinsky and said, "You think you're a man because you do what everybody does. But I want to tell you something the great Rabbi Hillel said: 'Where there are no men, be thou a man.' I want you to remember it."

Alinsky remembered that lesson for the rest of his life. After earning a doctorate in sociology and criminology at the University of Chicago, he founded the Back of the Yards Neighborhood Council in 1936. Using strategies that he would later implement across the country, Alinsky helped organize the citizens in a deteriorating Irish-Catholic neighborhood on Chicago's southwest side, helping them learn how to pressure city hall to improve their quality of life. In 1939, with funds that he secured from the Marshall Field Foundation, Alinsky founded the Industrial Areas Foundation (IAF), designed to empower average citizens to work on their own behalf to effect positive social change in their own communities. Alinsky moved around the country, organizing African-American employees at Eastman Kodak in Rochester, New York, steelworkers in Pittsburgh, and Chicano farmers in the southwestern United States (where he influenced the work of Cesar Chavez). Today, some thirty years after Alinsky's death, the IAF has fifty-five affiliates functioning in twenty-one states as well as in some foreign countries. Though working under different names that are created by the local affiliates, the organizations share a strategy of mobilizing labor, religious, and community groups to identify local issues of concern and then using their collective "people power" to pressure public officials to respond to those concerns.[1]

Alinsky's organizing model had a profound impact on the Jewish social activism of the 1990s. Alinsky taught that one could best effect social change by mobilizing people in their own communities to act on the issues that most directly affect their quality of life. While the 1980s witnessed the creation of a series of new national Jewish social justice organizations, the 1990s saw a trickle-down of this phenomenon to the local level. Jews were looking for ways to connect with other like-minded Jews to engage in social justice activity in the communities where they lived. As local Jewish federations followed the lead of their national parent bodies, focusing on an Exodus agenda of Israel advocacy, Jewish defense, and communal survival, many Jews were driven by their Sinai impulse to create Jewish ways to meet the needs of vulnerable populations in their midst.

Washington, D.C.

Simon Greer's upbringing on the Upper West Side of Manhattan was a far cry from the upbringing of Saul Alinsky. The child of parents who immigrated to America from England, he attended the upscale, private Ethical Culture Fieldston School in New York City's Riverdale neighborhood. After graduating from Vassar with a degree in American Studies, Simon moved to Poland to work for Solidarity, the union movement from which Lech Walesa emerged to lead Poland from a communist to a democratic state. Impressed by the example of what happens when working people acquire power, Greer returned to the United States to work as a community organizer in South Carolina. After a particularly difficult campaign organizing bus drivers, during which Greer was threatened with arrest, the bus company reversed itself and agreed to meet the workers' demands. Given the culture and history of exploiting black workers in this community, the odds against winning this labor struggle seemed overwhelming. Yet the drivers risked everything to demand what they felt was just. Upon receiving word of the victory, Greer was so surprised that the first image that came to his mind was that of Moses entering the Red Sea. Greer was inspired by the role model of Moses who risked everything, but who nonetheless succeeded in helping the children of Israel escape from their Egyptian oppressors.

When Greer moved to Washington, D.C., in 1997 to take a position with Jobs with Justice, a coalition of labor and religious groups advocating workers' rights around the United States, he was looking for a Jewish context in which he could live out the values that were already part of his secular, professional life. Taking a class on Abraham Joshua Heschel at a local synagogue, he met a rabbi/activist, David Shneyer, who told him of a group that existed in the 1960s and 1970s in Washington called Jews for Urban Justice. Unfortunately, that group disbanded more than twenty years earlier. Determined to fill that vacuum, in 1998 Simon organized a forum at the Hillel of George Washington University that featured several Jewish social justice activists from around the country. To everyone's surprise, about 100 people attended the forum. From that core Greer formed Jews United for Justice (JUFJ), a group committed to creating a progressive Jewish presence on pressing social and economic issues of the day affecting the local community.

The early activities of JUFJ were modest. Many of the twenty-somethings that came to JUFJ were already socially conscious and many had worked on a variety of progressive causes. JUFJ gave them the opportunity to explore what was Jewish about such work. JUFJ sponsored monthly Jewish text study sessions, led by local rabbis who linked the causes that JUFJ was mobilizing around with the ancient teachings of Jewish sages. At one such session, Greer learned the origin of the phrase "If I am not for myself, who will be for me; but if I am only for myself, what am I?"—a phrase that he had heard and used during his South Carolina days but without knowing its source. Finding out that the saying came from the second-century rabbi Hillel reinforced Simon's belief that Judaism could provide inspiration and guidance for social justice engagement. Another early JUFJ event was a Passover seder that featured a presentation by an African-born parking attendant, who was part of an emerging job action for better pay against the garage owners, and a film clip of a speech by Dr. Martin Luther King, Jr. The vast majority of JUFJ members did not attend synagogue regularly. About two-thirds were not affiliated with any Jewish institution. But JUFJ became a non-religious venue that fed the Jewish hunger of its participants.

JUFJ really got on the map in Washington in the winter of 2000. Progressive Montgomery, an organization in the heavily Jewish suburban Montgomery County, was organizing a living wage campaign. The group was trying to pressure the County Council to guarantee a minimum $10/hour salary for any county employee in the hope that this would, in turn, pressure nonprofit and private employers to similarly raise their wages from the federal minimum of $5.15/hour. One campaign tactic being considered was to publicize the plight of an African-American employee at the Jewish-sponsored Hebrew Home for the Aged. Illustrative of the plight of so many urban poor who cannot sustain themselves and their families at minimum wage, this worker, though working full-time, went "home" every night to a homeless shelter. The Jewish Community Council of Greater Washington, D.C., had initially come out against the living wage campaign, concerned about the impact that it might have on the network of Jewish nonprofits that struggled to keep labor costs down so that they could meet their budgets. In the hope of staving off the bad press about the Hebrew Home employee, the Council agreed to cosponsor with JUFJ a public forum at which four rabbis, representing each of the denominations of Judaism, would give testimony on the ethical teachings of the Jewish tradition that support the concept of a living wage for all workers. This modern *bet-din,* the equivalent of a Jewish legal court usually made up of three rabbis, received further press and attention because of the presence of Dr. Robert Pollin, an economist who was a national expert on living wage and also the son of one of Washington's most prominent Jewish philanthropists, sports entrepreneur Abe Pollin. Soon thereafter, the Jewish Community Council modified its stance and threw its support behind the living wage legislation after ensuring appropriate protections for nonprofit organizations.

While JUFJ can only claim a few hundred dues-paying members, close to 2,000 area Jews are on its mailing list. But even those numbers belie their influence in the community. Starting in 1998 JUFJ sponsored "Labor on the *Bimah,*" a campaign to get synagogues to devote some time on the shabbat of Labor Day weekend to speak about the issue of worker rights. JUFJ helped create a resource booklet filled with background information about the policy issues at stake and Jewish sources that address the way that Judaism expects employers to treat their employees. Some thirty-five local congregations now participate in the program annually, and the booklet was eventually distributed nationally. JUFJ also provided a Jewish presence at some work stoppages and strikes, including those of hotel workers, parking attendants, and grocery store workers. On occasion, leaders of JUFJ have sought meetings with the Jewish owners of businesses that are on the other side of labor disputes. Such meetings try to play on the owners' sense of fairness and Jewish ethics to be more forthcoming in their treatment of employees.

JUFJ has attracted a high percentage of young people not previously involved in any kind of organized Jewish activity. Through programs like "Labor on the *Bimah,*" some JUFJ members found themselves having meetings and even speaking at services at local congregations, drawing JUFJ members closer to the organized Jewish community. To bolster

JUFJ's efforts, the Endowment Fund of the Jewish Federation of Greater Washington, D.C., provided $20,000 to the group in 2000 to do education and outreach around Jewish social justice to attract Jews who would otherwise not be involved in the Jewish community.[2]

Occupying a similar niche in the Jewish social justice world of greater Washington, D.C., is Yachad: Jewish Housing and Community Development Corporation, a nonprofit organization founded in 1990. Yachad emerged out of the leadership of a domestic affairs committee of the Jewish Community Council. After the conclusion of a study sponsored by the Council revealed an urgent need for affordable housing and community revitalization in the inner city of Washington, several individuals created an independent organization to provide a Jewish counterpart to the churches and interfaith organizations that were already active on this issue.

Yachad sponsors several major initiatives. Its "Sukkot in April" program matches up volunteers from area synagogues with houses they identify in the inner city that are in need of upgrade and repair. Some twenty-five to thirty area congregations, from Orthodox to Reform, now send more than 500 volunteers on the same day to refurbish the homes of elderly, disabled, and low-income people. Yachad's Tikkun Olam Equity Fund provides seed money for housing and commercial development projects in some of Washington's most destitute neighborhoods. These difficult-to-get first dollars then leverage millions of additional dollars in public and private resources. A recent $20,000 loan from Yachad enabled a church to acquire an abandoned theater. The church then leveraged that loan into over $2 million in local and federal dollars for acquisition and renovation. Motivating this activity is the recognition that, in the inner city, churches stand at the very center of the residential community and are able to stimulate positive social networks and economic development in ways that outside agencies cannot.

Yachad's Faith to Faith Community Development Program goes even beyond loan dollars. By pairing a church community with a local synagogue, Yachad has been able to bring the pro bono expertise of Jewish architects, attorneys, bankers, contractors, and real estate agents into lower-income communities that can rarely afford such talent. Yachad's first Faith to Faith partnership involved Tifereth Israel, a D.C.-based Conservative synagogue, and Emory United Methodist Church. Since the launch of the partnership in 1998, the church has been able to renovate its parsonage into a community center and transitional housing for two families, buy and renovate a single-family house in the neighborhood, purchase and operate a day care establishment for use by many of its young families, and purchase and renovate an abandoned eight-to-twelve-unit apartment building. In all of these efforts, the members of Tifereth Israel allied with the members of Emory United, forging relationships and friendships across religious, racial, and economic divides that would never have otherwise happened.

One of Yachad's founders was Martin Blank, who works professionally in the field of community education, is active with the Jewish Community Council, and is a member of a local Conservative congregation. He recalls how Yachad overcame initial antipathy on the part of the local federation, which expressed concern at the organization's founding about having yet another Jewish organization compete for the financial resources of the local Jewish community. Yet as Yachad built closer and closer ties with congregations in the area, it came to be accepted not only as part of the Jewish landscape of the community, but also as a valuable addition to it. For the founders and many of the early pioneers of Yachad, getting the Jewish community to be at the forefront of a local issue that affected the non-Jewish community was essential. Yachad clearly has accomplished that. In addition, for many, participation in Yachad activities became a significant, if not a primary mode of identifying as Jews.[3]

Los Angeles, California

On the other side of the country, a similar niche was filled by a new organization called the Progressive Jewish Alliance (PJA). PJA emerged as a result of the controversial closure of the Los Angeles chapter of the American Jewish Congress. Historically, AJCongress had been the most liberal of the three major Jewish national defense agencies. In the 1990s, however, fiscal woes and an ideological shift to a more hawkish position on Israel in the New York-based national office created tensions with some chapters around the country.

The closing of the Los Angeles chapter of the American Jewish Congress in 1999 was a major Jewish news story. It threw fuel on a long-simmering fire that was both geographic and ideological. After metropolitan New York, the Los Angeles metropolitan area has the second largest concentration of Jews in the country. Even as the younger community developed a host of impressive Jewish institutions, such as the Simon Wiesenthal Center and the University of Judaism, it continued to play second fiddle to New York, which housed the vast majority of the national headquarters of Jewish life. The leadership of the Los Angeles AJCongress chapter was not prepared to fold its tent and go away quietly simply because New York said so. More significantly, the politics of the California group was decidedly left of that of the national office. Almost immediately upon the closing of the Los Angeles office, the chairperson of the now-disbanded board, Patsy Ostroy, announced the formation of the PJA with an agenda that would include economic justice, full inclusion of women, gays, and lesbians into the Jewish community, and support for a two-state solution to the Israeli-Palestinian conflict. Local rabbi Allen Freehling declared that the new organization would be true to the legacy of AJCongress founder, Rabbi Stephen Wise, advancing a vision of prophetic Judaism in the local Jewish community.[4]

Within a year of PJA's founding, enough local support was generated to enable the organization to hire Daniel Sokatch as its full-time director. A Jewish attorney from Boston in his early thirties who had spent a year in rabbinical school, Sokatch set about creating an organization quite different from the defense agency model of the AJCongress. PJA was going to be a grassroots social justice organization, engaging Jews in issues that would make a difference to at-risk populations in the local community. Furthermore, the work would be grounded in the teachings of Judaism.

Because members of PJA have a wide range of interests, the agenda of the organization is divided among several working groups. One group addresses issues of peaceful coexistence in the Middle East and the creation of a pluralistic and democratic state of Israel. Another working group focuses its energies on the civil rights infringements of the Patriot Act. PJA has made a mark on both the Jewish and the general community through more locally oriented projects like the Jewish Community Justice Project (JCJP). JCJP is the nation's first Jewish "restorative justice" project, and it was noteworthy enough to receive front-page coverage in the Sunday *Los Angeles Times* (June 20, 2004). In cooperation with the local judicial system, JCJP brings together nonviolent juvenile offenders and the victims of their crimes for mediation in lieu of incarceration. Using a team of mediators trained from the ranks of PJA members, offenders are brought close to the scene of their crime, admit their guilt, and come face to face with the victim of their crime. The result of the mediation is an agreed-upon act of restitution that might be monetary or might be in the form of compensatory service to the community. The program's goal is to keep offenders from entering the prison system, an experience that often leads to a downward spiral that practically assures repeat offenses. The program also weaves in the Jewish teachings of *teshuva,* repentance, and the belief that by treating the offender with respect, the juvenile is more likely to express remorse over his or her actions and take full advantage of the second chance that JCJP provides.

To date, PJA's signature project is its "No *Shvitz*" campaign, *shvitz* being the Yiddish word for "sweat." This campaign to stop the abysmal conditions and low pay of garment factories in the Los Angeles area actually predated PJA. Several Jewish organizations, including the soon-to-be disbanded Pacific Southwest office of the AJCongress, created the Los Angeles Jewish Commission on Sweatshops. The commission documented the growth of the garment industry in southern California, its resistance to unionization, and the resulting low pay and noncompliance with federal labor, health, and safety laws on the books. In its plan of action, published in January 1999, the commission committed to ongoing monitoring of the situation, a campaign of public education, and the creation of a broad interfaith effort to pressure the industry to upgrade pay and working conditions.

The commission's 1999 report dovetailed with the founding of PJA, and it was the PJA that ran with the initiative. It had all the elements that would make other organizing efforts attractive to newly created Jewish social justice organizations in the 1990s. There were Jewish ties to the issue. At the turn of the twentieth century in New York, the workers in the garment sweatshops were immigrant Jews. Now, 100 years later, Jews owned many of the factories, and the workers were mostly Latino and Asian. In 2002, PJA released an original booklet called *No Shvitz: Your One-Stop Guide to Fighting Sweatshops.* Designed for high school and college students, the booklet included the history of sweatshops, Jewish teachings that forbade the exploitation of workers, an expose on the extent of current abuses in the industry, and tips on how to organize citizen actions to help put an end to the practice. Both the attractive layout and the irreverent style made the book a big hit throughout the community. It was reviewed and widely covered in press reports from Spanish language papers, to union magazines, to the hip national Jewish magazine *Heeb*, which caters to a young Jewish audience. Indicative of the appeal of *No Shvitz*, Jewish students at UCLA organized their own PJA chapter. Both the college PJA chapter and high school groups throughout the area became mobilized around the sweatshop issue.

The campaign resulted in more than just good publicity. PJA was instrumental in the creation of a Garment Worker Center in downtown Los Angeles where the largely immigrant and poorly educated workers in the garment industry could go for free legal advice, counseling, and assistance in filing worker complaints against their employers. PJA also pressured the Los Angeles Unified School District to pass a procurement ordinance to ensure that all purchases of uniforms by schools had to be certified "sweat-free," meaning that the factories that produced the products had to meet federal standards on hours, conditions, and benefits.

In the first years after its founding, PJA met some resistance from leaders in the organized Jewish community who were nervous about a progressive organization whose agenda was somewhat at odds with that of the mainstream community. Over time, however, the PJA found a niche and earned the respect of former detractors. Of its 2,000 members, some 30 to 40 percent are young Jews in their twenties who had little if anything to do with the Jewish community prior to their PJA affiliation. By the year 2004, PJA could boast a budget of $600,000 and six staff people. In 2005 it opened a northern California office in the San Francisco Bay Area.

Ironically, PJA grew rapidly in its first few years, even as the local community relations office (JCRC), funded by the Jewish federation, dismissed its executive director and downsized its staff. Signaling PJA's growing acceptance, executive director Dan Sokatch is now part of a monthly gathering of Jewish agency executives in Los Angeles, and in 2002 the national Jewish paper, *Forward,* named Sokatch as one of the fifty most influential Jews in the country. Of equal note is the fact that many of the young Jews who were drawn to PJA became inspired by its emphasis on the teachings of the Jewish tradition that call Jews to social activism. Also worth noting is that many PJA members later joined a new congregation called IKAR, headed by Rabbi Sharon Brous, which emphasizes the relationship between Judaism and social justice.[5]

Minneapolis/St. Paul, Minnesota

Lest it be thought that the kind of Jewish social justice activity we have been exploring is restricted to large urban areas, it is instructive to look at the experience of the Twin Cities in Minnesota and the work of Jewish Community Action (JCA). The creation of JCA was spearheaded in 1995 by Frank Hornstein and Rachel Breen. Rachel was a native of Minneapolis who had spent the early years of her career working for a public interest group called Citizen Action in both Washington, D.C., and Seattle. Moving to New York, she got a job as a program officer with the Jewish Fund for Justice, where she noted that many interfaith coalitions around the country working on social justice issues lacked a Jewish presence. Such groups were not always sensitive to Jewish concerns. Many started out meetings with a prayer invoking Jesus or held meetings and demonstrations on the Jewish Sabbath. Still, she believed that those issues could be overcome if Jews got involved and were committed to the larger objectives of such coalitions. When she moved back to Minneapolis in her early thirties, Breen provided leadership to create just such a Jewish social justice organization.

Frank Hornstein was a Jewish activist who was working in the Twin Cities, first with Clean Water Action, an environmental organization, and later with Smart Growth, a group dedicated to responsible land use and growth in communities. Over several years, Hornstein was also struck by the absence of a Jewish presence at meetings and in coalitions devoted to the issues on which he was working. At the same time, he saw virtually every other faith community and civic constituency well represented. Both Hornstein and Breen had some familiarity with the Jewish Council for Urban Affairs in Chicago and they believed that such a model could be replicated in the Twin Cities. With an initial grant from a local foundation, Hornstein took part-time professional responsibility to lead Jewish Community Action.

JCA's agenda is divided into several areas, including affordable housing, community reinvestment, gun violence prevention, immigrant rights, and racial justice. The Affordable Housing Working Group (AHWG) works to build interracial and interfaith partnerships in order to promote the preservation and production of affordable housing. The AHWG successfully maintained the affordability of a development called Oak Grove Towers at a time when private development might have displaced thousands of residents, worked with pastors and community members in North Minneapolis to organize several events aimed at preserving affordable housing on the north side of the city, and coordinated an affordable housing conference attended by more than 150 people.

In St. Paul's Highland Park, the AHWG helped create GIFT, an interfaith affordable housing advocacy group, which won a commitment from the City Council to create 200 more affordable units. In coalition with other faith-based groups, JCA worked to create a county-wide affordable housing trust fund and to make $50 million of new money available for affordable housing in Minnesota.

The Community Reinvestment Working Group (CRWG) seeks to involve Jewish institutions, organizations, and individuals in investment in community-development financial institutions to promote the economic viability of urban communities. The CRWG, which has modeled its program on that developed by the Philadelphia-based Shefa Fund, has met with individuals and congregational committees to explain community reinvestment. Their first major success was a local Reform temple's (Temple Israel) investment of $25,000 in the Wendell Phillips Community Credit Union, a nonprofit, community-controlled financial institution.

In its other working groups JCA has worked in community coalitions to make handgun acquisition more restrictive and has sought to insure that immigrants are accorded their full civil liberties and receive appropriate public benefits when needed. It sponsors interfaith and interracial Passover seder celebrations and an ongoing Women's Jewish-Muslim dialogue group. On a regular basis, JCA sponsors *Tzedek* Institutes designed to teach Jews about the relationship between the Jewish tradition and social justice. These community-wide educational programs have been a key vehicle to attracting new and often unaffiliated Jews to JCA and its work.

As is the case with their counterpart organizations in Washington and Los Angeles, the mission statement of JCA speaks directly of the desire to honor the "ethical, religious, and cultural roots of Judaism's commitment to social justice." An additional parallel to sister organizations around the country was that the early years of JCA were characterized by an ambivalent relationship with the organized Jewish community. The local federation-funded community relations agency (JCRC) perceived JCA as too radical and too closely aligned with left-leaning organizations with which the Jewish community did not always see eye to eye. At the same time, JCA proved its effectiveness at drawing in Jews who otherwise would never be associated with the Jewish community. Trying to capitalize on JCA's appeal to the unaffiliated, the Minneapolis Jewish federation's endowment fund made a grant to JCA to run social justice skills training at area synagogues.

After founder Frank Hornstein left JCA in 2000 to make a successful bid for statewide elective office, he was succeeded by Vic Rosenthal. Previously drawn into the work of JCA as a volunteer, Rosenthal represents a fairly typical profile of the kind of Jew that JCA and its counterparts attract. Born in Yonkers, New York, Rosenthal's parents arranged for him to be tutored and celebrate a bar mitzvah at a neighborhood Orthodox synagogue. At the same time, his parents had little commitment to Jewish life, and Rosenthal felt little connection to his Jewish identity. When he moved to Minneapolis for a job, Rosenthal joined a synagogue primarily to provide his children with a place for rudimentary Jewish education and the obligatory bar mitzvah. JCA, however, tapped into a passion he had for social justice, and the Jewish framing of the work made the organization all the more intriguing for someone who, at mid-life, had so little knowledge of the religious tradition of which he was a part. Soon after Rosenthal took the helm of JCA, he became more involved in his synagogue, joined its board of directors, and also agreed to chair a committee at the local Jewish Community Center. The combination of social justice activities in collaboration with non-Jewish groups and Jewish study had worked its magic.[6]

Boston, Massachusetts

However impressive the grassroots efforts in Washington, D.C., Los Angeles, and the Twin Cities might be, they pale in comparison to what has taken place in Boston over the past fifteen years. To a large extent, the comparison is not totally fair. Unlike the profiles of the new start-up organizations in these other cities, the energy for social justice in Boston came from the organized Jewish community. In 1987, when Barry Shrage took the helm of the Boston Jewish federation, known as the Combined Jewish Philanthropies (CJP), he set out to create a different model for a Jewish community federation. A traditionally observant Jew, as well as a skilled communal professional who had previously worked at the highly regarded federation in Cleveland, Shrage hammered home the theme of a community of *Torah* (learning), *chesed* (acts of kindness), and *tzedek* (justice). At a time when his counterparts and the national federation system continued to be focused on a defense/survival agenda centering on the security of the state of Israel, Shrage sought to inspire the Jews of Boston with a positive vision for what Jewish life should be all about. Shrage's vision was given a considerable boost from the dynamic leadership of Rabbi David Gordis, the new president of the Boston Hebrew College. Soon Boston enjoyed a renaissance in Jewish learning through an adult Jewish education initiative called Meah, the revival of the Boston Hebrew College, and an explosive growth in Jewish day schools. Just when community relations agencies around the country were having their budgets squeezed and staff reduced, the Boston Jewish Community Relations Council grew to be the model JCRC in the country under the dynamic leadership of Nancy Kaufman.

Barry Shrage met Nancy Kaufman when she was working on a wide range of housing and welfare issues in the administration of Governor Michael Dukakis of Massachusetts. Nancy grew up in a Conservative synagogue in Brookline, Massachusetts, and is a self-described "child of the '60s." Active in the antiwar movement, she got a master's degree in community organizing and had her first professional successes doing community organizing for social change in several blue-collar suburbs north of Boston. During her tenure in state government, she and Kitty Dukakis, the Jewish wife of the governor, would often comment on how Catholic, Protestant, and other ethnic groups would be involved in the issues affecting the quality of life in the state (day care, mental health, housing, and education, for example), but how Jewish groups were almost never at the table for such discussions. Jewish groups would show up when there was an issue like hate crimes or religion in schools that directly affected the Jewish community. When Dukakis lost in his race for the White House in 1988, Kaufman became intrigued with the possibility of bringing her community organizing skills to the Jewish community. In the hiring process she did not mince any words. Her goal was to reengage the Jewish community in a social justice agenda. What happened in the ensuing decade in Boston was largely a result of the alignment of Nancy's vision with that set forth by Barry Shrage at the CJP, the umbrella that funds the JCRC.[7]

The Boston JCRC features many of the programs that are common to its counterparts across the country. It is active on Israel advocacy, providing support to the many college campuses in the areas that are experiencing heightened tensions during the second intifada. It sponsors a very active partnership with an adopted sister city, Dnepropetrovsk in Ukraine, sending regular delegations of Boston-area Jews to help that city's struggling Jewish community. The JCRC also lobbies the state legislature to help safeguard the grants that provide significant underwriting to communal agencies like the Jewish Family and Children's Service, Jewish Vocational Service, and the Hebrew Rehabilitation Center for the Aged.

What sets the Boston JCRC apart from its counterparts, however, is its extensive commitment to social justice organizing in the local community. It was the first community in the country to sign on to the effort of the National Jewish Coalition for Literacy (NJCL) to get Jews to engage in tutoring relationships with inner-city children in 1996. Today it continues to be one of the flagship communities for the NJCL in terms of number of volunteer tutors. In 1997, with a grant from the Nathan Cummings Foundation, the JCRC launched a new initiative called *Tikkun Ha'Ir* (repair of the city), the primary aim of which was the creation of sustainable partnerships between synagogues and urban community-based organizations and churches. The program's founders also hoped while training congregational laypeople and staff to make social justice more central to synagogue life. Within a few years, five area congregations joined the Greater Boston Interfaith Organization (GBIO), the local affiliate of the Saul Alinsky-inspired Industrial Areas Foundation (IAF). No community in the country had such a large Jewish presence in its respective local IAF effort. Not only did this partnership represent a significant commitment of money by these congregations, but the organizing strategy was one that engaged hundreds of synagogue members in intense, one-on-one conversations about the plight of at-risk populations in the greater Boston area.

Temple Israel, a large Reform temple located in Boston, was the pioneer in this effort, joining a coalition of groups trying to help raise the poverty-level wages of janitors in the city. Rabbi Jonah Pesner devoted a High Holy Day sermon to the subject in 2002 and then invited janitors to come to an event during the festival of Sukkot that same year to speak about their plight to members of the congregation. The involvement of a synagogue in a mobilization that primarily benefited immigrant, non-Jewish workers was notable enough to draw comment from the *New*

York Times in its coverage of the issue.[8] Another suburban congregation, Temple Beth Zion, which had a contract with one of the janitorial companies that was a target of the job action, soon also became involved in the issue. Soon thereafter, with the encouragement of the JCRC and a member of Temple Israel who also served in a leadership capacity with GBIO, seven synagogues plus the JCRC—as well as several independent Jewish groups—joined GBIO.[9]

Each of the congregations that participated in these mobilizations has its own story, but it is fair to say that each experienced unprecedented passion and the involvement of far more Jews in a hands-on social justice project than ever before. Building on this enthusiasm, the JCRC became a catalyst for three new congregations to fund a staff person who would specifically work within those congregations to build skills and mobilize support for ongoing local social justice organizing. In addition, in 2002, the JCRC began to sponsor an annual *Tzedek* Institute to bring together all of the Jews who were being energized around social justice activity, raise their skill level, and create additional momentum for the local efforts. An extension of the JCRC's commitment to social justice is serving as the Jewish partner to a state-wide One Family Campaign. This campaign pairs a synagogue with one specific homeless shelter, providing the opportunity for members to do everything from tutoring children in the shelter, to helping specific families transition from the shelter to permanent housing, to political advocacy on public policy issues affecting the state's homeless population.

The Boston JCRC staff estimates that their social justice efforts over the past ten years have touched close to 10,000 Jews, far surpassing the numbers of Jews engaged in Jewish-sponsored social justice activity anywhere else in the country. Breaking new ground in the field of Jewish community relations work has not always been easy. The JCRC has a wide array of program opportunities in both the field of direct service and advocacy. It has sometimes been criticized by more conservative elements of the community for positions it has taken on issues like tax cuts, gay marriage, and its "justice for janitors" campaign. At the same time, the Boston community has so fully engaged the social justice agenda that even a Republican who is a large contributor to AIPAC has come forward to provide major funding for the JCRC literacy effort, a prime example of how the Exodus and Sinai agendas are not necessarily mutually exclusive. In addition, the variety of projects sponsored by the JCRC has inspired some major local donors to significantly increase their financial commitments specifically to support the efforts of the community to do more programming in the area of social justice.[10] The budget of the agency jumped from half a million dollars and five staff people in 1990 to $2.5 million in 2004 with a staff of twenty-four, making it the largest JCRC in the country. It speaks to the potential interest of Jews in such engagement and the potential that can be tapped when the mainstream Jewish community endorses such an approach.

Synergies and Networks

While it is true that the grassroots efforts outlined in this chapter emerged a full decade after the creation of the national organizations profiled in Chapter 14, it is impossible to overstate the kind of cross-fertilization and synergy that are now taking place between the respective national and local orbits. The best example of this is the evolving work of the Jewish Fund for Justice.

The Jewish Fund for Justice (JFJ) was founded in 1984 to raise money from American Jews to benefit organizations working for economic and social justice around the country. The moving spirit behind JFJ, and its first board chair, was Si Kahn, a strongly identified Jew who moved to Arkansas in 1965 to work as a volunteer for the Student Nonviolent Coordinating Committee (SNCC). He stayed in Arkansas to work as a grassroots organizer for a host of labor and community groups. Si was the son of Rabbi Ben Kahn, a Conservative rabbi who served as national director of Hillel and later of B'nai Brith, and the nephew of Arnie Aronson, who worked on the staff of the National Community Relations Advisory Council and was one of the founders of the Leadership Conference for Civil Rights. He grew up seeing his father organize ministers in University Park, Pennsylvania, to boycott the barbershop that refused to cut the hair of the first black football players who were recruited to play for Penn State in the 1950s. After moving to Washington, D.C., he heard his uncle Arnie tell stories about his work with civil rights luminaries like A. Phillip Randolph, Roy Wilkins, and Martin Luther King, Jr. In 1982, Si began reaching out to other Jews who believed that it was important for there to be a more explicit Jewish financial investment in social justice efforts around the country, even if the organizations doing the work were not Jewish and Jews were rarely the direct beneficiaries of the work of the grantees. The Jewish Fund for Justice was modeled after the Campaign for Human Development, sponsored by the U.S. Catholic Conference.

One of JFJ's guiding principles is that the plight of the poor in America today recalls the conditions faced by a previous generation of immigrant American Jews living in America's inner cities. Funds raised by JFJ are directed to organizations that combat poverty and improve low-income communities and to education programs that engage Jews in social justice. From a modest start in 1985 of awarding $26,000, by 2003 JFJ had a $2.8 million budget and allocated 84 percent of those funds to programs advancing justice. Most of JFJ's grants support community-based organizing and advocacy on issues ranging from raising wages for the working poor, to creating jobs, to promoting affordable housing and health care.

The Jewish Fund for Justice was led from 1989 to 2005 by Marlene Provizer, a long-time Jewish professional who worked previously on the staff of the American Jewish Committee and the Jewish Council for Public Affairs. Raised in Boston, Provizer attended Conservative synagogue Kehillath Israel in Brookline, Massachusetts, and later continued her Jewish education at the Prozdor program sponsored by the Boston Hebrew College. She remembers being positively influenced by some outstanding young rabbis, but no one had a deeper impact on her than her maternal grandmother, who emigrated from Russia at the turn of the century. Together with her husband, she owned and ran a grocery store in Portsmouth, New Hampshire. Belonging to the sole (Orthodox) synagogue in a very Yankee town, Annie Yoffee modeled a life of *tzedakah* (charitable giving) and of service to others despite their own very modest circumstances. At the University of Chicago, Provizer recalls being impressed by the symbol of courage represented by the Hillel rabbi, Max Ticktin, who was arrested for providing young women with abortion counseling. Her first professional job was in Washington at the Children's Defense Fund in the 1970s, where she got hands-on experience working on policy issues related to poverty and the lingering effects of segregation. It was none other than Arnie Aronson, whom she met in his capacity at the Leadership Conference for Civil Rights, who convinced Provizer that she could make an impact on the domestic agenda of the Jewish community by going to New York to work for the Jewish Council for Public Affairs. It was this move into the orbit of Jewish communal organizations that would eventually bring Provizer to head up the organization started by Arnie Aronson's nephew.[11]

JFJ can take credit for being a catalyst for much of the work in local Jewish social justice organizing. In 1992, JFJ convened a conference for fifty activists from twenty JFJ-sponsored grassroots alliances between Jews and low-income individuals working on local issues like affordable housing, revitalizing neighborhoods, and fighting drugs and crime in the inner city. The conference energized the Jews who were doing the pioneering organizing on this front by allowing them to exchange ideas with like-minded activists from across the country. It also deepened the commitment of JFJ to promote more such activity through incentive grants. Over the next ten years, JFJ provided both financial and technical support to these local efforts and staffed a Jewish social justice network that kept Jewish activists abreast of one another's work and planted seeds for future collaborative efforts. In 2000, JFJ secured a grant from the Ford Foundation to link together the emerging Jewish social justice groups around the country and provide them with some technical assistance in growing these organizations. In 2003 JFJ published a guide for faith-based community organizing (FBCO), designed to encourage American synagogues to adopt this as a strategy that could both advance the Jewish vision of justice and energize the members of congregations.

Contributing to the JFJ-published guide to faith-based community organizing were a handful of rabbis and cantors who had already experienced the power of such tactics. The guide states that, despite Jewish leadership in the labor and civil rights movement, "Today we [Jews] have fewer enduring relationships with people of color, with low-income people, with people of other religions and backgrounds." It observes that many Jews have failed to get involved in key social and economic issues because of a mistaken belief that the highly organized Jewish community was already representing Jews on these issues. Seeing the growing privilege and insularity of the American Jewish community, the guide makes a strong case that faith-based community organizing can serve to strengthen a Jew's sense of purpose and make Judaism relevant to his or her life and community in new ways.[12] JFJ currently has a full-time staff person devoted to growing the network of congregations involved in local coalitions like the Greater Boston Interfaith Organization and to convening national conferences to make synagogue leaders more open to this kind of engagement.

A second example of the national ferment taking place around this new grassroots approach to social justice engagement is the Jewish Organizing Initiative (JOI), a program based in Boston and started by Michael Brown (JOI is not formally affiliated with the JCRC). Brown is a baby boomer who caught the tail end of the civil rights movement when he joined the march from Selma as a teenager. As he struggled with his relationship to Judaism, he became a professional community organizer. In the early 1990s, during a meeting of the National Organizers Alliance, Brown attended a Jewish caucus convened by Si Kahn, the founder of the Jewish Fund for Justice. Kahn said that it was time that the many Jews involved in the organizing world become more publicly open about their Jewishness. It struck a chord with Brown and he created the Jewish Organizing Initiative to blend his twin commitment to organizing and to Judaism. Starting in 1994, JOI began selecting ten to twelve young Jews each year, ages twenty-two to thirty, to move to Boston for a year during which they would receive stipends and engage in intensive training in Judaism, the Jewish community, social justice, and strategic community organizing. JOI is essentially training future leaders for this kind of organizing in the Jewish community.

The Shefa Fund, founded by Jeffrey Dekro in 1988, is a third organization whose programs are being adopted not only by some grassroots and progressive Jewish organizations like Jewish Community Action in Minneapolis, but by more mainstream Jewish organizations as well. Dekro is another child of the 1960s, raised in a committed Jewish family in Kansas City as the child of a Holocaust survivor. As an undergraduate at Brandeis, Dekro became involved with Jewish studies, progressive politics, and antiwar activity. After doing graduate work in Jewish mysticism at the University of Pennsylvania, Dekro got a job as a community organizer in Philadelphia where one of his projects was the creation of a revolving loan fund for religious institutions that needed help during the energy crisis of the early 1980s. Dekro conceived of the Shefa Fund as a *tzedakah* bank for foundations and Jewish contributors, enabling them to direct their dollars to a variety of peace-related and social and economic justice causes.

The Shefa Fund's most innovative project is its Tzedek Economic Development Campaign (TZEDEC). TZEDEC encourages Jewish institutions to invest some of their accumulated wealth in community development financial institutions (CDFIs) that are willing to make loans in low-income neighborhoods where most commercial banks fear to tread. For years, Christian organizations and churches have put sizable assets in such banks. This was not the case with the Jewish community. Through the Shefa Fund's efforts, this practice of investing communal dollars in accordance with social justice values has begun to catch on. Beginning with a breakthrough investment of a half-million dollars by the United Jewish Endowment Fund of Greater Washington Federation in 2000, the TZEDEC fund, now at $5 million, has been the catalyst for more than $17 million of investment in CDFIs, including a sizable portion of the endowment fund of the Union for Reform Judaism. One indicator of how the various Jewish social justice organizations are increasingly networked took place in 2005. Soon after Simon Greer—one of the founders of Washington's Jews United for Justice—succeeded Marlene Provizer as the executive director of the Jewish Fund for Justice, it merged with the Shefa Fund to create the Jewish Funds for Justice.

No survey of Jewish social justice in the last decade of the twentieth century would be complete without mention of the Jewish environmental movement. This is a subject worthy of its own treatment because of the significant number of Jews engaged in some form of environmental activism over the past two decades. Suffice it to say that Jewish environmentalism was a major part of the penetration of Jewish social justice into the grassroots of the American Jewish community in the 1990s. The first of numerous Jewish environmental organizations was Shomrei Adamah in 1988. The largest Jewish environmental group is the Coalition on the Environment and Jewish Life (COEJL), founded in 1993 as an outgrowth of a conference convened by Al Gore, Paul Gorman, and Carl Sagan. Parallel gatherings in collaboration with the U.S. Catholic Conference, The National Council of Churches, and the evangelical church community led to the creation of the National Religious Partnership for the Environment. These groups were formed to mobilize the faith communities of America to a higher level of consciousness about, and concern for, the planet's ecology. COEJL became the Jewish partner in this broad national coalition. While COEJL has its own board of directors and therefore functions with some degree of autonomy, it is a program of the Jewish Council for Public Affairs (JCPA) and is housed in their offices. Endorsed by the Jewish Theological Seminary (Conservative movement), the Religious Action Center (Reform movement), and twenty-six other national Jewish organizations, COEJL quickly became a notable presence on the national Jewish scene. Beginning in 1997 COEJL convened annual leadership conferences, mostly in conjunction with the annual meetings of the JCPA.

COEJL counts some fifty regional affiliates and independent initiatives all across the country. They include groups doing environmental education, action, and advocacy. Synagogues, schools, Jewish community centers, and other local Jewish organizations sponsor a wide range of environmental activities, such as environmental hikes, "Shabbat in the Woods," bike rides, and community clean-ups. Several independent groups and camps sponsor extended experiences in the wilderness that combine appreciation for nature with the teachings of Judaism. Similar to the other grassroots community organizing groups profiled in this chapter, the activists with COEJL are largely younger Jews for whom Jewish environmental activism is a central facet of their Jewish identity. COEJL has also published several books and curricula that connect environmental interest and commitment with Jewish values and classical texts. More than ten years after the creation of COEJL, it is clear that there is an entire Jewish environmental subculture in the country with an energy and dynamism all its own.

Tip O'Neill, the Boston congressman who served for many years as the speaker of the House of Representatives, used to say that "all politics is local." He spoke to the reality that people are most affected by the conditions and circumstances that they come into contact with day to day. The same observation can be made about the way that local Jewish social justice organizing is beginning to permeate the American Jewish community. In some ways, the phenomenon is still in its infancy. Yet there is no mistaking that a new movement is emerging that taps into a longing of American Jews to be engaged in Jewish social justice endeavors. This chapter profiled four communities in which some of the most exciting work is taking place. While similar efforts are taking place in other communities around the country, Jewish social justice organizing remains an experience that has become real for only a small subset of American Jewry. But when we combine the number of Jews who, under Jewish auspices, have engaged in some kind of community service activity, contributed money to help a non-Jew in need somewhere in the world, engaged in some Jewish environmental activism, or gotten involved in a community-based effort to bring about positive social change for people in need, we are describing a very significant sector of the American Jewish community. Indeed, there is substantial evidence that this kind of activity goes to the heart of how a majority of American Jews understand the meaning of their Jewish identity.

It is how American Jews encounter and internalize Sinai.

16

Reconciling Exodus and Sinai

It has been fifty years since Albert Vorspan and Rabbi Eugene Lipman coauthored a book published by the Reform movement called *Justice and Judaism*.[1] The book began with the story of a hypothetical synagogue board meeting at which trustees argued about the appropriateness of using the texts and wisdom of the Jewish tradition to take collective congregational action on a range of contemporary social and political issues. Assuming that the board would affirm such a direction, Lipman and Vorspan provided a book that would be a resource for the pursuit of social justice in a Jewish context.

Much has changed in the years since that book was published, the time horizon of the present volume. Jews have achieved an unprecedented level of socioeconomic success and have entered the top tiers of influence in the fields of business, science, the arts, academia, and public service. The organized Jewish community has succeeded in protecting Jewish interests at home and abroad and has also been a central player in making America a more just and equitable society. At the same time, successful integration has resulted in weakening ties to Judaism, a trend that can be seen in the statistics on intermarriage, in personal religious observance, and in affiliation rates with synagogues and secular Jewish organizations.

In the late nineteenth century, facing the challenge of preserving a traditional lifestyle while wanting to integrate into general European society, Jews heeded the motto coined by the Jewish enlightenment writer Yehuda Leib Gordon: "Be a man [*mencshen*] on the street, and a Jew at home." In other words, manifestations of particular Jewish identity were to be reserved for the private sphere so as not to be a barrier to full social integration. Yet in America, Jews are far more likely to be Jews in the street even when there is little Jewish content in their homes. "Jews in the street" refers to the unabashed way that Jewish organizations are prepared to advance Jewish interests, whether protesting anti-Semitism, lobbying for aid to Israel, or ensuring proper safeguards on church-state separation. But for many Jews who would not hesitate to take a public position on one of these issues, there is little commitment to Jewish learning or observance in the private sphere. In fact, the ever-expanding universe of "secular Jewish agencies" makes it possible for Jews to be formally affiliated with the Jewish community even if they never set foot into a synagogue or light shabbat candles in their homes.

The other major consequence of the successful integration of Jews into America is that the vast majority of Jews no longer need the organized Jewish community. In the 1950s, the sociologist Marshall Sklare conducted a series of landmark studies of a midwestern suburban Jewish community in a city he called Lakeville. He found that patterns of a distinctive Jewish lifestyle, such as keeping kosher and observing the Sabbath, had disappeared within the space of a single generation. At the same time, Jews showed a resistance to full assimilation into the gentile mainstream. The primary nature of their ongoing ethnic solidarity was "associationalism," the commitment to be with other Jews in social environments and through Jewish institutions with which Jews might affiliate.[2] The National Jewish Population Studies of 1990 and 2000 reveal that this willingness to affiliate with Jewish institutions has declined precipitously. At the close of the twentieth century, autonomy and individualism reign supreme, posing an unprecedented challenge to the efforts of the organized Jewish community to cultivate communal solidarity among American Jews. The one bright spot in the picture is the tenacity of Jewish identity. Even as the forms are highly personal and diverse, it seems that many Jews continue to seek out ways to express their Jewishness and use it as a primary way to define who they are and the ways in which they find meaning.[3]

Tribal versus Covenantal Identity

Throughout this book, I have used Exodus and Sinai as metaphors for twin impulses that are at work in Jewish history, Jewish community, and Jewish identity. The Exodus impulse is the tendency that has Jews come together in political and institutional arrangements to support the continuity of the group or "tribe." Forged out of the experience of enslavement in Egypt, the Exodus impulse is attuned to the threats to Jewish survival. In the biblical era, the Exodus impulse led the tribes of Israel to appeal to the prophet Samuel to allow them to form an army and defend the land of Israel against hostile invaders. In the modern era, the Exodus impulse makes it abundantly clear that without a Jewish homeland, the Jews will disappear in a world of competing nationalisms.

In the diaspora, the Exodus impulse gives rise to communal institutions that unite Jews and help Jews take care of one another, whether they live across the street or across the globe. The Exodus impulse is the intuitive sense that Jews have about threats to their group survival. It provides the impetus for Jews to create new organizations to address every new challenge that confronts the Jewish people. Thus, the United Jewish Appeal, the Jewish federation system, Soviet Jewry organizations, and AIPAC are all example of institutions created by Jews out of their Exodus impulse. Each identified a need of the Jewish community somewhere in the world and marshaled the resources to address that need. The Jews who support these institutions are those with the strongest ethnic/tribal identities. Almost by definition, they question the ethnic loyalty of Jews who do not support their causes. Because such organizations are very visible in the public square, they are central to the way that many Jews understand what it means to be a Jew. The Jews who rise to the professional and lay leadership of these organizations are often seen as the leaders of the Jewish community.

It needs to be said that the organizations I associate with the Exodus impulse are not without strong commitments to the ideals of justice and righteousness I identify with Sinai. The same Jewish historical consciousness that gave birth to the Exodus impulse also reminds Jews that they were once slaves in the land of Egypt. The Passover seder's theme of liberation is almost universally familiar to Jews, and the admonition "you shall not oppress the strangers for you were strangers in the land of Egypt" is virtually a communal ethic. Jewish communal organizations routinely raise money for disaster relief around the world, regardless of whether Jews live in the affected areas. During the war in the Balkans in the 1990s, the United Jewish Communities (UJC), the umbrella fundraising arm of the American Jewish community, raised $3.5 million through a Kosovo Relief Fund, which went for food and medical supplies to the victims of that war, few of whom were Jews. Even more impressively, UJC raised some $28 million in response to the Hurricane Katrina disaster in 2005, a tragedy that impacted hundreds of thousands in the Gulf States, mostly poor people of color. When the American Jewish Joint Distribution Committee mounted an emergency rescue of 2,100 people from the city of Sarajevo, under siege from Serb forces in 1993, Christian and Muslims were among the rescued, along with Jews. The Jewish Council for Public Affairs joined forces with the American Jewish World Service to mobilize the Jewish community to attend the Save Darfur: Rally to End Genocide in Washington, D.C., in April 2006. Observers estimated that over half the 75,000 in attendance were Jews. Examples of this kind of concern for humanity on the part of Jewish organizations could fill a book in itself.

Part II of this book went on at some length to explore and define the Sinai impulse. The biblical narrative challenges the Jewish people to live lives committed to justice and to holiness. The rabbinic tradition provides specific guidance for how both might be achieved in the world. I focused on those rabbinic values that specifically defined what this book has alternately described as social justice, prophetic Judaism, or the Sinai impulse. Those values included: compassion for others; a respect for the dignity of all of God's creation and creatures; the obligation to be pursuers of peace; the warning not to ignore the suffering of others; the requirement to seek harmonious relationships with non-Jews; the need to love the stranger in your midst; and seeking that which is right and true. Jews internalized these values so deeply that even as modernity weakened the tie between most Jews and their heritage, the attitudes and behaviors implicit in these values manifested themselves as an ethnic ethos. This explains why Jews were so prominent in the civil rights struggle, the persistence of liberal voting patterns despite socioeconomic trends that would suggest growing conservatism, and the leadership of Jews in so many organizations that are devoted to the welfare of society and the world.

Yet in the context of Jewish communal life, Jewish organizations are clear about their mandate to prioritize the needs of Jews, wherever they are in need or at risk. Of the two purposes of Judaism defined in Chapter 1—outer-directed justice and inner-directed holiness or distinctiveness—the organized Jewish community resonates most with the directive to be a distinct, if not a holy nation. It is the mandate to survive as a separate and unique people among the family of nations. The refusal of the National Conference for Soviet Jewry to link its struggle with that of political dissidents in the Soviet Union was not so much a rejection of the ethic to ally with others in need as it was a recognition of the organization's primary mission. Similarly, however sympathetic Jewish organizations may have been to the effort to create greater social equality in America, they could not endorse affirmative action programs advanced by black groups that included specific goals and timetables that would negatively impact Jews. Even though this stance of the organized Jewish community led to resentment from blacks and other liberal allies (many Jews included), Jewish leadership felt a responsibility to do what was necessary to ensure the future strength and viability of the Jewish people.

Modernity has thus brought into bold relief the growing gap between covenantal and tribal Jewish identity. In the modern world, Jews can choose to be part of the organized Jewish community, but it is a voluntary association. Tribal Jewish identity, which I have identified with the Exodus impulse, is relatively easy to define. The state of Israel is the single largest tribal Jewish polity. You are either a citizen of the state or not. A Jew living in the diaspora has the opportunity to express loyalty for the state of Israel by joining an organization that works to raise money or generate political support for the Jewish state. This, too, makes that Jew a member of the tribe. Jews can make a financial contribution to their local Jewish federation, which supports a wide range of local and international Jewish needs. Payment of this voluntary "tax" also essentially makes one member of the tribe. The same is true for memberships in synagogues and in Jewish cultural, philanthropic, public affairs, and/or educational organizations. While the population of the state of Israel continues to grow, the affiliation numbers in the rest of the Jewish world show a steady decline, a phenomenon that leads those very organizations to have a heightened sense that the future of the Jewish people is at risk. Those committed to the perpetuation of the Jewish community will continually be challenged to find ways to capture a larger market share of the Jews who do not choose to belong to the tribe in any tangible way.

It is here that understanding covenantal Jewish identity is so critical. I have identified covenantal Jewish identity with Sinai. Throughout the generations the rabbis recognized that the spirit of Abraham's legacy was as important as were the specific behavioral commandments that later made up the substance of Jewish life and observance. Rabbi Joseph Soloveitchick, perhaps the most respected Orthodox sage in the history of American Jewry, asserts that the *brit avot*, the covenant of Abraham and the patriarchs—a covenant with a universal thrust focused on the welfare of the entire world—was more important than the specific laws given in the Torah and in later rabbinic codes, laws intended to preserve Jewish particularity. The legacy of Abraham's response to God's call to righteousness and to justice shaped the values and consciousness of Jews for all time.[4]

In a similar vein, Rabbi Abraham Isaac Kook, who served as the first chief rabbi of Palestine from 1921 to 1935, believed that the early Zionists—who observed few, if any, of the ritual commandments of Judaism, and who wore their secularism proudly—were agents for a divine plan for the Jewish people in the world. Unlike Theodor Herzl, Kook did not see a Jewish homeland as primarily a place to provide safe refuge for persecuted Jews. Rather he believed that the upbuilding of Israel was part of a divine plan to bring healing to the entire world. This more universal understanding of Jewish faith and destiny is at the core of covenantal Jewish identity. Rabbi Kook challenged the normative rabbinic reading of the verse "thou shalt love your neighbor as yourself" as referring only to other Jews. He believed that Jews must read the verse to refer to all humanity.[5]

It is not easy for the organized Jewish community to assess how Jews might be living out covenantal Jewish identity when it is stripped of all elements of tribal association. It is easier to identify a Jew who takes on the particular details of Jewish observance and faith than it is to identify a Jew who has no such practice yet lives in accordance with Jewish ethical and moral principles. There is data that can tell you how many Jews belong to synagogues, how many contribute money to federations, and how many travel to Israel. You can also discover how many Jews keep kosher and how many light Chanukah candles. What cannot be as accurately determined, however, is how many Jews feel Jewish, or how many Jews view Judaism and Jewish ethics as an important part of their identity.

It is here that we enter the realm of what I have called Sinai consciousness, or what the sociologist Herbert Gans calls "symbolic ethnicity."[6] Many Jews define large parts of what drives their actions in the world through the context of the Judaic heritage, even when they have no Jewish affiliations or engage in any Jewish religious practice. Given the way that the Jewish community currently functions, such Jews are effectively defined as being outside of the tribe. It becomes a self-fulfilling prophecy. Jews who might otherwise be open to initiatives or programs of the Jewish community when such endeavors align with their values and ethics are driven away by an implicit attitude coming from communal institutions that they have "not paid their dues" to the tribe, not only financially but also by their lack of regular association with communal institutions.

Many of the Jews who traveled south for the civil rights struggle are prime examples of Jews who were, at least in part, motivated by covenantal identity. Debra Schultz found that even those Jewish women who were totally alienated by the Judaism of their suburban upbringings and who went south to "live their values" continued to have emotional ties to their Jewish roots. Many of the Jewish civil rights workers were the most marginal of Jews and yet, in the years that followed their active involvement in the South, they looked for ways to bring their passion for activism and justice to the Jewish community. One activist, Elaine DeLott Baker, sought in vain for a place in the Jewish community that would be welcoming and supportive of her commitment to compassion and ethics, values that she was able to live during her work in the civil rights movement. Her marriage to a Christian man made that search even more difficult. She finally gave up her effort to find a home in the Jewish community. Yet even as she today identifies as a practicing Buddhist, she identifies with Jewish culture as the foundation for the values that drove her activism and that have been the theme of her life.[7] Similarly, Emma Goldman, the anarchist who came to prominence in America in the early part of the twentieth century and who delighted in talking about how she had cast off her previous (European Jewish) life, was significantly influenced by the ethical teachings of prophetic Judaism.[8]

Saul Alinsky, who inspired the entire community organizing movement in America, would not have shown up on anyone's roster as an affiliated Jew. Yet his son recounts that every Sunday, after a family brunch, his father would gather the children around and read a portion of the Bible, drawing out from the passages key teachings about social justice to which his life was devoted. Only as an adult did David Alinsky discover that his father was actually following the weekly biblical portions as read in synagogues! As this anecdote suggests, in the last century tens of thousand of American Jews, from nationally prominent activists to those doing small acts of righteousness in their neighborhoods, identified with the spirit of Sinai in their attempts to create a more just society.[9]

The organized Jewish community is not very good at understanding and validating this kind of covenantal Jewish identity. The leadership of the American Jewish community often feels that the community is under siege and/or at risk. Any manifestation of anti-Semitism at home or abroad, and any threat to the security of the state of Israel, sends the community to its battle stations. When in this mode, the Jewish community has a tendency to circle the wagons and ostracize those Jews whose opinions stray too far from the party line, as evidenced by the experience of Breira in the 1970s and *Tikkun* magazine for much of its history. During rare moments, like the mid-1990s, when Israel seemed to be on the road to peace and the Jewish community did not feel besieged by outside enemies, the demons became internal. Predicting "death by demography," communal leaders sounded alarm bells over the results of Jewish population studies that showed soaring rates of intermarriage and assimilation and declining affiliation patterns. In either mode—under siege or at risk—the Jewish community tends to draw hard and fast lines on who belongs and who does not. And the harder the lines, the less likely that covenantal/Sinai Jews, whose identity is soft and ambivalent, will see themselves as part of the Jewish community.

It is here that the organized Jewish community has created for itself a catch-22 situation. In a social milieu in which fewer and fewer Jews deem ethnic affiliation a necessity, the Jewish community is nevertheless desperate to get marginally affiliated Jews to make overt commitments to communal institutions by joining Jewish organizations and contributing money to Jewish causes. The target audience is large. When one extrapolates from membership statistics and patterns of observance from recent Jewish population studies, it could be argued that over half of American Jewry are "potentially" affiliated Jews.[10] These Jews may be open to deeper involvement in the Jewish community but only on their terms. They don't feel that they need it. But if inspired and convinced that it will add meaning and purpose to their lives, they are "available." The form that their availability will take is very tentative. They are more likely to dabble in a Jewish event here, make a modest gift to a Jewish cause there, than they are to become flag-waving, highly affiliated Jews overnight. For a Jewish organization that invests money in some kind of outreach strategy, this is an unsatisfactory, short-term return. At the same time, the language used by Jewish organizations to rally the highly committed—constantly sounding the warning bell of imminent extinction—is the language least likely to attract marginal Jews to the fold. Why would anyone join a sinking ship if they did not have to?

The divide between Exodus/tribal Jews and Sinai/covenantal Jews is wide and getting wider. The Holocaust and the birth of the state of Israel were formative events for Exodus/tribal Jews. It would be hard to invent a more compelling narrative for why Jews need to band together, whether in a nation-state or through diaspora Jewish organizations, to protect themselves and watch out for each other in a hostile world. Yet those dual experiences are becoming more remote with every passing year. They are not the life experience of Jews born after World War II. And while Exodus Jews still see Israel as the biblical David doing battle against an array of Goliath enemies in the world and thus worthy of unqualified support, to the majority of Jews, the narrative is much more morally complex. Israel is no longer the engine to Jewish identity or to Jewish philanthropy that it once was.

Welcome to the Tribe: Why Jewish Particularism Is Okay

What then might draw marginal Jews closer to the Jewish community? I believe that social justice is one of the most compelling answers to that question.[11] It will not be a straight shot. There is much that stands in the way. But I will try to make the case.

It is critical to recognize how central social justice is to Jewish consciousness. The reason this book begins with an examination of the purpose of Judaism, and then develops the social justice theme as articulated through biblical and rabbinic texts that span more than a thousand years, is to give evidence of how deeply rooted the commitment to justice is in the psyche of the Jew. This is not a matter of aligning

Judaism with a passing political fad that is limited to one part of the planet over the last few decades. The concern for the stranger, the pursuit of justice and peace, the empathy for the poor, and the commitment to truth and fairness is buried deep in the soul of every Jew. It transcends denominational boundaries, geographical contexts, and historical eras. It is acted out by Jews who wear *kippot* (headcoverings) and by those who would not set foot in a synagogue. It is rooted in the sacred texts of the Jewish people, so it is familiar to the knowledgeable Jew. But in ways that only serendipity or faith can explain, it has become a large part of the identity of Jews even though they have never opened a single Jewish book. Despite the hand-wringing by those most committed to the continuity of the Jewish people, many Jews live the values of the Torah despite the fact that they have no formal affiliation with the Jewish community. It is what I have called Sinai consciousness.

What has helped to acculturate Jews into the communal ethic of righteousness and justice is the historical experience of the Jewish people. The admonition to "care for the stranger for you were once strangers in the land of Egypt" was not only about Egypt, just as the Passover seder was not just about Egypt. It was about the persecution of Jews in every era and in almost every place they lived. It developed in Jews a commitment to come to the aid of fellow Jews when circumstances made it possible. It developed in Jews an instinctual sympathy for others who similarly came to experience persecution and oppression. This explains the terrible guilt that American Jews felt about their failure to help their European coreligionists during the Holocaust. It explains why so many Jews rallied to the cause of civil rights for American blacks. It explains the Soviet Jewry movement and the development of an Israel lobby. It explains the prominence of Jews in organizations that work for the underprivileged and to protect human rights around the world. This culture of empathic compassion is what explains Jewish voting patterns and attitudes that defy the typical pattern that link rising socioeconomic status with growing political conservatism. Sinai consciousness, it turns out, is more tenacious than economic interests.

The way I understand the history of the last fifty years is that when Jewish communal organizations provided a context to work for the broader welfare of American society and the world, Jews pursued those goals with vigor. When, on the other hand, the organized Jewish community pursued its organizational mandates and missions largely focused on defense and survival—quite adeptly and appropriately, I might add—the Sinai consciousness of many Jews emerged elsewhere. One of the most welcome developments of recent years is the evidence of an unself-conscious Jewish identity among younger Jews, eager to combine their passion for justice with identification with the texts and values of the Jewish tradition. The Michael Schwerners and Andy Goodmans of today are not satisfied simply to ally with the most vulnerable members of our society. Increasing numbers of Jews are eager to root such behavior in the language of Jewish texts and to do the work under identifiable Jewish banners. This is cause for celebration, and it points to a healthy maturation of the American Jewish community.

What is unassailable is that social justice continues to be among the strongest factors that unite Jews. A 2000 study conducted by Steven M. Cohen and Leonard Fein under the auspices of a short-lived organization called Amos: The National Jewish Partnership for Social Justice asked the question, "Which of the following qualities do you consider most important to your Jewish identity?" Forty-seven percent cited "a commitment to social equality," 24 percent cited "religious observance," and 13 percent cited "support for Israel."[12]

Many will say that social justice is not enough. It certainly would fail the tribal loyalty test as defined in the minds of the stewards of the organized Jewish community. But take the hypothetical American Jew who is an active member of a human rights organization, an environmental organization, or a civil liberties organization, or who is active in local politics. Assume that this individual is not a member of any Jewish organization and gives no money to any Jewish causes. Engage this person in a conversation about what drives his or her volunteer and philanthropic activity, and in many cases we will find that it traces back to that person's Jewish roots, be it a grandparent role model, identification with one or more aspects of the Jewish historical narrative, or the reading of a book of Jewish fiction. Expose that person to a Jewish institution that speaks to his or her values, to a Jewish teacher who frames those values in the words of classical Jewish texts, to a social justice initiative sponsored by a Jewish organization, and there is a very good chance that such a person can be drawn closer to the Jewish community.

I know. I have been part of such education and outreach for three decades, and I can count hundreds of such Jews who "discovered" that there are Jewish institutions through which they can fulfill their personal passions. These Jews represent a gold mine of talent that is largely unrecognized and untapped by the organized Jewish community. The national and local Jewish social justice organizations and the handful of synagogues profiled in Chapters 14 and 15 are reaping the harvest of this very large pool of potentially affiliated Jews.

There are obstacles. The Amos study revealed a deep ambivalence on the part of those surveyed on whether they felt they needed to do their social justice work under Jewish auspices. Reflecting the same phenomenon uncovered by the 1990 and 2000 National Jewish Population Surveys, Jews are less and less likely to join Jewish organizations because they have so successfully integrated themselves into America. They don't need the communal support that was welcomed by their parents and grandparents when they first came to America, seeking a familiar context as an ethnic minority in a new milieu.

I would go one step further. I find that the younger the Jews, the more likely they are to manifest "post-tribal syndrome." Younger Jews tend to push away any and all elements of the Jewish heritage that smack of parochialism. The very elements of tribal connection that have kept the Jewish people united across the world for centuries are regarded with increasing disdain by younger Jews. Add to this bias a general suspicion of religious organizations that is supported by media revelations of unethical behavior by clergy and religious institutions and you begin to understand the deep aversion that many Jews have to associating themselves in any way with the Jewish community.

Ironically, beneath these biases lie many noble and commendable values and aspirations. One young Jewish social activist who now works for the Greater Boston Interfaith Organization, building relationships between synagogues in the Boston area and local community organizing efforts, recently reflected on his youth at a well-established Conservative synagogue in the suburbs of Washington, D.C. He was turned off by "empty ritual and an emphasis on couture over action." He contrasted his home congregation's $2 million capital campaign to make the synagogue more aesthetically pleasing to its upscale membership with a Lutheran church in Harvard Square, Cambridge, that launched a $1.5 million campaign to fix up its basement to better serve the homeless men and women served by the church's programs.[13] This is a harsh assessment, and not many religious institutions in America would pass this level of ethical scrutiny. Yet it is a good example how Sinai consciousness can drive many Jews away from Jewish institutions.

The same people who dismiss religion, and Judaism along with it, believe in many of the values I have examined in this book and would like to contribute to efforts that help such values influence the conduct of society. Yet in a world that is increasingly polarized and partisan, religions and religious institutions stand suspect. There is evidence to support the indictment. The Jewish community must be able to articulate why particularism is okay, why religion can be a force for good, and why Judaism is a worthy and morally compelling life path. The Jewish community desperately needs to attract these Sinai Jews. With each passing generation, they make up a larger and larger percentage of the American Jewish community. They will not resonate to the tribal appeals that worked for their parents or grandparents. They are, mostly, highly educated, affluent, and interested in those things that might give their lives added meaning and purpose. They will not affiliate with the Jewish community unless they resonate with a piece of the message. The Jewish community must make the case.

Why Judaism?

In Genesis chapter 4, God asks Cain about his brother, Abel, after Cain murdered him. Cain's answer was, "Am I my brother's keeper?" It was the wrong answer. Judaism teaches that we need to know both where our sister/brother is and be committed to extending our hand to that person in his/her time of need. "When any of your brothers [*acheycha*] are in need, do not harden your heart nor close your hand" (Deut. 15:7).

The Jewish tradition teaches that even if you have not caused a certain injustice, nonetheless "you are forbidden to hide your eyes from the situation" (Deut. 22:7). When a fellow human being is suffering persecution or is threatened with annihilation, "you shall not stand idly by while the blood of your neighbor is being shed" (Lev. 19:16). Judaism teaches that even if you are convinced that your efforts may fall far short of solving a given problem, you are forbidden to withdraw in despair over the futility of the mission. "It is not incumbent upon you to complete the task, but neither are you free to desist from trying" (*Ethics of the Ancestors* 2:16).

In short, Judaism brought into the world the notion of social responsibility. Abraham heard it in the call in the desert to "extend the boundaries of righteousness and justice." It is central to the covenant at Sinai.

Centuries before the creation of the modern nation-state that provided an array of social welfare and services to its citizens, the Jewish community created a network of mutual support for all the members of its community. As Jews were given the opportunity to become equal citizens of society in the modern period, Jews extended that ethic beyond the borders of the Jewish community. The Jewish community, wrestling as it has with its own anxieties about threats to its future—both from enemies outside and weakness from within—has a far from perfect record in keeping its Exodus and Sinai impulses in balance. But, at the same time, there is much that the Jewish community can be proud of in this regard.

From the earliest attempts to create community in America, Jews created multiple orbits of communal organization—social services, synagogues, cultural groups, defense agencies, homes for the elderly, schools, and so on. The federation system, now organized under the banner of United Jewish Communities, has played a central role as communal planner, fundraiser, and funder to provide for Jewish needs in local communities and in Israel and to Jews in distress all around the world. Today the network of national and local organizations that fall under the banner of Jewish social justice (profiled in Chapters 14 and 15) takes its place as an important expression of Jewish principles and values. These organizations build on a legacy of Jewish communal institutions in America that have contributed both to the welfare of Jews and also to the creation of a more just society for all. Even more importantly, these organizations represent a significant new portal of entry for covenantal Jews who might not otherwise be inclined to cast their lot with the Jewish community. Even more encouraging is to see how committed these organizations are to explicitly rooting their activity in the values of the Jewish tradition. Unlike the generation of Jews that became involved in the civil rights movement, contemporary Jews are eager to acquire a Jewish vocabulary for their social justice involvements, seeing themselves increasingly as responding to the same call that first drew Abraham. This is a generation that is prepared to self-consciously identify as children of the biblical prophets.

All indications are that Jewish social justice organizations will continue to grow, proliferate, and thrive. They fill a vacuum in the contemporary American setting for faith-based groups that can bring the power of religious witness to the injustices and abuses created by the political and economic systems in America and in the world. They also tap into the deep well of Sinai consciousness that continues to be part of the identity of so many American Jews. When Jewish organizations begin to speak Sinai language, and walk that talk, there are thousands of Jews, many of whom are marginally affiliated, who will respond.

All of this brings us back to the millennial tension in Judaism between Exodus and Sinai impulses. Every faith community is committed to the survival and perpetuation of its own. Judaism is not immune to these tendencies. Judaism has often fallen prey to the tendency, affecting all groups, to see itself in parochial terms, to believe that the interests of the group supersede all else. This is especially true in times of crisis. In modern times, this defensiveness extends to times when Israel is at risk, either from war, terrorism, or worldwide campaigns to discredit Zionism and the right of Jews to collective existence in their ancestral homeland.

Still, the Jewish tradition's universal teachings about responsibility toward all human beings and to the entire world continue to bring us back to the needed equilibrium between self-interest—the Exodus impulse—and the interests of humanity—the Sinai impulse. Even when, or perhaps especially when, the Jewish world tends toward the parochial, there are voices in our midst that call us back to our prophetic legacy to be agents for the repair of the entire world.

Rabbi Joseph Soloveitchik spoke to the tension between Exodus and Sinai in the consciousness of the Jewish people in another way:

> In order to explain the difference between the people of fate
> and the nation of destiny, it is worth taking note of the antithe-
> sis between camp (*machaneh*) and congregation (*edah*). The
> camp is created as a result of the desire for self-defense and is
> nurtured by a sense of fear; the congregation is created as a
> result of the longing for the realization of an exalted ethical
> idea and is nurtured by the sentiment of love.[14]

The Jewish community cannot realize its fullest potential to become a people of the covenant, committed to the ethical principles of righteousness and justice, if it remains in its tribal camp, paralyzed by fear and consumed by its perceived need to defend itself from every threat, real and imagined. It is true that without the proper communal mechanisms and political advocacy to properly defend the Jewish people at risk, no Jew would have the luxury to pursue the more lofty Sinai agenda that has been the focus of this book. At the same time, unless the Jewish community begins to give higher priority to an agenda of righteousness and justice—the agenda that started with the first Jew, Abraham—it will have confused the means and the ends. That prophetic legacy is why the Jewish people were put on this earth.

17

Conclusion

Responding to "the Call"

About fifteen years ago, I met an African-American homeless man who became one of my *rebbes,* a teacher who would introduce me to deep truths. I was leaving a hotel in downtown Washington, D.C., where I was in charge of a leadership seminar for high school students under the auspices of PANIM, an organization that I founded and still lead. The seminars are designed to train the next generation of Jewish leaders committed to Jewish values and social responsibility.

As I left the hotel I encountered this man who wore a broad grin and who was doing a little dance to a melody that only he could hear. He greeted me and I returned the greeting. He introduced himself as Jesse and I introduced myself as Sid. He asked what I was doing in this part of town and I told him. When I asked of him the same question, he told me that he was the "mayor." I happened to know the mayor of Washington, D.C., at the time, Marion Barry, so I asked Jesse if he was trying to hustle me. He assured me that he was not and he invited me to follow him a few blocks to meet the people in his "village." My curiosity got the better of my good judgment and I followed. We walked a few blocks in the Foggy Bottom section of Washington to the building that serves as the headquarters to the Federal Reserve, the government agency that oversees our country's money and monetary policies. In what only could be described as the height of irony, around the Federal Reserve building there were some thirty to forty homeless people, camped out with blankets and shopping carts that held all of their worldly possessions.

Jesse was excited by my curiosity and interest. He explained to me the harsh reality of life on the streets. He didn't blame others for his plight. He took responsibility for a series of bad decisions he had made that resulted in his homelessness. But he was also something of a crusader, and there was no denying his charisma and leadership skills. More than once he had been beaten up by local college students who had one beer too many. Knowing that other homeless people suffered a similar fate, he began to organize "his people" to come together every night to create a community of comradeship and mutual protection at the Federal Reserve. And just as people in premodern societies learned how to live off the land, Jesse had learned a lesson or two about how to survive the urban jungle. He pointed out to me that two features of the building made it an ideal shelter—the large overhang of the roof provided protection from the rain and the wide columns surrounding the building provided a barrier to the cold winds of winter. Jesse then pointed to the two armed guards across the street guarding one of the entrances to the State Department. Jesse had introduced himself to the guards and to his scheme and got their assurances that they would be available to help should any trouble come to Jesse's homeless village. Jesse's homeless friends were deeply indebted to him and they took to calling him "mayor," a title he was happy to brag about.

Thus here, not three blocks from the hotel used for my program, I had a great, if unconventional, example of leadership and social responsibility. I sensed that Jesse and his small homeless village had much to teach the teens who came on our program. Jesse was more than willing. The very next night I decided to bring the teen participants from my program onto the street to meet Jesse. He in turn took the kids around his village, introduced them to those who had gathered for the night, and invited them to sit down and talk to them in small clusters.

The experience turned out to be more powerful than I ever imagined possible. When we returned to the hotel, I invited the teens to talk about what they had experienced. They shared the stories they had just heard of people's lives: a Vietnam vet who could not find a job after he returned from fighting for his country; an auto mechanic who could not control his need for alcohol and who lost his job; an immigrant family of four without the proper papers to get gainful employment but in which the husband nevertheless worked odd jobs to buy food and clothing for his wife and two children. When I asked what the students took away from the experience, they began to articulate some of the core teachings of Judaism: the importance of acting toward others in a spirit of compassion (*chesed*); the dignity and worth of every human being (*k'vod habriot* and *b'tzelem Elohim,* the biblical teaching that every human being has within them a spark of God); and the need to reach out to the stranger and the most vulnerable in our midst (*ahavat ger*). The teens were not knowledgeable enough to invoke the biblical and rabbinic values. I did that. What fascinated them, however, was how values that Judaism brought into the world more than 3,000 years ago spoke directly to an experience that they had just lived through.

The encounter with human suffering had not only burst the comfortable bubble of these middle-class white Jewish teens from suburbia, it made them want to better understand what they could do about it. I once heard someone quip that rabbis have answers for questions that Jews no longer ask. Maybe. But in this circumstance, the teens were eager to explore the very values that shape the Jewish ethics of social responsibility.[1] These are values that motivate people to engage in political and social action on behalf of people in need.

Since that first experiment, I made visiting Jesse and the homeless village a regular feature of our program. We felt that students should not come to the homeless village empty-handed, so we suggested to all future seminar participants that they bring with them socks, gloves, scarves, and other useful items to distribute to the homeless. Sometimes we made sandwiches to give out. We provided briefings to the students on how to begin a conversation with a homeless person, since we knew that more than a few of our participants would be quite nervous. One night, Jesse asked me if it was all right to pray with the students. I said it was. He gathered them into a circle, asked them to hold hands, bowed his head, and offered: "God, thank You for these wonderful young people who took the time to visit me and my friends and make us feel good about ourselves. Bless them as they go on their way. And thank You for another day when You made sure that we got what we needed. Amen."

To a person, we were humbled by this expression of faith and gratitude from one who seemed to have so little, certainly far less than what any of us considered basic life necessities. Unbeknownst to Jesse (or, for that matter, to most of the Jewish teens present that night), his impromptu prayer paralleled a prayer that appears in the Jewish morning service: "Blessed are You, Sovereign of the universe, who provides for all of our needs [*sheasah li kol tzorki*]." I shared the parallel. Never before, and never since, have I been able to teach the spirit of *tefillah,* of prayer, as effectively as it was taught that night by Jesse. All the classes and lectures in the world do not equal the experience of actually helping another human being.

And Torah was never as powerfully understood as it was by Jewish teens among the homeless, on the street. Week after week, year after year, students walk away from their encounter transformed. To this day, we call the experience "Street Torah."

Why Religion?

We live in a world in which people are quick to find fault with people and institutions. The media feeds this phenomenon. Individuals in public office, or in the public eye, will endure higher scrutiny and greater criticism in the event of misdeeds than an average citizen. Similarly, nonprofit organizations whose mission it is to help others will be harshly criticized when evidence of misdeeds surface.

Religions cannot escape the harsh judgment of people, in part because they position themselves as standard bearers of moral and right action. Those who already have a low regard for organized religion can readily point to the sexual abuse problems of the Catholic Church, evangelical Protestant ministers who have enriched themselves with monies that church-goers intended for worthy causes, or Islamic fundamentalists who support violent actions against those whom they perceive as their enemies. Judaism comes in for its share of criticism as well. There are those who see it as overly legalistic, who see synagogues long on form and short on substance, or who see Jewish organizations as celebrating and honoring people of wealth without sufficient regard for character.

But upon closer examination, one could just as easily identify organized religion as a force that drives movements for positive social change—as sponsors of soup kitchens, homeless shelters, job training programs, after-school care, and programs to combat substance abuse. Faith communities, when they work, are places that get people to focus on ethical values that encourage greater kindness and generosity, one for the other. A recent book edited by Roger Gottlieb, *Liberating Faith: Religious Voices for Justice, Peace and Ecological Wisdom*, chronicles the words and actions of dozens of people of faith who, in the words of the volume's subtitle, serve as religious voices for justice, peace, and ecological wisdom.[2] They, and the religious traditions in whose voice they speak, make a difference.

It is precisely because of the rise of religious extremism, violence, and intolerance in the world today that we must reclaim the value of religion. This requires us to understand the difference between righteousness and self-righteousness. Righteousness is when we act toward others in a spirit of tolerance, justice, and compassion. Self-righteousness is when we come to be convinced that our own religion, lifestyle, or philosophy of living is superior to alternate paths. When we cross the line between righteousness and self-righteousness, we find ourselves in territory that leads to prejudice, hatred, and death.

In a similar way, there is good religion and bad religion. Bad religion is triumphant. It confuses ends and means. It places doctrines over people. It accepts injustice as a divinely ordained condition, beyond the ability of humanity to affect. It breeds self-righteousness.

Good religion recognizes that there are many equally valid paths to God. It puts a premium on acts of kindness and compassion for others. It is based on the belief that every person is made in the image of God. Good religion promotes the belief that a human being's duty here on earth is to repair a broken world. In the Jewish tradition, we call this concept *tikkun olam*.

Every religion has elements of good religion and bad. Ironically, when our loyalty to our own religion blinds us to the truth and wisdom of another's tradition, we go down the road that has given religion a bad name. This is why it is so easy to hate religion. This is why so many dismiss it. This is why so many have overlooked the possibilities that religion offers to create a reality more just, more compassionate, and more peaceful than the world in which we currently find ourselves.

The Bible gives us a paradigm of how religion can and has functioned in the world. We start out with an idyllic past in the first books of Genesis. God, representing the perfect unity of creation, fashions a perfect place on earth called Eden. Adam, the first human being, is conscious of a transcendent power beyond himself. From Adam, all humanity descends, and thus, the brotherhood of humanity. Soon, humanity is "out of Eden" and reality sets in. We see a world of murder, fratricidal jealousy, slavery, territorial conquest, alienation, disobedience, and punishment. This is not just the biblical story; it is our story. It is the world in which we live. It is the wilderness.

Starting with the idyllic past and then taking us through the wilderness of reality, the Bible leads us to understand its messianic vision of the future. We find it in many places in Scripture, but nowhere is it better articulated than in the Book of Micah chapter 4 (also paralleled in Isaiah ch. 2):

> It shall come to pass in the end of days that the mountain of
> God's house shall be established on the top of the mountains.
> And all nations shall come to it and we will walk in God's way.
> They shall beat their swords into plowshares and their spears
> into pruning hooks; nation shall not lift up sword against
> nation, neither shall they learn war any more.

Life is a journey through a wilderness filled with much pain and suffering, injustice, and inequality. Religion has the power to move us toward the messianic future. It is no coincidence that many of the most important movements for justice in the world have rallied around religious personalities whose leadership was deeply rooted in their respective faith traditions. Mahatma Ghandi used Hindu teachings to rally Indians against an unjust British occupation of their land. Dietrich Boenhoeffer used Protestant theology to articulate Christian opposition to Adolf Hitler. Dr. Martin Luther King, Jr., was a minister who used his pulpit to stir the conscience of America against the evils of racism. Desmond Tutu invoked Christian teachings about forgiveness and reconciliation to keep South Africa from plunging into a cycle of violent revenge after it succeeded in ridding itself of the white minority apartheid government. Elie Wiesel went from being a chronicler of the suffering of the Jewish people during the Holocaust to an international voice of conscience in the world, speaking on behalf of people experiencing oppression in every corner of the globe.[3]

These are examples of people whose lives bear witness to the incredible power of faith to stand up to evil and oppression and to rally people of conscience to a given cause. There are thousands of other such religious role models for social justice.

We wonder: What has given these individuals, what has given us, the strength to be, in the words of Martin Luther King, Jr., "drum majors for justice," in a world filled with poverty, oppression, and selfishness? Good religion gives people just such strength. A person of faith believes that good can triumph over evil despite the injustice they see in the world and lives his or her life in a way to make that belief true.

Social justice is to religion what love is to family. One is the institution; the other is a quality that makes the institution worthwhile. Just as a family without love is dysfunctional, so is a religion dysfunctional when it does not teach and manifest a deep commitment to social justice. It is a religion that has lost its way.

A person does not have to be a member of an organized religion to be kind, generous, or to act with compassion. At the same time it can be overwhelming to live in a world that contains so much suffering, pain, and injustice. Many good people come to the conclusion that there is nothing one person can do to change the basic order of the world. They shrink from public causes and civic engagements that require both time and money and often fail to achieve their stated objectives. They conclude that "the good life" means to provide for oneself and one's family and to live happily ever after.

Answering the Call

Judaism does not concur with this version of the "good life." The "call" that Abraham responded to in the desert (Gen. 18:6) was "to extend the boundaries of righteousness and justice in the world." Prophets like Amos, Isaiah, and Jeremiah railed at kings for creating societies that did not address the needs of the poor. They saved their most vehement rhetoric for the priests who dressed up in all their finery and tried to foist on the people Israel the notion that religion was no more than some incense, a ritual offering, and a few empty words.

It's about the stranger, they cried; it's about the widow, they cried; it's about the orphan, they cried. In the name of God, they declared: keep all your holy rituals and pious words. Religion is about caring for the needy in our midst.

How little things have changed. Our rabbis, priests, and imams are still overseeing all forms of religious activities that give people comfort. All too few make the social ills of our society a centerpiece of their religious communities. If any religion is to be relevant it must call its adherents to act upon the issues that affect the world. How we treat the poor is both a moral issue and a religious issue. How we protect our environment is both a moral issue and a religious issue. How we levy our taxes and spend state revenues is both a moral issue and a religious issue. How we reach out to try and understand people who do not share our faith, race, lifestyle, or ideology is both a moral issue and a religious issue.

Today, more than ever, religions are challenged to bring the wisdom of their respective traditions to bear on the moral crises besetting the human community. Religious leaders must challenge their adherents to respond to the same call that Abraham heard in the desert. Every human being has the ability "to extend the boundaries of righteousness and justice in the world." It needs to become the litmus test of true and good religion.

A Final Word of Torah

The Passover story introduces Jews to the theme of "slavery to redemption." It is a metaphor for the human experience. The story starts when Moses, a prince raised in the palace of the Pharaoh, sees an Egyptian beating a Hebrew slave. The text says, "He looked this way and that, and when he saw that there was no man [*ayn ish*], he slew the Egyptian ..." (Exod. 2:12). Moses saw the oppressed and the oppressor, saw no one intervene, and acted to protect the oppressed. At that moment, Moses crossed the threshold from the Egyptian identity in which he was raised to being part of the Jewish people, the people he then led to redemption. Moses's attempt to bring about justice, to side with the oppressed, defined his Jewish identity.

The phrase "there was no man" appears also in the Mishnah (*Ethics of the Ancestors* 2:6), although in the plural form. Most translate the line as: "In a place where there are no men [*ayn anashim*], strive to be a man." But the use of the phrase in the Moses story cannot be coincidental. *Ayn anashim* implies the moral cowardice that typifies the world. When Moses looked this way and that, he had hoped to find someone who would take moral responsibility for the injustice that was taking place. Being human, he, too, may have been reluctant to get involved. *Ayn anashim* means that no one was ready to take moral responsibility. Moses stepped forward.

Every moment of our lives we are challenged to moral responsibility. We are called upon to extend the boundaries of righteousness and justice. Most people choose to look the other way. The slave needs us to stop the hand of the taskmaster. The poor person needs us to find him or her a job. The stranger needs us as an ally to overcome the outcast status to which she or he has been consigned. The weak and oppressed need prophetic voices to speak truth to power. We assume, or hope, that someone else will intercede so as to absolve us of responsibility. But Judaism says that we cannot look the other way. We need to heed the passage from the Mishnah: "In a place where there is no one of moral courage, strive to be courageous."

Judaism calls upon Jews to stand up for what is right and to act with moral courage in a world that desperately needs it. That call, dating back to Abraham, is for the Jewish people to provide prophetic witness in a broken world that is in desperate need of repair.

All the rest is commentary.

Resource List of Jewish Social Justice/Community Service Organizations

Jews are heavily involved in organizations promoting social justice and community service in America—as professionals, as funders, and as volunteer leaders. But the Jewish community also has numerous organizations of its own that seek to create a more just and peaceful world. Below is a sampling of such organizations, divided into three categories: national organizations, local organizations, and single-issue organizations. Each provides a vehicle for those interested in pursuing the work of social justice discussed in this book.

National Organizations

Amcha—The Coalition for Jewish Concerns
3700 Henry Hudson Pkwy.
Riverdale, NY 10463
(718) 796-4730
www.amchacjc.org

Amcha—The Coalition for Jewish Concerns is an independent grassroots Jewish organization dedicated to raising a voice of conscience on behalf of endangered Jews. This worldwide effort includes countering anti-Semitism, advocating for Israel, preserving Holocaust memory, and other pro-Jewish activism.

American Jewish Committee
P.O. Box 705
New York, NY 10150
(212) 751-4000
www.ajc.org

AJC aims to promote pluralistic and democratic societies where all minorities are protected. In addition to its New York headquarters and Office of Government and International Affairs in Washington, D.C., AJC today operates thirty-three U.S. offices and eighteen international posts.

American Jewish Congress
825 Third Ave., Ste. 1800
New York, NY 10022
(212) 879-4500
www.ajcongress.org

The American Jewish Congress works to ensure the creative survival of the Jewish people through full participation in public life, inspiration from Jewish teachings and values, and liberal principles. It is dedicated to an activist and independent role, and committed to making its decisions through democratic processes.

American Jewish Joint Distribution Committee
711 Third Ave.
New York, NY 10017
(212) 687-6200
http://jdc.org

The American Jewish Joint Distribution Committee (JDC) serves as the overseas arm of the American Jewish community. Its mission is to serve the needs of Jews throughout the world, particularly where their lives as Jews are threatened or made more difficult. It sponsors programs of disaster relief, rescue, and renewal, and helps Israel address its most urgent social challenges. It is committed to the idea that all Jews are responsible for one another.

American Jewish Society for Service
15 E. 26th St., Rm. 916
New York, NY 10010
(212) 683-6178
www.ajss.org

AJSS's goal is to provide significant service to communities in need, and to inspire teens to put their Jewish values into action. It offers an experience of *tikkun olam* (repairing the world) for teens in its six-week summer program.

American Jewish World Service
45 W. 36th St., 10th Fl.
New York, NY 10018
(800) 889-7146
http://ajws.org

AJWS is an independent not-for-profit organization founded in 1985 to help alleviate poverty, hunger, and disease among the people of the world regardless of race, religion, or nationality. AJWS's service missions to third world countries provide opportunities for Jews to give direct service to some of the poorest communities in the world.

Anti-Defamation League
823 United Nations Plaza
New York, NY 10017
(212) 885-7970
www.adl.org

The ADL seeks to combat anti-Semitism and to secure justice and fair treatment for all citizens through law, education, and community relations. Its World of Difference program promotes understanding and tolerance.

Areyvut
1001 Avenue of the Americas, Ste. 1208
New York, NY 10018
(212) 813-2950
www.areyvut.org

Areyvut reaches out to Jewish day schools and congregational schools, regardless of affiliation, and offers a unique opportunity to create innovative and meaningful programs to make the values of *chesed*, *tzedakah*, and *tikkun olam* a reality for students and educators alike.

AVODAH: The Jewish Service Corps
443 Park Avenue South, 11th Fl.
New York, NY 10016
(212) 545-7759
www.avodah.net

AVODAH: The Jewish Service Corps integrates work for social change, Jewish learning, and community building. It provides an opportunity for young Jews to live out and deepen their commitments to Jewish life and social change through a year of work in low-income communities in New York City, Washington, D.C., and Chicago.

Institute for Public Affairs of the Orthodox Union
800 Eighth St. NW
Washington, DC 20001
(202) 513-6484
www.ou.org/public

As the public policy arm of the nation's largest representative Orthodox Jewish organization, the IPA works to protect Jewish interests and freedoms by providing government officials with informative policy briefings, advocating legislative and regulatory initiatives, and coordinating the grass-roots political activities of its constituent members.

The Jewish Coalition for Service
475 Riverside Dr., Ste. 1367
New York, NY 10115
(212) 870-2450
www.jewishservice.org

The mission of the Jewish Coalition for Service is to inspire everyone in the Jewish community to dedicate a part of their lives to full-time, hands-on volunteer service. More than fifty programs affiliated with the Coalition address pressing needs of communities and individuals, among both Jews and non-Jews.

Jewish Council for Public Affairs
443 Park Avenue South, 11th Fl.
New York, NY 10016
(212) 684-6950
www.jewishpublicaffairs.org

JCPA is the national coordinating body for the field of Jewish community relations. There are 13 national and 122 local Jewish community-relations agencies that seek to safeguard the rights of Jews in the United States, in Israel, and around the world, and protect, preserve, and promote a just American society.

Jewish FundS for Justice
330 Seventh Ave., Ste. 1401
New York, NY 10001
(212) 213-2113
www.jfjustice.org

The Jewish FundS for Justice is a national, publicly supported foundation with a commitment to combating poverty in the United States, and the injustices underlying it, as an essential part of our core identity and values as Jews. To fulfill its mission, JFSJ sponsors grant making, technical assistance, and education.

National Council of Jewish Women
53 W. 23rd St., 6th Fl.
New York, NY 10010-4204
(212) 645-4048
www.ncjw.org

The National Council of Jewish Women is a volunteer organization that has been at the forefront of social change for over a century. Inspired by Jewish values, NCJW takes a progressive stance on issues such as child welfare, women's rights, and reproductive freedom.

Religious Action Center of Reform Judaism
2027 Massachusetts Ave. NW
Washington, DC 20036
(202) 387-2800
http://rac.org

Since 1961, the RAC has educated and mobilized the American Jewish community on legislative and social concerns on issues ranging from Israel and Soviet Jewry to economic justice, civil rights, and religious liberty.

PANIM: The Institute for Jewish Leadership and Values
6101 Montrose Rd., Ste. 200
Rockville, MD 20852
(301) 770-5070
www.panim.org

PANIM is dedicated to the renewal of American Jewish life and to training the next generation of Jewish leaders with a focus on Jewish learning, values, and social responsibility. It serves over one hundred communities around the country with transformative programs combining Jewish learning with service and advocacy training.

Spark: Partnership for Service
3600 Clipper Mill Rd., Ste. 228
Baltimore, MD 21218
(410) 366-4151
www.sparkpfs.org

Spark works collaboratively with other Jewish organizations in developing resources, curricular materials, trainings and workshops, and programs to enhance and expand high quality Jewish community service.

Tikkun Magazine and the Tikkun Community
2342 Shattuck Ave., #1200
Berkeley, CA 94704
(510) 644-1200
www.tikkun.org

Tikkun magazine was started in 1986 as a literary forum for social justice and spirituality. The Tikkun Community is its advocacy arm, with chapters around the country. Tikkun sponsors periodic conferences that include spiritual activists from many different faith communities.

Tzedek Hillel
800 Eighth Street NW
Washington, DC 20001-3724
(202) 449-6500
www.hillel.org/tzedek/about

Framed by the Jewish imperatives of *tzedakah* (righteousness), *gemilut chasadim* (acts of loving kindness), and *tikkun olam* (repair of the world), the Tzedek Hillel program engages and empowers college students in meaningful public service through its affiliated campus Hillel organizations.

Local Organizations

Bet Tzedek—The House of Justice
145 S. Fairfax Ave., Ste. 200
Los Angeles, CA 90036
(323) 939-0506
www.bettzedek.org

Bet Tzedek provides free legal assistance to more than 10,000 people regardless of race or religion. It has three locations and representatives at over thirty senior centers throughout Los Angeles County.

Jews for Racial and Economic Justice
135 W. 29th St., Ste. 600
New York, NY 10001
(212) 647-8966
www.jfrej.org

JFREJ was founded to fill the need for progressive Jewish leadership in confronting the growing racial and ethnic tension and economic disparity within New York City. Utilizing community organizing, political education, and media advocacy, JFREJ works to end all forms of hatred and oppression.

Jews United for Justice
2027 Massachusetts Ave. NW
Washington, DC 20036
(202) 483-1945
www.jufj.org

Jews United for Justice seeks to organize a visible Jewish presence and takes action for economic and social justice in the Washington, D.C., area.

Jews United for Justice—St. Louis
P.O. Box 460346
St. Louis, MO 63146
(314) 993-9643
www.jujstl.org

Jews United for Justice—St. Louis is dedicated to working in coalition with partners and allies for the goals of economic, social, and racial justice in the St. Louis metropolitan area. JUJ was organized to be a progressive presence in the Jewish community and a Jewish presence in the progressive community.

Jewish Alliance for Law and Social Action
18 Tremont St., Ste. 320
Boston, MA 02108
(617) 227-3000
www.jewishalliance.org

The Jewish Alliance for Law and Social Action is a membership-based nonprofit organization based in Boston. It is dedicated to being a strong, progressive, intergenerational voice, inspired by Jewish teachings and values, for social justice, civil rights, and civil liberties.

Jewish Community Action
2375 University Ave. West, Ste. 150
St. Paul, MN 55114
(651) 632-2184
www.jewishcommunityaction.org

Jewish Community Action's mission is to bring together Jewish people from diverse traditions and perspectives to promote understanding and take action on social and economic justice issues in Minnesota.

Jewish Council on Urban Affairs

618 S. Michigan Ave.
Chicago, IL 60605
(312) 663-0960
www.jcua.org

Since 1964, JCUA has brought a Jewish voice and Jewish community involvement to efforts that help build coalitions, promote advocacy, and address issues that affect Chicago's most at-risk communities.

Jewish Organizing Initiative

99 Chauncy St., Ste. 600
Boston, MA 02111
(617) 350-9994
www.jewishorganizing.org

The Jewish Organizing Initiative (JOI) offers young adults a chance to work for justice and create a meaningful Jewish community that can support and sustain them in working for justice. Drawing from Jewish heritage, JOI focuses on community organizing as a strategy for social change.

Jewish Youth for Community Action

1300 Grand Ave.
Piedmont, CA 94610
(510) 547-2424, ext.110
www.jycajustice.org

JYCA is a leadership development and community organizing project for Jewish teens that involves teens in leadership of the program at every level. Teens are involved in leadership training, peer education, and community organizing and have been involved in a range of issues, including the fight against anti-immigration and youth incarceration statewide ballot initiatives.

Progressive Jewish Alliance
5870 West Olympic Blvd.
Los Angeles, CA 90036
(323) 761-8350
www.pjalliance.org

Bay Area Office:
409 Liberty St.
El Cerrito, CA 94530
(510) 527-8640

PJA educates, advocates, and organizes on issues of peace, equality, diversity, and justice, as a progressive voice in the Jewish community and a Jewish voice in the progressive community. Since 1999, PJA has created a new model of Jewish community organizing, and has reinvigorated the progressive Jewish landscape in Los Angeles.

The Shalom Center
6711 Lincoln Dr.
Philadelphia, PA 19119
(215) 844-8494
www.shalomctr.org

The Shalom Center brings Jewish and other spiritual thought and practice to bear on seeking peace, pursuing justice, healing the earth, and celebrating community.

Tekiah: A Jewish Call to Action
31 Leroy St., #2
Dorchester, MA 02122
(617) 894-2319
www.tekiah.org

Tekiah is an alliance of progressive Jewish activists, community organizers, and lay leaders in Greater Boston, committed to mobilizing the Jewish community to work for a fundamental, systemic change in American society. Tekiah organizes around issues of local and global human rights and economic justice.

Yachad
1776 Massachusetts Ave. NW, Ste. 810
Washington, DC 20036
(202) 296-8563
www.yachad-dc.org

Yachad is the Jewish Housing and Community Development Corporation of Greater Washington, D.C., which mobilizes the resources of the Jewish community to support commercial and housing redevelopment, creating new opportunities for both skilled Jewish professionals and Jewish volunteers of all ages to put into action two central Jewish values: *tikkun olam* (repairing the world) and *tzedakah* (righteousness).

Single Issue Organizations

The Abraham Fund
9 E. 45th St.
New York, NY 10017
(212) 661-7770
www.abrahamfund.org

The Abraham Fund works to advance coexistence, equality, and cooperation among Israel's Jewish and Arab citizens by creating and operating large-scale initiatives, cultivating strategic grassroots projects, and conducting public education and advocacy that promote its vision of shared citizenship and opportunity for all of Israel's citizens.

ADAMAH: Jewish Environmental Fellowship
Isabella Friedman Jewish Retreat Center
307 7th Ave., Ste. 900
New York, NY 10001
(212) 242-5586
www.isabellafreedman.org/adamah

ADAMAH: The Jewish Environmental Fellowship is a three-month leadership training program for Jewish young adults ages twenty through twenty-nine that integrates organic farming, sustainable living, Jewish learning, leadership, and contemplative spiritual practice.

American Israel Public Affairs Committee (AIPAC)
440 First St. NW, Ste. 600
Washington, DC 20001
(202) 639-5200
http://aipac.org

AIPAC lobbies for a strong U.S.-Israel relationship. With 100,000 members across all fifty states, it is considered one of America's most effective lobby groups.

Americans for Peace Now
1101 14th St. NW, 6th Fl.
Washington, DC 20005
(202) 728-1893
www.peacenow.org

APN's mission is to help Israel and Shalom Achshav (Peace Now in Israel) to achieve a comprehensive political settlement of the Arab-Israeli conflict consistent with Israel's long-term security needs and its Jewish and democratic values.

American ORT
817 Broadway, 10th Fl.
New York, NY 10003
(212) 353-5800
www.aort.org

ORT provides the skills and knowledge needed for individuals to obtain jobs and live independently and with dignity through vocational programs throughout the country. It serves both Jews and non-Jews.

Brit Tzedek v'Shalom, Jewish Alliance for Justice and Peace
11 E. Adams, Ste. 707
Chicago, IL 60603
(312) 341-1205
www.btvshalom.org

The mission of Brit Tzedek v'Shalom, the Jewish Alliance for Justice and Peace is to educate and mobilize American Jews in support of a negotiated two-state resolution of the Israeli-Palestinian conflict.

CAMERA: Committee for Accuracy in Middle East Reporting in America
P.O. Box 428
Boston, MA 02456
(617) 789-3672
www.camera.org

The Committee for Accuracy in Middle East Reporting in America is a media-monitoring, research, and membership organization devoted to promoting accurate and balanced coverage of Israel and the Middle East.

Coalition on the Environment and Jewish Life (COEJL)
443 Park Avenue South, 11th Fl.
New York, NY 10016
(212) 532-7436
www.coejl.org

COEJL aims to enact a distinctively Jewish programmatic and policy response to the environmental crisis. Closely associated with and housed at the Jewish Council for Public Affairs, COEJL has affiliated groups around the country that operate under various names.

Hadassah, The Women's Zionist Organization of America
50 W. 58th St.
New York, NY 10019
(800) 664-5646
http://hadassah.org

Hadassah is the largest women's, largest Jewish, and largest Zionist membership organization in the United States. Hadassah founded and funds Hadassah Medical Organization in Jerusalem, and was nominated for the Nobel Peace Prize in 2005 for its work for peace in the Middle East.

Hazon
829 Third Ave., 3rd Fl.
New York, NY 10022
(212) 644-2332
www.hazon.org

Hazon's mission is to create and support a range of programs, especially (though not exclusively) focused on Jewish outdoor and environmental education, in order to bring joy and meaning to people's lives and thus to foster new vision in the Jewish community and the world beyond.

Hebrew Immigrant Aid Society

333 Seventh Ave., 16th Fl.
New York, NY 10001-5004
(212) 967-4100
http://hias.org

Started in New York City by a group of Jewish immigrants who found sanctuary in the United States after fleeing persecution in Europe, HIAS offers food, shelter, and other aid to countless new arrivals from around the world.

Israel Policy Forum

165 E. 56th St., 2nd Fl.
New York, NY 10022
(212) 245-4227
www.israelpolicyforum.org

Founded in 1993 in the wake of the Oslo Accords, Israel Policy Forum (IPF) is dedicated to mobilizing American Jews in support of sustained U.S. diplomatic efforts in the Middle East.

Jewish Labor Committee

25 E. 21st St.
New York, NY 10010
(212) 477-0707
www.jewishlaborcommittee.org

The Jewish Labor Committee is an independent secular organization that helps the Jewish community and the trade union movement work together on important issues of shared interest and concern. The organization has helped promote intergroup relations and engender support for the state of Israel and Jews in and from the former Soviet Union.

Jewish Peace Fellowship

P.O. Box 271
Nyack, NY 10960-0271
(845) 358-4601
www.jewishpeacefellowship.org

JPF establishes the right of Jews to be recognized as conscientious objectors to war and provides counseling for objectors. It also has a program of publications, meetings, and actions.

Jewish Voice for Peace
1611 Telegraph Ave., Ste. 806
Oakland, CA 94612
(510) 465-1777
www.jewishvoiceforpeace.org

Jewish Voice for Peace is a diverse and democratic community of activists inspired by Jewish tradition to work together for peace, social justice, and human rights. They support the aspirations of Israelis and Palestinians for security and self-determination.

Keshet
284 Amory St., Building G, 2nd Fl.
Jamaica Plain, MA 02130
(617) 524-9227
www.boston-keshet.org

Keshet seeks to create a fully welcoming and inclusive Jewish community for gay, lesbian, bisexual, and transgender (GLBT) Jews in Greater Boston. It also develops leadership for change among GLBT Jews and allies to effect concrete changes in Jewish institutions' policies and cultures. Above all, Keshet is a place for GLBT Jews to come together, celebrate, and explore their Jewish identities in an affirming environment.

MAZON: A Jewish Response to Hunger
1990 South Bundy Dr., Ste. 260
Los Angeles, CA 90025
(310) 442-0020
www.mazon.org

MAZON collects and allocates donations from the Jewish community to prevent and alleviate hunger among people of all faiths and backgrounds.

National Conference on Soviet Jewry
2020 K St. NW, Ste. 7800
Washington, DC 20006
(202) 898-2500
www.ncsj.org

NCSJ works to safeguard the individual and communal political rights of Jews living in the former Soviet Union and to secure their religious and political freedoms.

National Jewish Coalition for Literacy
134 Beach St.
Boston, MA 02111
(617) 423-0063
www.njcl.net

The National Jewish Coalition for Literacy, with affiliated projects around the United States, is the organized Jewish community's vehicle for mobilizing volunteer tutors and reading partners for at-risk children in kindergarten through third grade throughout the United States.

National Jewish Democratic Council
P.O. Box 75308
Washington, DC 20013-5308
(202) 216-9060
www.njdc.org

Founded in 1990, the National Jewish Democratic Council is the national voice of Jewish democrats. The organization works to influence democratic politicians and leaders to address the concerns of Americans. It supports a variety of policies, including the separation of church and state, a strong U.S.-Israel relationship, and reproductive freedom.

New Israel Fund
1101 14th St. NW, 6th Fl.
Washington, D.C. 20005
(202) 842-0900
www.nif.org

Founded in 1979, NIF pioneered the funding of Israel's social change organizations and advocacy groups, and is widely credited with transforming the social justice and human rights communities in Israel. NIF has funded more than seven hundred fifty non-governmental organizations with approximately $300 million in twenty-six years.

North American Conference on Ethiopian Jewry
132 Nassau St., Ste. 412
New York, NY 10038
(212) 233-5200
www.nacoej.org

NACOEJ's mission is to help Ethiopian Jews survive in Ethiopia, assist them in reaching Israel, aid in their absorption into Israeli society, and preserve their unique and ancient culture.

Rabbis for Human Rights—North America
P.O. Box 1539
West Tisbury, MA 02575
(508) 696-1880
www.rhr-na.org

RHR—North America is a rabbinic organization dedicated to education, advocacy, prayer, and action in support of human rights. Its initial focus has been on supporting the work of Rabbis for Human Rights in Israel. New initiatives are now underway focusing on the issue of torture.

Republican Jewish Coalition
50 F St. NW, Ste. 100
Washington, DC 20001
(202) 638-6688
www.rjchq.org

The RJC promotes involvement in Republican politics among its members and encourages Republican leaders to support views and interests of the American Jewish community. The organization supports principles of free enterprise, a strong national defense, and an internationalist foreign policy.

Seeds of Peace
370 Lexington Ave., Ste. 401
New York, NY 10017
(212) 573-8040
www.seedsofpeace.org

Seeds of Peace is dedicated to empowering young leaders from regions of conflict with the leadership skills required to advance reconciliation and coexistence. Its program includes an International Camp in Maine, follow-up programming at the Seeds of Peace Center for Coexistence in Jerusalem, international youth conferences, regional workshops, educational and professional opportunities, and an adult educator program.

Toward Tradition
P.O. Box 58
Mercer Island, WA 98040
(206) 236-3046
www.towardtradition.org

Toward Tradition works to advance America toward the traditional Judeo-Christian values by advocating for faith-based American principles of constitutional and limited government, the rule of law, representative democracy, free markets, a strong military, and a moral public culture.

Interviews

Interviewees are listed alphabetically. The position(s) associated with each name refers to what was relevant at the time of the interview and may not reflect current positions. If a city is not listed, it is because the position was national in scope. JCRC stands for Jewish Community Relations Council, the standard name for that agency in a given community that is charged with the Jewish community's public affairs, defense, and social justice functions.

Batya Abramson-Goldstein, director, JCRC of St. Louis

David Alinsky, son of Saul Alinsky, community organizer and founder of the Industrial Areas Foundation

Diana Aviv, director, Washington Office, Council of Jewish Federations

Ellen Bernstein, founder, Shomrei Adamah

Martin Blank, board member, Yachad: Jewish Housing and Community Development Corporation of Greater Washington

Lorraine Blass, senior associate, United Jewish Communities

Hyman Bookbinder, Washington director, American Jewish Committee

Heather Booth, director, Amos

Rachel Breen, co-founder, Jewish Community Action, Minneapolis, MN

David Cohen, president, Common Cause; co-founder, Advocacy Institute

Steven M. Cohen, sociologist, Hebrew University

Rabbi Rachel Cowan, program officer, The Nathan Cummings Foundation

Jeffrey Dekro, founder/president, The Shefa Fund

Leonard Fein, founder, MAZON, Amos, and the National Jewish Coalition for Literacy

Jerry Fowler, director, Committee on Conscience, U.S. Holocaust Memorial Museum

David Gad-Harf, executive director, JCRC of Metropolitan Detroit

Misha Galperin, executive vice president, Jewish Federation of Greater Washington, D.C.

Fran Godine, board member, Greater Boston Interfaith Organization, Boston, MA

Marcia Goldstone, executive director, JCRC of Greater Indianapolis

Jerry Goodman, executive director, National Conference on Soviet Jewry

Marlene Gorin, director, JCRC of Greater Dallas

Cynthia Greenberg, director, Jewish Social Justice Network

Simon Greer, founder, Jews United for Justice, Washington, D.C.

Malcolm Hoenlein, executive vice-president, Conference of Presidents of Major American Jewish Organizations

Jonathan Jacoby, president, Israel Policy Forum

Rabbi Douglas Kahn, executive director, JCRC of San Francisco

Si Kahn, founder, Jewish Fund for Justice

Mitchell Kamin, executive director, Bet Tzedek—The House of Justice, Los Angeles

Nancy Kaufman, executive director, JCRC of Greater Boston

Lew Kreinberg, co-founder, Jewish Council on Urban Affairs, Chicago

Meyer Laikin, director, Boston Synagogue Organizing Project

Rabbi Michael Lerner, editor, *Tikkun* Magazine

Ari Lipman, organizer, Greater Boston Interfaith Organization

Audrey Lyon, executive director, Yachad: Jewish Housing and Community Development Corporation of Greater Washington

Rabbi Michael Miller, executive vice president, JCRC of New York City

Shelly Moskowitz, president, Jews United for Justice, Washington, D.C.

Nahma Nadich, director of social justice programs, JCRC of Greater Boston

Micah Naftalin, director, Union of Councils for Soviet Jewry

Mark Pelavin, associate director, Religious Action Center for Reform Judaism

Rabbi Jonah Pesner, Temple Israel, Boston

Gary Posen, board member, Holy Blossom Temple, Toronto, Canada

Marlene Provizer, executive director, Jewish Fund for Justice

Jane Ramsey, executive director, Jewish Council on Urban Affairs, Chicago

M. J. Rosenberg, director of policy analysis, Israel Policy Forum

Hannah Rosenthal, executive vice president, Jewish Council for Public Affairs

Vic Rosenthal, executive director, Jewish Community Action, Minneapolis, MN

Larry Rubin, executive vice president, National Jewish Community Relations Council

John Ruskay, executive vice president, UJA-Federation of New York

Rabbi David Saperstein, co-director, Religious Action Center for Reform Judaism

Eric Schockman, executive director, MAZON: A Jewish Response to Hunger

Rabbi Barry Schwartz, Congregation Mkor Shalom, Cherry Hill, NJ

Rabbi Gerold Serotta, co-founder, Breira, New Jewish Agenda

Jerry Shestack, founder, Lawyers Committee for Human Rights; chairman, International League for Human Rights

Barry Shrage, executive vice president, Combined Jewish Philanthropies, Boston

Burt Siegel, director, JCRC of Greater Philadelphia

Dara Silverman, executive director, Jews for Racial and Economic Justice, New York

Rabbi Joel Soffin, Temple Shalom, Succasunna, NJ

Daniel Sokatch, executive director, Progressive Jewish Alliance, Los Angeles

Jay Tcath, executive vice president, JCRC of Metropolitan Chicago

Karla Van Praag, synagogue social justice organizer, JCRC of Greater Boston

Albert Vorspan, co-director, Religious Action Center for Reform Judaism

Rabbi Arthur Waskow, founder/director, The Shalom Center

Julie Weill, director, Faith-Based Community Organizing Initiative of the Jewish Fund for Justice

Eileen Weiss, co-founder, Jews Against Genocide, New York

Marilyn Wise, board member, Beth Emeth/Bais Yehuda Synagogue, Toronto, Canada

Endnotes

Chapter 1

1. See Mordecai Kaplan, *The Future of the American Jew* (New York: Macmillan, 1948), 211–230.
2. K. Kohler, "The Mission of Israel and Its Application to Modern Times," CCAR Yearbook, XXIX (1919), cited in Daniel Jeremy Silver, "A Lover's Quarrel with the Mission of Israel," in *Contemporary Reform Jewish Thought,* ed. Bernard Martin (Chicago: Quadrangle Books, 1968), 145–160. Silver's article provides a rich compendium of thoughts on the mission-of-Israel concept that spans the spectrum from classical rabbinic views to modern interpretations like Kohler's.

Chapter 2

1. These themes are addressed well in Jacob Katz, *Out of the Ghetto: The Social Background of Jewish Emancipation, 1770–1870* (Cambridge, MA: Harvard University Press, 1973).
2. Babylonian Talmud, *Betza* 32b.
3. Leo Baeck, *This People Israel: The Meaning of Jewish Existence* (Philadelphia: Jewish Publication Society, 1965), 402.
4. Michael Walzer, *Exodus and Revolution* (New York: Basic Books, 1985). This interpretation can be found on pp. 102–104, but an analysis of the entire book has informed this chapter.
5. Samson Raphael Hirsch, *Commentary on the Torah, Vayera* (New York: P. Feldheim, 1948).
6. David Hartman, "Auschwitz or Sinai?" in *A Heart of Many Rooms: Celebrating the Many Voices within Judaism* (Woodstock, VT: Jewish Lights, 1999), 259–266.
7. Baeck, *This People Israel,* 402.

Chapter 3

1. Babylonian Talmud, *Sanhedrin* 6b.
2. Babylonian Talmud, *Ta'anit* 23a.
3. Nahum Glatzer, *In Time and Eternity: A Jewish Reader* (New York: Schocken, 1943), 94–95.

Chapter 6

1. Abraham J. Heschel, *The Prophets* (Philadelphia: Jewish Publication Society, 1962), 16.
2. I owe this insight to Joshua Perry.

Chapter 7

1. Harris poll, October 15, 2003.
2. See the collection of essays by Heschel compiled in Susannah Heschel, ed., *Moral Grandeur and Spiritual Audacity* (New York: Farrar, Straus and Giroux, 1996).
3. See Arthur Green, *Ehyeh: A Kabbalah for Tomorrow* (Woodstock, VT: Jewish Lights, 2003).

Chapter 8

1. For a full treatment of this subject see Elliot Dorff, *To Do the Right and the Good: A Jewish Approach to Modern Social Ethics* (Philadelphia: Jewish Publication Society, 2002), ch. 3.
2. Samson Raphael Hirsch, *Horeb: A Philosophy of Jewish Laws and Observances* (Brooklyn, NY: Soncino Press, 1962), 392–393.
3. See Ernst Simon, "The Neighbor (*Re'a*) Whom We Should Love," in *Modern Jewish Ethics: Theory and Practice,* ed. Marvin Fox (Columbus: Ohio State University Press, 1975), 29–56.

Chapter 9

1. Public address at Faneuil Hall, Boston, MA, July 1915. See www.wzo.org.il/en/resources/view.asp?id=1639.
2. Speech to the Eastern Conference of Reform Rabbis, in New York, June 1915. See www.wzo.org.il/en/resources/view.asp?id=1639.

3. See Horace Kallen, *Culture and Democracy in the United States* (1924; repr. New York: Arno Press, 1970); Mordecai Kaplan, *The Future of the American Jew* (1948; repr. New York: Reconstructionist Press, 1967); and Milton Konvitz, *Judaism and the American Idea* (Ithaca, NY: Cornell University Press, 1978).

4. To learn more about this, see David Wyman, *The Abandonment of the Jews: America and the Holocaust 1941–1945* (New York: Pantheon, 1984), or Haskel Lookstein, *Were We Our Brother's Keepers? The Public Response of American Jews to the Holocaust, 1938–1944* (New York: Hartmore House, 1985).

5. Many comment on the dizzying array of abbreviations used by insiders to talk about the numerous organizations in American Jewish life. I will use the abbreviations for brevity's sake. No abbreviation is more confusing than that of the National Community Relations Advisory Council (NCRAC), which served as an organization of organizations. In the 1950s, the word "Jewish" was inserted into the name to make it the National Jewish Community Relations Council (NJCRAC). In 1998 the name was changed to the Jewish Council for Public Affairs (JCPA). The organizations are one and the same.

6. AIPAC actually began as the American Zionist Council in 1951, founded by Si Kenan. It changed its name to the American Israel Public Affairs Committee in 1959.

7. This began to erode somewhat in the 1990s when the ZOA became unhappy with AIPAC's support for Israel's dovish Labor government and began to make independent representations to public officials advocating a more hawkish stance. Similarly, more dovish American Jewish groups have tried to get the ear of public officials to support a more even-handed and conciliatory approach in the Middle East. Neither they nor the ZOA have come close to rivaling AIPAC in terms of the size of its staff, its access to Israeli officials, or its influence on Congress and the White House. See Chapter 12 for fuller details on this issue.

8. For an excellent treatment of how the Jewish community has conducted its Israel advocacy efforts over the past fifty years, see Martin Raffel, "History of Israel Advocacy," in *Jewish Polity and American Civil Society*, ed. Alan Mittleman, Jonathan D. Sarna, and Robert Licht (Lanham, MD: Rowman & Littlefield, 2002), 103–180.

9. See J. J. Goldberg, *Jewish Power: Inside the American Jewish Establishment* (Reading, MA: Addison-Wesley, 1996) for a full treatment of how powerful the American Jewish community became during these years.

10. See Steven Windmueller, "Defenders: National Jewish Community Relations Agencies" and Michael Kotzin, "Local Community Relations

Councils and Their National Body," both in Mittleman et al., *Jewish Polity,* 13–102. These efforts will be looked at in greater detail in Chapter 10.

11. Recollection of David Cohen, interview by author, September 29, 2004.

12. These estimates are cited in Marshall Breger, "Jewish Activism in the Washington 'Square'," in *Jews and the American Public Square,* eds., Alan Mittleman, Jonathan D. Sarna, and Robert Licht (Lanham, MD: Rowman & Littlefield, 2002), 157, 175.

13. *Washington Post,* September 5, 2004: A10. For a fuller treatment of the role of AIPAC in the American political arena, see Hedrick Smith, *The Power Game: How Washington Works* (New York: Ballantine, 1989).

14. The 2000 election came down to the electoral votes of the state of Florida. When the Supreme Court refused to order a recount of questionable ballots in that state, the electoral votes and the presidency went to George W. Bush.

15. Joseph Lieberman, introduction to *Jews in American Politics,* ed. L. Sandy Maisel and Ira Forman (Lanham, MD: Rowman & Littlefield, 2001), xxi.

16. Cited in Robert St. John, *Jews, Justice, and Judaism* (Garden City, NY: Doubleday, 1969), 275.

17. Irving Kristol, "The Liberal Tradition of American Jews," in *American Pluralism and the Jewish Community,* ed. S. M. Lipset (New Brunswick, NJ: Transaction, 1990), 115.

18. The survey and its analysis are summarized in Anna Greenberg and Kenneth Wald, "Still Liberal After All These Years?" in Maisel and Forman, *Jews in American Politics,* 162–193.

19. A good comparison study of Jewish attitudes on a range of social issues, done twelve years earlier, is Steven M. Cohen, "The Dimensions of American Jewish Liberalism," American Jewish Committee, 1989.

20. Greenberg and Wald, "Still Liberal," 187.

21. Michael Pelavin, "To Build a Better America: The Unfinished Agenda of the Jewish Communal Relations Field," 1989–1990 Joint Program Plan, National Jewish Community Relations Advisory Council, 70–73.

22. Hyman Bookbinder, "The Wrong Way to Appeal to Jewish Voters," *New York Times,* March 30, 1984: A1.

23. Maisel and Forman, *Jews in American Politics,* xxii.

Chapter 10

1. *New York Times,* July 24, 1994: 1, 15.

2. See Marc Dollinger, introduction to *Quest for Inclusion: Jews and Liberalism in Modern America* (Princeton, NJ: Princeton University Press, 2000).

3. See Edward Shapiro, *A Time for Healing: American Jewry Since World War II* (Baltimore, MD: Johns Hopkins University Press, 1992), 1–7.

4. Murray Friedman, *What Went Wrong? The Creation and Collapse of the Black-Jewish Alliance* (New York: Free Press, 1995), 133. This volume and Jonathan Kaufman, *Broken Alliance: The Turbulent Times Between Blacks and Jews in America* (New York: Scribner's, 1988) are the two best books for a comprehensive treatment of this subject.

5. Arthur Liebman, *Jews and the Left* (New York: Wiley, 1979), 68.

6. Friedman, *What Went Wrong?*, 188–189.

7. Debra L. Schultz, *Going South: Jewish Women in the Civil Rights Movement* (New York: New York University Press, 2001), 162–174.

8. See Susannah Heschel, "Theological Affinities in the Writings of Joshua Heschel and Martin Luther King, Jr.," in *Black Zion: African-American Religious Encounters with Judaism,* ed. Yvonne Chireau and Nathaniel Deutsch (New York: Oxford University Press, 1999), 168–186.

9. Arthur Hertzberg, "The Present Casts a Dark Shadow," *Jewish Heritage* 6 (Winter 1963–64), 12–15.

10. Michael Staub, *Torn at the Roots: The Crisis of Jewish Liberalism in Postwar America* (New York: Columbia University Press, 2002), 89.

11. Al Vorspan and David Saperstein, *Jewish Dimensions of Social Justice: Tough Moral Choices of Our Time* (New York: UAHC Press, 1998), 207–210.

12. Interview with Al Vorspan, October 14, 2004.

13. Robert Weisbord and Arthur Stein, *Bittersweet Encounter: The Afro-American and the American Jew* (New York: Greenwood Publishing Group, 1970), 139.

14. Staub, *Torn at the Roots,* 100.

15. Although beyond the scope of this limited treatment, to be fair it needs to be noted that Jesse Jackson has built extremely strong ties to the Jewish community in the decades following his offensive remark in the 1980s. To date, there has been no similar rapprochement with Louis Farrakhan.

16. Operation Understanding was set up in Philadelphia in 1985 by black congressman (and reverend) William H. Gray and George Ross, the chairman of the Philadelphia chapter of the AJCommittee. It identifies a few dozen African-American and Jewish teens for a yearlong exploration of their respective community's history. The program was expanded to Washington, D.C., and several other communities in the 1990s.

Chapter 11

1. Albert Chernin, "Making Soviet Jews an Issue" in *A Second Exodus: The American Movement to Free Soviet Jews,* ed. A. Chernin and M. Friedman (Hanover, NH: Brandeis University Press, 1999), 30–32.

2. This in itself was indicative of a newfound willingness of Jews—in this case, those in public life—to speak out for a Jewish cause. Neither Sol Bloom, who served as chairman of the House Foreign Affairs Committee, nor Sam Rosenbaum, who was counsel to President Roosevelt, spoke out on issues affecting Jews. Bloom and Rosenbaum were more typical of Jews who rose to prominence in public life. Both could have exercised considerable influence on the Soviet Jewry issue.

3. Cited in Yossi Klein Halevi, "Jacob Birnbaum and the Struggle for Soviet Jewry," *Azure,* no. 17 (Spring 2004), 27–57.

4. Elie Wiesel, *The Jews of Silence* (New York: Holt, Rinehart and Winston, 1966), 126–127.

5. See J. J. Goldberg, *Jewish Power: Inside the American Jewish Establishment* (Reading, MA: Addison-Wesley, 1996), ch. 7. It should be noted that Goldberg argues that the Jewish community played too tough in the application of Jackson-Vanik on the Soviets. The failure of the Jewish community to support trade concessions in the face of growing numbers of Jews being allowed to emigrate from the Soviet Union led the Soviets to close the doors on emigration again in the early 1980s.

6. William Orbach, *The American Movement to Aid Soviet Jews* (Amherst: University of Massachusetts Press, 1979), 4.

7. Michael Staub, *Torn at the Roots: The Crisis of Jewish Liberalism in Postwar America* (New York: Columbia University Press, 2002), 206.

8. Ibid., 209.

9. Ibid., 219.

10. Natan Sharansky, *Fear No Evil* (New York: Random House, 1988), xxii.

11. Interview with Jerome Shestack, November 2, 2004. Shestack served as chairman of the International League for Human Rights for more than twenty years.

12. For a full treatment of this conflict, see Steven Windmueller, "The Noshrim War: Dropping Out," in Chernin and Friedman, *A Second Exodus,* 161–172.

13. Interviews with Jerry Goodman, former director of the NCSJ (October 26, 2004), and Micah Naftalin, national director of the UCSJ (November 3, 2004). Also see Walter Ruby, "The Role of Nonestablishment Groups," in Chernin and Friedman, *A Second Exodus,* 215–218.

14. Speech delivered December 10, 1986. See www.eliewieselfoundation.org.
15. http://xroads.virginia.edu/~CAP/HOLO/holo.htm.
16. Recollection by author.
17. Recollection of this campaign, the Jewish role in it, and the final Senate hearing can be found in Hyman Bookbinder, *Off the Wall: Memoirs of a Public Affairs Junkie* (Cabin John, MD: Seven Locks Press, 1991), 137–140. For more on the issue of genocide and how it has played out in the American public policy arena, see Samantha Power, *A Problem from Hell: America and the Age of Genocide* (New York: Basic Books, 2002).

Chapter 12

1. Edward Shapiro, *A Time for Healing: American Jewry Since World War II* (Baltimore, MD: Johns Hopkins University Press, 1992), 208.
2. See Jonathan S. Woocher, *Sacred Survival: The Civil Religion of American Jews* (Bloomington: Indiana University Press, 1986).
3. Cited in Leonard Fein, *Where Are We? The Inner Life of America's Jews* (New York: Harper and Row, 1988), 86.
4. Ibid., 75.
5. An excellent treatment of the rise of AIPAC as the central pro-Israel lobby is J. J. Goldberg, *Jewish Power: Inside the American Jewish Establishment* (Reading, MA: Addison-Wesley, 1996), ch. 8.
6. An excellent analysis of the rise and fall of Breira is Michael Staub, *Torn at the Roots: The Crisis of Jewish Liberalism in Postwar America* (New York: Columbia University Press, 2002), ch. 8. The quote from Arthur Lelyveld is cited in Goldberg, *Jewish Power,* 209. Rabbi Gerry Serotta, a leader of both Breira and later New Jewish Agenda, provided invaluable context for the two organizations. Interview with Gerry Serotta, October 18, 2004.
7. See Martin Raffel, "History of Israel Advocacy," in *Jewish Polity and American Civil Society,* ed. Alan Mittleman, Jonathan D. Sarna, and Robert Licht (Lanham, MD: Rowman & Littlefield, 2002).
8. The Kahan Commission Report also led to the resignation of then-Defense Minister Ariel Sharon, who was instrumental in implementing the Israeli incursion into southern Lebanon to rid the area of Islamic militias responsible for launching attacks on northern Israeli villages.
9. Bennet Yanowitz, "Democracy and Discipline in the American Jewish Community," NJCRAC Program Plan, 1983–84, 20–22. There are numerous examples of ever more public criticisms of Israeli policies by prominent American Jews such as the letter addressed to Prime Minister Yitzhak Shamir, on the occasion of his speech to the 1989 General

Assembly of the Council of Jewish Federations, that essentially said: Do not mistake the respect we show you for our approval of your policies. The letter ran in the *New York Times,* the *Los Angeles Times,* and the *Jerusalem Post.* The letter was signed by forty-one leaders of the most prominent organizations in the American Jewish community, including AIPAC and the Presidents Conference. For a full treatment on dissent from Israeli policies and the American Jewish organizations that led that effort, see Marla Brettschneider, *Cornerstones of Peace: Jewish Identity Politics and Democratic Theory* (New Brunswick, NJ: Rutgers University Press, 1996).

10. Goldberg, *Jewish Power,* 349–350.
11. Steven M. Cohen, "Amoral Zionists, Moralizing Universalists and Conditional Doves," *Moment* (August 1989), 56–57.
12. Ibid.
13. 2003 Annual Survey of American Jewish Opinion, American Jewish Committee.
14. Steven M. Cohen and Arnold M. Eisen, *The Jew Within: Self, Family and Community in America* (Bloomington: Indiana University Press, 2000), 144.
15. National Jewish Population Study 2000–01, United Jewish Communities.
16. Amy Sales-Leonard Saxe, "Particularism in the University: Realities and Opportunities for Jewish Life on Campus," Cohen Center for Modern Jewish Studies, Brandeis University, 2006, pp. 24–26.
17. This portrait emerges from the interviews appearing in Cohen and Eisen, *The Jew Within,* 144–151. See also my observations, Sidney Schwarz, "Between Conscience and Solidarity," *Forward,* July 5, 2002.
18. Fein, *Where Are We?,* 98.
19. "What Really Happened in Jenin," Jerusalem Center for Public Affairs, vol. 1, no. 22, May 2002.
20. Steven M. Cohen study sponsored by the Zionist Education Department of the Jewish Agency, December 2004/January 2005.
21. M. J. Rosenberg, "Letting Israel Sell Itself," *IPF Friday,* no. 218 (March 18, 2005).
22. Richard Cohen, "Israel's Day of Light," *Washington Post,* July 3, 2004: A27.

Chapter 13

1. See Murray Friedman, *What Went Wrong? The Creation and Collapse of the Black-Jewish Alliance* (New York: The Free Press, 1995), 319–325.
2. See Marc Dollinger, *Quest for Inclusion: Jews and Liberalism in Modern America* (Princeton, NJ: Princeton University Press, 2000), 164–165.

3. Ibid., 189.
4. *Jewish Spectator,* February 29, 1964, cited in Michael Staub, *Torn at the Roots: The Crisis of Jewish Liberalism in Post-War America* (New York: Columbia University Press, 2002), 92.
5. Dollinger, *Quest for Inclusion,* 202–203.
6. Ibid.
7. See J. J. Goldberg, *Jewish Power: Inside the American Jewish Establishment* (Reading, MA: Addison-Wesley, 1996), ch. 6.
8. Murray Friedman, *The Utopian Dilemma: New Political Directions for American Jews* (Washington, D.C.: Ethics and Public Policy Center, 1985), 55–66.
9. Steven M. Cohen, "Attitudes of American Jews in Comparative Perspective," Center for Jewish Community Studies, 2000.
10. See Charles Silberman's treatment of the issue in *A Certain People: American Jews and Their Lives Today* (New York: Summit Books, 1985), 337–340. The study was Jerome Chanes, *Anti-Semitism in America Today: Outspoken Experts Explode the Myths* (New York: Birch Lane Press, 1995).
11. Steven M. Cohen, "Content or Continuity: Alternative Bases for Commitment," American Jewish Committee, 1991, 24.
12. 1998 Annual Survey of American Jewish Opinion, American Jewish Committee, pp. 14–15.
13. Cohen, "Attitudes of American Jews," 34.
14. Cited in Leonard Fein, *Where Are We? The Inner Life of America's Jews* (New York: Harper and Row, 1988), 148.
15. Ibid.
16. Goldberg, *Jewish Power,* 74–76.
17. See my book, Sidney Schwarz, *Finding a Spiritual Home: How a New Generation of Jews Can Transform the American Synagogue* (Woodstock, VT: Jewish Lights, 2003) for a full treatment of the new Jewish spirituality. On the larger phenomenon of the changing agenda of the American Jewish community, see Sidney Schwarz, "Hold the Eulogy, Jewish Renaissance on the Rise," *Conservative Judaism,* vol. 56 (2004, special supplement), 57–68.
18. www.mfa.gov.il. Statement by Deputy Foreign Minister Michael Melchior to the Durban Conference, delivered by Ambassador Mordecai Yedid, head of Israeli delegation, September 3, 2001.
19. See Phyllis Chesler, *The New Anti-Semitism: The Current Crisis and What We Must Do About It* (San Francisco: Jossey-Bass, 2003).
20. Many of these observations come from the author's first-hand experiences. The author attended the Solidarity Rally for Israel in April 2002 and heard the crowd's reaction to Paul Wolfowitz and witnessed the jostling of

groups with peace-themed banners. The *Forward,* on June 7, 2002, reported on the exclusion of a pro-peace Jewish group from a Jewish community-sponsored rally in Seattle, Washington, "Clash of Seattle Jews Seen as Sign of the Times." The interview with the unnamed Democratic Hill staffer was conducted on October 5, 2004. Conversations with Jewish activists and college students—left, right, and center—are part of the author's everyday work at PANIM.

21. Dollinger, *Quest for Inclusion,* 164–165.

22. Michael Staub, *Torn at the Roots: The Crisis of Liberalism in Postwar America* (New York: Columbia University Press, 2002).

23. Marshall Breger, "For Ourselves and for Others: Defining Jewish Interests," in *The New Jewish Politics,* ed. Daniel Elazar (Lanham, MD: University Press of America, 1988), 60.

24. Ibid., 61–63.

25. The organization during Chernin's tenure was still called the National Jewish Community Relations Advisory Council but we use the current name for consistency and clarity to the reader.

26. Albert Chernin, "The Liberal Agenda: Is It Good or Bad for the Jews?" *Journal of Jewish Communal Service,* vol. 67, no. 3 (Spring 1991), 166, 173.

27. Murray Friedman, "Jewish Public Policy: Its Unexamined Premises," *Journal of Jewish Communal Service,* vol. 67, no. 3 (Spring 1991), 174–179.

28. Interviews with: Burt Siegel, Philadelphia JCRC, August 27, 2004; Jay Tcath, Chicago JCRC, August 27, 2004; David Gad-Harf, Detroit JCRC, August 23, 2004; Nancy Kaufman, Boston JCRC, August 11, 2004; Rabbi Douglas Kahn, San Francisco JCRC, September 10, 2004; Batya Abramson-Goldstein, St. Louis JCRC, September 10, 2004; Marcia Goldstone, Indianapolis JCRC, September 14, 2004; Marlene Gorin, Dallas JCRC, September 10, 2004; Diana Aviv, Washington Office, United Jewish Communities, November 12, 2004; and Hannah Rosenthal, national JCPA executive, August 11, 2004.

29. For a description of how large donors are seizing more and more control of the Jewish communal apparatus and affecting the policy direction of communal agencies, see James Besser, "The Golden Rule of Jewish Leadership," *Los Angeles Jewish Journal,* March 11, 2005.

30. Interview with Larry Rubin, July 13, 2005.

31. J. J. Goldberg, "Family Fued," *The Jewish Week* (New York), November 5, 1999: 16; and "The Face-Off Over the Jewish Liberal Agenda," *The Jewish Week* (New York), November 12, 1999: 18.

32. Michael Kotzin, "Local Jewish Community Relations Councils and Their National Body," in *Jewish Polity and American Civil Society*, ed. Alan Mittleman, Jonathan D. Sarna, and Robert Licht (Lanham, MD: Rowman & Littlefield, 2002), 93–98. Rubin already identified this trend in public Jewish life ten years earlier; see Larry Rubin, "The Emerging Jewish Public Affairs Culture," in *American Pluralism and the Jewish Community*, ed. Seymour Martin Lipset (New Brunswick, NJ: Transaction Publishers, 1990), 193–201.

Chapter 14

1. Statistics are drawn from Larry Mishel, Jared Bernstein, and Heather Boushey, *The State of Working America, 2002-2003* (Ithaca, NY: Cornell University Press, 2003).
2. Interview with Lew Kreinberg, November 10, 2003.
3. Interview with Jane Ramsey, October 20, 2004.
4. Story cited in Arthur Waskow, *The Bush Is Burning: Radical Judaism Faces the Pharaohs of the Modern Superstate* (New York: Macmillan, 1971), 12–15. Also interview with Arthur Waskow, October 6, 2004.
5. See Preface to Michael Lerner, *Jewish Renewal: A Path to Healing and Transformation* (New York: Grosset/Putnam, 1994). Additional insights came from interview with Michael Lerner, September 14, 2004.
6. See *Tikkun* Magazine, November/December 2001: 49–63.
7. Michael Lerner, "*Tikkuning* the Road Map," *Tikkun* Magazine, July/August 2003: 7–10.
8. I served as one of three coauthors of that curriculum, along with Rabbi Marc Gopin and Rabbi Mark Levine. In 1998 PANIM published a complementary curriculum designed for Jewish day schools entitled *Jews, Judaism and Civic Responsibility*, coauthored by Zvi Nierman, Joshua Perry, Sid Schwarz, and Michoel Shepard.
9. Interview with Leonard Fein, September 24, 2004.
10. Interviews with Gary Posen, June 9, 2005, and Marilyn Wise, June 3, 2005.
11. Interview with Rabbi Joel Soffin, October 13, 2004.
12. Interview with Rabbi David Saperstein, August 6, 2004.
13. Rabbi Irving Greenberg, "Personal Service: A Central Jewish Norm for Our Time," *Contact*, vol. 4, no.1 (Autumn 2001), 3–4.
14. Steven M. Cohen and Arnold M. Eisen, *The Jew Within: Self, Family and Community in America* (Bloomington: Indiana University Press, 2000), 188.

15. Anna Greenberg and Kenneth Wald, "Still Liberal After All These Years? The Political Behavior of American Jews," in *Jews in American Politics,* ed. L. Sandy Maisel and Ira Forman (Lanham, MD: Rowman & Littlefield, 2001), 162–193.

Chapter 15

1. Personal background on Alinsky was garnered from an interview with his son, David Alinsky, November 11, 2004, and from an interview with him posted on the web, www.progress.org/2003/alinsky4.htm. His philosophy is best summarized in his book, *Rules for Radicals: A Practical Primer for Realistic Radicals* (New York: Vintage Books, 1971).
2. Interviews with Simon Greer, October 13, 2004, and Shelly Moskowitz, chairman of the board of JUFJ, on October 5, 2004.
3. Interview with Martin Blank, October 14, 2004.
4. Tom Tugend, "LA AJCongress Chapter Secedes over Ideology and Finances," Jewish Telegraphic Agency, March 16, 1999.
5. Interview with Daniel Sokatch, September 24, 2004. About 35 percent of the early membership of IKAR was made up of PJA members, with Sokatch serving on the board.
6. Interview with Vic Rosenthal, October 5, 2004.
7. Interview with Barry Shrage, October 21, 2004, and Nancy Kaufman, November 12, 2004.
8. "Janitors in the Boston Area Are Threatening to Strike," *New York Times,* September 29, 2002, section 1: 28.
9. Interview with Rabbi Jonah Pesner, October 22, 2004, and Fran Godine, volunteer leader in the GBIO effort, October 21, 2004. Another high-profile GBIO-led mobilization was a campaign to improve the pay and working conditions of Haitian health care workers.
10. Nancy Kaufman, "Recapturing Our Soul: A Vision of Community Relations," *Journal of Jewish Communal Service,* vol. 78, no.1 (Fall 2001), 20–31. Also, Kaufman interview.
11. When Marlene Provizer stepped down from her position as director of the Jewish Fund for Justice in 2005, she was succeeded by Simon Greer, who was the founder of Washington's Jews United for Justice.
12. *Faith-Based Community Organizing: A Unique Social Justice Approach to Revitalizing Synagogue Life,* Jewish Fund for Justice, 2003, pp. 2–5.

Chapter 16

1. Albert Vorspan and Eugene Lipman, *Justice and Judaism: The Work of Social Action* (New York: Union of American Hebrew Congregations, 1955).
2. Marshall Sklare, *America's Jews* (New York: Random House, 1971), ch. 4.
3. Steven M. Cohen and Arnold M. Eisen, *The Jew Within: Self, Family and Community* (Bloomington: Indiana University Press, 2000), ch. 8.
4. Comment of Rabbi Joseph Soloveitchik, in Abraham Besdin, *Man of Faith in the Modern World* (Hoboken, NJ: KTAV, 1989), 67–69.
5. *Maamrei HaReAYaH (Teachings of Rav Kook)*, p. 252, cited in Rav Yehuda Amital, "The Significance of Rav Kook's Teaching for Our Generation," in *The World of Rav Kook's Thought*, Benjamin Ish Shalom and Shalom Rosenberg (New York: Avi Chai Foundation, 1991), 434.
6. For a fuller discussion of "secular" Jewish identity see Seymour Martin Lipset and Earl Raab, *Jews and the New American Scene* (Cambridge, MA: Harvard University Press, 1995), 66, 175.
7. Debra Schultz, *Going South: Jewish Women in the Civil Rights Movement* (New York: New York University Press, 2001), ch. 6.
8. See Richard Drinnon, *Rebel in Paradise* (New York: Alfred Knopf, 1931), 3–29.
9. Interview with David Alinsky, November 11, 2004. An inspiring book that is totally devoted to chronicling acts of kindness, mostly by Jews, and the linkage of those acts to Jewish teachings is Jack Doueck, *The Chesed Boomerang: How Acts of Kindness Enrich Our Lives* (New York: Yagdil Torah Publications, 1998).
10. In one section, the NJPS breaks down the numbers as follows: 28 percent highly affiliated, 28 percent moderately affiliated, and 44 percent unaffiliated. However, these numbers were based exclusively on memberships in JCCs, synagogues, or other Jewish organizations. In another section, under "Jewish connections," the same survey revealed more than 70 percent observing Chanukah, 67 percent observing Passover, and 65 percent reading Jewish content books and magazines. In other words, if the criterion is not rigidly defined as just dues-paying membership, a significant portion of the category that the study labels "unaffiliated" are better classified as "potentially affiliated." This is how I arrive at these rough estimates.
11. "One of" because I believe that there are three elements to a renaissance Jewish agenda that has a chance to attract young and marginally affiliated Jews, the other two being spirituality and serious Jewish learning. My

book *Finding a Spiritual Home: How a New Generation of Jews Can Transform the American Synagogue* (Woodstock, VT: Jewish Lights, 2003) makes the case for spirituality. The case for how the new Jewish agenda needs to replace the older, defense/survival agenda can be found in my article "Hold the Eulogy: Jewish Renaissance on the Rise," *Conservative Judaism*, no. 56 (2004).

12. The study, "American Jews and their Social Justice Involvement: Evidence from a National Survey," was released in 2000 and used to launch Amos, which got some initial foundation support and functioned for a few years with a board and small staff. But the organization struggled to define its mission and find its niche in the American Jewish community and folded after the initial grants expired. Interviews with Heather Booth, November 19, 2004, and Leonard Fein, September 24, 2004. It should be noted that the study's findings about the centrality of social justice to Jewish identity were consistent with findings of a major study twenty-five years earlier of the Jews of "Lakeville." See Marshall Sklare and Joseph Greenbaum, *Jewish Identity on the Suburban Frontier* (Chicago: University of Chicago Press, 1979), ch. 3.

13. Ari Lipman, "From Woodrow Avenue to Woodrow Avenue: The Path of an Organizer and a Jewish Community," *Reconstructionist*, vol. 68, no. 1 (Fall 2003), 24–32.

14. Joseph Soloveitchik, *Fate and Destiny: From the Holocaust to the State of Israel* (Hoboken, NJ: KTAV, 1992), 57–60. I am indebted to Barry Shrage for suggesting this excerpt.

Chapter 17

1. Chapter 8 outlines a representative sample of these values, and the antecedent ideas from biblical literature that lay the foundation for these values are outlined in Chapters 3–7.

2. Roger Gottlieb, ed., *Liberating Faith: Religious Voices for Justice, Peace, and Ecological Wisdom* (Lanham, MD: Rowman & Littlefield, 2003).

3. It was for this human rights activism that Elie Wiesel won the Nobel Peace Prize in 1986.

Bibliography

Arendt, Hannah. *The Jew as Pariah: Jewish Identity and Politics in the Modern Age.* New York: Grove Press, 1978.

Baeck, Leo. *This People Israel: The Meaning of Jewish Existence.* Philadelphia: Jewish Publication Society, 1965.

Bellah, Robert N., Richard Madsen, William M. Sullivan, Ann Swidler, and Steven M. Tipton, eds. *Habits of the Heart: Individualism and Commitment in American Life.* New York: Harper and Row, 1985.

Berger, Peter L. *The Sacred Canopy: Elements of a Sociological Theory of Religion.* Garden City, NY: Doubleday, 1969.

Biale, David. *Power and Powerlessness in Jewish History.* New York: Schocken, 1996.

Bookbinder, Hyman. *Off the Wall: Memoirs of a Public Affairs Junkie.* Cabin John, MD: Seven Locks Press, 1991.

Breger, Marshall, ed. *Public Policy and Social Issues: Jewish Sources and Perspectives.* Westport, CT: Praeger, 2003.

Brettschneider, Marla. *Cornerstones of Peace: Jewish Identity Politics and Democratic Theory.* New Brunswick, NJ: Rutgers University Press, 1996.

Broyde, Michael, and John Witte, Jr., eds. *Human Rights in Judaism: Cultural, Religious and Political Perspectives.* Northvale, NJ: Jason Aronson, 1998.

Brustein, William. *Roots of Hate: Anti-Semitism in Europe Before the Holocaust.* New York: Cambridge University Press, 2003.

Chanes, Jerome. *Antisemitism in America Today: Outspoken Experts Explode the Myths.* Secaucus, NJ: Birch Lane Press, 1995.

Chesler, Phyllis. *The New Anti-Semitism: The Current Crisis and What We Must Do About It.* San Francisco: Jossey-Bass, 2003.

Cohen, Naomi W. *Not Free to Desist.* Philadelphia: Jewish Publication Society of America, 1972.

Cohen, Steven M. *American Modernity and Jewish Identity.* New York: Tavistock Publications, 1983.

———. "Content and Continuity: Alternative Bases for Jewish Commitment." American Jewish Committee, 1991.

————. "The Dimensions of Jewish Liberalism." American Jewish Committee, 1989.

————. "The Political Attitudes of American Jews." American Jewish Committee, 1984.

————., and Arnold M. Eisen. *The Jew Within: Self, Family and Community in America.* Bloomington: Indiana University Press, 2000.

Cohn-Sherbok, Dan. *On Earth As It Is in Heaven: Jews, Christians and Liberation Theology.* Maryknoll, NY: Orbis, 1987.

Dershowitz, Alan. *Chutzpah.* Boston: Little, Brown, 1991.

Dinnerstein, Leonard. *Antisemitism in America.* New York: Oxford University Press, 1994.

Dollinger, Marc. *Quest for Inclusion: Jews and Liberalism in Modern America.* Princeton, NJ: Princeton University Press, 2000.

Dorff, Elliot N. *To Do the Right and the Good: A Jewish Approach to Modern Social Ethics.* Philadelphia: Jewish Publication Society, 2002.

————. *The Way Into* Tikkun Olam *(Repairing the World).* Woodstock, VT: Jewish Lights, 2005.

Dorrien, Gary. *The Neoconservative Mind: Politics, Culture, and the War of Ideology.* Philadelphia: Temple University Press, 1993.

Doueck, Jack. *The Chesed Boomerang: How Acts of Kindness Enrich Our Lives.* New York: Yagdil Torah Publications, 1998.

Drachman, Edward. *Challenging the Kremlin: The Soviet Jewish Movement for Freedom, 1967–1990.* New York: Paragon House, 1991.

Eisen, Arnold. *Rethinking Modern Judaism: Ritual, Commandment, Community.* Chicago: University of Chicago Press, 1998.

Elazar, Daniel. *Community and Polity: The Organizational Dynamics of American Jewry.* Philadelphia: Jewish Publication Society of America, 1980.

Elazar, Daniel, ed. *The New Jewish Politics.* Lanham, MD: University Press of America, 1988.

Ellis, Marc. *Toward a Jewish Theology of Liberation.* Maryknoll, NY: Orbis, 1987.

Fein, Leonard. "Smashing Idols and Other Prescriptions for Jewish Continuity." Nathan Cummings Foundation, 1994.

————. *Where Are We? The Inner Life of America's Jews.* New York: Harper and Row, 1988.

Feingold, Henry. *Lest Memory Cease: Finding Meaning in the American Jewish Past.* Syracuse, NY: Syracuse University Press, 1996.

Findley, Paul. *They Dare to Speak Out: People and Institutions Confront Israel's Lobby.* Chicago: Lawrence Hill Books, 1989.

Fishman, Sylvia Barack. *A Breath of Life: Feminism in the American Jewish Community.* Hanover, NH: Brandeis University Press, 1995.

Fox, Marvin ed. *Modern Jewish Ethics: Theory and Practice.* Columbus: Ohio State University Press, 1975.

Friedland, Michael B. *Lift Up Your Voice Like a Trumpet: White Clergy and the Civil Rights and Antiwar Movements, 1954–1973.* Chapel Hill: University of North Carolina Press, 1998.

Friedman, Murray, ed. *Commentary in American Life.* Philadelphia: Temple University Press, 2005.

———. *The Neoconservative Revolution: Jewish Intellectuals and the Shaping of Public Policy.* New York: Cambridge University Press, 2005.

———. *The Utopian Dilemma: American Judaism and Public Policy.* Washington, D.C.: Ethics and Public Policy Center, 1985.

———. *What Went Wrong? The Creation and Collapse of the Black-Jewish Alliance.* New York: Free Press, 1995.

———, and Albert Chernin, eds. *A Second Exodus: The American Movement to Free Soviet Jews.* Hanover, NH: Brandeis University Press, 1999.

Gans, Herbert. "Symbolic Ethnicity: The Future of Ethnic Groups and Cultures in America." *Ethnic and Racial Studies* 2, 1979.

———. "Symbolic Ethnicity and Symbolic Religiosity: Toward a Comparison of Ethnic and Religious Acculturation." *Ethnic and Racial Studies* 17, 1994.

Gilman, Sander. *Jewish Self-Hatred: Anti-Semitism and the Hidden Language of the Jews.* Baltimore, MD: John Hopkins University Press, 1986.

Ginsberg, Benjamin. *The Fatal Embrace: Jews and the State.* Chicago: University of Chicago Press, 1993.

Goldberg, J. J. *Jewish Power: Inside the American Jewish Establishment.* Reading, MA: Addison-Wesley, 1996.

Goldscheider, Calvin. *Jewish Continuity and Change: Emerging Patterns in America.* Bloomington: Indiana University Press, 1986.

———, and Alan S. Zuckerman. *The Transformation of the Jews.* Chicago: University of Chicago Press, 1984.

Goldstein, Sidney, and Calvin Goldscheider. *Jewish Americans: Three Generations in a Jewish Community.* Lanham, MD: Unversity Press of America, 1985.

Gottlieb, Roger, ed. *Liberating Faith: Religious Voices for Justice, Peace and Ecological Wisdom.* Lanham, MD: Rowman & Littlefield, 2003.

Grose, Peter. *Israel in the Mind of America.* New York: Schocken, 1984.

Hartman, David. *A Heart of Many Rooms: Celebrating the Many Voices within Judaism.* Woodstock, VT: Jewish Lights, 2002.

Herberg, Will. *Protestant, Catholic, Jew: An Essay in American Religious Sociology.* Chicago: University of Chicago Press, 1983.

Hertzberg, Arthur. *The Jews in America: Four Centuries of an Uneasy Encounter: A History.* New York: Columbia University Press, 1997

Himmelfarb, Milton. *The Jews of Modernity.* New York: Basic Books, 1973.

Hirsch, Richard. *The Way of the Upright: A Jewish View of Economic Justice.* New York: Union of American Hebrew Congregations, 1973.

Hoffman, Charles. *The Smokescreen: Israel, Philanthropy, and American Jews.* Silver Spring, MD: Eshel Books, 1989.

Isaacs, Stephen D. *Jews and American Politics.* Garden City, NY: Doubleday, 1974.

Jacobs, Paul. *Is Curly Jewish? A Political Self-Portrait Illuminating Three Turbulent Decades of Social Revolt, 1935–1965.* New York: Vintage Books, 1973.

Joselit, Jenna Weissman. *The Wonders of America: Reinventing Jewish Culture 1880–1950.* New York: Hill and Wang, 1994.

Katz, Jacob. *Out of the Ghetto: The Social Background of Jewish Emancipation, 1770–1870.* Syracuse, NY: Syracuse University Press, 1998.

———. *Tradition and Crisis: Jewish Society at the End of the Middle Ages.* Syracuse, NY: Syracuse University Press, 2000.

Kaufman, Jonathan. *Broken Alliance: The Turbulent Times Between Blacks and Jews in America.* New York: Simon and Schuster, 1995.

Kliksberg, Bernardo. *Social Justice: A Jewish Perspective.* Hewlett, NY: Gefen Publishing, 2003.

Kosmin, Barry A., Sidney Goldstein, Joseph Waksberg, Nava Lerer, Ariella Keysar, and Jeffrey Scheckner. *Highlights of the CJF 1990 National Jewish Population Survey.* New York: Council of Jewish Federations, 1991.

Kushner, Tony, and Alisa Solomon, eds. *Wrestling with Zion: Progressive Jewish-American Responses to the Israeli-Palestinian Conflict.* New York: Grove Press, 2003.

Lazerwitz, Bernard, J. Alan Winter, Arnold Dashevsky, and Ephraim Tabory. *Jewish Choices: American Jewish Denominationalism.* Albany: State University of New York Press, 1998.

Lerner, Michael. *Jewish Renewal: A Path to Healing and Transformation.* New York: Grosset/Putnam, 1994.

Levin, Nora. *While Messiah Tarried: Jewish Socialist Movements, 1871–1917.* New York: Schocken, 1977.

Liebman, Arthur. *Jews and the Left.* New York: John Wiley, 1979.

Liebman, Charles S., and Steven M. Cohen. *Two Worlds of Judaism: The Israeli and American Experiences.* New Haven, CT: Yale University Press, 1990.

Lipset, Seymour Martin, ed. *American Pluralism and the Jewish Community.* New Brunswick, NJ: Transaction, 1990.

Lipset, Seymour Martin, and Earl Raab. *Jews and the New American Scene.* Cambridge, MA: Harvard University Press, 1995.

Lubet, Steven. *Chutzpah: A Jewish Liberation Anthology.* San Francisco: New Glide Publications, 1977.

Lurie, Walter. *Strategies for Survival: Principles of Jewish Community Relations.* New York: KTAV, 1982.

Maisel, Sandy, and Ira Forman, eds. *Jews in American Politics.* Lanham, MD: Rowman & Littlefield, 2001.

Mittleman, Alan, Jonathan Sarna, and Robert Licht, eds. *Jewish Polity and American Civil Society.* Lanham, MD: Rowman & Littlefield, 2002.

———. *Jews and the American Public Square.* Lanham, MD: Rowman & Littlefield, 2002.

Moore, Deborah Dash. *At Home in America: Second Generation New York Jews.* New York: Columbia University Press, 1981.

Novak, David. *Jewish Social Ethics.* New York: Oxford University Press, 1992.

Pogrebin, Letty Cottin. *Deborah, Golda, and Me: Being Female and Jewish in America.* New York: Anchor Books, 1992.

Polner, Murray, and Naomi Goodman, eds. *The Challenge of Shalom: The Jewish Tradition of Peace and Justice.* Philadelphia: New Society Publishers, 1994.

Porter, Jack Nusan, and Peter Dreier, eds. *Jewish Radicalism: A Selected Anthology.* New York: Grove Press, 1973.

Prell, Riv-Ellen. *Fighting to Become Americans: Jews, Gender, and the Anxiety of Assimilation.* Boston: Beacon Press, 1999.

Raphael, Marc Lee. *A History of the United Jewish Appeal, 1939–1982.* Chico, CA: Scholars Press, 1982.

Ringer, Benjamin B. *The Edge of Friendliness: A Study of Jewish-Gentile Relations.* New York: Basic Books, 1967.

Roth, Sol. *Halakhah and Politics: The Jewish Idea of the State.* New York: KTAV, 1988.

Sacks, Jonathan. *To Heal a Fractured World: The Ethics of Responsibility.* New York: Schocken, 2005.

Salzman, Jack, and Cornel West, eds. *Struggles in the Promised Land: Towards a History of Black-Jewish Relations in the United States.* New York: Oxford University Press, 1997.

Schneier, Marc. *Shared Dreams: Martin Luther King, Jr. and the Jewish Community.* Woodstock, VT: Jewish Lights, 1999.

Schultz, Debra L. *Going South: Jewish Women in the Civil Rights Movement.* New York: New York University Press, 2001.

Schwartz, Richard. *Judaism and Global Survival.* New York: Lantern Books, 2002.

Schwarz, Sidney. *Finding a Spiritual Home: How a New Generation of Jews Can Transform the American Synagogue.* Woodstock, VT: Jewish Lights, 2003.

Schwarz, Sidney, Marc Gopin, and Mark Levine, eds. *Jewish Civics: A Tikkun Olam/World Repair Manual.* Rockville, MD: PANIM, 1994.

Schwarz, Sidney, Zvi Nierman, Joshua Perry, and Michoel Shepard. *Jews, Judaism and Civic Responsibility.* Rockville, MD: PANIM, 1998.

Shapiro, Edward. *A Time for Healing: American Jewry Since World War II.* Baltimore, MD: Johns Hopkins University Press, 1992.

Shatz, David, Chaim Waxman, and Nathan Diament, eds. *Tikkun Olam: Social Responsibility in Jewish Thought and Law.* Northvale, NJ: Jason Aronson, 1997.

Silberman, Charles. *A Certain People: American Jews and Their Lives Today.* New York: Summit Books, 1985.

Silver, Daniel Jeremy, ed. *Judaism and Ethics.* New York: KTAV, 1970.

Simons, Howard. *Jewish Times: Voices of the American Jewish Experience.* New York: Anchor Books, 1990.

Sklare, Marshall. *America's Jews.* New York: Random House, 1971.

——. *Observing America's Jews.* Hanover, NH: Brandeis University Press, 1993.

——, and Joseph Greenblum. *Jewish Identity on the Suburban Frontier: A Study of Group Survival in the Open Society.* Chicago: University of Chicago Press, 1979.

Soloveitchik, Joseph. *Fate and Destiny: From the Holocaust to the State of Israel.* Hoboken, NJ: KTAV, 2000.

Sorin, Gerald. *The Prophetic Minority: American Jewish Immigrant Radicals, 1880–1920.* Bloomington: Indiana University Press, 1985.

St. John, Robert. *Jews, Justice, and Judaism.* Garden City, NY: Doubleday, 1969.

Staub, Michael. *Torn at the Roots: The Crisis of Jewish Liberalism in Postwar America.* New York: Columbia University Press, 2002.

Stember, Charles Herbert. *Jews in the Mind of America.* New York: Basic Books, 1966.

Strum, Philippa. *Louis D. Brandeis: Justice for the People.* New York: Schocken, 1989.

Svonkin, Stuart. *Jews Against Prejudice: American Jews and the Fight for Civil Liberties.* New York: Columbia University Press, 1997.

Tivnan, Edward. *The Lobby: Jewish Political Power and American Foreign Policy.* New York: Simon & Schuster, 1987.

Urofsky, Melvin I. *A Voice That Spoke for Justice: The Life and Times of Stephen S. Wise.* Albany: State University of New York Press, 1982.

Vorspan, Albert. *Great Jewish Debates and Dilemmas: Jewish Perspectives in Conflict in the Eighties.* New York: Union of American Hebrew Congregations, 1980.

―――, and Eugene Lipman. *Justice and Judaism: The Work of Social Action.* New York: Union of American Hebrew Congregations, 1956.

―――, and David Saperstein. *Jewish Dimensions of Social Justice: Tough Moral Choices of Our Time.* New York: Union of American Hebrew Congregations, 1998.

―――. *Tough Choices: Jewish Perspectives on Social Justice.* New York: Union of American Hebrew Congregations, 1992.

Walzer, Michael. *Exodus and Revolution.* New York: Basic Books, 1985.

―――, Menachem Lorberbaum, and Noam J. Zohar, eds. *The Jewish Political Tradition,* vols. 1 and 2. New Haven, CT: Yale University Press, 2000.

Waxman, Meyer. *Judaism: Religion and Ethics.* New York: Thomas Yoseloff, 1958.

Wiesel, Elie. *A Jew Today.* New York: Vintage Books, 1979.

Wisse, Ruth. *If I Am Not for Myself: The Liberal Betrayal of the Jews.* New York: Free Press, 1992.

Wolfe, Robert. *Remember to Dream: A History of Jewish Radicalism.* Jewish Radical Education Project, 1994.

Woocher, Jonathan S. *Sacred Survival: The Civil Religion of American Jews.* Bloomington: Indiana University Press, 1986.

Wyman, David. *The Abandonment of the Jews: America and the Holocaust, 1941–1945.* New York: New Press, 1998.

Index

PAN*i*M
The Institute for Jewish Leadership and Values

Since 1988, PANIM: The Institute for Jewish Leadership and Values has been training and inspiring the next generation of Jewish leaders through programs that integrate Jewish learning, values and social responsibility. Programs include:

Panim el Panim
Four-day leadership seminars exploring public policy and social activism through a Jewish lens

Jewish Civics Initiative
A year-long service learning program and curriculum adopted by over 25 communities nationwide

Summer JAM (Judaism, Activism, Mitzvah work)
A month-long program on the campus of The George Washington University for teens passionate about politics, community service and Judaism

J-Serve
A national day of community service for Jewish teens

PANIM Fellowship Program
A year-long fellowship for outstanding college graduates offering Jewish learning, professional mentoring, and experience as a professional on the staff of PANIM

Israel Education and Advocacy Seminar
A seminar focused on the place of Israel in one's Jewish identity that gives participants advocacy skills they can use to support the Jewish state

Jewish Teen Leaders Fellowship
A year-long program focusing on leadership, service and social action with teens from cities across the country. The program includes a summit in Washington, D.C. and mini-grants for innovative J-Serve projects.

w w w . p a n i m . o r g

Bar/Bat Mitzvah

The JGirl's Guide: The Young Jewish Woman's Handbook for Coming of Age
By Penina Adelman, Ali Feldman, and Shulamit Reinharz
An inspirational, interactive guidebook designed to help pre-teen Jewish girls address the spiritual, educational, and psychological issues surrounding coming of age in today's society.   6 x 9, 240 pp, Quality PB, 978-1-58023-215-9 **$14.99**
Also Available: **The JGirl's Teacher's and Parent's Guide**
8½ x 11, 56 pp, PB, 978-1-58023-225-8 **$8.99**
Bar/Bat Mitzvah Basics: A Practical Family Guide to Coming of Age Together
Edited by Cantor Helen Leneman 6 x 9, 240 pp, Quality PB, 978-1-58023-151-0 **$18.95**
The Bar/Bat Mitzvah Memory Book, 2nd Edition: An Album for Treasuring the
Spiritual Celebration *By Rabbi Jeffrey K. Salkin and Nina Salkin*
8 x 10, 48 pp, Deluxe HC, 2-color text, ribbon marker, 978-1-58023-263-0 **$19.99**
For Kids—Putting God on Your Guest List: How to Claim the Spiritual Meaning
of Your Bar or Bat Mitzvah *By Rabbi Jeffrey K. Salkin*
6 x 9, 144 pp, Quality PB, 978-1-58023-015-5 **$14.99** *For ages 11–13*
Putting God on the Guest List, 3rd Edition: How to Reclaim the Spiritual
Meaning of Your Child's Bar or Bat Mitzvah *By Rabbi Jeffrey K. Salkin*
6 x 9, 224 pp, Quality PB, 978-1-58023-222-7 **$16.99**; HC, 978-1-58023-260-9 **$24.99**
Also Available: **Putting God on the Guest List Teacher's Guide**
8½ x 11, 48 pp, PB, 978-1-58023-226-5 **$8.99**

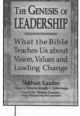

Tough Questions Jews Ask: A Young Adult's Guide to Building a Jewish Life
By Rabbi Edward Feinstein 6 x 9, 160 pp, Quality PB, 978-1-58023-139-8 **$14.99** *For ages 12 & up*
Also Available: **Tough Questions Jews Ask Teacher's Guide**
8½ x 11, 72 pp, PB, 978-1-58023-187-9 **$8.95**

Bible Study/Midrash

**Abraham's Bind & Other Bible Tales of Trickery, Folly, Mercy
and Love** *By Michael J. Caduto*
Re-imagines many biblical characters, retelling their stories and highlighting their foibles and strengths, their struggles and joys. Readers will learn that God has a way of working for them and through them, even today.
6 x 9, 224 pp, HC, 978-1-59473-186-0 **$19.99** *(A SkyLight Paths book)*
Ancient Secrets: Using the Stories of the Bible to Improve Our Everyday Lives
By Rabbi Levi Meier, PhD 5½ x 8½, 288 pp, Quality PB, 978-1-58023-064-3 **$16.95**

The Genesis of Leadership: What the Bible Teaches Us about Vision,
Values and Leading Change *By Rabbi Nathan Laufer; Foreword by Senator Joseph I. Lieberman*
Unlike other books on leadership, this one is rooted in the stories of the Bible, and teaches the values that the Bible believes are prerequisites for true leadership.
6 x 9, 288 pp, HC, 978-1-58023-241-8 **$24.99**
Hineini in Our Lives: Learning How to Respond to Others through 14 Biblical Texts and
Personal Stories *By Norman J. Cohen* 6 x 9, 240 pp, Quality PB, 978-1-58023-274-6 **$16.99**
Moses and the Journey to Leadership: Timeless Lessons of Effective Management from
the Bible and Today's Leaders *By Dr. Norman J. Cohen* 6 x 9, 250 pp, HC, 978-1-58023-227-2 **$21.99**
Self, Struggle & Change: Family Conflict Stories in Genesis and Their Healing Insights for
Our Lives *By Norman J. Cohen* 6 x 9, 224 pp, Quality PB, 978-1-879045-66-8 **$18.99**
The Triumph of Eve & Other Subversive Bible Tales *By Matt Biers-Ariel*
5½ x 8½, 192 pp, HC, 978-1-59473-040-5 **$19.99** *(A SkyLight Paths book)*
Voices from Genesis: Guiding Us through the Stages of Life *By Norman J. Cohen*
6 x 9, 192 pp, Quality PB, 978-1-58023-118-3 **$16.95**

Or phone, fax, mail or e-mail to: **JEWISH LIGHTS** Publishing
Sunset Farm Offices, Route 4 • P.O. Box 237 • Woodstock, Vermont 05091
Tel: (802) 457-4000 • Fax: (802) 457-4004 • www.jewishlights.com
Credit card orders: (800) 962-4544 (8:30AM–5:30PM ET Monday–Friday)
Generous discounts on quantity orders. SATISFACTION GUARANTEED. Prices subject to change.

Congregation Resources

The Art of Public Prayer, 2nd Edition: Not for Clergy Only *By Lawrence A. Hoffman*
6 x 9, 272 pp, Quality PB, 978-1-893361-06-5 **$19.99** *(A SkyLight Paths book)*

Becoming a Congregation of Learners: Learning as a Key to Revitalizing
Congregational Life *By Isa Aron, PhD; Foreword by Rabbi Lawrence A. Hoffman*
6 x 9, 304 pp, Quality PB, 978-1-58023-089-6 **$19.95**

Finding a Spiritual Home: How a New Generation of Jews Can Transform the
American Synagogue *By Rabbi Sidney Schwarz*
6 x 9, 352 pp, Quality PB, 978-1-58023-185-5 **$19.95**

Jewish Pastoral Care, 2nd Edition: A Practical Handbook from Traditional &
Contemporary Sources *Edited by Rabbi Dayle A. Friedman*
6 x 9, 528 pp, HC, 978-1-58023-221-0 **$40.00**

Jewish Spiritual Direction: An Innovative Guide from Traditional and Contemporary
Sources *Edited by Rabbi Howard A. Addison and Barbara Eve Breitman*
6 x 9, 368 pp, HC, 978-1-58023-230-2 **$30.00**

The Self-Renewing Congregation: Organizational Strategies for Revitalizing
Congregational Life *By Isa Aron, PhD; Foreword by Dr. Ron Wolfson*
6 x 9, 304 pp, Quality PB, 978-1-58023-166-4 **$19.95**

Spiritual Community: The Power to Restore Hope, Commitment and Joy
By Rabbi David A. Teutsch, PhD 5½ x 8½, 144 pp, HC, 978-1-58023-270-8 **$19.99**

The Spirituality of Welcoming: How to Transform Your Congregation into a
Sacred Community *By Dr. Ron Wolfson* 6 x 9, 224 pp, Quality PB, 978-1-58023-244-9 **$19.99**

Rethinking Synagogues: A New Vocabulary for Congregational Life
By Rabbi Lawrence A. Hoffman 6 x 9, 240 pp, Quality PB, 978-1-58023-248-7 **$19.99**

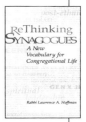

Children's Books

What You Will See Inside a Synagogue
By Rabbi Lawrence A. Hoffman and Dr. Ron Wolfson; Full-color photos by Bill Aron
A colorful, fun-to-read introduction that explains the ways and whys of Jewish
worship and religious life.
8½ x 10½, 32 pp, Full-color photos, HC, 978-1-59473-012-2 **$17.99** *For ages 6 & up* *(A SkyLight Paths book)*

The Kids' Fun Book of Jewish Time
By Emily Sper 9 x 7½, 24 pp, Full-color illus., HC, 978-1-58023-311-8 **$16.99**

In God's Hands
By Lawrence Kushner and Gary Schmidt 9 x 12, 32 pp, HC, 978-1-58023-224-1 **$16.99**

Because Nothing Looks Like God
By Lawrence and Karen Kushner
Introduces children to the possibilities of spiritual life.
11 x 8½, 32 pp, Full-color illus., HC, 978-1-58023-092-6 **$16.95** *For ages 4 & up*

Also Available: **Because Nothing Looks Like God Teacher's Guide**
8½ x 11, 22 pp, PB, 978-1-58023-140-4 **$6.95** *For ages 5–8*

Board Book Companions to *Because Nothing Looks Like God*
5 x 5, 24 pp, Full-color illus., SkyLight Paths Board Books *For ages 0–4*

What Does God Look Like? 978-1-893361-23-2 **$7.99**

How Does God Make Things Happen? 978-1-893361-24-9 **$7.95**

Where Is God? 978-1-893361-17-1 **$7.99**

The Book of Miracles: A Young Person's Guide to Jewish Spiritual Awareness
By Lawrence Kushner. All-new illustrations by the author
6 x 9, 96 pp, 2-color illus., HC, 978-1-879045-78-1 **$16.95** *For ages 9 and up*

In Our Image: God's First Creatures
By Nancy Sohn Swartz 9 x 12, 32 pp, Full-color illus., HC, 978-1-879045-99-6 **$16.95** *For ages 4 & up*

Also Available as a Board Book: **How Did the Animals Help God?**
5 x 5, 24 pp, Board, Full-color illus., 978-1-59473-044-3 **$7.99** *For ages 0–4* *(A SkyLight Paths book)*

Current Events/History

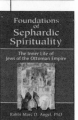

The Story of the Jews: A 4,000-Year Adventure—A Graphic History Book
Written & illustrated by Stan Mack
Witty, illustrated narrative of all the major happenings from biblical times to the twenty-first century. 6 x 9, 288 pp, illus., Quality PB, 978-1-58023-155-8 **$16.95**

Hannah Senesh: Her Life and Diary, the First Complete Edition
By Hannah Senesh; Foreword by Marge Piercy; Preface by Eitan Senesh
6 x 9, 352 pp, HC, 978-1-58023-212-8 **$24.99**

The Jewish Prophet: Visionary Words from Moses and Miriam to Henrietta Szold and A. J. Heschel *By Rabbi Dr. Michael J. Shire*
6½ x 8½, 128 pp, 123 full-color illus., HC, 978-1-58023-168-8
Special gift price $14.95

Foundations of Sephardic Spirituality: The Inner Life of Jews of the Ottoman Empire
By Rabbi Marc D. Angel, PhD 6 x 9, 224 pp, HC, 978-1-58023-243-2 **$24.99**

Judaism and Justice: The Jewish Passion to Repair the World
By Rabbi Sidney Schwarz
6 x 9, 250 pp, HC, 978-1-58023-312-5 **$24.99**

Ecology

Ecology & the Jewish Spirit: Where Nature & the Sacred Meet
Edited by Ellen Bernstein 6 x 9, 288 pp, Quality PB, 978-1-58023-082-7 **$16.95**

Torah of the Earth: Exploring 4,000 Years of Ecology in Jewish Thought
Vol. 1: Biblical Israel: One Land, One People; Rabbinic Judaism: One People, Many Lands
Vol. 2: Zionism: One Land, Two Peoples; Eco-Judaism: One Earth, Many Peoples
Edited by Arthur Waskow
Vol. 1: 6 x 9, 272 pp, Quality PB, 978-1-58023-086-5 **$19.95**
Vol. 2: 6 x 9, 336 pp, Quality PB, 978-1-58023-087-2 **$19.95**

The Way Into Judaism and the Environment
By Jeremy Benstein 6 x 9, 224 pp, HC, 978-1-58023-268-5 **$24.99**

Grief/Healing

Against the Dying of the Light: A Parent's Story of Love, Loss and Hope
By Leonard Fein
5½ x 8½, 176 pp, Quality PB, 978-1-58023-197-8 **$15.99**

Grief in Our Seasons: A Mourner's Kaddish Companion *By Rabbi Kerry M. Olitzky*
4½ x 6½, 448 pp, Quality PB, 978-1-879045-55-2 **$15.95**

Healing of Soul, Healing of Body: Spiritual Leaders Unfold the Strength & Solace in Psalms *Edited by Rabbi Simkha Y. Weintraub, CSW*
6 x 9, 128 pp, 2-color illus. text, Quality PB, 978-1-879045-31-6 **$14.99**

Jewish Paths toward Healing and Wholeness: A Personal Guide to Dealing with Suffering *By Rabbi Kerry M. Olitzky; Foreword by Debbie Friedman.*
6 x 9, 192 pp, Quality PB, 978-1-58023-068-1 **$15.95**

Mourning & Mitzvah, 2nd Edition: A Guided Journal for Walking the Mourner's Path through Grief to Healing *By Anne Brener, LCSW*
7½ x 9, 304 pp, Quality PB, 978-1-58023-113-8 **$19.99**

The Perfect Stranger's Guide to Funerals and Grieving Practices
A Guide to Etiquette in Other People's Religious Ceremonies *Edited by Stuart M. Matlins*
6 x 9, 240 pp, Quality PB, 978-1-893361-20-1 **$16.95** *(A SkyLight Paths book)*

Tears of Sorrow, Seeds of Hope: A Jewish Spiritual Companion for Infertility and Pregnancy Loss *By Rabbi Nina Beth Cardin*
6 x 9, 192 pp, HC, 978-1-58023-017-9 **$19.95**

A Time to Mourn, A Time to Comfort, 2nd Edition: A Guide to Jewish Bereavement *By Dr. Ron Wolfson*
7 x 9, 384 pp, Quality PB, 978-1-58023-253-1 **$19.99**

When a Grandparent Dies: A Kid's Own Remembering Workbook for Dealing with Shiva and the Year Beyond *By Nechama Liss-Levinson, PhD*
8 x 10, 48 pp, 2-color text, HC, 978-1-879045-44-6 **$15.95** *For ages 7–13*

Holidays/Holy Days

Rosh Hashanah Readings: Inspiration, Information and Contemplation
Yom Kippur Readings: Inspiration, Information and Contemplation
Edited by Rabbi Dov Peretz Elkins with Section Introductions from Arthur Green's These Are the Words
An extraordinary collection of readings, prayers and insights that enable the modern worshiper to enter into the spirit of the High Holy Days in a personal and powerful way, permitting the meaning of the Jewish New Year to enter the heart.
RHR: 6 x 9, 400 pp, HC, 978-1-58023-239-5 **$24.99**
YKR: 6 x 9, 368 pp, HC, 978-1-58023-271-5 **$24.99**

Jewish Holidays: A Brief Introduction for Christians
By Rabbi Kerry M. Olitzky and Rabbi Daniel Judson
5½ x 8½, 144 pp, Quality PB, 978-1-58023-302-6 **$16.99**

Leading the Passover Journey: The Seder's Meaning Revealed,
the Haggadah's Story Retold *By Rabbi Nathan Laufer*
Uncovers the hidden meaning of the Seder's rituals and customs.
6 x 9, 224 pp, HC, 978-1-58023-211-1 **$24.99**

Reclaiming Judaism as a Spiritual Practice: Holy Days and Shabbat
By Rabbi Goldie Milgram
7 x 9, 272 pp, Quality PB, 978-1-58023-205-0 **$19.99**

7th Heaven: Celebrating Shabbat with Rebbe Nachman of Breslov
By Moshe Mykoff with the Breslov Research Institute
5⅛ x 8¼, 224 pp, Deluxe PB w/flaps, 978-1-58023-175-6 **$18.95**

The Women's Passover Companion: Women's Reflections on the
Festival of Freedom *Edited by Rabbi Sharon Cohen Anisfeld, Tara Mohr, and Catherine Spector*
Groundbreaking. A provocative conversation about women's relationships to Passover as well as the roots and meanings of women's seders.
6 x 9, 352 pp, Quality PB, 978-1-58023-231-9 **$19.99**

The Women's Seder Sourcebook: Rituals & Readings for Use at the
Passover Seder *Edited by Rabbi Sharon Cohen Anisfeld, Tara Mohr, and Catherine Spector*
Gathers the voices of more than one hundred women in readings, personal and creative reflections, commentaries, blessings, and ritual suggestions that can be incorporated into your Passover celebration.
6 x 9, 384 pp, Quality PB, 978-1-58023-232-6 **$19.99**

Creating Lively Passover Seders: A Sourcebook of Engaging Tales, Texts & Activities
By David Arnow, PhD 7 x 9, 416 pp, Quality PB, 978-1-58023-184-8 **$24.99**

Hanukkah, 2nd Edition: The Family Guide to Spiritual Celebration
By Dr. Ron Wolfson. Edited by Joel Lurie Grishaver.
7 x 9, 240 pp, illus., Quality PB, 978-1-58023-122-0 **$18.95**

The Jewish Family Fun Book: Holiday Projects, Everyday Activities, and Travel Ideas
with Jewish Themes *By Danielle Dardashti and Roni Sarig. Illus. by Avi Katz.*
6 x 9, 288 pp, 70+ b/w illus. & diagrams, Quality PB, 978-1-58023-171-8 **$18.95**

The Jewish Gardening Cookbook: Growing Plants & Cooking for Holidays
& Festivals *By Michael Brown* 6 x 9, 224 pp, 30+ b/w illus., Quality PB, 978-1-58023-116-9 **$16.95**

The Jewish Lights Book of Fun Classroom Activities: Simple and Seasonal
Projects for Teachers and Students *By Danielle Dardashti and Roni Sarig*
6 x 9, 240 pp, Quality PB, 978-1-58023-206-7 **$19.99**

Passover, 2nd Edition: The Family Guide to Spiritual Celebration
By Dr. Ron Wolfson with Joel Lurie Grishaver 7 x 9, 352 pp, Quality PB, 978-1-58023-174-9 **$19.95**

Shabbat, 2nd Edition: The Family Guide to Preparing for and Celebrating the Sabbath
By Dr. Ron Wolfson 7 x 9, 320 pp, illus., Quality PB, 978-1-58023-164-0 **$19.99**

Sharing Blessings: Children's Stories for Exploring the Spirit of the Jewish Holidays
By Rahel Musleah and Rabbi Michael Klayman
8½ x 11, 64 pp, Full-color illus., HC, 978-1-879045-71-2 **$18.95** *For ages 6 & up*

Inspiration

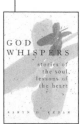

God's To-Do List: 103 Ways to Be an Angel and Do God's Work on Earth
By Dr. Ron Wolfson 6 x 9, 150 pp, Quality PB, 978-1-58023-301-9 **$15.99**

God in All Moments: Mystical & Practical Spiritual Wisdom from Hasidic Masters
Edited and translated by Or N. Rose with Ebn D. Leader
5½ x 8½, 192 pp, Quality PB, 978-1-58023-186-2 **$16.95**

Our Dance with God: Finding Prayer, Perspective and Meaning in the Stories of Our
Lives *By Karyn D. Kedar* 6 x 9, 176 pp, Quality PB, 978-1-58023-202-9 **$16.99**

Also Available: **The Dance of the Dolphin** (HC edition of *Our Dance with God*)
6 x 9, 176 pp, HC, 978-1-58023-154-1 **$19.95**

The Empty Chair: Finding Hope and Joy—Timeless Wisdom from a Hasidic Master,
Rebbe Nachman of Breslov *Adapted by Moshe Mykoff and the Breslov Research Institute*
4 x 6, 128 pp, 2-color text, Deluxe PB w/flaps, 978-1-879045-67-5 **$9.95**

The Gentle Weapon: Prayers for Everyday and Not-So-Everyday Moments—
Timeless Wisdom from the Teachings of the Hasidic Master, Rebbe Nachman of Breslov
Adapted by Moshe Mykoff and S. C. Mizrahi, together with the Breslov Research Institute
4 x 6, 144 pp, 2-color text, Deluxe PB w/flaps, 978-1-58023-022-3 **$9.99**

God Whispers: Stories of the Soul, Lessons of the Heart *By Karyn D. Kedar*
6 x 9, 176 pp, Quality PB, 978-1-58023-088-9 **$15.95**

An Orphan in History: One Man's Triumphant Search for His Jewish Roots
By Paul Cowan; Afterword by Rachel Cowan. 6 x 9, 288 pp, Quality PB, 978-1-58023-135-0 **$16.95**

Restful Reflections: Nighttime Inspiration to Calm the Soul, Based on Jewish Wisdom
By Rabbi Kerry M. Olitzky & Rabbi Lori Forman 4½ x 6½, 448 pp, Quality PB, 978-1-58023-091-9 **$15.95**

Sacred Intentions: Daily Inspiration to Strengthen the Spirit, Based on Jewish Wisdom
By Rabbi Kerry M. Olitzky and Rabbi Lori Forman 4½ x 6½, 448 pp, Quality PB, 978-1-58023-061-2 **$15.95**

Kabbalah/Mysticism/Enneagram

Awakening to Kabbalah: The Guiding Light of Spiritual Fulfillment
By Rav Michael Laitman, PhD 6 x 9, 192 pp, HC, 978-1-58023-264-7 **$21.99**

Seek My Face: A Jewish Mystical Theology *By Arthur Green*
6 x 9, 304 pp, Quality PB, 978-1-58023-130-5 **$19.95**

Zohar: Annotated & Explained
Translation and annotation by Daniel C. Matt; Foreword by Andrew Harvey
5½ x 8½, 176 pp, Quality PB, 978-1-893361-51-5 **$15.99** *(A SkyLight Paths book)*

Cast in God's Image: Discover Your Personality Type Using the Enneagram and Kabbalah
By Rabbi Howard A. Addison
7 x 9, 176 pp, Quality PB, Layflat binding, 20+ journaling exercises, 978-1-58023-124-4 **$16.95**

Ehyeh: A Kabbalah for Tomorrow
By Arthur Green 6 x 9, 224 pp, Quality PB, 978-1-58023-213-5 **$16.99**

The Enneagram and Kabbalah, 2nd Edition: Reading Your Soul
By Rabbi Howard A. Addison 6 x 9, 192 pp, Quality PB, 978-1-58023-229-6 **$16.99**

Finding Joy: A Practical Spiritual Guide to Happiness *By Dannel I. Schwartz with Mark Hass*
6 x 9, 192 pp, Quality PB, 978-1-58023-009-4 **$14.95**

The Flame of the Heart: Prayers of a Chasidic Mystic *By Reb Noson of Breslov. Translated by
David Sears with the Breslov Research Institute* 5 x 7¼, 160 pp, Quality PB, 978-1-58023-246-3 **$15.99**

The Gift of Kabbalah: Discovering the Secrets of Heaven, Renewing Your Life on Earth
By Tamar Frankiel, PhD 6 x 9, 256 pp, Quality PB, 978-1-58023-141-1 **$16.95;**
HC, 978-1-58023-108-4 **$21.95**

Kabbalah: A Brief Introduction for Christians
By Tamar Frankiel, PhD 5½ x 8½, 208 pp, Quality PB, 978-1-58023-303-3 **$16.99**

The Lost Princess and Other Kabbalistic Tales of Rebbe Nachman of Breslov
The Seven Beggars and Other Kabbalistic Tales of Rebbe Nachman of Breslov
Translated by Rabbi Aryeh Kaplan; Preface by Rabbi Chaim Kramer
Lost Princess: 6 x 9, 400 pp, Quality PB, 978-1-58023-217-3 **$18.99**
Seven Beggars: 6 x 9, 192 pp, Quality PB, 978-1-58023-250-0 **$16.99**

See also *The Way Into Jewish Mystical Tradition* in Spirituality / The Way Into... Series

Life Cycle
Marriage / Parenting / Family / Aging

Jewish Fathers: A Legacy of Love
Photographs by Lloyd Wolf. Essays by Paula Wolfson. Foreword by Rabbi Harold Kushner.
Honors the role of contemporary Jewish fathers in America. Each father tells in his own words what it means to be a parent and Jewish, and what he learned from his own father. Insightful photos.
10¾ x 9⅞, 144 pp with 100+ duotone photos, HC, 978-1-58023-204-3 **$30.00**

The New Jewish Baby Album: Creating and Celebrating the Beginning of a Spiritual Life—A Jewish Lights Companion
By the Editors at Jewish Lights. Foreword by Anita Diamant. Preface by Rabbi Sandy Eisenberg Sasso.
A spiritual keepsake that will be treasured for generations. More than just a memory book, *shows you how—and why it's important*—to create a Jewish home and a Jewish life. 8 x 10, 64 pp, Deluxe Padded HC, Full-color illus., 978-1-58023-138-1 **$19.95**

The Jewish Pregnancy Book: A Resource for the Soul, Body & Mind during Pregnancy, Birth & the First Three Months
By Sandy Falk, MD, and Rabbi Daniel Judson, with Steven A. Rapp
Includes medical information, prayers and rituals for each stage of pregnancy, from a liberal Jewish perspective. 7 x 10, 208 pp, Quality PB, b/w photos, 978-1-58023-178-7 **$16.95**

Celebrating Your New Jewish Daughter: Creating Jewish Ways to Welcome Baby Girls into the Covenant—New and Traditional Ceremonies *By Debra Nussbaum Cohen; Foreword by Rabbi Sandy Eisenberg Sasso* 6 x 9, 272 pp, Quality PB, 978-1-58023-090-2 **$18.95**

The New Jewish Baby Book, 2nd Edition: Names, Ceremonies & Customs—A Guide for Today's Families *By Anita Diamant* 6 x 9, 336 pp, Quality PB, 978-1-58023-251-7 **$19.99**

Parenting As a Spiritual Journey: Deepening Ordinary and Extraordinary Events into Sacred Occasions *By Rabbi Nancy Fuchs-Kreimer* 6 x 9, 224 pp, Quality PB, 978-1-58023-016-2 **$16.95**

Parenting Jewish Teens: A Guide for the Perplexed
By Joanne Doades 6 x 9, 200 pp, Quality PB, 978-1-58023-305-7 **$16.99**

Judaism for Two: A Spiritual Guide for Strengthening and Celebrating Your Loving Relationship *By Rabbi Nancy Fuchs-Kreimer and Rabbi Nancy H. Wiener; Foreword by Rabbi Elliot N. Dorff* Addresses the ways Jewish teachings can enhance and strengthen committed relationships. 6 x 9, 224 pp, Quality PB, 978-1-58023-254-8 **$16.99**

Embracing the Covenant: Converts to Judaism Talk About Why & How
By Rabbi Allan Berkowitz and Patti Moskovitz 6 x 9, 192 pp, Quality PB, 978-1-879045-50-7 **$16.95**

The Guide to Jewish Interfaith Family Life: An InterfaithFamily.com Handbook
Edited by Ronnie Friedland and Edmund Case 6 x 9, 384 pp, Quality PB, 978-1-58023-153-4 **$18.95**

Introducing My Faith and My Community
The Jewish Outreach Institute Guide for the Christian in a Jewish Interfaith Relationship
By Rabbi Kerry M. Olitzky 6 x 9, 176 pp, Quality PB, 978-1-58023-192-3 **$16.99**

Making a Successful Jewish Interfaith Marriage: The Jewish Outreach Institute Guide to Opportunities, Challenges and Resources *By Rabbi Kerry M. Olitzky with Joan Peterson Littman*
6 x 9, 176 pp, Quality PB, 978-1-58023-170-1 **$16.95**

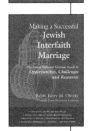

The Creative Jewish Wedding Book: A Hands-On Guide to New & Old Traditions, Ceremonies & Celebrations *By Gabrielle Kaplan-Mayer*
9 x 9, 288 pp, b/w photos, Quality PB, 978-1-58023-194-7 **$19.99**

Divorce Is a Mitzvah: A Practical Guide to Finding Wholeness and Holiness When Your Marriage Dies *By Rabbi Perry Netter; Afterword by Rabbi Laura Geller.*
6 x 9, 224 pp, Quality PB, 978-1-58023-172-5 **$16.95**

A Heart of Wisdom: Making the Jewish Journey from Midlife through the Elder Years
Edited by Susan Berrin; Foreword by Harold Kushner
6 x 9, 384 pp, Quality PB, 978-1-58023-051-3 **$18.95**

So That Your Values Live On: Ethical Wills and How to Prepare Them
Edited by Jack Riemer and Nathaniel Stampfer
6 x 9, 272 pp, Quality PB, 978-1-879045-34-7 **$18.99**

Meditation

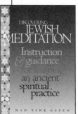

The Handbook of Jewish Meditation Practices
A Guide for Enriching the Sabbath and Other Days of Your Life
By Rabbi David A. Cooper Easy-to-learn meditation techniques.
6 x 9, 208 pp, Quality PB, 978-1-58023-102-2 **$16.95**

Discovering Jewish Meditation: Instruction & Guidance for Learning an Ancient
Spiritual Practice *By Nan Fink Gefen*
6 x 9, 208 pp, Quality PB, 978-1-58023-067-4 **$16.95**

A Heart of Stillness: A Complete Guide to Learning the Art of Meditation
By David A. Cooper 5½ x 8½, 272 pp, Quality PB, 978-1-893361-03-4 **$16.95** *(A SkyLight Paths book)*

Meditation from the Heart of Judaism: Today's Teachers Share Their
Practices, Techniques, and Faith *Edited by Avram Davis*
6 x 9, 256 pp, Quality PB, 978-1-58023-049-0 **$16.95**

Silence, Simplicity & Solitude: A Complete Guide to Spiritual Retreat at Home
By David A. Cooper 5½ x 8½, 336 pp, Quality PB, 978-1-893361-04-1 **$16.95**
(A SkyLight Paths book)

The Way of Flame: A Guide to the Forgotten Mystical Tradition of Jewish
Meditation *By Avram Davis* 4½ x 8, 176 pp, Quality PB, 978-1-58023-060-5 **$15.95**

Ritual/Sacred Practice/Journaling

The Jewish Dream Book: The Key to Opening the Inner Meaning of
Your Dreams *By Vanessa L. Ochs with Elizabeth Ochs; Full-color illus. by Kristina Swarner*
Instructions for how modern people can perform ancient Jewish dream practices
and dream interpretations drawn from the Jewish wisdom tradition.
8 x 8, 128 pp, Full-color illus., Deluxe PB w/flaps, 978-1-58023-132-9 **$16.95**

The Jewish Journaling Book: How to Use Jewish Tradition to Write
Your Life & Explore Your Soul *By Janet Ruth Falon*
Details the history of Jewish journaling throughout biblical and modern times, and
teaches specific journaling techniques to help you create and maintain a vital journal,
from a Jewish perspective. 8 x 8, 304 pp, Deluxe PB w/flaps, 978-1-58023-203-6 **$18.99**

The Book of Jewish Sacred Practices: CLAL's Guide to Everyday & Holiday
Rituals & Blessings *Edited by Rabbi Irwin Kula and Vanessa L. Ochs, PhD*
6 x 9, 368 pp, Quality PB, 978-1-58023-152-7 **$18.95**

Jewish Ritual: A Brief Introduction for Christians
By Rabbi Kerry M. Olitzky and Rabbi Daniel Judson
5½ x 8½, 144 pp, Quality PB, 978-1-58023-210-4 **$14.99**

The Rituals & Practices of a Jewish Life: A Handbook for Personal Spiritual
Renewal *Edited by Rabbi Kerry M. Olitzky and Rabbi Daniel Judson*
6 x 9, 272 pp, illus., Quality PB, 978-1-58023-169-5 **$18.95**

The Sacred Art of Lovingkindness: Preparing to Practice
By Rabbi Rami Shapiro 5½ x 8½, 176 pp, Quality PB, 978-1-59473-151-8 **$16.99**
(A SkyLight Paths book)

Science Fiction/Mystery & Detective Fiction

Mystery Midrash: An Anthology of Jewish Mystery & Detective Fiction
Edited by Lawrence W. Raphael; Preface by Joel Siegel
6 x 9, 304 pp, Quality PB, 978-1-58023-055-1 **$16.95**

Criminal Kabbalah: An Intriguing Anthology of Jewish Mystery & Detective Fiction
Edited by Lawrence W. Raphael; Foreword by Laurie R. King
6 x 9, 256 pp, Quality PB, 978-1-58023-109-1 **$16.95**

Wandering Stars: An Anthology of Jewish Fantasy & Science Fiction
Edited by Jack Dann; Introduction by Isaac Asimov
6 x 9, 272 pp, Quality PB, 978-1-58023-005-6 **$16.95**

More Wandering Stars: An Anthology of Outstanding Stories of Jewish Fantasy and
Science Fiction *Edited by Jack Dann; Introduction by Isaac Asimov*
6 x 9, 192 pp, Quality PB, 978-1-58023-063-6 **$16.95**

Spirituality

The Adventures of Rabbi Harvey: A Graphic Novel of Jewish Wisdom and Wit in the Wild West *By Steve Sheinkin*
Jewish and American folktales combine in this witty and original graphic novel collection. Creatively retold and set on the western frontier of the 1870s.
6 x 9, 144 pp, Full-color illus., Quality PB, 978-1-58023-310-1 **$16.99**

Ethics of the Sages: *Pirke Avot*—Annotated & Explained
Translation and Annotation by Rabbi Rami Shapiro
5½ x 8½, 192 pp, Quality PB, 978-1-59473-207-2 **$16.99** *(A SkyLight Paths book)*

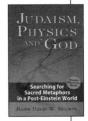

A Book of Life: Embracing Judaism as a Spiritual Practice
By Michael Strassfeld 6 x 9, 528 pp, Quality PB, 978-1-58023-247-0 **$19.99**

Meaning and Mitzvah: Daily Practices for Reclaiming Judaism through Prayer, God, Torah, Hebrew, Mitzvot and Peoplehood *By Rabbi Goldie Milgram*
7 x 9, 336 pp, Quality PB, 978-1-58023-256-2 **$19.99**

The Soul of the Story: Meetings with Remarkable People
By Rabbi David Zeller 6 x 9, 288 pp, HC, 978-1-58023-272-2 **$21.99**

Aleph-Bet Yoga: Embodying the Hebrew Letters for Physical and Spiritual Well-Being
By Steven A. Rapp. Foreword by Tamar Frankiel, PhD and Judy Greenfeld. Preface by Hart Lazer.
7 x 10, 128 pp, b/w photos, Quality PB, Layflat binding, 978-1-58023-162-6 **$16.95**

Entering the Temple of Dreams
Jewish Prayers, Movements, and Meditations for the End of the Day
By Tamar Frankiel, PhD, and Judy Greenfeld
7 x 10, 192 pp, illus., Quality PB, 978-1-58023-079-7 **$16.95**

Does the Soul Survive? A Jewish Journey to Belief in Afterlife, Past Lives & Living with Purpose *By Rabbi Elie Kaplan Spitz; Foreword by Brian L. Weiss, MD*
6 x 9, 288 pp, Quality PB, 978-1-58023-165-7 **$16.99**

First Steps to a New Jewish Spirit: Reb Zalman's Guide to Recapturing the Intimacy & Ecstasy in Your Relationship with God *By Rabbi Zalman M. Schachter-Shalomi with Donald Gropman* 6 x 9, 144 pp, Quality PB, 978-1-58023-182-4 **$16.95**

God in Our Relationships: Spirituality between People from the Teachings of Martin Buber *By Rabbi Dennis S. Ross* 5½ x 8½, 160 pp, Quality PB, 978-1-58023-147-3 **$16.95**

Judaism, Physics and God: Searching for Sacred Metaphors in a Post-Einstein World
By Rabbi David W. Nelson 6 x 9, 368 pp, Quality PB, inc. reader's discussion guide, 978-1-58023-306-4 **$18.99**;
HC, 352 pp, 978-1-58023-252-4 **$24.99**

The Jewish Lights Spirituality Handbook: A Guide to Understanding, Exploring & Living a Spiritual Life *Edited by Stuart M. Matlins*
What exactly is "Jewish" about spirituality? How do I make it a part of my life? Fifty of today's foremost spiritual leaders share their ideas and experience with us.
6 x 9, 456 pp, Quality PB, 978-1-58023-093-3 **$19.99**

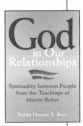

Bringing the Psalms to Life: How to Understand and Use the Book of Psalms
By Daniel F. Polish 6 x 9, 208 pp, Quality PB, 978-1-58023-157-2 **$16.95**;
HC, 978-1-58023-077-3 **$21.95**

God & the Big Bang: Discovering Harmony between Science & Spirituality
By Daniel C. Matt 6 x 9, 216 pp, Quality PB, 978-1-879045-89-7 **$16.99**

Minding the Temple of the Soul: Balancing Body, Mind, and Spirit through Traditional Jewish Prayer, Movement, and Meditation *By Tamar Frankiel, PhD, and Judy Greenfeld*
7 x 10, 184 pp, illus., Quality PB, 978-1-879045-64-4 **$16.95**
Audiotape of the Blessings and Meditations: 60 min. **$9.95**
Videotape of the Movements and Meditations: 46 min. **$20.00**

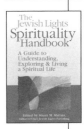

One God Clapping: The Spiritual Path of a Zen Rabbi *By Alan Lew with Sherril Jaffe*
5½ x 8½, 336 pp, Quality PB, 978-1-58023-115-2 **$16.95**

There Is No Messiah ... and You're It: The Stunning Transformation of Judaism's Most Provocative Idea *By Rabbi Robert N. Levine, DD*
6 x 9, 192 pp, Quality PB, 978-1-58023-255-5 **$16.99**

These Are the Words: A Vocabulary of Jewish Spiritual Life
By Arthur Green 6 x 9, 304 pp, Quality PB, 978-1-58023-107-7 **$18.95**

Spirituality/Lawrence Kushner

Filling Words with Light: Hasidic and Mystical Reflections on Jewish Prayer
By Lawrence Kushner and Nehemia Polen
5½ x 8½, 176 pp, HC, 978-1-58023-216-6 **$21.99**

The Book of Letters: A Mystical Hebrew Alphabet
Popular HC Edition, 6 x 9, 80 pp, 2-color text, 978-1-879045-00-2 **$24.95**
Collector's Limited Edition, 9 x 12, 80 pp, gold foil embossed pages, w/limited edition silkscreened print, 978-1-879045-04-0 **$349.00**

The Book of Miracles: A Young Person's Guide to Jewish Spiritual Awareness
6 x 9, 96 pp, 2-color illus., HC, 978-1-879045-78-1 **$16.95** *For ages 9 and up*

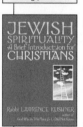

The Book of Words: Talking Spiritual Life, Living Spiritual Talk
6 x 9, 160 pp, Quality PB, 978-1-58023-020-9 **$16.95**

Eyes Remade for Wonder: A Lawrence Kushner Reader *Introduction by Thomas Moore*
6 x 9, 240 pp, Quality PB, 978-1-58023-042-1 **$18.95**

God Was in This Place & I, i Did Not Know: Finding Self, Spirituality and Ultimate Meaning 6 x 9, 192 pp, Quality PB, 978-1-879045-33-0 **$16.95**

Honey from the Rock: An Introduction to Jewish Mysticism
6 x 9, 176 pp, Quality PB, 978-1-58023-073-5 **$16.95**

Invisible Lines of Connection: Sacred Stories of the Ordinary
5½ x 8½, 160 pp, Quality PB, 978-1-879045-98-9 **$15.95**

Jewish Spirituality—A Brief Introduction for Christians
5½ x 8½, 112 pp, Quality PB, 978-1-58023-150-3 **$12.95**

The River of Light: Jewish Mystical Awareness
6 x 9, 192 pp, Quality PB, 978-1-58023-096-4 **$16.95**

The Way Into Jewish Mystical Tradition
6 x 9, 224 pp, Quality PB, 978-1-58023-200-5 **$18.99**; HC, 978-1-58023-029-2 **$21.95**

Spirituality/Prayer

Pray Tell: A Hadassah Guide to Jewish Prayer
By Rabbi Jules Harlow, with contributions from many others
8½ x 11, 400 pp, Quality PB, 978-1-58023-163-3 **$29.95**

Witnesses to the One: The Spiritual History of the *Sh'ma* *By Rabbi Joseph B. Meszler; Foreword by Rabbi Elyse Goldstein* 6 x 9, 176 pp, HC, 978-1-58023-309-5 **$19.99**

My People's Prayer Book Series

Traditional Prayers, Modern Commentaries *Edited by Rabbi Lawrence A. Hoffman*
Provides diverse and exciting commentary to the traditional liturgy, helping modern men and women find new wisdom in Jewish prayer, and bring liturgy into their lives. Each book includes Hebrew text, modern translation, and commentaries from all perspectives of the Jewish world.

Vol. 1—The *Sh'ma* and Its Blessings
7 x 10, 168 pp, HC, 978-1-879045-79-8 **$24.99**
Vol. 2—The *Amidah*
7 x 10, 240 pp, HC, 978-1-879045-80-4 **$24.95**
Vol. 3—*P'sukei D'zimrah* (Morning Psalms)
7 x 10, 240 pp, HC, 978-1-879045-81-1 **$24.95**
Vol. 4—*Seder K'riat Hatorah* (The Torah Service)
7 x 10, 264 pp, HC, 978-1-879045-82-8 **$23.95**
Vol. 5—*Birkhot Hashachar* (Morning Blessings)
7 x 10, 240 pp, HC, 978-1-879045-83-5 **$24.95**
Vol. 6—*Tachanun* and Concluding Prayers
7 x 10, 240 pp, HC, 978-1-879045-84-2 **$24.95**
Vol. 7—Shabbat at Home
7 x 10, 240 pp, HC, 978-1-879045-85-9 **$24.95**
Vol. 8—*Kabbalat Shabbat* (Welcoming Shabbat in the Synagogue)
7 x 10, 240 pp, HC, 978-1-58023-121-3 **$24.99**
Vol. 9—Welcoming the Night: *Minchah* and *Ma'ariv* (Afternoon and Evening Prayer) 7 x 10, 272 pp, HC, 978-1-58023-262-3 **$24.99**
Vol. 10—Shabbat Morning: *Shacharit* and *Musaf* (Morning and Additional Services) 7 x 10, 240 pp, HC, 978-1-58023-240-1 **$24.99**

Spirituality/Women's Interest

The Quotable Jewish Woman: Wisdom, Inspiration & Humor from the Mind & Heart
Edited and compiled by Elaine Bernstein Partnow
6 x 9, 496 pp, HC, 978-1-58023-193-0 **$29.99**

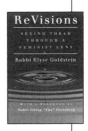

The Knitting Way: A Guide to Spiritual Self-Discovery *By Linda Skolnick and Janice MacDaniels* 7 x 9, 240 pp, Quality PB, 978-1-59473-079-5 **$16.99** *(A SkyLight Paths book)*

The Quilting Path: A Guide to Spiritual Self-Discovery through Fabric, Thread and Kabbalah
By Louise Silk 7 x 9, 192 pp, Quality PB, 978-1-59473-206-5 **$16.99** *(A SkyLight Paths book)*

The Divine Feminine in Biblical Wisdom Literature: Selections Annotated & Explained *Translated and Annotated by Rabbi Rami Shapiro*
5½ x 8½, 240 pp, Quality PB, 978-1-59473-109-9 **$16.99** *(A SkyLight Paths book)*

Lifecycles, Vol. 1: Jewish Women on Life Passages & Personal Milestones
Edited and with Introductions by Rabbi Debra Orenstein
6 x 9, 480 pp, Quality PB, 978-1-58023-018-6 **$19.95**

Lifecycles, Vol. 2: Jewish Women on Biblical Themes in Contemporary Life
Edited and with Introductions by Rabbi Debra Orenstein and Rabbi Jane Rachel Litman
6 x 9, 464 pp, Quality PB, 978-1-58023-019-3 **$19.95**

Moonbeams: A Hadassah Rosh Hodesh Guide *Edited by Carol Diament, PhD*
8½ x 11, 240 pp, Quality PB, 978-1-58023-099-5 **$20.00**

ReVisions: Seeing Torah through a Feminist Lens *By Rabbi Elyse Goldstein*
5½ x 8½, 224 pp, Quality PB, 978-1-58023-117-6 **$16.95**

The Women's Haftarah Commentary: New Insights from Women Rabbis on the 54 Weekly Haftarah Portions, the 5 Megillot & Special Shabbatot
Edited by Rabbi Elyse Goldstein 6 x 9, 560 pp, HC, 978-1-58023-133-6 **$39.99**

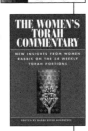

The Women's Torah Commentary: New Insights from Women Rabbis on the 54 Weekly Torah Portions *Edited by Rabbi Elyse Goldstein*
6 x 9, 496 pp, HC, 978-1-58023-076-6 **$34.95**

The Year Mom Got Religion: One Woman's Midlife Journey into Judaism
By Lee Meyerhoff Hendler 6 x 9, 208 pp, Quality PB, 978-1-58023-070-4 **$15.95**

See Holidays for *The Women's Passover Companion: Women's Reflections on the Festival of Freedom* and *The Women's Seder Sourcebook: Rituals & Readings for Use at the Passover Seder.* Also see Bar/Bat Mitzvah for *The JGirl's Guide: The Young Jewish Woman's Handbook for Coming of Age.*

Travel

Israel—A Spiritual Travel Guide, 2nd Edition
A Companion for the Modern Jewish Pilgrim
By Rabbi Lawrence A. Hoffman 4¼ x 10, 256 pp, Quality PB, illus., 978-1-58023-261-6 **$18.99**
Also Available: **The Israel Mission Leader's Guide** 978-1-58023-085-8 **$4.95**

12-Step

100 Blessings Every Day: Daily Twelve Step Recovery Affirmations, Exercises for Personal Growth & Renewal Reflecting Seasons of the Jewish Year
By Rabbi Kerry M. Olitzky; Foreword by Rabbi Neil Gillman
4½ x 6½, 432 pp, Quality PB, 978-1-879045-30-9 **$15.99**

Recovery from Codependence: A Jewish Twelve Steps Guide to Healing Your Soul
By Rabbi Kerry M. Olitzky 6 x 9, 160 pp, Quality PB, 978-1-879045-32-3 **$13.95**

Renewed Each Day: Daily Twelve Step Recovery Meditations Based on the Bible
By Rabbi Kerry M. Olitzky and Aaron Z.
Vol. 1—Genesis & Exodus: 6 x 9, 224 pp, Quality PB, 978-1-879045-12-5 **$14.95**
Vol. 2—Leviticus, Numbers & Deuteronomy: 6 x 9, 280 pp, Quality PB, 978-1-879045-13-2 **$18.99**

Twelve Jewish Steps to Recovery: A Personal Guide to Turning from Alcoholism & Other Addictions—Drugs, Food, Gambling, Sex ...
By Rabbi Kerry M. Olitzky and Stuart A. Copans, MD; Preface by Abraham J. Twerski, MD
6 x 9, 144 pp, Quality PB, 978-1-879045-09-5 **$14.95**

Theology/Philosophy/The Way Into... Series

The Way Into... series offers an accessible and highly usable "guided tour" of the Jewish faith, people, history and beliefs—in total, an introduction to Judaism that will enable you to understand and interact with the sacred texts of the Jewish tradition. Each volume is written by a leading contemporary scholar and teacher, and explores one key aspect of Judaism. *The Way Into...* series enables all readers to achieve a real sense of Jewish cultural literacy through guided study.

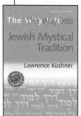

The Way Into Encountering God in Judaism
By Neil Gillman
For everyone who wants to understand how Jews have encountered God through-out history and today.
6 x 9, 240 pp, Quality PB, 978-1-58023-199-2 **$18.99**; HC, 978-1-58023-025-4 **$21.95**
Also Available: **The Jewish Approach to God:** A Brief Introduction for Christians
By Neil Gillman
5½ x 8½, 192 pp, Quality PB, 978-1-58023-190-9 **$16.95**

The Way Into Jewish Mystical Tradition
By Lawrence Kushner
Allows readers to interact directly with the sacred mystical text of the Jewish tradition. An accessible introduction to the concepts of Jewish mysticism, their religious and spiritual significance and how they relate to life today.
6 x 9, 224 pp, Quality PB, 978-1-58023-200-5 **$18.99**; HC, 978-1-58023-029-2 **$21.95**

The Way Into Jewish Prayer
By Lawrence A. Hoffman
Opens the door to 3,000 years of Jewish prayer, making available all anyone needs to feel at home in the Jewish way of communicating with God.
6 x 9, 224 pp, Quality PB, 978-1-58023-201-2 **$18.99**

The Way Into Judaism and the Environment
By Jeremy Benstein
Explores the ways in which Judaism contributes to contemporary social-environmental issues, the extent to which Judaism is part of the problem and how it can be part of the solution.
6 x 9, 288 pp, HC, 978-1-58023-268-5 **$24.99**

The Way Into *Tikkun Olam* (Repairing the World)
By Elliot N. Dorff
An accessible introduction to the Jewish concept of the individual's responsibility to care for others and repair the world.
6 x 9, 320 pp, HC, 978-1-58023-269-2 **$24.99**

The Way Into Torah
By Norman J. Cohen
Helps guide in the exploration of the origins and development of Torah, explains why it should be studied and how to do it.
6 x 9, 176 pp, Quality PB, 978-1-58023-198-5 **$16.99**; HC, 978-1-58023-028-5 **$21.95**

The Way Into the Varieties of Jewishness
By Sylvia Barack Fishman
Explores the religious and historical understanding of what it has meant to be Jewish from ancient times to the present controversy over "Who is a Jew?"
6 x 9, 250 pp, HC, 978-1-58023-030-8 **$24.99**

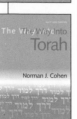

Theology/Philosophy

Christians and Jews in Dialogue: Learning in the Presence of the Other
By Mary C. Boys and Sara S. Lee; Foreword by Dr. Dorothy Bass
6 x 9, 240 pp, HC, 978-1-59473-144-0 **$21.99** *(A SkyLight Paths book)*

The Death of Death: Resurrection and Immortality in Jewish Thought
By Neil Gillman 6 x 9, 336 pp, Quality PB, 978-1-58023-081-0 **$18.95**

Ethics of the Sages: Pirke Avot—Annotated & Explained
Translation & Annotation by Rabbi Rami Shapiro
5½ x 8½, 208 pp, Quality PB, 978-1-59473-207-2 **$16.99** *(A SkyLight Paths book)*

Evolving Halakhah: A Progressive Approach to Traditional Jewish Law
By Rabbi Dr. Moshe Zemer 6 x 9, 480 pp, Quality PB, 978-1-58023-127-5 **$29.95**;
HC, 978-1-58023-002-5 **$40.00**

Hasidic Tales: Annotated & Explained
By Rabbi Rami Shapiro; Foreword by Andrew Harvey
5½ x 8½, 240 pp, Quality PB, 978-1-893361-86-7 **$16.95** *(A SkyLight Paths Book)*

Healing the Jewish-Christian Rift: Growing Beyond our Wounded History
By Ron Miller and Laura Bernstein; Foreword by Dr. Beatrice Bruteau
6 x 9, 288 pp, Quality PB, 978-1-59473-139-6 **$18.99** *(A SkyLight Paths book)*

A Heart of Many Rooms: Celebrating the Many Voices within Judaism
By David Hartman 6 x 9, 352 pp, Quality PB, 978-1-58023-156-5 **$19.95**

The Hebrew Prophets: Selections Annotated & Explained
Translation & Annotation by Rabbi Rami Shapiro; Foreword by Zalman M. Schachter-Shalomi
5½ x 8½, 224 pp, Quality PB, 978-1-59473-037-5 **$16.99** *(A SkyLight Paths book)*

A Jewish Understanding of the New Testament
By Rabbi Samuel Sandmel; Preface by Rabbi David Sandmel
5½ x 8½, 368 pp, Quality PB, 978-1-59473-048-1 **$19.99** *(A SkyLight Paths book)*

Keeping Faith with the Psalms: Deepen Your Relationship with God Using the Book
of Psalms *By Daniel F. Polish* 6 x 9, 320 pp, Quality PB, 978-1-58023-300-2 **$18.99**;
HC, 978-1-58023-179-4 **$24.95**

A Living Covenant: The Innovative Spirit in Traditional Judaism
By David Hartman 6 x 9, 368 pp, Quality PB, 978-1-58023-011-7 **$20.00**

Love and Terror in the God Encounter
The Theological Legacy of Rabbi Joseph B. Soloveitchik
By David Hartman 6 x 9, 240 pp, Quality PB, 978-1-58023-176-3 **$19.95**;
HC, 978-1-58023-112-1 **$25.00**

The Personhood of God: Biblical Theology, Human Faith and the Divine Image
By Dr. Yochanan Muffs; Foreword by Dr. David Hartman
6 x 9, 240 pp, HC, 978-1-58023-265-4 **$24.99**

Tormented Master: *The Life and Spiritual Quest of Rabbi Nahman of Bratslav*
By Arthur Green 6 x 9, 416 pp, Quality PB, 978-1-879045-11-8 **$19.99**

Traces of God: Seeing God in Torah, History and Everyday Life
By Neil Gillman 6 x 9, 240 pp, HC, 978-1-58023-249-4 **$21.99**

We Jews and Jesus: Exploring Theological Differences for Mutual Understanding
By Rabbi Samuel Sandmel; Preface by Rabbi David Sandmel
6 x 9, 176 pp, Quality PB, 978-1-59473-208-9 **$16.99** *(A SkyLight Paths book)*

Your Word Is Fire: The Hasidic Masters on Contemplative Prayer
Edited and translated by Arthur Green and Barry W. Holtz
6 x 9, 160 pp, Quality PB, 978-1-879045-25-5 **$15.95**

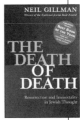
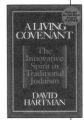

I Am Jewish
Personal Reflections Inspired by the Last Words of Daniel Pearl
Almost 150 Jews—both famous and not—from all walks of life, from all around
the world, write about Identity, Heritage, Covenant / Chosenness and Faith,
Humanity and Ethnicity, and *Tikkun Olam* and Justice.
Edited by Judea and Ruth Pearl
6 x 9, 304 pp, Deluxe PB w/flaps, 978-1-58023-259-3 **$18.99**; HC, 978-1-58023-183-1 **$24.99**
Download a free copy of the *I Am Jewish Teacher's Guide* at our website:
www.jewishlights.com

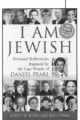

About Jewish Lights

People of all faiths and backgrounds yearn for books that attract, engage, educate, and spiritually inspire.

Our principal goal is to stimulate thought and help all people learn about who the Jewish People are, where they come from, and what the future can be made to hold. While people of our diverse Jewish heritage are the primary audience, our books speak to people in the Christian world as well and will broaden their understanding of Judaism and the roots of their own faith.

We bring to you authors who are at the forefront of spiritual thought and experience. While each has something different to say, they all say it in a voice that you can hear.

Our books are designed to welcome you and then to engage, stimulate, and inspire. We judge our success not only by whether or not our books are beautiful and commercially successful, but by whether or not they make a difference in your life.

For your information and convenience, at the back of this book we have provided a list of other Jewish Lights books you might find interesting and useful. They cover all the categories of your life:

Bar/Bat Mitzvah	Life Cycle
Bible Study / Midrash	Meditation
Children's Books	Parenting
Congregation Resources	Prayer
Current Events / History	Ritual / Sacred Practice
Ecology	Spirituality
Fiction: Mystery, Science Fiction	Theology / Philosophy
Grief / Healing	Travel
Holidays / Holy Days	12-Step
Inspiration	Women's Interest
Kabbalah / Mysticism / Enneagram	

Stuart M. Matlins, Publisher

Or phone, fax, mail or e-mail to: **JEWISH LIGHTS Publishing**
Sunset Farm Offices, Route 4 • P.O. Box 237 • Woodstock, Vermont 05091
Tel: (802) 457-4000 • Fax: (802) 457-4004 • www.jewishlights.com
Credit card orders: **(800) 962-4544** (8:30AM–5:30PM ET Monday–Friday)
Generous discounts on quantity orders. SATISFACTION GUARANTEED. Prices subject to change.

For more information about each book, visit our website at www.jewishlights.com